THE

RACES OF BRITAIN

THE

RACES OF BRITAIN

A CONTRIBUTION TO

The Anthropology of Western Europe

BY

JOHN BEDDOE

M.D., F.R.S., &c.

Ex-President of the Anthropological Society of London and of the Bristol Naturalists' Society
Foreign Associate of the Anthropological Society of Paris
Corresponding Member of the Anthropological Society of Berlin
Honorary Member of the Anthropological Societies of Brussels and of Washington
and of the Philosophical Institute of Bath

THE CLIVEDEN PRESS
Suite 520, 1629 K Street, N.W.
Washington, D.C. 20006

Reprint of the 1885 edition originally
published by J.W. Arrowsmith,
Quay Street, Bristol, England

Cliveden Press edition
Suite 520, 1629 K Street, N.W.
Washington, D.C. 20006

Manufactured in The United States of America

TO

Rudolf Virchow

AND

Paul Topinard

AND

TO THE MEMORY OF

Paul Broca

AND

Joseph Barnard Davis

This Work is Dedicated.

PREFACE.

THE present volume is to a great extent an expansion or development of a manuscript Essay, which in 1868 carried off the great prize of the Welsh National Eisteddfod. This prize, consisting of one hundred guineas, contributed by an accomplished and public-spirited Welshman, Mr. A. Johnes, of Garthmyl, and supplemented by a promise of fifty more from the funds of the Eisteddfod Committee, had been competed for, without success, during four successive years, by numerous candidates, two at least of whom—Mr. L. Owen Pike and Dr. Nicholas—had published their essays.

The successful work, however, though composed expressly for the occasion, was really the outcome of a great part of the leisure of fifteen years devoted to the application of the numerical and inductive method to the ethnology of Britain and of Western Europe. Their fruit, though satisfactory to the accomplished arbiter (the late Lord Strangford), did not appear to me ripe for publication. Having since then added largely to my material, and accumulated as great a store of observations as my opportunities are likely to afford, I now offer my conclusions and opinions to my brother anthropologists and to the public. In doing so, it has seemed best to present to them also the greater part of the facts and figures on which these opinions have been founded. Those relating purely to stature and bulk are not, however, republished; as they have been the subject of a monograph in the *Anthropological*

Memoirs, and have also been extensively utilized by Mr. Charles Roberts and Sir Rawson Rawson, in the Anthropometric Reports of the British Association.

Since the publication of my *Contribution to Scottish Ethnology*, one of the earliest pieces of work in this field, in 1853, the scientific value of numerical observations on colour as well as stature, conducted on a large scale, has come to be generally acknowledged; and under Virchow and Ranke in Germany, Vanderkindere in Belgium, Meyer and Kopernicki in Poland, Kollmann, Guillaume, and others in Switzerland, and Guibert in Brittany, statistics of great extent and value, and arranged more or less on the same plan as my own, have been accumulated and published; while in France, Topinard hopes to induce the Government to carry out, on a national scale, and on my system, a similar investigation.

The ever-increasing rapidity of local migration and intermixture, due to the extension of railways and the altered conditions of society, will in the next generation almost inextricably confuse the limits and proportions of the British races; and it is a source of satisfaction to me that I have laboured to seize on fleeting opportunities, and to observe and record phenomena, which, however trivial they may appear from some points of view, may for generations to come retain some biological and historical value.

I owe a heavy debt of gratitude to many friends, and to some whom I do not even personally know, for assistance in the work; but the only one I can here mention is Mr. David Davies, who has lent his valuable aid in the revision of the proofs, during my absence from England. Most of the drawings were executed by Mr. Norman Hardy.

Table of Contents.

FRANKS.

FROM TERRA COTTA FIGURES FOUND NEAR NYMEGEN AND XANTEN.

After Lubach

BELGÆ.

FROM THE MONUMENT OF JOVINUS AT REIMS.

THE RACES OF BRITAIN.

CHAPTER I.

On Methods.

IT was the ancient controversy respecting the colour of the hair of the Kelts, then burning briskly enough, and even now still smouldering, that led me to begin systematic numerical observations in physical anthropology. Very little reading sufficed to show me that, if it was a difficult task to ascertain the complexional peculiarities of the Kelts of 2000 years ago, it was a no less puzzling one to determine those of their supposed representatives at the present day. It is of little use to appeal to current opinion, or the results of casual observation. The eye may rest upon a great many sets of features in the course of a long day's travel, but the mind will retain but few of them photographed on the tablet of memory; and those few will probably be such as have presented striking peculiarities, or have belonged to the persons brought most frequently and nearly into the company and contact of the observer. This fact, together with the inveterate tendency of so many scientific observers, to see everything as they wish and expect it to be, rather than as it is, may account for the striking discrepancies among ethnological writers on this simple matter of fact. Thus it comes to pass that some attribute blue, others black eyes to the majority of the Irish; some describe the men of Kent as particularly fair, others as "assimilated to the dark-complexioned inhabitants of the opposite coast." The minister of Wick, in his Statistical Account of the place, described his parishioners as "having for the most part dark brown or black hair, and dark complexions; remarkably few having red or yellow hair." My own impressions on visiting the town were quite of an opposite nature, and were confirmed by an enumeration of the complexional characters of more than 300 individuals.

Similar discrepancies are manifested whenever any one attempts to define the prevailing complexion of the continental Teutonic peoples, or of the Slavonic, or of almost any other race or tribe. Take, for example, the Croats. One of two observant travellers talks of their "shaggy black locks," and another of "their Slavonian characteristics of blue eyes and fair hair." I could quote two or three other descriptions of their persons, which only agree in differing every one from the other.

Taking note of all these contradictions, and considering, moreover, that the material to be worked upon lay ready to hand in streets and market-places, not hidden away in museums and charnel-houses, I resolved to make observations on colour phenomena on a large scale, so as to afford to anthropologists some trustworthy material whereon to build, or at least to test the permanence of characteristics which were by some treated as fugitive, by others as well-nigh everlasting. How far I have succeeded in the first-mentioned object it will be for such of my readers to determine who shall have borne with me to the end. With regard to the second, it is, doubtless, natural that a subject to which one has given much time and labour should gradually increase in apparent importance under one's eyes, and that he who has given more attention to colour than to form should be disposed unduly to exalt the value of the first. Be that as it may, I have come to estimate very highly the permanence of the colours of hair and eyes. It is, of course, impossible for an evolutionist to regard them as *absolutely* permanent. But one may readily conceive, as I do, that whenever a distinct and tolerably homogeneous breed has been established, its colours may remain very much the same so long as the conditions of natural selection remain nearly identical. There are naturalists of eminence who regard these characters as fugitive, nay, almost accidental, so to speak, compared with the form of bones, especially of the skull-bones. "Colour," I once heard Sir Henry Rawlinson say, at an ethnological gathering, "is no part of type." From this view I strongly dissent. In the same family, in the same tribe, variations in head-form are usually about as notable as variations in complexion. There is as much to show for Schaafhausen's notion, that civilisation tends to widen the head, as for another very prevalent idea, that it tends to darken the hair. Indeed, it is more easy to reckon up agencies which might operate on the head-form than such as might alter the colour of the iris. Of the latter, the only feasible one that occurs to me is an increase or diminution in the amount of light to which the organ is habitually exposed;[*] but the former are many, *e.g.*, changes in the soil, or in the food produced therefrom, or in the character of the diet, increasing or lessening the supply of phosphate of lime;[†] changes in civilisation, involving greater or less employment of certain portions of the brain; and so forth.

Unfortunately we have not the same kind of evidence respecting colour in past ages as we have respecting form. We know by the

---

[*] Thus natural selection, in a dark, cloudy climate like that of the West of Ireland, may have tended to lighten the colour of the eye, the protection of much dark pigment being unnecessary.

[†] See Durand de Gros on the population of the Aveyron, in the *Bulletins de la Société d'Anthropologie*.

evidence of our own eyes that flattened leg-bones and perforated humeri were common in certain ancient races, and that they are now very uncommon in their supposed descendants, or at any rate in the present occupiers of the same countries. But as to whether red hair was more common then than now, we cannot have the same assurance : such hair as has come down to us from individuals of ancient races is generally stained and altered, so as to be untrustworthy evidence ; and the representations of colour on walls and vases are evidently conventional, and afford, at the best, only material for inferential argument. , Finally, the descriptive statements of ancient geographers and historians, even when obviously intended to be careful and accurate, are liable to two qualifications, one of which is our ignorance of the precise shade of meaning their contemporaries and countrymen attached to certain adjectives of colour, and the other is our ignorance of the personal equation of the observer, the latter objection, of course, applying equally to the statements of modern travellers and naturalists, whose nomenclature of colours and shades often differs very widely. Thus almost all French anthropologists say that the majority of persons in the north of France are blond ; whereas almost all Englishmen would say they were dark, each set of observers setting up as a standard what they are accustomed to see around them when at home. What is darkish brown to most Englishmen would be chestnut in the nomen-clature of most Parisians, and perhaps even blond in that of Auvergne or Provence ; an ancient Roman might probably enough have called it sufflavus, or even flavus. Nor is this difference of personal equation confined to observers who differ in nationality, or who dwell among populations which differ strikingly from each other in colour. The plan for obviating this difficulty devised by the illustrious Broca, though very useful as regards the hues of skin and irides, is less so for those of the hair, which are not flat tints ; and the scale of hair-colours contrived for the Anthropometric Committee of the British Association by General Pitt-Rivers, was found of little practical use for the same reason.

My first observations were vitiated by faulty classification ; but I soon settled down into the system to which I have since adhered, and which recommended itself chiefly by its convenience, as it generally enabled me to locate an individual in his proper class and division on a very cursory inspection.

I acknowledge three classes of eyes, distinguished as much by shade as by colour—light, intermediate or neutral, and dark. To the first class are assigned all blue, bluish-gray and light gray eyes (cærulei, cinereo-cœrulescentes, cœsii). These correspond to the five blue types of Broca, 11, 12, 13, 14, 15, and to No. 10, his lightest green. It was perhaps a mistake to include the darkest blue (No. 11) in this category, as in an unfavourable light it is liable to be confounded with "black."

In the third class I put the so-called black eyes, and those usually called brown and dark hazel. These correspond to the deeper shades of Broca's orange, green, and violet-gray, Nos. 1, 2, 3, 6, 7, 16, 17, 18.

To the second, or neutral class, remain dark gray, brownish-gray, very light hazel or yellow, hazel-gray, formed by streaks of orange radiating into a bluish-gray field, and most shades of green, together with all the eyes of whose colour I remain uncertain after an ordinarily close inspection. These correspond pretty exactly, I believe, to 4, 5, 8, 9, 19, and 20.

Each of my three classes of eyes is sub-divided into five, in accordance with the accompanying colour of hair:

Class R includes all shades which approach more nearly to red than to brown, yellow, or flaxen.

Class F (fair) includes flaxen, yellow, golden, some of the lightest shades of our brown, and some pale auburns in which the red hue is not very conspicuous.

Class B includes numerous shades of brown, answering nearly, I believe, to the French chatain and chatain-clair, but perhaps less extensive on the dark side.

Class D corresponds nearly with the French brun, most of their brun-foncés, and the darkest chatains, and includes the remaining shades of our brown up to

Class N (niger), which includes not only the jet-black, which has retained the same colour from childhood, and is generally very coarse and hard, but also that very intense brown which occurs in people who in childhood have had dark brown (or in some cases deep red) hair, but which in the adult cannot be distinguished from coal-black, except in a very good light.

When unable to decide in which of two columns (*e.g.*, B or D) an individual ought to be inscribed, I divide him between the two, by a Solomonian judgment, and set down ½, or ·5, in each of them.

When engaged in this work I set down in his proper place on my card of observation every person (with the exceptions to be mentioned presently) whom I meet, or who passes me within a short distance, say from one to three yards. As a rule, I take no note of persons who apparently belong to the upper classes, as these are more migratory and more often mixed in blood. I neglect those whom I suppose to be under age—fixing the point roughly at 18 or 20 for men, 17 or 18 for women—as well as all those whose hair has begun to grizzle. Thus I get a fairly uniform material to work upon, though doubtless the hair of most people does darken considerably between 20 and 40 or 50. In order to preserve perfect fairness, I always examine first, out of any group of persons, the one who is nearest, rather than the one to whom my attention is most drawn. Certain colours of the hair, such as red, certain shades of the eye, such as light gray, can be discerned at a very considerable distance; but I take no note of anyone who does not approach me so nearly that I can recognise the more obscure colours. Much allowance needs to be made for the varying effects of light.

Direct sunlight is better avoided when possible; I always choose the shady side of a street on a sunny day. Considerable difficulties are created by the freaks of fashion. I once visited Friesland, in order to study the physical type of that region. Conceive my disappointment when I found myself surrounded by comely damsels and buxom matrons, not one of whom suffered a single yellow hair to stray beyond her lace cap or silver-gilt head-plate. When I began to work in England dark hair was in fashion among the women; and light and reddish hues were dulled with greasy unguents. In later years fair hair has been more in vogue; and golden shades, sometimes unknown to nature, are produced by art. Among men, on the other hand, the close cropping of the head, borrowed from the French, makes comparisons difficult. Fortunately, most vagaries of this kind are little prevalent in the classes among whom I seek my material.

It may be objected that there is no security that many of the persons observed may not be aliens to the place or neighbourhood wherein they are encountered. Certainly, there is no such security. But if a sufficient number of observations be secured, and the upper and other notoriously migratory classes (who are mostly easy of recognition) be excluded, the probability is immense that the great majority of the remainder have been born within a moderate radius of the centre of observation; and the majority will determine the position of the community in my chromatic scale.

A ready means of comparing the colours of two peoples or localities is found in the Index of Nigrescence. The gross index is gotten by subtracting the number of red and fair-haired persons from that of the dark-haired, together with twice the black-haired. I double the black, in order to give its proper value to the greater tendency to melanosity shown thereby; while brown (chestnut) hair is regarded as neutral, though in truth most of the persons placed in B are fair-skinned, and approach more nearly in aspect to the xanthous than to the melanous variety.

$$D + 2N - R - F = \text{Index}.$$

From the gross index the net, or percentage index, is of course readily obtained.

It must not be supposed that, in devoting so much time and care to the collection of facts relating to colour, I was influenced by any excessive estimate of their importance. My chief inducement was the great abundance of the material, which, from a scientific point of view, was running to waste. The same thing might indeed be said of the heads of the British population; for they were also generally neglected by ethnologists, whatever phrenologists might be doing, the former being almost entirely absorbed in ancient craniology. But there was a very important difference between these two lines of enquiry: the one could be pursued without the concurrence of the subjects, the other could not.

Had there been anything like a complete craniological record, had there even been anything approaching the amount of ancient and mediæval material that can be used in France or Switzerland, one might have neglected the heads of one's contemporaries, in consequence of the obstacle just mentioned; but in truth the record is anything but complete or satisfactory, notwithstanding the exertions of Davis and Thurnam, of Bateman, of Greenwell and Rolleston, of Daniel Wilson, James Hunt, and Pitt-Rivers. This lamentable defect arises partly from the destructive ignorance of our earlier antiquaries, who, while they carefully collected every fragment of a potsherd from the barrows they explored, utterly neglected, and exposed to decay, the often more important osseous remains. Even now " finds " frequently occur, the benefit of which is lost to anthropology, from the absence of qualified observers, and the lack of knowledge or interest in the finders and their neighbours. It is not long since there existed several mediæval ossuaries in England, systematic observations in which might have been of some value; but with the exception of those at Hythe, Rothwell, and Micheldean, they have all, I fear, been destroyed. Thus a very fine one at Ripon was destroyed, unmeasured and undescribed, by the late Dean Macneile, and another in the crypt of Tamworth was turned out to make room for a heating apparatus. These misfortunes are the more to be regretted, inasmuch as we really do not possess sufficient osseous material in our museums for determining the form and size of the skull of the modern Englishman. The few we have are in great part those of criminals, lunatics, and paupers. In this respect, owing to a prejudice, from some points of view respectable, we are behind most European nations; and when, in such works as those of Topinard and De Quatrefages, we see comparisons drawn between the ordinary skull-forms of different countries, England is usually conspicuous by its absence.

On account of this dearth of material, I have measured a considerable number of living British heads, and shall make use of the results of these measurements in the present volume. As no accredited method existed when the work was begun, it was necessary to frame one. The difficulties in the way were considerable, and certainly were but partially overcome. It was necessary to avoid fatiguing or irritating the subjects; yet it was desirable to obtain as many data as possible suitable for comparison with those taken from ancient crania. With much regret I abandoned the use of Mr. Busk's excellent craniometer, and with it all radial measurements, because it sinned against the former of these requirements, and restricted myself to the use of the index callipers and graduated tape.

There are few points on the living head that are positively identifiable; and I was compelled to retain the use of some which are open to the objection of not being so. Some of the tape measures are affected by the variations in quantity and length of hair, though to a less extent than might be supposed. The following are those which I have been accustomed to take:

A. With the callipers. (*a*) Lengths.

    1. Maximum length from the glabella.

    2. Length from the inion or occipital tuberosity to the most prominent part of the frontal curve.

    3. Glabello-inial length.

    4. Maximum length according to Barnard Davis, *i.e.*, from the ophryon, or the flat space above the glabella.

By the use of these four it is possible, in pursuance of one of Broca's suggestions, to work out the degree of prominence of the occiput, of the forehead, and of the glabella, and thus to compensate in some degree the lack of radial measurements.

    5. Vertico-mental length, or maximum length of the whole head from crown to chin.

(*b*) Breadths.

    6. Frontal minimum breadth, just above the brows.

    7. Breadth at the stephanion, or maximum frontal. This is very uncertain; in many heads it is impossible to be sure whereabout the stephanion is.

    8. Zygomatic breadth, maximum.

    9. Auricular breadth, gotten, in accordance with Broca's recommendation, at the pit just in front of the helix, and above the condyle of the jaw and the root of the zygoma. This is a valuable measurement, the point being so easily identifiable. In conjunction with No. 11, it yields information as to the breadth of the base of the skull.

    10. Maximum breadth, wherever found, and where found.

    11. Mastoid breadth. Taken at the most prominent part of the external mastoid curve. This is very faulty, from the difficulty of fixing on the same point in different heads, the shape of the mastoid protuberances varying much.

B. With the tape. (*c*) Circumferences.

    12. Circumference in the line of length 1.

13.	do.	do.	do.	2.
14.	do.	do.	do.	3.
15.	do.	do.	do.	4.

13, 14, and 15 are of comparatively little value, seldom adding anything to the information given by 1, 2, 3, 4, 9, and 10. I often omit them.

(c) Arcs.

16. From the nasal notch to the inion, or occipital tuberosity.

17. From opposite the centre of one auricular meatus to that of the other, in a vertical line. This is very useful. Taken in connexion with 1 and 16, it gives a fair idea of the height of the head; but it has disadvantages, of which the chief is the uncertainty of the vertical line.

18. From the centre of one meatus to that of the other, along the superciliary ridges and the glabella. Indicates the comparative frontal and occipital development.

It is perhaps unfortunate, especially in view of the great attention now given to the facial bones, that I have seldom taken the length from the chin to the nasal notch, nor the breadth nor length of the nose. It has been my custom, however, to sketch the facial portrait by means of a few initial letters. Thus F., Sc., Pr., Br., Aq., Si., Ang. sketches a man of Fair complexion, Scutiform face, with Prominent brows, Broad cheekbones, Aquiline and Sinuous nose, and Angular chin.

I have spoken of the necessity and frequent difficulty of obtaining the consent of the owner of the head to be examined. His reluctance may sometimes be overcome by means of money, without going to the extent of the new hat always jocularly demanded in such cases. Sometimes other means have proved successful. I cannot resist detailing those by which I succeeded in obtaining a valuable series of head-measurements in Kerry. Our travelling party consisted of Dr. Barnard Davis, Dr. T. Wise, Mr. Windele, and myself. Whenever a likely little squad of natives was encountered the two archæologists got up a dispute about the relative size and shape of their own heads, which I was called in to settle with the callipers. The unsuspecting Irishmen usually entered keenly into the debate, and before the little drama had been finished were eagerly betting on the sizes of their own heads, and begging to have their wagers determined in the same manner.

CHAPTER II.

Prehistoric Races.

THANKS to Boyd Dawkins, and Lubbock, and Evans, and a number of other workers at home and abroad, we know, or at least conjecture with some confidence, a great deal about the surroundings and mode of life of palæolithic man in Western Europe—nay, even about his intellectual development, on which the very spirited and even artistic drawings and carvings he has left us throw some little light. But about his physical type we know next to nothing. Nothing like a strong case, so far as I am aware, has yet been made out for the palæolithic position of any ancient skull discovered in England. The scepticism which some English anthropologists extend to the position of crania generally reputed palæolithic by continental writers—*e.g.*, those of Cro-Magnon on the one hand, and those of Furfooz on the other—may, perhaps, be overstrained; but though England was, doubtless, a part of the continent of Europe at the date generally assigned to these skulls, it would not necessarily follow that the race even of Furfooz should have extended its habitat into this country.

If our palæolithic race were really the ancestors of the Eskimos, or at least their near relations, as Boyd Dawkins would have them to be, it is at least possible that they may have left descendants behind them to mingle their blood with the neolithic races and their descendants of to-day. Now I think some reason can be shown for suspecting the existence of traces of some Mongoloid race in the modern population of Wales and the West of England.

Their most notable indication is the oblique or Chinese eye, with its external angle in a horizontal plane a little higher than the internal one. This is usually accompanied by an almond-like form of the opening, and a peculiar thickness of the upper eyelid: these latter characters may occur without the obliquity of the opening, but with a physiognomy referable to the same type.

I have notes of 34 persons with oblique eyes. Their heads include a wide range of relative breadth, from 72 to 86·6; and the average index of latitude is 78·9, which is not much greater than the average of England and Wales. But in other points the type stands out distinctly. The cheek-bones are almost always broad; the brows oblique, in the same direction as the eyes; the chin, as a rule, narrow or angular; the nose is often concave or flat, seldom arched; and the mouth is rather inclined to be prominent. The forehead usually recedes a little; the inion is placed high, and the naso-inial arc is rather short (13·8 inches), so as to lead one to suppose that the cerebellum is scarcely covered by the posterior lobes. The *iris is usually hazel or brown, and the hair straight, dark brown, black, or reddish.* This type seems to be common in Wales, in West Somerset, and especially in Cornwall.

Colour of Eyes—Six blue or blue-gray, 1 gray, 3 dark gray, three hazel-gray or neutral brown, 16 hazel, 5 brown.

Colour of Hair—Two red, 1 red-brown, 1 dark chestnut, 6 brown, 4 darkish brown, 15 dark brown, 1 brown-black, 2 black.

Locality—Wales, 8; Dean Forest (Welsh surnames), 2; East Somerset, 2; Mid Somerset, 3; West Somerset, 6; Devon, 4; Cornwall, 5; other counties, 4.

No instance of this type has turned up among the (comparatively few) heads from the East of England which I have had opportunity for measuring, and very few from Ireland. I believe, however, that specimens of it might easily be found in the mountainous parts of Connaught, especially on the borders of Sligo and Roscommon. I have seldom noticed it in Scotland, but it occurs in Shetland. Dr. Mitchell mentions the obliquely-set eye in his description of one of his Scottish types, "the Irish Celt or Firl;" but though I am acquainted with the type he evidently had in mind, I cannot recognise in it any resemblance to the Finns of Finland, nor to the pattern of features just described.

There is an Irish type, known to Mr. Hector Maclean, and admirably described by him,* which I am disposed to derive from the race of Cro-Magnon, and that none the less because, like some other Irish types, it is evidently common in Spain, and furnishes, as Maclean remarks, the ideal portrait of Sancho Panza. It is said to be pretty common in the Hebrides, but rare in the Highlands. In the West of Ireland I have frequently seen it; but it is curious, psychologically, that the most exquisite examples of it never would submit to measurement. Though the head is large, the intelligence is low, and there is a great deal of cunning and suspicion.

There are, however, in my lists more than 40 persons who are noted as prognathous, or, more exactly, "having prominent mouths;" 29 of these are English, 5 Welsh, and 11 Irish; roughly speaking, about 6 per cent. of the English, 8 per cent of the Welsh, and 20 per cent. of the Irish list. The "Mongoloids" and the "prognathous" overlap each other in six instances; but except in these cases there are very decided points of difference. The latter have longer and narrower heads; their index of breadth is but 76·5, and in the bare skull would never exceed 80. The cheek-bones are much narrower (135 against 141 millimetres), but almost invariably prominent in the face. The usual form of the forehead is flat, narrow, and square; that of the chin,

* *Anthropol. Review*, Vol. IV., p. 218.

narrow and often receding ; that of the nose, oftener concave than straight, oftener straight than sinuous or aquiline, usually prominent at the point, with the long slitty nostrils, which, whencesoever derived, are a characteristic of the modern Gaels.   The flatness of the temporal region, which comes out in the narrowness of the diameter at the root of the zygoma, gives to the norma verticaolis that coffin- or pear-shape which Daniel Wilson ascribes to the Celts.*   The hair is generally very dark and *often curly*, but the eyes are more often blue or light- or dark-gray than of any shade of brown ; they belong to the blue and violet scales of Broca rather than to the orange.

This is evidently the Gaelic type of Mr. D. Mackintosh,† whom I rank with Hector Maclean as one of the best observers and recorders of local physiognomy.   Mackintosh finds these people very numerous in Dorset and Devon, especially towards Exmoor ; and several of my specimens came from that quarter.   It may be worth notice that there was a large immigration from Ireland into North Devon in the sixteenth century, during one of the perpetually recurring seasons of civil strife in that island.   I should think, however, that such immigrants were probably Anglo-Irish from the towns and coast-districts, and not Gaels at all, and that they returned to Ireland during the next interval of peace.

This one character of prognathism, taken separately, may be objected to as being of small value ; but there is, as I have shown, a very great similarity in other respects among the individuals who present it.   It will scarcely do to ascribe it, as is often done, to the effect of misery and oppression on the physique of the race.   The average stature of my 34 was 5 ft. 7·6 in. (1·717 metre) : my material is taken mostly from the labouring classes, yet in the prognathous list appears one of the ablest and most distinguished clergymen in Wales.   I have also noticed it in the portraits of some well-known Welsh bards ; in fact, eloquence, or at least readiness of speech, seems to be a general characteristic of the type.

While Ireland is apparently its present centre, most of its lineaments are such as lead us to think of Africa as its possible birthplace ; and it may be well, provisionally, to call it Africanoid, applying the name Atlantean, which has been suggested, to the widely-diffused Ibero-Berber race type, of which it is probably a subdivision, in spite of the wide difference in the form of the jaws between it and the Basque type of Zaraus, the best accredited Iberian standard.

Though I believe this Africanoid type to have been of very high antiquity, it must be acknowledged that we have no evidence carrying back its presence, in any of the British Isles, beyond the polished stone period.   But the best authenticated ancient skulls from Ireland may have belonged to it ; for example, the three from the Phœnix Park tumuli (of which two are figured in the *Crania Britannica*), and those from the

---

* *Prehistoric Annals of Scotland.*   † *Anthrop. Review,* Vol. IV., p. 15.

bed of the Nore at Borris.* These show the inclination to prognathism to be of remote date in Ireland, as well as the peculiar form of low, straight brow that still prevails there, and which is connected with low, square, horizontal orbits.

COMPARATIVE TABLE OF MONGOLOID AND AFRICANOID TYPES.

HAIR	LIGHT EYES.						NEUTRAL EYES.					
	Red.	Fair.	Brown.	Dark.	Black.	Total.	Red.	Fair.	Brown.	Dark.	Black.	Total.
Mongoloids (34)...	1	—	2	3	—	6	·5	—	2·5	2	—	5
Africanoids (35)...	1·5	2·5	6	8		18	—	—	·5	2·5	1	4

HAIR:	DARK EYES.						Stature.	Weight.	Index of Nigrescence.
	Red.	Fair.	Brown.	Dark.	Black.	Total.			
Mongoloids...	1·5	—	4	15	2·5	23	5 ft. 7 in.	151·3	64·7
Africanoids...	—	—	1·5	7	4·5	13	5 ft. 7·6 in.	147·6	70

	HEADS, BREADTH.					
	Frontal Minimum.	Zygomatic.	Auricular.	Maximum.	Length.	Index.
Mongoloid (10) ...	4·25	5·67	5·54	6·08	7·70	78·9
Africanoid (13) ...	4.20	5·29	5·15	5·94	7·76	76·6

The Neolithic Period.

Since Daniel Wilson asserted the priority in Britain of the kymbe-kephalic or boat-shaped skull, and Thurnam broached his theory of "long barrows, long heads; round barrows, round heads," so much evidence has been produced in favour of their views, and so little against them, that they may be regarded as fairly established. The frequent— nay, almost general—use of the tumuli and cairns of previous popula- tions by later comers raises a difficulty sometimes as to which may have been the primary, which the secondary interment; and mistakes may have been made in many instances. We may probably, however, put almost entire trust in the list of skulls from long barrows and chambered tumuli, given in the *Crania Britannica*. This list was drawn up, I believe, by Dr. Barnard Davis, who, at the time of its construction, had not become a convert to the long-barrow hypothesis of his colleague, and, consequently, was free from any unconscious bias, which might have led him in some instances to weed out the broader heads as secondary interments. There are 31 skulls sufficiently perfect to yield the pro- portions of both breadth and height, as well as length; and the

* Figured in Laing and Huxley's *Prehistoric Remains of Caithness.*

latitudinal index comes out as low as 71·6, and the altitudinal at 72·6, the latter being taken, after the method of Ecker, from the plane of the occipital foramen, and being larger than the preferable method of Broca would make it.

Rolleston, operating on 10 skulls from the long barrows near Swell, in Gloucestershire, obtained average indices of 72·8 for breadth, and 76·5 for height; and Garson, from 5 Oreadian skulls, which he attributes to the same period, gets a breadth index so low as 70·3. D. Wilson got from 9 of what he considered " primitive skulls " an index of 71·6; but his mode of selection was open to criticism.

But though these figures are probably adequate to give us a correct idea of the general form of cranium in the tenants of long barrows, it must not be taken for granted that they represent accurately the entire population of the neolithic period. We know well, from the light thrown on the ethnological history of Southern Germany by Ecker and Ranke and Von Hölder, that it is quite possible for a large section of the population to be, during long periods, almost entirely unrepresented in the ordinary burial-grounds. The Mongoloid type, which I have already described, if it be really a race-type, and not merely a harmonious concurrence of fortuitous characters, probably existed in this country before the neolithic period, and was akin to or descended from the Belgian race of Furfooz. My Africanoid type, whose index of breadth, measured on the skull, would be about 74·5, may be a mere variety of the long-barrow race. But there are other skulls, or series of skulls, which have been measured and minutely described by careful observers, such as Huxley and Busk, and which are assigned to the neolithic period, but which depart considerably, in their general proportions, from the typical long-barrow cranium. Thus, the cave-skulls of Perth-y-Chwareu,* in North Wales, seem to have a fairly arched contour, and an index of 76·5; while Laing and Huxley's Caithness skulls yield an index of 75·1.† I doubt whether quite sufficient attention has been paid to the greater breadth of these Perth-y-Chwareu and other cave skulls, as compared to those found in long and chambered barrows. After all, though the difference between an index in breadth of 71½ and 76½ is a mere trifle when we are dealing with individuals, it is of some importance when it represents the *averages* of two sets of skulls. We may talk of these Perth-y-Chwareu men as long-heads; but their heads were, to say the least of it, quite as broad as those of modern Welshmen, and rather broader than those of our modern West of England folk, or of the old Anglo-Saxons. Either they were a different race to the neolithic folk of the long barrows, or we need to enquire into the causes of the difference of the twain. When no less an anatomist than Johannes Ranke starts afresh the doctrine that form of brain may depend on ossification of sutures rather than the opposite, it may be time to reconsider the doctrine of Barnard Davis, that the skulls of the long-barrows, or at least the

* Boyd Dawkins's *Cave Hunting*, pp. 168-171.   † *Prehistoric Remains of Caithness*, p. 161.

extreme examples of narrowness among them, owed their form to premature synostosis, however the liability to such a process might have arisen. The so-called "river-bed" skulls, again, have for the most part a rather broad form, with a general resemblance to late or modern types, Irish or English, according to their place of origin; but there is, I apprehend, no particular reason for attributing to these the great antiquity sometimes claimed for them.*

It is almost certain that no considerable body of people now exists in any part of Europe who would yield so low an index—that is, who have skulls so long and narrow—as the occupants of our long barrows. Yet, at the age when dolmens and chambered tumuli began to be built, there is reason to think that extreme dolichocephaly was the prevailing type throughout most of the west and north-west of Europe, from the Baltic to the Straits of Gibraltar.

French anthropologists think there were two palæolithic races of long-heads in their country—those of Canstadt and of Cro-Magnon—before the neolithic long-heads, the first constructors of dolmens, came in from the north-east. If so, it is likely enough that the third race was a blond one, identical with the Tamahu, who are supposed to have imported dolmen-building and the fair complexion into North Africa, and who are portrayed with blue eyes and light hair upon the Egyptian monuments of 1500 B.C. Or, if not, the Tamahu may have been a subsequent wave of long-heads, but the first of the succession of blond northern conquerors, and may have taken up the dolmen type of civilisation, so to speak, as in the historical period the Normans accepted the civilisation of the conquered Frenchmen of Neustria.

The division of the European long-heads is at present sufficiently well marked into a northern blond race or races, extending from Flanders far to the north and east, around the North Sea and the Baltic, and a southern brown race, in Spain, Sardinia, Southern Italy, &c., which extends into Northern Africa. Cross exceptions in colour occur, however, not only in individuals, where they might arise from "sporting," but in considerable masses of population. Thus, certain Berber tribes—especially, it is said, some who dwell in districts where dolmens are very common—contain a large proportion of blonds; while, on the other hand, we have in the western parts of the British Isles, as I shall hereafter show, a notable concurrence of long heads and dark hair; and M. Hamy finds in the dark-haired people of Dalecarlia descendants of the southern long-heads.† These exceptions are sufficient to prevent us from too hastily accepting the notion, commonly held ever since the days of Galen and of Celsus, that the colour of the hair

---

* Dr. Henry Bird, on the strength of observations on certain small, ill-developed skulls from small "tump" barrows, mostly in Gloucestershire, believes in another race prior to the long-barrow men. But the evidence is insufficient.

† The only Dalecarlian I have ever seen had gray eyes and rather dark hair and complexion; his cephalic index was only 73·4, which would be 71·4 in the skull.

depends simply on temperature and latitude; yet, though they indicate that hereditary influence overbears every other factor in determining the distribution of pigment, they must not be taken as proving that no other factor has any power whatever. If, on the one hand, we find that upwards of 3,000 years of Africa have not turned the descendants of the Tamahu into brunettes, we acknowledge, on the other, that their colour was probably developed and fixed for them in some original home in the temperate and comparatively sunless north. If it be true that a dark-haired type is even now flourishing in Dalecarlia, it probably found its way thither by following from the south the gradual northward migration of the reindeer. The history of the British Isles is that of an irregular or intermittent current of invasion from the neighbouring continent—invasion of ideas, of customs, and of arts, even more than of human beings. Anthropologically, Britain has been always a stage farther back in development than the Continent. Thus, in France more than one type of broad-headed men already existed before the building of dolmens was conceived or learned; but it was the pure long-headed race who established the practice in England, though it is not impossible that the race of Furfooz may have existed among them in a state of serfdom.

The comparative date of interments in cists is usually very uncertain: this mode of burial probably preceded, and was contemporary with, the erection of long barrows and galleried tumuli, and certainly it survived them. But we may say with some confidence that most kinds of early round barrows came into vogue with the introduction of bronze, and that bronze and the bronze culture were brought into Britain by a broad-headed race.

The average index of breadth of 80 skulls whose measurements are given in the *Crania Britannica*, and which were not found in long barrows or chambered tumuli, is as high as 82; that of height, according to Dr. Davis's system, being about 76, which would probably be over 70 on the basio-bregmatic plan. Among the 80 are probably a considerable number not belonging to the bronze period; and if these could be identified and subtracted (which is impossible), the breadth might have been greater. On the other hand, Dr. Davis measured the length of skulls, not from the glabella, or most prominent point between the superciliary ridges, but from the plain of the forehead, nearly an inch higher, in order to avoid the frontal sinuses, and approach more nearly to the length of the brain; and this procedure, in a frowning, beetle-browed head, such as were those of most specimens of the bronze race, would somewhat increase the relative breadth. Thus, Davis and Virchow, measuring nearly the same series of stone-age skulls at Copenhagen, got average indexes, the former of 78, the latter of 77·3. Moreover, there appeared to Barnard Davis to be a certain degree of parieto occipital flattening in most of the round-barrow crania, the result, probably, of laying the infant's head on a cradle-board or other hard substance.*   On the whole, however, we cannot be far wrong in describing the British skulls of the bronze period as distinctly brachy-cephalic; and this seems to have been the case in Scotland † as well as in England.   Whether it was so in Ireland also we have not material for forming a judgment; but it is probable that the bronze race did not settle numerously in Ireland, though MacFirbis's traditional account of the Tuatha de Danaan, the large, fair, vengeful race, skilled in music and in magical arts (*i.e.*, bringing with them a higher civilisation), may, perhaps, point to them.

Whence came this race?   Its strong resemblance to a type which abounds in the stone-age tombs of Denmark has struck several observers,‡ the principal points of resemblance being the rounded form, the great parietal breadth, the great development of the superciliary ridges, and the prominent nose and chin.   Except that the parietal breadth is moderate, these characters all occur also in the Sion type of His and Rutimeyer, the fathers of Swiss anthropology, who ascribe it to the Helvetii; and there are skulls which the Swiss savans refer to a mixed type—simply, as it seems to me, on account of their greater breadth—which bear a yet closer resemblance.§   The same characters appear in the modern Walloons, the descendants of the Belgæ, and, with some attenuation—due, it may be, to admixture with the generally long-headed aborigines and Germanic conquerors—radiate from the Ardennes into the north-east of France, to enter into the composition of the Kimric race of Edwards and Broca.   Virchow‖ remarks that the Danish skulls of the iron period, which are very long, gave him the impression of belonging to a different race from those of the stone period: "Sie machen den Eindruck, als seien sie einem anderen Volke angehörig;" whereas he evidently thinks the Borreby type is represented to a considerable extent in the present population of Zealand, which, so far as we are aware, possesses an intermediate index of head-breadth.   I myself found one of 80·6, which would be 78 or 79 in the skull, in 14 Isle-Danes.¶

Looking at these facts in the light of the statements of the classical authors respecting the Cimbri, their original location in or about Jutland, and their south-westerly movement into Belgic Gaul, one is disposed to think the Borreby skulls may have belonged to a race, if not identical, yet nearly allied to the Cimbri, which may have been partly subdued,

---

* For my own part, I am disposed to think too little importance is attached to the mode of nursing infants, as an exaggerating cause of brachycephaly. I believe it to be operative in this way in some parts of Germany; *e.g.*, Nassau.

† D. Wilson, *Archæol. and Prehist. Annals of Scotland*, pp. 168-171.

‡ Especially Rolleston, *British Barrows*, p. 631, &c.   He remarks also (p. 712) that the frequent occurrence of amber in round barrows is an argument for the Baltic origin of the tenants.

§ See further on, in the chapter on Switzerland, a diagrammatic comparison of skulls of these three types.

‖ "Die Altnordischen Schaedel zu Kopenhagen." *Archiv für Anthropologie.*

¶ Beddoe *On the Headform of the Danes*, "Anthrop. Memoirs." See also British Assoc. "Report on Facial Characteristics;" respecting the prominence of the super-ciliary ridges in some of the modern Danes.

partly expelled by a long-headed race of conquerors, Danish or Anglian, and which may have found its way across the Rhineland and Northern Gaul, acquiring the bronze civilisation on the way, into the British Islands. For other kinds of evidence, for or against this view, I must refer to the next chapter.

Whencesoever they came, the men of the British bronze race were richly endowed, physically. They were, as a rule, tall and stalwart; their brains were large; and their features, if somewhat harsh and coarse, must have been manly and even commanding. The chieftain of Gristhorpe, whose remains are in the Museum of York, must have looked a true king of men, with his athletic frame, his broad forehead, beetling brows, strong jaws, and aquiline profile.

What has become of them? Perhaps they were never more than a dominant caste. At all events, continued admixture with other types, in the course of upwards of two thousand years, might well tone down their more salient characters, except in a moderate proportion of instances, in which atavic heredity may have preserved the type. Mr. Park Harrison, who has paid much attention to the point, finds that in those individuals who retain it in its greatest purity, the lips are thin and straight, the ear long and pear-shaped, the eyes bluish-gray, and the hair light; and I am disposed to agree with him, though I think the colour less constant than the form. Among the men whom I have measured in the West of England and in Wales, 82 had heads with a breadth index of more than 80. The colours of their hair and eyes are given below, reduced to percentages; and it will be seen that they are very much lighter, generally speaking, than those of the rest of the local population:

HAIR:	LIGHT EYES.						NEUTRAL EYES.						DARK EYES.						Index of Nigrescence.
	Red.	Fair.	Brown.	Dark.	Nig.	Total.	Red.	Fair.	Brown.	Dark.	Nig.	Total.	Red.	Fair.	Brown.	Dark.	Nig.	Total.	
	4·3	20	26·2	12·8	—	63·3	—	2·4	3·6	9·7	1·2	16	·6	·6	6·1	10·3	1·8	20·5	10·9

It has been noted that the great development of the brows, and the transverse furrow on the forehead above them, are shared by this type with the Australians and some other savage races, as well as by the ancient Canstadt race, who have even been thought to retain in these points a Simian characteristic. Ranke and Kollmann say well, however, that points of likeness to the anthropoid apes are distributed variously among the different races of mankind, but that none of them can be taken in themselves to imply intellectual or moral inferiority. King Robert Bruce's skull was of the Canstadt type, and Savonarola's approached it. Certain it is that the British bronze type is found frequently—I should say with disproportionate frequency—among our best as well as our ablest and strongest men.

There is no distinct craniological or sepulchral evidence of the settlement of any subsequent race in Britain before the advent of the

Romans. Historically, indeed, we know that immigration from Gaul continued after iron had begun to take the place of bronze. What manner of men the immigrants probably were I shall discuss in the next chapter, on other kinds of evidence. Meantime, I may say that the people whose land the Romans invaded, whatever their chiefs may have been, were not themselves, in the mass, of the bronze type. The interments which we call Romano-British vary considerably; but more often than not, I think, they exhibit a type which Professor Wilson and I used to call the Celtic, and which he ascribed to a race of invaders posterior in date to the bronze folk. The name Celtic is better avoided for several reasons, and chiefly because our late master, Paul Broca, limited it, on grounds which he thought sufficient, to the race of men that predominates in the old Celtic Gaul, from Bretagne to Savoy, whose short, thick-set figures and large, broad heads and faces are entirely different from the characters of the people in question. Wilson gave the name of "pear-shaped" to the skulls of these supposed Celtic invaders: the term was not, perhaps, very happy; nor is that of "coffin-shaped," which I suggested, much better. In fine, these skulls are intermediate in length and breadth between the long-barrow and the round-barrow forms: they have the prominent occiput of the former, with some degree of the parietal dilatation of the latter, and a long, flattened temporal region, gradually widening out to the point of maximum breadth, which is generally rather far back. This character belongs to neither of the other types, but seems to me a probable result of their partial fusion. If the existence and prevalence of this type were not brought about in this way, it must either have been the direct descendant of the river-bed and cave men, or have been imported by very numerous invaders from Belgic Gaul. Its resemblance to some forms that occur in Scandinavia, and in the Reihengraber of South Germany, is commented on by Huxley (*Prehis. Remains of Caithness*), and certainly the general proportions of all three are very much alike; so much so that they might be difficult to distinguish with certainty, especially if the lower jaw were not present. Still, the British type usually differs in some details from the Scandinavian: the temporal flatness, particularly, is more marked; the forehead is flatter and squarer; and the eye deeper set, not to speak of differences in colour. The Anglo-Saxon type inclines rather more to be elliptic in the norma verticalis (*i.e.*, when viewed from above); the orbits are more rounded, the chin rounder, the jaw broader, the brows more arched and less prominent. Moreover, the general distribution of the British type through the three kingdoms tells strongly, though not absolutely, against its being a late importation. The only apparent loop-hole of escape for those who think so seems to me to be the following: What if the Milesians, a race, by hypothesis, of Gaelic-speaking conquerors from Spain, perhaps somewhat darkened as to hair by Iberian admixture— what if they overran Ireland in force and naturalised their type there, while long-headed Belgæ did the same thing in England and Wales?

CHAPTER III.

Britain before Cæsar and Claudius.

WE may now proceed to discuss the ethnological position of Britain, especially its southern part, when the invasion of Cæsar brought it within the domain of history.

Cæsar was informed, and believed, that the interior of the island was inhabited by an aboriginal race, and that those tribes who inhabited the maritime parts had passed over the Channel, and had mostly retained the names of the States from which they had proceeded. The lists of the tribes of the south and east of England, which we find in the works of the classical geographers, appear to corroborate this last statement; at the same time, it does not exactly follow from such similarity of name that the Morini and Attrebates of Britain, for example, were identical with the Morini of Flanders and the Attrebates of Artois. Derivations for these names, and those of most of the other tribes, may easily be found in the Welsh language, and were probably significant in the Belgic; in which case similarity of position, rather than derivation of blood, may have been the cause of identity of name; and the Morini of Dorset, to return to our example, may have been so called because, equally with the Morini of Belgium, they were seated on the coast, and not from being a colony of that tribe.

Tacitus affirms that the language of the Britons was "haud multum diversus" from that of the Gauls; and we have the authority of Strabo that the dialects of Belgic and Celtic Gaul were very similar. So little curiosity had the Romans in general about the languages of barbarians, that we are not entitled to conclude, from the silence of Tacitus and the geographers, that there were no great diversities of the kind in that part of Britain known to them; still, Tacitus did found speculations as to the diverse origin of the tribes on their physical aspect, and did not altogether ignore the evidence of language in other cases.* His doing thus, by the way, adds to the probability that in his day the Silurians had ceased to speak an Iberian tongue, if they ever had so spoken; for if it had not been so, Tacitus might have used their language, as well as their curly hair and swarthy countenances, to sustain his theory of their Spanish connection.

Again, the words acknowledged to be old Gallican (such as petorritum) are generally allowed to be explicable by the modern Kymric;

* See the *Germania*, with reference to the Œstiæi and Gothini.

and there is a great resemblance between the Kymric and the Gallic local names, though both in Gaul and in Britain there are linguistic indications of the presence of Gaels.* The names found on British coins—Boduoc, Commius, Dubnovellaunus, Tasciovanus, &c.—may be, in some cases certainly are, both Gallic and Welsh; and the same may be said of the names of the chieftains of Kent, mentioned by Cæsar; but none of them seem to be Germanic. The religious institutions also were alike on both sides of the Channel; so, on the whole, were the arms and ornaments: the torc equally adorned the necks of the Boian warriors, of Boadicea, and of the sons of Llywarch Hên, and of the 363 Kymric chiefs who marched in insolent confidence to the fight of Cattraeth; though the British cetra or target may have been Iberian or Gaelic, not Gallic.†

It is strange, in the face of all this evidence, inferential and circumstantial though it may be, that some weighty authors have favoured the idea of the Germanic character of the Belgæ as a people. Even Palgrave gave it a doubtful adhesion; and Latham does not always and altogether oppose it. The grounds alleged in its support appear to me extremely weak.

They are: firstly, the difficulty of accounting otherwise for the rapid Saxonization of England; secondly, the nearer approach of the Welsh than of the Gaelic to the German tongue; thirdly, certain statements of Cæsar and others as to the German origin of *some* of the continental Belgæ; and, fourthly, the possibility of the Galatians of Asia having been Germans.

The consideration of the first of these objections may be deferred to to my fifth chapter. The second hardly touches the question: the ancestors of the modern Welsh, in blood and language, were the Silures, Demetes, Ordovices, Ottadini, &c.; and these are scarcely suspected of having belonged to the recent Belgic immigration. Very early Belgian colonies, to which the Fir-bolg may possibly be ascribed, might be Keltic or Ibero-Keltic, but must have occurred before anyone dates the appearance of Germans to the west of the Rhine.

As for the third objection, that there were already, in Cæsar's day, some truly Teutonic tribes on the left bank of the Rhine, is probable enough, though their presence there was pretty surely recent.

Though Cæsar had been told by the Celtic Gauls that most of the Belgæ were of German descent, more precise information seems not to

---

* Guest and Peacock. The former thought the Belgic tongue was Gaelic rather than Kymric; and Leo, quoted by Taylor, partially supports him. Taylor, *Words and Places*. Davies, *Celtic Researches*. But most of their examples are doubtful. Basil Jones, *Vestiges of the Gael*. But the local names given by him may have been of later introduction, though probably not.

† *Cran. Brit.* Much confusion arises from the likeness, in their modern forms, of the words Gallic and Gaelic. Some French writers reason from their supposed identity.

have confirmed this statement; for he subsequently specifies* four small tribes—the Condrusi, Eburones, Cœresi, and Pœmani—as Germans, apparently to the exclusion of the other and greater tribes. And even the Eburones, by the way—if we may draw an inference from the name of their great war-chief, Ambiorix—were but doubtful Teutons. Tacitus, who evidently aimed at accuracy in the matter, allows only the Tribocci, Nemetes, and Vangiones, all close to the Middle Rhine, in the modern Elsass, to be "haud dubie Germanos;" adding, that the Treviri and Nervii affected a Germanic origin because it gratified their vanity. The modern population of Hainault, the ancient territory of the Nervii, is Walloon in language and in physical type,† notwithstanding its having been occupied by the Franks; and therefore is *probably* not of German origin. To the Treviri I will return presently, as their case is important. The Gallicism of the great tribes of the Remi, Bellovaci, Suessiones, and Attrebates has hardly ever been doubted; and the name of the last-mentioned, and the fact that Divitiacus of Soissons made conquests in Britain, lead us to derive some, at least, of the British Belgæ from this quarter.

Gallic skulls from the region of the Bellovaci, so far as I have seen, differ considerably in general from those of the Merovingian Franks, but much resemble certain skull-types common in the West of England; and these skull-types are of very old date in Belgium and Northern France, occurring in remains from the sepulchral caves of Nogent, as well as at later periods. And the figures of the provincials on the monument of Jovinus, in the Cathedral of Reims, beautifully discriminated in type as they are from the Roman Governor, are equally and conspicuously unlike the modern Germans in feature; while, notwithstanding the great influx of German Franks that must have poured into the Belgic provinces in times subsequent to that of Jovinus, the modern inhabitants of Reims are mostly quite unlike Germans in complexion, and exhibit, equally with the monumental figures, the tall frames, square foreheads, and long, sharply-drawn features, which constitute William Edwards's Kymric type.‡ The same complexion and features continue to prevail, with little modification, as one journeys north-eastwards through the Ardennes, as far as Liege and Verviers (where many of the Walloon inhabitants reminded me strongly of Cornishmen); but they suddenly change, and give way to German characteristics, when we cross the frontier of the Walloon dialect in the direction of Mechlin or Aachen. Seldom can we see an ethnological line so distinctly drawn as that between the Walloons and the Flemings, though for hundreds of years they have been under the same government. My own observations show the facts pretty clearly, the indices of nigrescence for the Flemish-speaking country varying from a minus number up to + 26, and those for the Walloon districts

---

* *Bell. Gall.*, ii.4.　　　　　† Vanderkindere, *Recherches, &c.*

‡ See the frontispiece for a comparison of the Belgic with the old Frankish type; the latter still visible in the peasantry of the Lower Rhine.

from 28 to 61; but the beautifully displayed statistics of Professor Vanderkindere are equally distinct, and far more extensive and weighty. Of the 26 arrondissements into which Belgium is divided, in 14 of which Flemish is spoken, and in 12 Walloon, every one of the 14 shows more blonds and fewer brunettes than any one of the 12. At the same time, M. Houzé demonstrates a decided difference in the breadth of the head between the Flemings and the Walloons. It is difficult not to be convinced that we have here to do with a real ethnic frontier, and that we have on the north a Germanic, on the south an old Belgic type. I may be reminded that the old Reihengraber type, to which the Franks and Alemanni are supposed to have belonged, was long-faced as well as long-headed. So it was, to some extent, but not so remarkably and generally as the Kymro-Belgic form I have been describing. Moreover, it both was and is usually combined with fair hair; whereas we have seen that the Walloon type includes comparatively dark hair in the present day; and in all probability, though the chiefs, the true Galatæ, were fair, the mass of the old Belgæ was of old something like what it is now.

The modern Trèves is now within the limits of the German tongue. I should say that the German physical type also prevails there, though not so as to overpower all others; but the city, lying as it does on the eastern side of the principal masses of frontier hill-country, may probably have been Germanised during the great westward movement of the Ripuarian Franks in the fifth century.

But the main point of interest about the city, for us, is the fact, avouched by Jerome, that the Asiatic Galatians spoke the language of Trèves. Now nobody, until lately, ever dreamed of denying the Gallicism of the Galatians. Niebuhr, having made the Treviri Germans in spite of Tacitus, evaded the difficulty by the futile explanation that Jerome's Galatians were not Galatians at all, but Goths from Thrace. In this, I believe, no one has followed him; and Latham has rather severely characterised the criticism in his *Germania*. But others have made the Galatians German, on the ground that the names of the two chiefs who led them across the Hellespont, Leonarius and Lutarius, are very like the German Leonhard and Lothar (as they certainly are). To this, however, a sufficient answer seems to be, that of the three principal Galatian tribes, the Tectosages undoubtedly, and the Trocmi and Tolistoboii apparently, bore Celtic names; and that the same may be said of their subordinate tribes, the Tosiopi and Teutobodiaci; of most of their chiefs, *e.g.*, Brennus, Bitoetus, Deiotarus, Brogitarus, Bogodiatorus; and of some of their towns, *e.g.*, Eccobriga and Tolosochorion. Taylor (*Words and Places*) gives a list of local names in Galatia, containing some others that might support my argument; but he seems to be in error when he quotes several which embrace the root Mag or Myg to show the Gaelicism of the Galatians; some at least of these words, such as Magnesia, having existed long prior to the arrival of the Galatians in Asia, though they may possibly date from that of the Kimmerians.

In the Triads the Belgæ seem to be spoken of as "the refuge-taking Men of Galedin;" and the part of South Britain extending between Kent and Somerset—*i.e.*, precisely the part which the Belgæ did certainly occupy—is called Arlechwedd Galedin in a list of the divisions of Britain.* To return to the physical characteristics of the Belgæ, we know that they appeared to the swarthy Romans to be a tall and rather fair race; but if they had been generally so tall and fair as the Germans, Caligula would have had no need to choose the tallest of them, and dye their hair, when he wished to make them pass for German captives.

On the whole, I have little difficulty in concluding that the Belgæ—though there was in some of their tribes, and perhaps in the noble and military caste throughout, some infusion of German blood; and though former waves of long-headed and light-complexioned warriors, Kymric or Galatic, may have rolled over their country and mixed blood with them in earlier ages—were a Celtic-speaking and, to some extent in blood and physique, a Celtic or Celtiberian people in Gaul, Asia, and Britain.

There remain, however, still some arguments from other quarters in favour of the presence of Germans in Britain at this early period.

Of these, one is derived from the statements in the Triads, and elsewhere in the old Welsh literature, respecting the Coranied; another from the mention by Ptolemy of Petuaria and a Gabrantuicorum Sinus, in the country of the Parisii, north of the Humber. The Coranied are said in the Triads to have been one of the races who came into Britain in a hostile manner, and to have come from the land of Pwyl, which is by some interpreted to mean the marshy lands (pools) at the mouths of the Rhine, but by Lord Strangford, who discredited the whole story, to have been some mediæval Welshman's notion of Poland. They are also said to have treacherously made common cause with the Saxons in their invasions. In the tale of Lludd and Llewelys, in the Mabinogion, are some fantastic stories about them, in which they are represented as a race of magicians (reminding one somewhat of the Tuatha de Danaan of Ireland) who were destroyed by King Lludd. According to E. Davies,† one of this race was called Cawr or Cor, a giant; in the plural, Coried or Corion. All this sounds very mythical; still, to those who find in the Jotuns of Scandinavian mythology merely the primitive Finnish inhabitants, it will present little difficulty. The Coranied are identified with the Coritavi or Coritani of the Romans, from the similarity of the first syllable in each word, from a statement that the Coranied settled about the Humber, and from the name of Ratis Corion having been applied to Leicester, seemingly the chief town of the Coritavi. The only grounds for making the Coranied and Coritavi (allowing them to be the same) Germans are, their siding with the Saxons, and having a Latin name ending in AVI, like the undoubtedly Germanic tribes of the Batavi and Chamavi. I entirely disagree with this view, for the following reasons:

* Iolo MSS., p. 477.   † *Celtic Researches*, p. 200.

They are supposed to have occupied the counties of Lincoln, Nottingham, Derby, Leicester, Rutland, and part of Northamptonshire; and in these counties I can find no Roman station whose name appears to be Teutonic; while the important town of Margidunum, near Southwell, in Nottinghamshire, bears a name almost certainly Celtic, and Ratis Corion does the same; and Nottingham would seem to have remained Celtic long enough for its Welsh name not to have been altogether forgotten even in the time of Alfred; for Asser says it was called in Welsh, Tigguocobauc. Again, if the Coritavi were Germans, and were overlaid by successive strata of Angles and Danes, one may reasonably expect to find the Teutonic physical type prevalent over their whole area to a degree not found elsewhere in Britain. Now, in the northern part of the Coritanian area it is really very prevalent, but in the southern (Leicestershire and Northamptonshire) there is, if I may judge by the colours of the hair and eyes, a strong non-Teutonic element. The following table shows a great difference between Lincoln and Leicester, Nottingham and Northampton, in these respects, there being a much larger proportion of dark hair in the two more southern towns:

	Number Observed.	COLOUR OF HAIR: Red.	EYES LIGHT.					EYES NEUTRAL.					EYES DARK.					Index of Nigrescence.
			Fair.	Brown.	Dark.	Nig.	Red.	Fair.	Brown.	Dark.	Nig.	Red.	Fair.	Brown.	Dark.	Nig.	
Lincoln...........	500	2	15	35·2	8·5	·2	·4	1·2	5·2	4·4	·2	·9	1·3	8·1	15·8	1·7	12·3
Leicester	540	3	13·9	26·6	7·1	·1	·8	1·6	6·6	6·8	·2	·4	1·3	7·8	19·9	3·7	20·8
Nottingham......	700	3·7	15·3	24·6	9·9	·3	1	1·8	6·1	5·1	·1	1·1	1·4	9	18·2	2·2	14·1
Northampton ...	300	3	9·8	35·6	13·3	·8	·3	·7	3·5	4·5	—	·3	·5	5·3	18·7	3·8	31·1

Professor Phillips, than whom no ethnologist was a keener observer, once visited Leicestershire, with the expectation of finding a strongly-marked Scandinavian type predominant there; but he was surprised to find a dark-haired type, which he supposed to be Celtic, equally prevalent. This may easily be accounted for, and that without treating the traditions about the Coranied as altogether spurious, as Lord Strangford thought them, if we suppose the Coritavi to have been a colony of Celtic Belgæ; but, unless we throw aside the evidence of physical type, we can hardly conceive how they can possibly have been Germans. Moreover, the silence of Tacitus respecting any suspicion of there being Germans in the island, except the Caledonians, is of weight on the same side.

The names Petuaria and Gabrantuicorum Sinus do certainly, at the first blush, look rather Teutonic than Celtic; but the suggestion of Mr. Isaac Taylor, that the Parisi or Parisii may have been Frisians, does not commend itself to my mind. The name of the Frisians was too well known to have been thus distorted; and Ptolemy would probably have called them φρισσονες or φρισιοι, as Procopius did subsequently. If Whitaker's etymology* be trustworthy in this instance, as I incline to think, the

* *History of Manchester*, i., 45.

Parisi were simply Paruis, herdsmen, and the Gabrantic goatherds. Thus fades away, bit by bit, all the evidence in favour of the presence of Germans in the southern part of Great Britain before the Roman period.

Tacitus, whose ideas are always entitled to consideration, thought the Caledonians were of German origin; but the only grounds he assigned for this opinion were their huge limbs and fiery-red hair (*rutilæ comæ, magni artus*). If their language had been German, he would probably have known and mentioned the fact, as he mentioned the Gallic language of the Gothini and the Œstiæi. Modern philologists do not, I believe, pay any respect to the notion of Jamieson, that Teutonic names existed in the north-east of Scotland prior to the arrival there of the Angles and the Norsemen. The red hair and large limbs are still prevalent in Athol and Marr and Badenoch (see 51, 52, 53, &c., in my Scottish table); but all we can say of them is that they point to an origin from the northern rather than from the Mediterranean long-headed races. The Caledonians might have come over from Denmark, and yet borne their Celtic name; but to one who looks at them from the point of view of the physical anthropologist, it may seem more likely that they were a Gaelic or a Pictish tribe, with a strong dash of the athletic broad-headed element.

In Ireland the name of the Cauci suggests a Frisian colony; but I know of nothing else to favour the notion. The Irish traditions indicate that there, as in Great Britain and in France, successive swarms of fair-haired invaders overlay the dark-complexioned aborigines; but that any of them were German, in the strict sense, is improbable. It may be worthy of remark that the inhabitants of the Aran Isles, in Galway Bay, are reputed to be descended from the Firbolg, who were masters of Ireland before the advent of the Tuatha-de-Danaan, and that they have nearly the same long-featured, long-headed type already spoken of as common in the Belgic region of Northern France. In this connexion, the opinion of Dr. Guest, that the Belgic dialect belonged rather to the Gaelic than to the Kymric branches of the Celtic tongues, becomes very suggestive.

There remain other questions, similar to that of the presence of Germans in England before Cæsar, which present still greater difficulties; such as the following: Were there considerable remains of the Gael among the Cymry and the Lloègrians of England and Wales? Was there a notable proportion of Iberian blood among the Britons, especially the Silures and the people of Cornwall? Who were the original Lloegrians? and had they any connexion with the Ligurians beyond the similarity of their names? Did the Phœnicians really trade directly with Cornwall? and if so, did they leave there any traces of their blood?

Until of late years, almost all we had to show for our belief in the existence of an Iberian substratum in our population were, the conjecture of Tacitus respecting the Silures; the length of head in the long-barrow people and some other neolithic men; the resemblance

between the Welsh cave-men and Busk's Gibraltar skulls; and the supposed greater frequency of dark hair, especially in the west, than could
otherwise be well accounted for.   I hope to be able, in a later portion of
this book, considerably to define and strengthen the evidence of physical
characteristics.   In the meantime, I will say that dark eyes and dark
hair, often curly, are still very frequent in Siluria, but that the dark
colours are not much less so in Dyfed and Gwynedd, the other ancient
divisions of Wales.   Dark and even black hair is abundant also in
Cornwall and Devon, and in those parts of Scotland and the North of
England where Kymric blood may well be supposed to remain in large
proportion, such as Upper Galloway, Strathaven, and Allendale.   And
Strabo says that in his time the Britons were somewhat (taller and)
darker-haired than the Gauls; so that we must suppose that rather
dark hair was frequent among the ancient Britons in general, though
perhaps especially so among the Silures.   I am prepared to admit that
a physiognomy strikingly Iberian (or Basque-like, at least) is commoner
in South Wales than in any other part of Great Britain.   Many photographs of Basques, and some of Bearnese, are recognised, both by myself
and by an observant Welsh anthropologist to whom I have submitted
them, as being in no respect different from some of the ordinary types of
feature in South Wales.*

Anthropologists have long been awaiting the appearance of some
philologist fully qualified to determine the important problem whether
there be really an Euskarian or Iberian element in the Kymric languages,
or, if so, whether it be equally or more potent in the Gaelic and Erse.
The existence of such an element had been boldly asserted, and super-
ciliously denied or ignored, until recently Professor Rhys has answered
our call with the assurance that the element which physical phenomena
has led us to look for does really exist; that it is to be found in
Gaelic rather than in Kymric, and in Pictish rather than in Gaelic;
and that the Iberian symptoms among the Silures must be accounted for
by their having been, in part at least, Gaelic before they became Kymric
in language.

Professor Rhys's opinion is clear and consistent, and may be recon-
ciled with physical facts better than any other hypothesis on the subject,
as I shall subsequently demonstrate.   The well-reasoned affirmation of
Skene, that the Pictish language was, phonetically, intermediate between
Gaelic and Kymric, is the principal obstacle in its way, and that is not,
perhaps, insurmountable.   The Pictish of Skene, and even of Bede, may
have been the Celtic language in the form which it took in the mouth
of the Picts; and it is noteworthy that the Picts had been brought
intimately into contact with tribes some of which spoke Brythonic, and
some Gaelic dialects.

The evidence in favour of the importance of Phœnician intercourse
with Britain, and of the introduction of at least some little Punic blood

* Greatheed made the same remark, *Archæologia*, xvi.

into Cornwall, may be found in the chapter of the *Crania Britannica* on the " Historical Ethnology of Britain." The statements of Diodorus and others certainly lead one to suppose that the intercourse had had a considerable effect; for the grave, black-robed people, described as inhabiting Cornwall, nowise remind us of the British dress, aspect, or character. Traffic with the Phœnicians must have involved intercourse with Spain, but to what extent is quite inscrutable. The maritime position of Cornwall, and its many good harbours, have led to the introduction of a variety of ethnological types and elements, of which the Semitic is one : the Iberian was pretty surely there previously. That the long-barrow race can have been a ruling caste of Phœnicians does not seem possible.

The presence of Gaelic-speaking folk in Great Britain has already been touched upon. The subject has been chiefly in the hands of the philologists, and the evidence upon it has been gradually growing stronger. There are those who think the long-barrow race, if Iberian in blood, were Gaelic in speech ; and they adduce Gaelic etymologies for the names of places where chambered barrows and other megalithic monuments exist.[*] If the bronze race spoke Kymric, as is generally believed, and if the long-barrow people still spoke Iberian, it is a little difficult to identify the Gael in the craniological calendar.

The opinion of Lhuyd, that most of the river-names of Great Britain must have been bestowed by the Gaels, is not capable of complete proof, from the near relation of the two branches of the Celtic, but it appears likely enough. Some of them are, perhaps, older still, dating from the Iberian or pre-Gaelic period.[†] Bishop Basil Jones supplies, in a work which seems to me a model of dispassionate criticism,[‡] a considerable amount of evidence of the presence of Gaels in the coast districts of North Wales and in Brecon at or soon after the time of the Roman invasion, and Professor Rhys a good deal more—weak in detail, and of a presumptive and inferential character, for the most part, but strong in the aggregate—to indicate that the greater part of Wales was more or less Gaelic even to the later period when the Kymric Britons from the north subjugated the whole of that country; and that Devon, on the evidence of the Ogham inscriptions, was still partly Gaelic during the Roman dominion.

The presence of Irish physical types in Wales may, of course, be accounted for by the common ethnological elements in the diverse branches of the Celtic-speaking folk, or by the later immigrations from Ireland ; but if I am correct in my belief, based on repeated observations, that persons of thoroughly Gaelic aspect [§] are common in the

---

[*] Thus Dr. Henry Bird.   [†] Hyde Clarke.   [‡] *Vestiges of the Gael.*

[§] That is, with dark brown hair, gray eyes, long heads, flat in the temporal and prominent in the upper occipital region ; with cheek-bones prominent rather than broad ; jaws often prominent, but somewhat narrow. Such persons are occasionally, but rarely, seen in other parts of the south and even of the east of England. Dr. Mackintosh found them plentiful in Dorset.

Mendips and in Exmoor, while we know of no Irish immigration into Mendip during the historical period, and while these are precisely the districts into which a conquered race might flee for refuge, the fact furnishes a slight additional argument in favour of the views of Lhuyd and his followers.

As for the Lloegrwys, the view that identifies them with the Belgæ is nowise favoured by the Triads, which speak of them as very near akin to the Cymry, and distinguish from both of them the men of Galedin, who were pretty certainly, and the Coranied, who, if anything, were probably, Belgic. The assertion that the Lloegrwys came from Gwasgwyn or Gascony would be in no way decisive, even if we could at all trust to it as anything but a mediæval fiction; for the Volcæ Tectosages of Tolosa appear to have been the same people with the Tectosages of Galatia, and these latter, as we have seen, spoke Belgic; so that Belgic tribes had penetrated pretty early as far as the Garonne. The temptation to identify them with the Ligurians is very strong; but whatever the old Ligurians were, they differed considerably from the Cymry. As met with in north-western Italy, they seem to have been a very broad-headed race—brachycephalic, indeed, to a degree very rarely met with in our islands, even in isolated cases.* The theory that connects the Lloegrwys with the river Liger (Loire) is less open to objection. On the whole, we shall run least risk of violating probabilities based on the Triads, and on what little we know or surmise of their physical characteristics and language, if we suppose them to have partaken somewhat of the blood of that great stock which, whether we call it Ligurian, or Celtic, or Arvernian, has survived the conquests and migrations of upwards of 20 centuries in the centre and south of France, and furnished the ancestry and the physical type, and perhaps the language too, of the swarthy, broad-headed people who prevail there to this day.

The Brythons may have been derived from a more northern part of Gaul, where the tribe of the same name inhabited Picardy, and accordingly partaken more of the Belgic blood. The physical characteristics of the descendants of the Strathclyde Brythons are nearer to those of the Walloons than are those of the modern Welsh. The great stature of the men in some of the vales of Upper Galloway, where Strathclydian blood is probably pretty well preserved, is very remarkable, and distinguishes them from their relations in the Principality. The average stature of upwards of 70 men in the Glenkens district, measured by the Rev. George Murray, of Balmaclellan, exceeded 5 ft. 10¾ in. (179 centimeters); and in some other districts about the Border, where the old British blood is more or less mingled with Anglian, Norse, or Gaelic, it is little less remarkable.†

* Nicolucci, in 10 old skulls from Liguria, found an average length-index of 86·7. Calori has shown that brachycephalism prevails in Northern Italy generally. Language and head-form both indicate that their connexion was with the Southern Celts rather than with the Iberians.

† Beddoe On Stature and Bulk, pp. 32-43. Report of the Anthrometrical Committee of the British Association.

To sum up this chapter, the natives of South Britain, at the time of the Roman conquest, probably consisted mainly of several strata, unequally distributed, of Celtic-speaking people, who in race and physical type, however, partook more of the tall blond stock of Northern Europe than of the thick-set, broad-headed, dark stock which Broca has called Celtic, and which those who object to this attribution of that much-contested name may, if they like, denominate Arvernian. Some of these layers were Gaelic in speech, some Cymric; they were both superposed on a foundation principally composed of the long-headed dark races of the Mediterranean stock, possibly mingled with the fragments of still more ancient races, Mongoliform or Allophylian. This foundation-layer was still very strong and coherent in Ireland and the north of Scotland, where the subsequent deposits were thinner, and in some parts wholly or partially absent. The most recent layers were Belgic, and may have contained some portion or colouring of Germanic blood; but no Germans, recognisable as such by speech as well as person, had as yet entered Britain.

CHAPTER IV.

The Roman Period.

TO what extent was the ethnological position of Britain modified during the Roman period?

This question may be analysed into several, and made to read as follows: Was the destruction of the native Britons extensive? What was the magnitude and character of the immigration brought about by the Romans? Did the Gaels on the west, or the Saxons and kindred tribes on the east coast, effect any considerable settlements before the departure of the Romans?

With the exception of the campaigns of Suetonius, it does not appear that the reduction of southern Britain to a province was attended with any extraordinary destruction of life. Agricola and some other generals who took part in it are described as men of exceptional mildness. Still, the tender mercies of the Romans were cruel; and when Tacitus put into the mouth of Galgacus that famous sentence, "Ubi solitudinem faciunt, pacem appellant," he must have felt that there were pretty good grounds for the charge he thus made against his countrymen. The Iceni and other tribes who joined in the revolt of Queen Boadicea may probably have been almost exterminated; but the relations of the empire with the Germans at that period were not such as to justify the conjecture of some writers, that the vacant seats of the Iceni were filled up with settlers from the German coast, a conjecture that seems to me baseless and extravagant.

In process of time Britain was traversed by numerous great roads, and studded with Roman colonies and stations and villas, the remains of which are found generally, it is true, in the immediate neighbourhood of the roads, but sometimes at a considerable distance from them. In Gloucestershire, Somerset, Kent, Essex and Hampshire, and along the line of Hadrian's wall, the Roman or Romanised population must have been considerable; and even in the more remote, rugged, and unattractive parts of the island it is difficult to get more than a few miles away from some trace or other of Roman occupation. On the other hand, in situations favourable for the preservation of such remains—for example the Wiltshire downs—are found the vestiges of British hut-villages, whose date is fixed in the Roman period, and sometimes rather late in that period, by the evidence of coins disinterred.

Different writers have taken very different views of the position of the native races under the Roman *regime*, views varying from that of Whitaker, who believed that most of the British tribes retained under the Roman sovereignty some remains of their autonomy (pretty much as Sikkim, for example, does under the British, notwithstanding the existence within its limits of important British stations like Darjiling), to those of Thomas Wright, who seemed to think that hardly any British blood was left except among the servile peasantry, the towns having been occupied exclusively by the people of mixed or diverse descent introduced by the Romans from every other part of the empire.

The population of Italy, already, at the beginning of the Imperial period, exhausted by the selfish policy and destructive wars of the Roman aristocracy, could hardly, even during an occupation of 350 years, have spared enough of their increase to re-people Britain, while they were equally or more intensely engaged in colonising Spain, Gaul, Africa and the Danubian countries. The Spaniards had almost an equal period allowed to them for the colonisation of their American dominions, where they had to do with nations who may be said, without any glaring error, to have borne to them in respect of civilisation and military character something like the same relation that the inhabitants of Western Europe did to the Romans. But except in Chili, where the climate is particularly congenial to European constitutions, and where the aboriginal population was but scanty, they did not succeed in making themselves the numerical majority; and as soon as the stream of immigration was cut off, their numbers and importance, relatively to the aboriginal races, began to decline.

But the Roman system of transferring the military population of every subject territory, in small bodies, to various other parts of their dominions, where they could not help losing their own nationalities, and acquiring that of their masters, renders this analogy of very little value. The Romans may be said to have had at their command, as Romanising agents, as large a proportion of the population of their whole empire as they found it convenient to levy for military purposes. The *Notitia Imperii* shows us that bodies of Syrians, Cilicians, Spaniards, Moors, Thracians, Dalmatians, Frisians, &c., formed the military colonists of the stations in Britain; and when even the emperors themselves were often not of Italian birth, and the most trusted officers and governors provincials or even barbarians, we have no reason to suppose that any notable proportion of genuine Roman blood found its way to this country. "No doubt," says Mr. Wright, "the colonists of these towns were accompanied or followed by their relations and friends; and as evidently they were recruited from their own countries, they must have gone on increasing and strengthening themselves. They were all, however, obedient to Roman laws and institutions, used the Latin tongue, and had, indeed, become entirely Romanised." It is doubtful, however, whether a settlement of Moors, for example, could have even maintained its numbers without large and constant immigration. So extensive was the empire, that the natives of its southern and eastern borders could hardly have become fairly acclimatised to the cold and humid regions of the north-west. I shall return to this point presently; it is of some importance in explaining the disappearance, in most cases, of all traces of the blood of these colonists, a disappearance which may also depend, in part, on the heterogeneous character of the Romanised population taken *en masse*, which would render its potency, in breeding, very inferior to that of a comparatively uniform and pure-bred race like the British rural population, among which it was dispersed. If we seek for light by investigating the effect of Roman occupation on language and physical type in other countries than our own, we find the evidence somewhat diverse and doubtful, yet not without interest and value. Thus we find that a comparatively short occupation sufficed to destroy the old language of Dacia, and to modify, in the opinion of some observers, the Dacian physical type by the introduction of an Italian one, which has not even yet been quite worked out; that a much longer occupation replaced the Iberian tongues by a Romance language in the greater part, but not the whole, of Spain; and that it was only just long enough to produce the same effect in Gaul, where a Celtic tongue survived the Roman dominion, but had already received its death-blow, so that it languished and died out. In both the latter cases the physical type seems to have been a little, probably only a little, modified. The case of Armorica would be very valuable for our purpose, if we were not in the dark as to the extent and effects of the immigration into that country from Britain, from the time of Maximus (the Maxen Wledig of the Welsh) downwards. We know that the Veneti, the leading people of Armorica, had been ruthlessly extirpated as far as possible by Cæsar, and that the whole country had been, like Britain, seamed with Roman roads and dotted with towns and villas. So far the cases are parallel. But a few hundred years afterwards, there having been no disturbing agencies of any great account in the meantime, except the immigration from the kindred and like-historied land of Britain, we find scarcely a trace left of the blood, language, polity or religion of the Romans; and the chief enemy which Christianity has had to struggle against, and which it is said not to have succeeded in altogether eradicating even in our own day, is a Paganism attaching itself to the dolmens, the maenhirs, and the natural objects of the country, evidently the direct descendant of that which ruled before the introduction of the Roman ideas.

Very similar would probably have been the history of our own country but for the interference of the Saxons. In proportion as the central authority grew weak, the spirit of nationality among the Britons seems to have revived. About the second and third centuries of the Roman dominion we find, so far as I am aware, hardly a trace of a truly British name, owing, as I conceive, to the fact that every Briton of consideration, in public transactions, such as dedications, &c., used a

Latin name in compliance with fashion, though he probably enough bore among his own people a purely Celtic one, pretty much as a Maori chief nowadays has very frequently two names, one of which is an English one, often borrowed from some friendly colonist.

About the year 408 we come upon a " Count," an officer of rank and talent, and the main pillar of the usurper Constantine's fortunes, who bore the name of Gerontius. Whether this was the Greek Γερόντιος, or a translation of the Welsh Geraint, I cannot say; but thereafter, with the exception of those supposed to be members of the Ambrosian family, we find none but Celtic names among the chiefs of the British people.

If any part of England, except perhaps Kent and Essex, was more thoroughly Romanised than the rest, it must have been the tract traversed by the wall of Hadrian. To the import of the disappearance of the names of almost all the towns on the wall I shall have occasion to revert in a succeeding chapter; it has, I think, in conjunction with similar facts in other quarters, an important bearing on the nature of the Saxon conquest. But I wish now to point out that in the only instance, out of 19, in which the Roman name has survived, that of Carlisle, the ancient Lugubalia, the Welsh Caer-luel, that name sounds very like a Welsh one latinised; and that the only other, in which any relation at all between the old and the new name can be made out, is that of Magna, now Carvoran, where Carvoran seems to be a Celtic name signifying "the great castle," probably meant as a translation of Magna: from this I draw the inference that Magna had lapsed into barbarism and Britannicism before that region was conquered by the Angles.

If we extend this examination to England in general, we shall find that throughout the whole land the Roman local names that survive bear but a small proportion to the British ones; and that where such Roman local names do still exist they are usually British ones latinised, e.g., Lincoln, Wroxeter, Cirencester, &c. Spinæ, the modern Speen, is, however, a notable exception; Pennocrucium (Penkridge) and Brocavium (Brougham) perhaps only apparent ones. The Kentish instances I pass by for the present.

It does not seem possible to extract anything of value respecting this period from Geoffrey of Monmouth, nor yet from the fragments of uncertain date and origin contained in the Iolo MSS. If we could give any credit at all to them, they would add weight to the opinion of Whitaker, that British chiefs continued to hold a certain sway over their own compatriots, much as the chiefs of Arab tribes in Algeria are allowed to do at present by their French masters. There is indeed one set of traditional accounts which, though contradictory in themselves chronologically and genealogically, must surely contain some kernel of fact; I mean those relating to the presence of Gael in Wales, and especially in Gwynedd and the modern Breconshire, which I have already referred to. Professor Rhys points out that Serigi, the Irish chieftain said to have been expelled from North Wales, is probably Sitric the Norseman (Sigtryg with the silken beard?) pre-dated several hundred years; but though he distrusts much of the evidence of the presence of the Gaels in the third or fourth century, he does not doubt the fact. The real doubt is, whether the Gaels were Irish invaders, the Scoti mentioned as having raided in Wales in the time of King Niall-of-the-Nine-Hostages, or were the original occupants of the country. The latter theory is supported not only by the numerous arguments adduced by the Bishop in its favour, but by the extreme improbability that the Romans would have allowed the Irish Gael to acquire by violence settled possession of a large portion of one of their provinces.

This destruction of the Gaelic dominion in Wales by the northern Cymry, under the leadership of the sons of Cunedda, seems to have taken place somewhere about the time of the supposed invasion of Kent by Hengist; but we may as well note here, by anticipation, the probable ethnological results. The Gael in Gwynedd were not extirpated; and ages afterwards we hear of the fifteen royal tribes who were regarded as pure in blood, because uncontaminated by marriages with the descendants of the conquered Gwyddel (Gael). A large part of the population may have remained Gwyddelian in blood, and even in sympathies, for some generations; else how should we account for the position, as national heroes, sorcerers though they be, which is held in the Mabinogion by the princes of that race, Gwydion ap Don and Math ap Mathonwy? The account of the occupation of Garth Mathrin (Brecon) by the Gwyddel is tolerably clear, and contains no discrepancy or improbability; and we are told that their descendants continued to dwell there in the historical period, intermixed with the other natives.

Meanwhile certain intertribal movements were taking place in Ireland and Scotland, of which we know very little with any approach to certainty. The power of the Milesians, probably a Celtiberian race from Spain, who are described by Mac Firbis as traditionally "white of skin, brown of hair," may have been still growing at the expense of prior Celtic-speaking conquerors, and of the Cruithne or Picts, who still remained a separate nationality in parts of Ulster, if not elsewhere. Whether the early Oghams belonged to them or to some of the prior conquerors may be a little doubtful; but I think Mr. Brash and General Pitt-Rivers have made out a strong case for their having been the work of a tribe who crossed over from Spain to Munster, and perhaps also to Devonshire. The Scots, a Milesian tribe, or at least under Milesian leadership, were beginning to make settlements on the western side of the country to which they were to transfer their name.

So much for the ethnic movements on the western side of the islands. Those on the eastern side about the same period were also of importance; but that importance has, I think, been exaggerated. I mean the gradual or successive introductions of Germanic blood into the coast-lands, extending between Portsmouth and the Wash, which Kemble, Palgrave, and several other modern writers on this portion of our history, including all those in whom scepticism is so strong that they prefer conjecture to tradition, regard as having amounted to a thorough Germanisation of the whole region, so as to entitle it to be called "the Saxon shore" by as full a right as it had acquired two hundred years later. I prefer to range myself in this matter on the weaker side, if that can be called the weaker side, which, though few in number, includes the powerful authority of Dr. Guest.

The designation of Litus Saxonicum appears to me no more to imply that the Saxons had occupied the country than that of the " Welsh Marches " implied that the Welsh occupied West Worcestershire in the twelfth century. There was a corresponding Litus Saxonicum in Gaul, in parts of which, and especially about Bayeux and in Artois, Saxons may have been actually settled, nay, did settle, either then or at a later period; but the name in that instance was extended to the whole coast of Brittany, and we have no reason whatever, historical, linguistic, or physico-anthropological, for supposing that the Saxons ever settled except on very small portions of that coast. It is extremely improbable, considering the troublesome piratical habits of the Saxons, that the Romans would have chosen to constitute a complete fringe of them* on a coast abounding with inlets and harbours admirably adapted for carrying on their favourite occupation. But if it is meant that not only the coast, but the inland parts bounded on the west by a line drawn from Portsmouth to the Wash, had been re-peopled with Saxons by the Romans, these further difficulties arise:

Why was the Comes Litoris Saxonici not rather called Comes Provinciæ Saxonicæ, or by some equivalent title? When and whence was so immense a multitude of Saxon captives obtained, from a people whose own territory was not then conterminous with that of Rome, and who appear to have confined themselves to maritime expeditions? How is it that in the *Notitia Imperii* we find no evidence of the imposition of new local names in the interior by the colonists, which, if the settlement had been of the character and magnitude claimed for it, would almost certainly have taken place, considering the passion for bestowing new names which their subsequent history shows the Saxons to have had.

The argument, then, based on the words " Litus Saxonicum " may perhaps be dismissed; but there are other grounds for supposing the existence in Britain of a considerable Teutonic population introduced by the Romans. In the first place, as Wright remarked, the longer the empire endured the more dependent it became on the swords of the Germans; and so that race may gradually have come to predominate in

---

* According to the *Notitia*, the second legion lay at Richborough, and auxiliaries in the other garrisons along the Saxon shore, Dalmatians, Sarmatians, Belgic Gauls Tungrians, but NO SAXONS.—GUEST, *Early English Settlements in South Britain*

the military colonies, in several of which Tungrians and Batavians were stationed from the first. Moreover, we have precise statements as to the introduction of other bodies of Germans on several occasions. Thus Marcus Aurelius brought over a multitude of Marcoman captives, and Probus did the same with such Vandals and Burgundians as he had taken, as well as a number of Alemanni. Crocus, an Alemannic king or chief, was one of Constantine's supporters when he was proclaimed emperor at York, and had doubtless a following of his own nation ; and the Bucinobantes, a small Alemannic tribe from near Mayence, were transported into Britain by Valentinian, and are supposed to have been located at Buckenham in Norfolk, under their chief Fraomar.

These are all the facts of the kind mentioned by Kemble, or, I believe, by any other authority, Saxon, British, or modern ; and I venture to express the opinion that they are, though of course not unimportant, scarcely sufficient to bear the weight of inference erected upon them. They do not strike me as of the magnitude required to account for a great ethnic change in an extensive country, which seems at the time to have been pretty thickly inhabited ; for they all occurred long after the supposed destruction of the Iceni, and it is not likely that the best corn district in Britain should have been allowed to lie waste during all that time. The tribes mentioned were of the High German division, and traces of High-Germanism in England are indistinct.* Some might say, moreover, that the somewhat elaborate Teutonic social and agrarian system, which Kemble and Palgrave describe as prevailing in Saxon England, and as having been imported from the continental Saxonland, could hardly have grown up, or been reproduced, among a number of colonists scattered in a strange country among alien neighbours, and subjected either to Roman military discipline or to Roman civil government.

This position, however, is completely turned by those who, like Seebohm and Coote, deny that the English land-laws and social organisation (apart from that of a mere military caste) were German rather than Roman, and who, accordingly, hold that the majority of the population of Eastern England descend from ancestors who were here before the Anglo-Saxon conquest. These opinions are supported with great ability and learning, and must be further discussed bye-and-bye.

Meanwhile, we may suppose that towards the close of the Roman period—let us say in the year 400, between the usurpations of Maximus and of Constantine—the Romanised population of the towns, under the influence of bad government, dissensions at home and invasions from abroad, were beginning to decline in numbers and importance; while the British people, who, still retaining their (as I believe Celtic) language and partially their institutions, occupied most of the intervening country, probably maintained their numbers and increased in relative importance; for in the decline of civilisation it is the most cultivated

* See, however, Seebohm, especially as to the word Gebur (= villan), p. 394.

portion of the community which suffers most and relatively dwindles. There may have been, in some parts of the East of England, limited Teutonic settlements still retaining the memory of their ethnic character, and possibly their language; if so, they may have been ready, as the Welsh say the Coranied were, to side with Saxon invaders; but evidence of the fact is awanting. In the western parts the Roman power had probably waned still more than in the east and south: the Celtic tribes were doing pretty much what was right in their own eyes; and the extrusion or subjection of the Gaelic inhabitants of Wales by the Cymric tribes of the north had probably already begun. With migrations under Maximus, or subsequently, from Britain to Armorica, we need not much concern ourselves: they would be rather an overflowing than an extrusion of the native race; but the uniform statement, found not only in the suspected and much-abused Gildas, but in every native reference to the period, that the Romans ultimately *departed* from Britain, cannot be neglected altogether. We need not and cannot suppose that there was an universal emigration of the citizens. London and Anderida, for example, were well inhabited in the next generation; and so too, it would seem, were some towns in Kent and Essex. But the wealthy planters, no longer safe under the government of their mother-country, would in many cases return thither, leaving their splendid villas and estates and the British serfs who tilled their fields; and with the military force would go the merchants and skilled artizans who ministered to it, and to whom it assured peace and employment; and thus in a short time the towns would probably be drained of the best portion of their population, including almost all those who were more Romans than Britons. A single generation had not passed away when St. Germanus, in his attempts to evangelise the island, found himself dealing with chiefs whose very names a Roman would probably be unable to pronounce; though a few families, like that of Ambrosius, might for a generation or two continue to pride themselves on their Roman descent and cultivation.

CHAPTER V.

The Anglo-Saxon Conquest and Period.

WHO were the Saxons, Angles and Jutes? When and whence did they come? and to what extent did they modify or displace the previous population of the Eastern parts of Britain?

The last of these questions includes by far the most interesting and important part of the inquiry we are engaged upon, and it is the one respecting which there has been the widest diversity of opinion; but we must give a little attention, in the first place, to the other two.

A great deal has been written on the relations of the words Angle and Saxon, and of the peoples designated thereby. Latham, in particular, has discussed the matter, according to his wont, very learnedly; though it can hardly be said that he has made it much clearer. I am disposed to think, indeed, that he has made it in some points a little more obscure, owing to his too great solicitude about the connexion of particular tribes with particular dialects. The great changes that have taken place in the limits of the several languages and dialects of North Germany since the period when we know, on good historical authority, that *tribal* migrations had almost ceased in the lands between the Rhine and the Eyder and Trave; the manner and extent to which the Old-Saxon * and the Danish have yielded to the Platt-Deutsch, the Platt-Deutsch to High Dutch, and the Frisian to all its neighbours, while all traces of the Wendish have silently disappeared, should make us very cautious in arguing on the relations of our Teutonic dialects to those of the mainland, the more so as we have not in general the means of making the comparison between contemporary stages of these dialects. The tribal names we have to do with—those of the Jutes, Saxons, Angles and Frisians—were certainly not applied, by the only ancient authorities we have, with anything like the exactness we expect from them. It has been doubted—hypercritically, I think—whether "Saxon"

---

* It is quite possible, if, as Mr. Howorth supposes, the Saxons were a tribe of conquerors from beyond the Elbe, while the descendants of the Cherusci, Chamavi, &c., were their lœts or churls, that the language of these latter was always Platt-Deutsch, rather than Old-Saxon.

was even a native name; at all events, it has for upwards of a thousand years been bestowed by the Celts upon populations the greater portion of which do not appear ever to have acknowledged it. The limits of confederacies like those of the Franks, Saxons and Frisians (to which we may perhaps add the Angles likewise, who seem to have sometimes included the Warini) varied from time to time, and by no means always coincided with the limits of the dialects. Hengist (if Hengist ever existed, as I believe he did) was probably a Frisian. The Frisians about Tonning have a tradition that he sailed from that port; but Bede supposed him to have been a Jute, and the Welshmen, who "fled from him like fire," called him a Saxon; while the Chronicle, in recording the fact, speaks of him and his warriors as Engle; so that by one and another authority he is made to belong in turn to each of the four tribes in question. I do not wish to deny the existence of differences, physical as well as dialectic, between the Frisians and the Saxons, understanding by the latter name the modern inhabitants of Northern Westphalia and Hanover, &c., Holstein and part of Sleswick. But Zeuss looked upon those of the latter kind as mere developments. He says: "Die Angel-sachsen und Friesen noch Sprachdenkmaler haben, die mehren Jahnhunderte hinaufreichen, und unter sich in naher Verwandtschaft, ferner dem Oberdeutschen oder Gothischen stehen. Angelsachsisch und Altfriesisch sind als spätere Fortbildungen aus gemeinschaftlichen Grunde, dem Ingœvischen Sprachzweige, zu betrachten." Even now the likeness of some of the Frisian dialects to "Saxon" English and to Lowland Scotch is extremely close, though the Frisian naturally retains more archaic forms. It may be worth while to note that the name *seax* for a knife, said to have been peculiar to the Saxons, is found in the Saterlandish as *sox*, by the side of *knif*.

The Frisian physical type is one of great interest to the anthropologist, partly on historical grounds, partly by reason of the remarkable and almost peculiar media among which they live. They are an extremely fair and very comely people. Professor Johannes von Müller once made some remarks to me on this point, noting particularly the beauty of the women, which, he said, had struck him immediately on crossing the frontier from a Saxon district. My own observations corroborated those of von Müller. I found the Frisians, from the Zuyder Zee, through Groningen (a Saxonised district), to beyond the Ems, a taller, longer-faced, more universally blond and light-eyed folk than the Saxons, the latter being very often hazel-eyed, even when their

Official (children).			Beddoe (adults).		
		BROWN EYES, per cent., with			
Aurich	Light hair	7·87	Leewarden and Groningen	Chestnut, &c., hair...	5·5
	Dark hair	5·60		Dark hair	6·5
Leer	Light hair	9·44	Leer	Chestnut, &c.	8·5
	Dark hair	6·84		Dark hair	5·8
Munster District	Light hair	13·65	Munster District	Chestnut, &c.	9·
	Dark hair	6·20		Dark hair	8·3

hair is light.* Dr. D. Lubach, who, as a Hollander, has had greater opportunities than I, distinguishes a Frisian from a Hollandish or Low Dutch type, assigning to the former a taller and more slender frame, a longish-oval flat skull, with prominent occiput ; a long-oval face, with flat cheek-bones ; a long nose, straight or aqiline, the point drooping below the wings ; a high under-jaw, and a well-developed chin ; the skin very fair ; the hair of all colours, but seldom very dark. To his Low-Dutch type he gives a shorter, more thick-set frame, with shorter neck and broader shoulders ; a rounder, broader, less flattened head, little or no projection of occiput ; a rounder face, more prominent cheek-bones ; a nose short, low-bridged ; the chin various, sometimes receding and pointed ; the skin and hair more often dark than in the Frisian type. In the former I recognise the Frisian of D. Macintosh, "not less English," says he, "than the Saxon," and very common in the north of Kent ; the latter is comparatively rare in England, but spreads upwards along the Rhine, and furnished studies of boors to Ostade and Teniers.

The cranial form of the Frisians has been studied with great care and labour by Virchow. Its most uniform and remarkable character is its lowness, its small vertical elevation. It seems, as Virchow himself says, that the brain develops somewhat in breadth to make up for this ; for though, in passing through the country, one gets the impression that the people have long and *narrow* heads, and though the facial features and the general form of the head itself are of the dolicho-cephalic cast, yet the breadth index, in both old and recent skulls, seems to average as high as 77 or 78, and is often much higher. Withal, the length and narrowness of the nasal opening is remarkable and pretty constant, according with Lubach's description of the nose in the present population, but differing from that of the Merovingian Franks.

As for their relations with the Saxons proper, and the degree of probability of their having united in the conquest or settlement of England, it should be noted that some three or four centuries later than the supposed date of Hengist's invasion, a sort of tribal antipathy seems to have existed between the Frisians and the Saxons, which continued in being, more or less, for centuries after Witikind's Saxons had cut off a Frisian army levied by Charlemagne for foreign service. But there is no evidence that I am aware of of any such mutual hostility at an earlier period than the eighth century as would have prevented some com-munity of action in the invasion of England. Combination among Germanic tribes for similar purposes was notoriously common about the time of the wandering of nations ; and the confederates were often separated far more widely in language and customs than the Saxons and Frisians can possibly have been. Thus, the Cimbri,

* See my tables for Holland and Germany. This difference is confirmed by the more recent official colour-census of Germany.

Teutones, Tigurini, whatever they were, must have differed *inter se :* thus, Ariovistus led several tribes to the field against Cæsar ; and, later, the Alans accompanied the Vandals, and the Huns furnished cavalry to the Goths.

Who, then, were the true Saxons, excluding any Frisians who may sometimes have passed by that name ?

There are two or three possible hypotheses respecting them. The name may not have been native, but may have been one fixed on them by others ; in which case it is easier to believe that the Frisians were often included under it. Secondly, it may have been applied to the Cheruscans, Angrivarians, and neighbouring tribes, at a later period than that of Varus and Arminius. This is not very likely, as the Saxons were already known to Ptolemy, who placed them much further to the north-east than the Cherusci. Thirdly, they may have been a martial and aggressive tribe (as we know they had the reputation of being), and may have spread from the neighbourhood of the Elbe over the Weser country, subduing the prior occupants, and becoming the dominant class. This latter opinion, which is that of Mr. Howorth, appears, on the whole, most probable. It accounts best for the disappearance, or perhaps rather the non-appearance, of the Anglo-Saxon speech in the region which the Old English called " Old Saxony," which they erroneously looked upon as their old home because their kindred had come to occupy it since their separation.

We are told that the Thuringians, after their subjugation by the Franks (aided, apparently, by the Saxons), were reduced in status, their nobles becoming simple freemen, their freemen descending to the rank of lazzi or serfs. Thus it may have been with the tribes of Germanic race who were conquered by the Saxons or by the Jutes. I am more disposed to look on the Kentish lœts as freemen of the lower rank, who accompanied their lords to England, than as being *en masse* prior occupants, Romano-British or Belgic.

The true Angles seem to have been the most northern tribe of the Saxon confederation, and to have dwelt beyond the Ditmarshian Frisians, to whom or to the Frisians of Western Sleswick they may have been indebted for the means of passage to Britain, though some of them may have extended as far as the Elbe, and thus possessed an independent way of access to the North Sea. The Saxons who were not Angles may have had similar relations with the Southern Frisians ; but, from the description we have of their daring seamanship, it is probable that in the fourth and fifth centuries they had direct access to the sea, possibly by the Elbe if not the Weser. Mr. Kemble found near Stade (a very Frisian region, anciently Chaukian), and also far up the Weser, certain mortuary urns, rare or unknown in other parts of Germany, but known to occur in Suffolk, Warwickshire, Derbyshire, the Isle of Wight, and other parts of England. They may, perhaps, have belonged to a particular tribe of Saxons, for nobody, I believe, locates any Angles on the Weser; but it is noteworthy, as indicating the admixture of the conquering tribes in England, and the community of enterprise just now insisted on, that the districts mentioned are commonly called Anglian or Jutish.

Who the Jutes were is perhaps the most difficult part of the question. Latham and others prefer to make them Goths from a Visigothic State in Normandy. I believe them to have been a Gothic tribe, a part of the one which gave name to Jutland, but not Danes; the true Danes were then farther east. That some Visigoths from Gaul took part in the conquest I would readily admit, as I would admit also the concurrence of Franks from the Rhine, and of Saxons from the new settlements of that people in what was afterwards Normandy. But the West Jutland dialect, like all the others that have been mentioned, has its points of close resemblance to current English, and I see little reason to discredit the old view respecting the Jutes. That they were to some extent a distinct tribe is supported by the positive assertions of Bede, by the statements of the Saxon Chronicle, and by the occurrence of similar and peculiar forms of ornament (the Kentish fibulas) in the settlements ascribed to them. On the other hand, the similarity of the mark, or patronymic place-names, and the other place-names in Kent and in other parts of England, forbids us to imagine an exclusive Jutish nationality.*

I have already spoken of the physical type of the ancient and modern Frisians: that of the other old inhabitants of the region, whence the invaders are supposed to have come, remains to be studied. The prehistoric material is, unfortunately, scanty. That dolichocephali existed between the Rhine and the Trave and Oder, as they did to the west and to the east of those limits, may be taken for certain: the discoveries at Minsleben, for example, are sufficient to prove this; but whether brachycephali were contemporary, though probable, is not proven. They were present in Belgium, we know, at a very early period. Dupont's discoveries, and, above all, Arnold's Sclaineux skulls of the neolithic age, with their breadth-index of 81 to 88, furnish us, probably, with a reason why the modern Walloons have rather broad heads, as well as some modern Zealanders. We have already noted the occasional occurrence of very broad heads among the Frisians (Virchow); but whether these should be taken to be other than the frontier instances of a variable type, or the results of the influence of a peculiar medium, the alluvial marsh-lands of the North Sea,† on the blond long-headed type, may be doubtful.

Further to the north, in the direction of the possible home of the Jutes, the skulls that have come down to us from the bronze and early

* A.D. 586, Tytila, the son of Uffa, ruled in East Anglia. His name is very like that of the Ostrogothic king Totila. Were the Uffings Jutes?

† Is it inconceivable that some defect of phosphatic salts in the soil, and thence in the food, might have some influence in this direction?

iron ages are long and very narrow;* and probably this would be the prevailing type among invaders from that quarter; though doubtless the short-headed type, with high vault and prominent brows, must also have been in existence there, subject or incorporated.

To the south of Jutland and Frisia, in the remaining parts of Holland and of North-Western Germany, though the countenance and general aspect of the people does not vary much in different districts, the breadth-index does, apparently, vary more than in some other countries. Sasse and Lubach, operating on considerable numbers of skulls, up to 20 from one locality, have found the average index vary from 75 to 80 or more, not to speak of the remarkably round heads which occur about the mouth of the Scheldt.† The breadth does not increase as one proceeds from north to south, within the limits just mentioned; the Flemings, at least, have an index of about 76. (Houzé, Virchow.) For the southern part of the Old Saxon country—Westphalia, Brunswick, &c.—there is, I believe, very little information. In 13 living men of Northern Hanover and East Friesland, I found a mean index of 79·2, which in the skull would be about 77.

So far, the modern inhabitants of these countries would appear to differ little in the most important article of head-form from those of the East of England, though they may have in some districts a tendency to greater breadth. The race elements cannot have altered much since the era of the Saxon conquest : the only new ones worth mentioning that have been introduced having been, firstly, the Slavonic captives, reduced to slavery and brought westwards during the Germanisation of the country beyond the Elbe; and, secondly, the refugees from the south during the religious wars. These elements, if they had any effect at all, would tend to enlarge the prevailing indices.

We have, however, fortunately, a valuable accession to our knowledge of the physical type of North-West Germany in the paper of Dr. Gildemeister, in the *Archiv fur Anthropologie* for 1878. It embraces full details of the measurements of 103 skulls, from old burying-grounds at Bremen, some dating from the beginning of the Christian period, and the whole yielding, says Gildemeister, " ein Bild der Bevölkerung Bremen's etwa zwischen dem 9 und 14 Jahrhundert." One would expect to find a (so-called) Saxon population, with some Frisian blood, but very little other admixture.

Gildemeister divides this remarkable collection under three types, assigning 72 to the grave-row (Reihen-Graber) series; 26 to what he supposes to be a Frisian type, but which, unfortunately I think, he styles Batavian; 5 to a brachycephalic one, unnamed. I do not feel sure that the division between the first and second type is fully warranted, for

---

* Virchow, *Archiv. f. A.* 1873.

† At Saaftingen, below Antwerp, the index of 11 skulls from a submerged churchyard was found to be 86·4, while the same crania belonging to Antwerp yielded one of 77.—M. Kemna, in *Bulletins of the Paris Society* for 1877.

reasons which will be more easily comprehended after inspection of the accompanying diagram (opposite) and table, which I have constructed from Dr. Gildemeister's data:

	Maximum Length.	Inial Length.	Frontal Breadth.	Mastoid Breadth.	Maximum Breadth.	Circumference.	Ear-height.	Occipital Length.	Longitudinal Arc.	Breadth Index.	Height Index.	Nose Index.
In Graverow, Males... 46	190·2	180·5	97·2	129·3	139·7	532·6	118·9	98·7	377	73·6	71·6	46·6
Females 26	182·7	170·8	93·7	...	137·8	...	115·4	...	...	75·2	71·4	47·9
Batavian, Males 10	192	183·2	98·2	131·4	151·4	551·5	116·3	98·7	379	79·7	66·1	47·3
Females 13	180·9	170	97·1	...	143·1	...	111·3	...	...	79.2	68·1	51·4
Brachycephal (Males?) 5	175·4	170	99·4	134·8	153·4	524·2	121	93	367	86·9	75·4	45
Whole Series, Males 63	190·8	181·3	97·6	130	143	536·6	118·9	98·7	378	75·8	70·8	46·6
Females 40	181·8	170·5	...	...	...	...	...	...	...	76·6	70·5	49
Both sexes 103	...	...	...	...	...	...	...	...	...	76·1	70·7	...

When the breadth-indices have been arranged diagrammatically, after the method which Kollmann and Galton especially have utilised, it will be seen that, though the series is somewhat irregular, it does not depart very greatly from the line of a curve whose maximum point would be about 77; not very much higher than the average, which, it will be seen, would be about 76·1. But when the series is dissected into three, though the small Batavian division yields a tolerably uniform curve, the Graverow one, which, after culminating at 75, should gradually descend to zero at 85, comes to an abrupt conclusion at 79-80.

If we construct a diagram of the height-indices, the result is much the same; there is a much nearer approach to a regular and satisfactory curve if we throw together the three divisions of Dr. Gildemeister. On the other hand, it must be confessed that variations so great as from 66 to 89 in the index of breadth, and from 59 to 82 in that of height, are very unusual in an unmixed race; in which, indeed, the highest possible authority (Broca) says they should not exceed something between 10 and 15. The differences between the Graverow and Batavian divisions which appear in the measurements are not very great: the latter are more exuberant laterally, in the temporo-parietal region, distinctly lower, and somewhat more capacious; but in occipital projection and breadth of base there is hardly any difference. The 5 brachycephalic males are so different from the "Batavians," in almost every point except the absolutely large breadth, that if we concede a several origin to the latter, we certainly must do so to the former. In that case, they may probably be referred to the Disentis type of Switzerland and Swabia.

These two subdivisions excluded, the whole remainder, nearly three-fourths of the entire series, may be taken as the mediæval representatives of the Saxons of Witikind, if not of Hengist. They pretty closely

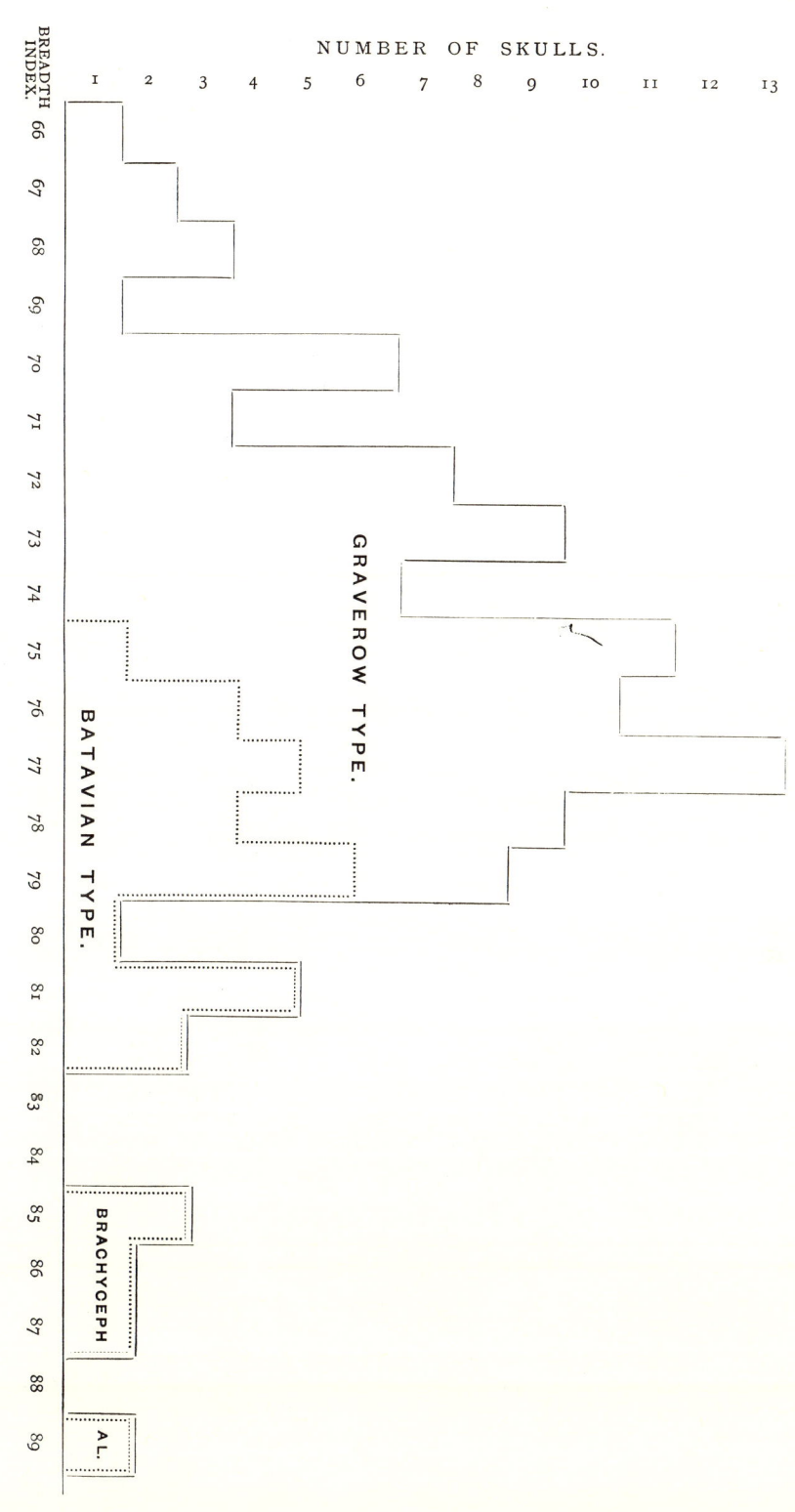

resemble the remains we possess of the other Germanic conquerors of the fourth and fifth century, the Merovingian Franks,[*] the Burgundians, the Alemanni at an early date when little mixed, and even the Goths, if the cemetery at Almuneçar be really Gothic. The resemblance is not one merely of breadth, but extends to the general contour, both facial and cranial. Very constant are the projection of the occiput, the post-parietal flattening, the somewhat roof-like norma occipitalis, the rounding of the frontal region as viewed from above, the prominent chin, the nearly vertical cheek-bones. Small differences there are, which may have been tribal, though certainly not constant. Thus, the nasal index is said to be larger in the Franks (as also in many of the modern Hollanders, who may represent the Salian Franks) than in the Graverow men of Swabia, the oldest Alemans. In Gildemeister's Saxons it will be seen to be small (46·6 in the males): what it was in the Anglo-Saxon I regret to be unable to affirm with any confidence; the point could be settled only by very careful and leisurely measurement. There are differences also in the degree of development of the superciliary ridges, which may have been more tribal than individual; and here Gilde-meister's Saxons, and the Saxon conquerors of England, were perhaps, as a rule, less rugged in feature than the Franco-Thuringians. On the whole, I believe the Saxons, Franks, Burgundians,[†] and Alemanni to have been branches, but lately separated, from one great blond and long-headed stock, which may have been the Hermionian of Tacitus. Differences of dialect, known to have existed at a later period, but fairly conjectured, from the personal names, to have been already in being, may have been developments partly due to the conquest of, or intercourse with, people of other tongues. In this department, philology may be trusted to follow in the steps of anthropology, so soon as these shall have been firmly planted. Anthropologists had long been crying out for the remains of an Iberian or pre-Celtic language in the British Isles before their philological brethren woke up to the consciousness of their existence. Mongolian or Ugrian types had been recognised, though less distinctly; and now Ugrian grammatical forms are being dimly discerned in the Welsh and Irish.[‡]

On the whole, the following theory of the origin of the "Anglo-Saxons" may be put forth as probably not far from the truth:

The first invasion was made in Kent by certain of the northern Frisians and their neighbours the Jutes. Its success encouraged the more adventurous spirits in all the country near the coast, from the Rhine to beyond the Eyder, to follow their example. As a rule, the more northern of the invaders attacked the more northern parts of the

---

[*] Burgundians of Savoy, lat. ind. 74·9 (Hovelacque); Merovingians, 76·3 (Broca). The figures given by Ecker, His, and Von Holder, for the Alemanni, are much the same.

[†] De Mortillet says the contents of Franks and Burgundian tombs are almost identical; the same brooches, beads, belt-plates, pottery, &c. The Saxon paraphernalia are nearly the same. [‡] Elton, p. 167.

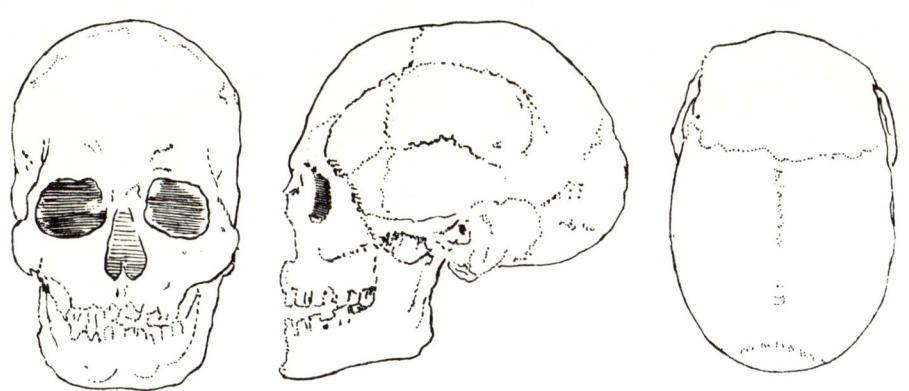

GILDEMEISTER'S GRAVEROW TYPE.

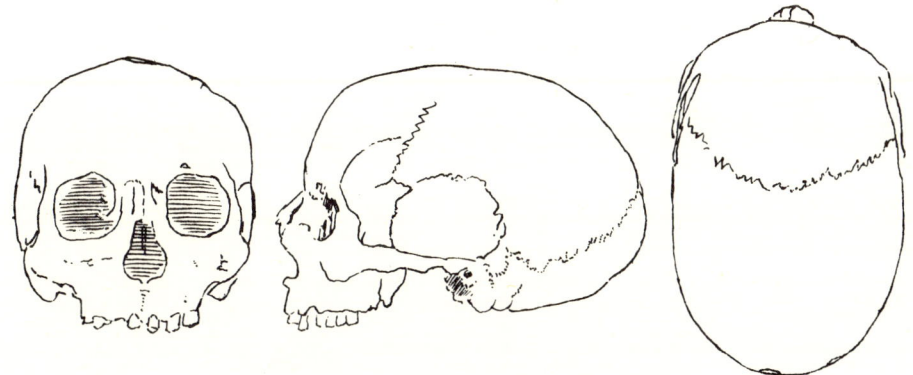

GILDEMEISTER'S GRAVEROW TYPE,
BREMEN.

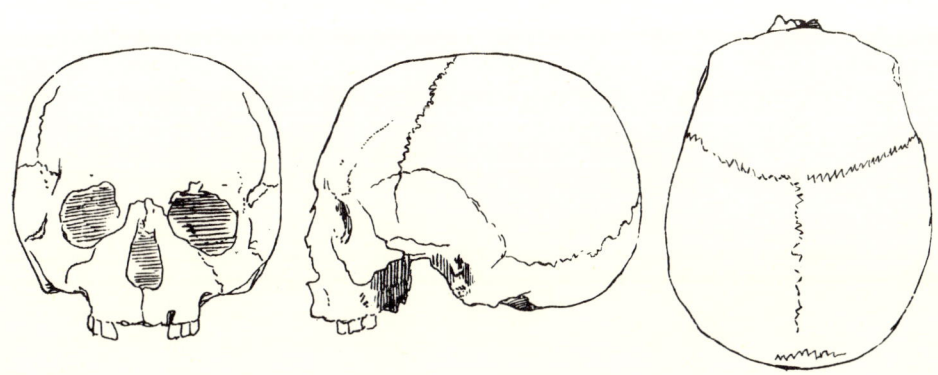

GILDEMEISTER'S BATAVIAN TYPE.

ARROWSMITH, BRISTOL

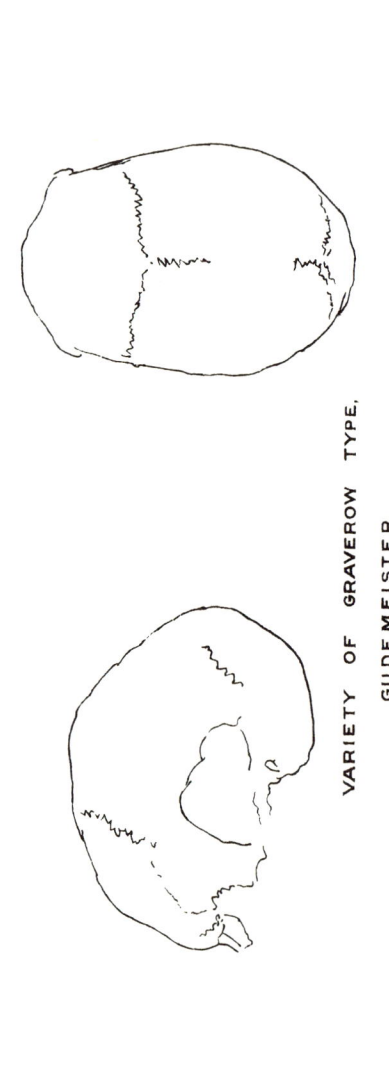

VARIETY OF GRAVEROW TYPE,

GILDEMEISTER.

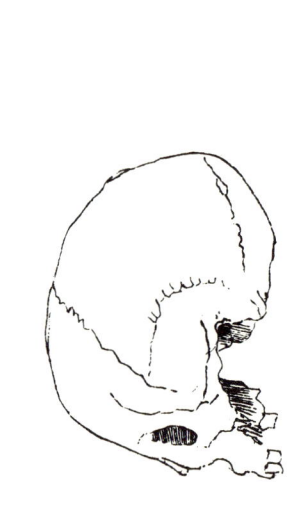

GILDEMEISTER'S BATAVIAN TYPE.   FEMALE.

ARROWSMITH   BRISTOL

island, landing about the Yare, the Wash, the Humber, or even the Forth; and these caused a preponderance of the Anglian dialect, which leaned somewhat towards the Danish, in those regions; while the southern pirates, from the Rhine, the Yssel, the Ems, the Weser, and, above all, the Elbe, occupied the south-eastern parts of the island. Certain Visigoths from Normandy may have joined with the Jutes, who, by hypothesis, were a remnant of their kindred who had never hitherto left the neighbourhood of the Baltic, in supporting the great invasion by Cerdic; and they acquired lands in the Isle of Wight and the district of Meon; but as the southern or true Saxons much predominated in that quarter, they ultimately adopted the dialect of their neighbours.* Spite of any possible shades of difference in language, the evidence of a common national feeling among them, a consciousness of racial identity, was very strong. In Beowulf even the Danes are spoken of as if of the same race. The national traditions and national heroes were common; the kings drew, or believed they drew, their origin from the same sacred family; their religion was the same; their laws differed little. Not that in these half-military, half-piratical, colonisations this kind of congruity among the invaders was likely to have been much considered: the principle of selection, if selection there was any, was probably that of the Jomsburg vikings, who cared little for nationality in comparison with prowess.†

The date of arrival of the Saxons (or Jutes) in England has been much debated. I trust I have shown some reasons for my belief that only piratical descents, not leading to permanent settlements, had taken place before the abandonment of Britain by the Romans. How soon after that event the Saxon colonisation began is a matter of less importance. Haigh brings forward a good deal of evidence to show that it was in 428; but it may have been as late as 449, the commonly received date.

In considering the manner and extent of the earlier conquests of the Saxons, as I shall continue to style them in order to avoid any ambiguity that might arise from calling them English, one finds oneself compelled to make an estimate of the credibility of the only author who could have written from personal knowledge or direct information, namely, Gildas. Gildas has been fiercely assailed of late years, chiefly by those writers who hold strong views as to the predominance of the British element in the modern English people. No doubt his work is liable to the strongest objections: meagre in fact, copious in words, stuffed with sounding

---

* There is an argument against the importance of any Visigothic constituent of the invasion, which I do not remember to have seen noticed. The Goths in France were already Christians of the Arian sect.

† Jarl Hakon, of Norway, after his battle with the Jomsburgers, was presiding at the beheading of his prisoners. His son induced him to spare eighteen of them, among whom was found a Welshman, named Björn. The fact is a warning not to trust too much to the linguistic character of proper names. (Note by Lord Strangford.—Welsh-man is as likely as not to mean Italian or Frenchman, without any further specification. Björn may have been an Orsini from Rome.)

epithets, it is evidently the production of a monk who, himself more than half a barbarian, outdid, through affectation, the faults of civilised writers. Some portion of what he relates is, no doubt, incorrect and exaggerated, but there seems no reason to suspect him of wilful falsification. Unfortunately, his aim was not so much to give us the historical facts of the conquest, as to improve the whole affair for the benefit of his countrymen. The book must be taken for what it may be worth, which would not be very much, indeed, if we had anything better to substitute. It contains one famous passage,* which, having been quoted by both Bede and Nennius, has greatly aided in bringing about the popular belief that in most parts of England the Britons were either exterminated or utterly enslaved. To the consideration of this I shall return after a while.

Our other principal authorities for the Saxon Conquest are Bede, Nennius, the *Annales Cambriæ* and *Brut y Tywysogion*, which, however, are extremely meagre on the points which concern us; the genuine poems of Aneurin and Llywerch Hên, and, above all, the Saxon Chronicle. To these may be added the works of numerous chroniclers who founded their works mainly upon the last-mentioned storehouse of facts, including Ethelwerd, Henry of Huntingdon, and many others. In some cases these later chroniclers seem to have had access to sources of information lost to us; but in other of their amplifications it is pretty clear that they sacrificed truth to what they thought literary effect.

Putting together what we can gather from all these writers, we obtain a pretty fair account of the gradual conquest of Wessex, and some idea of that of Northumbria, and even of Sussex and Kent; but as to that of the rest of Eastern Britain we are left in the dark in a most remarkable manner.

The great gaps in the story might be partly filled up if we could, with Mr. Haigh, trust in other authorities which are generally regarded as spurious or valueless. I confess that the work of this laborious author has educed from what at first sight appears a mere chaos and farrago of invention a certain number of not improbable conjectures. I would not be too ready to deny that there may have been a period of savage warfare preceding that of settlement, during which the whole east of Britain may have been ravaged, and in which the Frankish king Childeric may have played a considerable part. But on the whole the ordinarily received view, shorn of certain features which are obviously conjectural and untrustworthy, such as the deeds of Port and Wihtgar, seems more probable.

Kent, then, appears to have been conquered not at a stroke, but gradually, after several battles in which the invaders were not uniformly

---

* Itaque nonnulli miserarum reliquiarum in montibus deprehensi āceroatim jugulabantur; alii fame confecti accedentes, manus hostibus dabant in œvum servituri, si tamen non continuo trucidarentur, quod altissimæ gratiæ stabat in loco; alii transmarinas petebant regiones, cum uludatu magno, &c.

successful. The conquest of Sussex was also gradual; the natives were in one city at least utterly extirpated, but they seem to have retained their hold on the great forest of Andred for a further indefinite period. Meanwhile settlements were being made all along the eastern coast, but no important states were constituted. Towards the end of the fifth century Cerdic (?) and Cynric began the reduction of Hampshire and Berkshire, which were the nucleus of the important kingdom of Wessex, and they even occupied some portions of Oxfordshire; while Surrey, so far as we can see, may have been still British. Meanwhile Essex was being settled. From the evidence of mixed Saxon and Roman occupation, such as coins, &c., in some towns of Essex, it may be that this conquest was not so much a war of extermination as that of eastern Wessex seems to have been. Towards the middle of the sixth century Ida began in earnest the reduction of Northumbria, on the coast of which Anglian and Frisian settlements had been going on for some time; he overthrew the Britons in the great battle of Cattraeth, and appears to have displaced and compelled southwards some of the tribes that opposed him. In the latter part of the same century the monarchy of East Anglia is said to have been formed; but probably the North and the South Folk had previously constituted independent tribes. The vigorous line of princes who ruled in Wessex meanwhile pushed their conquests northward and westward, carrying their arms as far as Bedford, which was still Celtic (571), and acquiring (577) all the country up to Gloucester, including that town. How far beyond this Ceawlin extended his dominions is doubtful; but there is reason to think that he overran most of the valley of the Mid-Severn, which, however, must have been lost to him, but not necessarily lost to the Saxons, by the defeat of Wodnesburgh in 591. Dr. Guest ingeniously showed the probability that the Damnonian kingdom for some time after these events still included the upper valley of the Bristol Avon and the western borders of Wilts. The history of Wessex is thenceforward that of a succession of contests against the Damnonian Welshmen, and occasional extensions of the frontier by further conquests from them. In 658 the Welsh were driven across the Parret, which seems to have been the boundary for some time afterwards, though in Ine's time (722) Taunton was already within the Saxon frontier. The conquest of Dorset is obscure; that of Devon was probably not effected till the time of Egbert, and cannot then have been altogether complete, though the statement that the Dene fought the Wealas at Gafulford must be taken to imply the existence of a Saxon military colony, at the least, in Devon. The reported birth of Wilfrid at Crediton, in the seventh century, is worth noting. Possibly small local settlements of Saxons on the banks of the navigable rivers preceded the conquest; certainly my figures indicate that a blond population is found precisely in those quarters. Still, there was a half-independent British community in Exeter till the time of Athelstan, who "drove them out," *i.e.*, probably, put an end to the corporate or separate legal existence of the Welshmen, both there and elsewhere east of the Tamar. In Cornwall they retained some shadow of independence yet awhile.

So much for the history of the South of England, as it bears on our subject. That of the north is less clear, and that of the centre very scanty. Theodoric, son of Ida, is said by Nennius to have been besieged by Urien, Morgant, and other Welsh chieftains, in Holy Island, for three days. This may imply that the British frontier in Bernicia had not yet been thrust back so very far from the coast; otherwise the Anglian king could hardly have been so successfully surprised. Ethelfrid Fleisawr, the ravager, who acceded in 592, seems to have extended greatly the limits both of his kingdom and of Anglian colonisation. "Rex fortissimus et gloriæ cupidissimus," says Bede in an important and often-quoted passage, "qui plus omnibus Anglorum primatibus, gentem vastavit Britonum. . . Nemo enim in Tribunibus, nemo in Regibus, plures eorum terras, exterminatis vel subjectis indigenis, aut tributarias genti Anglorum, aut habitabiles fecit." As only about sixty years intervened between the death of Ethelfrid and the birth of Bede, this evidence that from some districts the natives were entirely driven out seems to be very valuable. It is probable that Lancashire, Cumberland, and indeed all the country west of the mountains, remained altogether Celtic for some time longer, though doubtless they paid tribute to Ethelfrid. The little British state of Elmet, about Leeds, endured till the time of Edwin, who expelled the king, and probably also the inhabitants;* for their mere subjection would hardly have been noticed among the achievements of a king who, according to Bede, was suzerain of all the Britons, including the men of Gwynedd, Anglesea, and Man. In Edwin's reign, at least during the earlier part of it, the Mercian kingdom had not yet been constituted: this is indicated not only by the direct statement of the chroniclers, but by the whole history of the political relations between Edwin and Cwichelm of Wessex. I shall endeavour, hereafter, to augment, by inferential evidence of other kinds, the probability that great part of Mercia was really colonised from Deira, or by way of the Humber and the Trent.

Under Penda, Mercia seems to have reached as far as the Severn, though even this is uncertain. Under Wulfere, a little later, Merwald, his brother, is spoken of as ruling in West Hecana (Herefordshire), but this can only indicate a sort of peninsular extension of Mercia.

The growth of the Northumbrian states was checked for a time by the gallant efforts of the Welsh prince Cadwallon, who was probably the ruler of the Northern Cumbrians as well as of North Wales,† as the scene of some of his battles is placed at least as far north as Tynedale. After his defeat and death, Oswy and Ecgfrid for a time must have held

---

* The modern inhabitants of Elmet are a remarkably fair race. (See Tables for Yorkshire.)

† This is asserted by certain Welsh authorities.—*Cambrian Register*, ii., 527.

at least the suzerainty over the whole country from the Mersey to the
Forth, and from the Humber to the Mull of Galloway; and it would
appear from the statements of Bede that under the latter monarch some
portions of the newly subjugated territory were actually colonised.
Cartmel in Furness was British; but the gift of the land by Ecgfrid to
the see of Lindisfarne, " with all the Britons thereupon," implies a very
complete subjection of the district to the Northumbrian power. So
does the establishment of a Bishop at Whithern in Galloway, and the
apparently English name of that place. After Ecgfrid's defeat and
death among the Picts many of his conquests were lost; but Herebert,
the anchorite, an Angle, dwelt near Carlisle; and there was a monastery
on the Dacre river, near Penrith, whereof the names of the abbot,
Suidbert, and a presbyter, Thuidred, prove the Saxon character. That
near Hexham English was the language of the lower orders is indicated
by the story of the dumb man cured by John, Bishop of Hexham. But
in 731 the Northumbrian kingdom still extended its limits beyond those
of the English language; for Bede, writing in that year, remarks of the
Britons, " quippe qui quamvis ex parte sui sunt juris, nonnullâ tamen ex
parte Anglorum sunt servitio mancipati." Another flow of the tide of
Northumbrian power took place about the middle of the eighth century,
when King Eadbert conquered Kyle (Mid-Ayrshire) and took Dum-
barton. From that time until the Danish conquests the independent
British dominion was probably restricted to the most rugged and infertile
parts of the ancient Cumbrian kingdom, and of these only the districts
north of the Solway. But that the population of parts, at least, of
Cumberland, Westmoreland, Furness, &c., remained British in language
and feeling is rendered more than probable by the reconstitution of a
southern Cumbrian state in the latter half of the ninth century, when
the English were too much occupied in resisting the incursions of the
Danes to defend the outlying portions of their territory. In the
Lothians and Tweeddale the Anglian population, once established,
always remained predominant.

The state and position of the Mercian and Welsh frontier must have
fluctuated considerably from the time of its formation. We have seen
that Ceawlin of Wessex may have been the first conqueror of the middle
as well as of the lower portion of the Severn valley. Cynddylan, Prince
of Powys, is thought to have been the Condidan slain by him at the
great battle of Deorham; and in his elegy by Llywarch Hên are allusions to the destruction by the enemy of Cynddylan's city on the Tren
or Tern. So, at least, the poem is generally read. Moreover, near the
same time, Gwên, the valiant son of Llywarch, was slain at the ford of
Morlas, close to the present frontier, though we are not distinctly told
that his enemies were Saxon. It has been suggested by Dr. Guest that
in the same campaign in which the battle of Fethanleage (Faddiley in
Cheshire?) was fought Ceawlin destroyed Wroxeter, and overran the
whole country as far as Cheshire; and I am disposed to embrace this

view. But the portion of Hwiccia which had been conquered in this and preceding campaigns seems to have broken off the yoke of Wessex in the year 591, at the battle of Wanborough. As this battle was won by a combined force of Britons and rebellious Saxons, we are left in doubt who retained the supremacy over Hwiccia, which, however, was undoubtedly a Saxon land a century later. Its dialect is a southern one to this day, though it remained a sub-kingdom of Mercia after the seventh century. Though there were, as has been already mentioned, Saxon settlers (Magesætas) in the district between Severn and Wye (*May*hill, between Ross and Gloucester), it was not till the reign of Offa that the Welsh were deprived of all Salop and of Herefordshire north-east of the Wye. Indeed it is difficult to account for the paucity of hundreds, *i.e.*, of free population, and the entire absence of history during the early part of the Saxon period, in Staffordshire and East Cheshire, except by supposing that these districts were still little more than border-lands. In the early part of the ninth century the process of pushing the march westwards was still going on. In 823, according to the *Brut-y-Tywysogion*, the Saxons took the kingdom of Powys into their possession. But here, as in Northumbria, the further progress of the Saxon arms and frontier was checked by the Danish invasions; and for two centuries more the Wye and Offa's Dyke may be said, roughly speaking, to have been the boundary of the nations, though Welshmen probably remained east of those boundaries in considerable numbers, obeying English law, just as they did in West Wessex when the laws of Ine were compiled.

Ethnological changes in other parts of the British Isles than England and Southern Scotland, during the period we have been considering, were probably but inconsiderable. Professor Rhys holds that in Scotland north of the Forth vacillations occurred in the relative position and power of the Brythonic (Cymric), true Gaelic, and Pictish elements, the last of which he supposes, as we have seen, to have been still more or less Iberian or Ivernian in language in the early part of this period, basing his belief partly on the use of interpreters by the Gael Columba in his communications with some of the Pictish people. There can be little doubt, however, that the Caledonians were a Gaelic people; and that they, who were classed as Picts by the Romans, continued to exist and flourish in the Central Highlands, where their type as described by Tacitus is still nowise uncommon, though intermixed with another which was probably Iberian.

In the west of Scotland the true Scotic Irish streamed over at intervals into Argyle and the neighbouring isles; and the Irish Cruithne, or Picts, similarly crossed over the narrow channel into Galloway, where they, reinforcing probably a pre-existing tribe of their own kindred, maintained a separate tribal existence for some hundreds of years, being still recognisable at the Battle of the Standard in 1138. In Ireland itself, meanwhile, no new element was added to the population; nor does it appear that continued intestine warfare brought about any considerable changes in those which already existed: only the Cruithne, doubtless, were gradually melting away into the Gaelic-speaking mass.

We may now proceed to consider the evidence to be derived from proper names of persons, from statements and allusions which occur in the documents of the period, and from the nature of laws and social usages, as to the ethnological character of the subjects of the Heptarchy. The evidence of local names, and the most important of all, that of physical type and characteristics, must be reserved for a later stage.

One is struck with the extreme rarity of names apparently British, not only in the history, but in the documents of the whole period. Kemble has found a few in the earliest charters contained in his *Codex Diplomaticus;* but there is nothing discoverable that can be compared with what we find, for example, in Gaul under the Frankish kings, where persons with Latin names very frequently appear, not only as churchmen, but as councillors and leaders.

The name of Coifi, the heathen priest under King Edwin, who was first of the Northumbrians to embrace Christianity, may easily be derived from the Celtic, but hardly from the Teutonic. There is no corresponding fact in Wessex; but we meet there with one equally noteworthy in another rank, the name of Ceadwalla, the savage conqueror of Wight and Sussex, being clearly Welsh, and its owner being claimed by the Welsh as a countryman and their king, by the name of Cadwallader. There is, however, no sign in the histories of any revolution favourable to the Britons about that time; and Ine, his cousin, who succeeded, carried on wars of conquest against them, and allowed a smaller weregild for their slaughter than for that of Englishmen. No Celtic name appears in the genealogies assigned to Ceadwalla; and it can hardly be doubted that, if British at all, he was so by the mother's side only, which would probably be enough to account for his name, and for that of his brother Mul (the mule, half-breed).

There is, however, one portion of Mercia, and by no means the one in which the presence of un-Saxonised Celts might have been looked for from its geographical position, in which two very Celtic-looking names do occur. Ovin is noticed by Bede in the ancient *History of Ely*, as primus ministrorum of Etheldreda (A.D. 670?), and is thought to have had the administration of the Isle of Ely.* His monument is now in the Cathedral there. And when Ethelfled's men, in 916, stormed Derby, one of her captains, of the race of the Lords of Ely (South Gyrwa), and called in the Welsh annals Gwynan, set fire to the town-gate. If, in connexion with these names, we consider that the Fen country long constituted separate districts, called North and South Gyrwa, but very thinly peopled, having indeed only 600 hydes in each; when we call to mind the story of St. Guthlac, who, about A.D. 700, was surrounded by night, in his cell near Croyland, by a crowd of enemies, and from their

* Palgrave, II., ccciii.

rough and guttural speech imagined them to be Britons, by whom the country was then much harassed, though they turned out, to the saint's great relief, to be only devils, and not Welshmen; and when we find in the history of Ramsey* that that neighbourhood was, even in the time of Canute, liable to "the infestation of British thieves," and that in the regulations of the Thegna gild of Cambridge, probably in the reign of Ethelred, provision is made for the slaughter of a Welsh churl, and that at half-price, we shall probably agree that a case is made out in favour of the Britons having remained as Britons in the neighbourhood of the Fens much longer than in most parts of England. I hope to show, further on, some little evidence of a physical character in support of this view.

The use of the words Wealh *(a Welshman)*, Wylisc *(Welsh)*, &c., is not infrequent in the ancient Saxon laws. These words do not, however, occur in the ordinances of the Kentish kings, though the frequent mention of "esnes" and "theows" shows that the servile class was numerous. One would infer that the Welsh language, and with it the distinction of race, had become extinct by the time of King Ethelbert, which is inconsistent with the notion of any considerable portion of the native population having been suffered to remain in Kent by the conquerors. If Mr. Kemble be correct in his reckoning of the Kentish weregilds, the Kentish ceorl was valued at half the worth of an eorl; whereas in Wessex the ratio of values was as 1 to 3 at least, or 6 in the case of the full thane; in Mercia, as 1 to 6; and in Northumbria, 1 to 7½. These differences may be connected with the relatively higher value of the simple freeman among the Frisians and Franks† than among the Saxons and Angles, whose original constitution appears to have been more aristocratic. But, at all events, the relatively high weregyld of the Kentish churl makes it very improbable that he was, as a rule, of British descent.

We have some valuable material in the often-quoted laws of Ine of Wessex, who lived at a period when the prevalence of Christianity had in some small degree mitigated the horrors of wars of conquest, and who had himself reduced West Somerset to be part and parcel of Wessex. Under Ine a Welshman might be free, might own or rent land, and might by holding five hydes attain the rank, or rather value, of a sixhyndman. We hear of no other sixhyndman, as Robertson remarks; and it may be that he was in a class by himself, below all thanes of true Saxon blood, who were twelfhynd. A distinction was still drawn, too, between the English and the Welsh churl. The life of

* Quoted by Palgrave.

† The weregylds in Kent (see Robertson, *Scotland under her Early Kings*, for the most comprehensive statement of weregylds) seem to agree in proportion with those of the Salian Franks, who probably took some part in the colonisation of that county. Grimm, quoted by Kemble, makes those of the continental Saxons resemble those of our Angles; but those of the Thuringian Angles differed from both. For an indication of the greater political importance of the churls of Kent, see Thorpe, *Laws of Athelstan*, II.

the former was valued at 200 shillings; but that of the latter, though he held a hyde of land, was but 120 shillings; and if he had none he was rated at 60 shillings, the price of a theow or slave. We may infer that in a considerable portion of the Wessex of that period (about A.D. 700) Welshmen and Englishmen lived intermixed under English law; and though the former, as the conquered race, were subjected to some derogatory legal provisions, they were not altogether deprived of their lands, and remained too numerous and powerful to be treated without some consideration. It by no means follows, however, that this intermixture extended to the eastern portion of Wessex, which had been conquered before the introduction of Christianity, when community of religion had not begun to soften national antipathies. In Mercia the eorl was worth six times as much as the ceorl; the probability of the latter being generally of British origin is somewhat greater, therefore, than in Eastern Wessex. From Northumberland we have precise information in the fragment entitled "The North People's Law,"* which, however, Kemble, without reason assigned, seems to consider a suspicious authority. It sets the value of a churl's life at 200 shillings, while that of the lowest rank of thane is not less than 1,500. This comparative elevation of the upper ranks may have taken place subsequently to the Danish conquest; for it is not probable, from the nature of that conquest, that any considerable number of churls were Danish. The socman does not appear at all under that name; he may have been a development of the Danish leysing or of the churl. Welshmen are provided for almost as in Wessex, a landholder of that race being worth 120 shillings, and a simple Welsh freeman 70 shillings; a churl may rise to be a thane, but it is not stated that a Welshman may do so. These provisions for Welshmen are to be accounted for by the continued existence of the British language as well as the British race, under Danish and Norse as well as Anglian Northumbrians, in Cumbria and Craven. This latter district, from which we have evidence of a singularly interesting kind, derived from the contents of caves, that civilised Britons took refuge there from Anglian or other invaders, is generally supposed to be the commot of Carnoban, spoken of in one of the Triads as having remained British in speech. The name Carnavy or Cornaby, said to be applied by the peasantry of Warwickshire to a district in the centre of that county, raises a suspicion whether the commot of Carnoban may not have been in the forest of Arden rather than in the wilderness of Craven.† One is tempted to refer the name to the tribe whom the Romans called Cornavii, and who are located to the east and north-east of the Severn. The population of both these districts retains decided marks of pre-Anglian descent.

There is a passage in the law of the Northumbrian priests (a code also of date subsequent to the Danish conquest) which has been held

* Thorpe, i., 186.
† Carnoban in Deifyr, says the Triad. But "in Deifyr" may be a gloss.

to imply the continued presence of Welshmen, acknowledged as such, throughout the whole country, a thing on other grounds very improbable. "If a King's Thane," it is said, "make denial, let twelve be named to him; and let him take twelve of his kinsmen, and twelve Waller-wents; and if it fail," &c., &c. "If a land-owning man make denial, then let be named to him of his equals as many Wents as to a King's Thane," &c.; "if a ceorlish man make denial, then let be named to him of his equals as many Wents as to the others," &c., &c. Thorpe supposes these Waller-wents to have been Britons of Cumbria; but it seems obvious that an inhabitant of the centre of Deira (and York is mentioned in the law) could not have been expected to import twelve Britons from Cumbria, beyond the mountains, to be his jury or compurgators. Bosworth says: "Wallerwents, peregrini, *i.e.*, Britanni ita dicti a Saxonibus." But as this is the only passage in which the word occurs, it seems to me easier to suppose that it means simply "strangers," "strangers in blood," as distinguished from kinsmen, and has no reference to race or nation, than to believe that there were in the Danish period, in the neighbourhood of York, such numbers of land-holding Welsh-speaking men that a dozen of them could be readily got together for every legal proceeding. There is no other reference in the code to the existence of Welshmen.*

It is ordered in the *Judicia Civitatis Lundoniæ*, respecting a runaway slave, "that the same be done unto him as to a Wylisc thief, or that he be hanged." It is difficult to credit the existence of Welsh brigands near London so late as the reign of Athelstan. Perhaps it would be better to understand the phrase as meaning "a servile thief," "a slave who steals." Abimelech gave to Abraham, according to a Saxon translation, "oxen and sheep, Welshmen and Welshwomen (wealas and wylna)."† So, when in the Laws of Ethelred ‡ it is agreed that "neither they (the Danes) nor we harbour the other's Wealh, nor the other's thief, nor the other's foe," we can hardly translate the word Wealh otherwise than by "slave." It is a fact of fearful significance that the very name of a brave though unfortunate nation should have descended to mean, in their enemies' mouths, a bondsman; but we have another example of it in the desecration to the same purpose, by the Germans, of the national name with which the Slavonians had gratified their own pride.

Another document of great importance for our present purpose is the will of King Alfred, in which he bequeaths to his younger son all the lands he has "on Wealcynne bûtan Triconscire." Triconscire

---

* There were several landowners with Celtic names (Murdoch, Gilpatrick, &c.) in Yorkshire just before the Norman conquest; but the names were of Gaelic, not of Cymric type, except perhaps Maban and Artor; and there can be little doubt that they had been introduced from Scotland through Lothian, where Angles and Scots were then intermixed.

† Bosworth.   ‡ Thorpe, i., 289.

seems to have been a part of Somerset, which may very well have been Welsh then as in Ine's day; but in the enumeration of the other lands "on Wealcynne" are included Stureminster (in Dorset) and Ambresbyrig, which has always been supposed to mean Ambresbury = Amesbury in Eastern Wiltshire. On this some writers have founded the statement that Wiltshire and Dorset still used the Welsh language in Alfred's time. The premises are not sufficient for the conclusion. East Dorset may have been Saxon, though Sturminster was not so as yet. Or these districts may have been still recognised in common parlance as Welsh country, though no longer under Welsh law or Welsh in speech; just as all Monmouthshire is commonly spoken of, by Somerset and Gloucestershire men, as being in Wales, though it is legally an English county, and though the Cymric language has long ago receded behind the Usk. Finally, if Amesbury (supposing Amesbury to be the Ambresbyrig mentioned, which seems pretty clear)—if, I say, Amesbury was in the Wealcynne, Chippenham, far to the west of it, was not; for it was not included in the grant, but subsequently given to his youngest daughter. I am inclined to think that Amesbury, or Ambresbyrig, may have really remained Celtic when all the surrounding region had been Saxonised, much as there is some reason for supposing Glastonbury to have done. Ambresbyrig was a sacred place to the Welsh; it was the seat of one of their three famous choirs and the royal residence* of Caradoc Vreichvras, and they may have clung to and around it long after they had yielded most of Wiltshire to the undisturbed possession of their conquerors. Dr. Guest has succeeded in rendering it probable that the country about Bradford and Malmesbury remained British after Bristol and Devizes and Mere had been subdued. Alfred's gifts, during his lifetime, to Asser, consisted generally of parishes in the western, *i.e.*, British portion of his dominions; and there was a certain congruity in this, Asser being a Welshman. Why, then, was Ambresbyric (with Banwell in North Somerset) his first gift to Asser? On my hypothesis nothing could be more natural.†

Another important field for argument is afforded by the various points of resemblance between the Welsh and Saxon, and, again, the Roman and Saxon legal and social systems. The former part of the subject has been worked out by Palgrave and Kemble; the latter by Wright, Pearson, and Coote, to whom also Seebohm, though taking an independent line, is in some respects a powerful auxiliary. All these take more or less strongly what may be called the negative, or anti-Germanic, side of the question; the positive or *de novo* theory, which denies any considerable survival of pre-Saxon usages, has been main-

---

* Guest.

† The inhabited valleys of Central and Southern Wiltshire, separated as they are by tracts of upland pasturage, have comparatively little intercourse with each other. It will be seen from my tables that the inhabitants of these valleys differ much in physical type, and probably in blood.

tained chiefly by Guest and Stubbs, followed by Freeman and Green. I shall not attempt to discuss the whole of this great and difficult subject, nor even to epitomise it, but only to refer briefly to a few important points.

Palgrave and Kemble, while agreeing as to the survival of usages dating from before the fifth century, diverged in their views as to the nature of the population from whom they were derived. Palgrave believed the Belgians to have been the ruling race of Britain before the Romans, and to have been ethnologically the same as the Frisians and Saxons ; while Kemble, relying on that very equivocal term, " the Saxon shore," supposed the eastern part of Britain to have been thoroughly Germanised under the Romans. Both were, therefore, prepared to make much of the resemblances between the British and the Saxon laws. " These resemblances," says Palgrave, " must be sought principally in the tenures of lands, in the territorial organisation of the country, and perhaps in the constitution of the tribunals which were founded on that division. . . . They agreed in their usages respecting crimes and punishments ; they agreed in allowing the homicide to redeem his guilt by making compensation to the relations of the slain ; they agreed in the use of trial by ordeal and by compurgation. . . . The question whether such analogous customs be of British or Saxon origin is little more than a mere verbal dispute, very difficult to decide, and perfectly useless when decided." Most of the usages alluded to in the foregoing passage were common to many of the northern nations, and had probably been the common property of at least several branches of the Aryan stock. For example, the general principle of the were-gyld was common to Saxons, to Cymry, to all the Germanic tribes, as well as other peoples. When we come to look into details, we find them varying widely. The elaborate system of were-gylds in the Laws of Howel Dda bears little resemblance to that of any one of the Saxon codes ; and the complicated territorial division, which is said to have prevailed among the Cymry, but which one is tempted to suppose to have been rather the ideal of a legislator than a system actually carried out in its integrity, can hardly be recognised under the Saxons. Palgrave, indeed, treats the British maenawl as the possible origin of the Saxon township ; but as $12\frac{1}{2}$ maenawls = 50 trefs constituted a commot, and 25 maenawls a cantred (literally a hundred), it is difficult to see how the divisions in the two cases can be made to run parallel. Four trefs constituted a maenawl ; but if we make the township the equivalent of the tref, our difficulties are not lessened ; and the argument which Palgrave derives from the constant appearance of Four Men as deputies from the township, whom he supposes to have been originally the representatives of the Four Trefs of which the Maenawl was composed, will fall to the ground. If, indeed, this system had really been in force throughout Britain at the era of the Roman Conquest, one would hardly look for its persistence throughout the continuance of the

Roman dominion. Again, the supposition that the Saxon conquest was a mere substitution of a new military aristocracy for a native one, or for the Roman rulers lately withdrawn, with little interference with the body of the people, or with the laws and usages that governed them— that, in short, it was very like the Norman conquest—can hardly be entertained by those who have any respect for Mr. Kemble's views as to the nature of the Mark and the constitution of a Saxon settlement; though Coote and Seebohm may consistently do so.

The election of the tun-gerefa, or reeve, by the villans (allowing that it existed during the Saxon period) is used by Palgrave to increase the probability of the churls being really the representatives or descendants of a subjugated race; and he brings forward the analogy of the practice in the Levant, where a *Greek* community, for example, elects its native magistrate, who is its head and representative in all its dealings with the Turkish Government. The fact founded on is correctly stated; but as Turkish villages and communities equally elect their own head-men, I cannot see that the election of the reeve is any indication of the alien nationality of the churls: it is equally consistent with that and with the other view.

The name and institution of gavelkind furnish a stronger argu-ment. The usage was general in Wales, as applied to the lands of free tenants, though restrained from operating beyond the third generation; while in England it was of limited and local application; nor has it ever been suggested that the Welsh derived the custom from the English. It is positively affirmed, however, by Sumner that the Welsh, though they previously used the custom, took the name from the English. On the other hand, the Welsh language affords a clear and unstrained etymology for it; viz.: *gavael*, a grasp, and thence a holding; and *cenedyl*, kindred or family. The Irish have both the thing, the name, and a probable etymology (*gabal-cined*); and there is choice of one fair Germanic deriva-tion (*gafol*, *tributum*, a gift); and of one which seems common to German and Celtic, *Gabel* or *Gable*, a fork, the angle of a roof; in both of which the essential idea seems to be that of division. If the Saxons took the usage from the Welsh, how came it that it was adopted in one of the counties which had been most Romanised, and which was earliest and most completely Saxonised, viz., Kent,* and not in those whose conquest was late, and conducted with less barbarity and slaughter, such as Devon and Somerset, or those where there is reason to think that the British population long retained their language and distinct national character, such as Huntingdonshire?

If these considerations, however, are not sufficient to rebut the common opinion on the subject, then we have in the existence of gavel-kind among the free tenants of Kent a strong presumption that the churls who followed this custom were mainly of British descent, and

---

* Pearson would perhaps have said that it was because the eastern part of Kent was acquired by peaceable cession, and only the western by fighting.

a fortiori that the bulk of the population in most other parts of England is so; for several lines of proof combine to show that the north and east, at least, of Kent, are among our most Teutonic districts.*

The difference between the Salic villa and the Anglo-Saxon tun, the former not being necessarily subject to any lord, while the latter always was so, has also been used as an indication that the Saxon churls were the remains of the conquered Britons; but, in truth, the continental Franks, as well as the Frisians, were always less aristocratic in their polity than the Saxons. If we may accept the Saxon tradition as of any value, their churls were really the descendants of the subjugated Thuringians, who had first occupied the lands about the Elbe. The same ranks or castes existed among the Saxons on the Continent and in Britain; and as the churls bore arms, we cannot doubt that many of them accompanied the nobles in the invasion of Britain. It is necessary that we rid ourselves of the idea that our Saxon ancestors were a kind of democratic community with universal suffrage; if they ever had been such a community, they had ceased to be so before they emerged into history.

From Angeln, indeed, if we believe Bede, almost the entire population migrated, and it remained a desert until his day. If, then, a portion at least of the churls of insular Anglia were not of continental descent, what had become of the churls of Angeln? Had they become nobles, *i.e.*, eorls or athelings, in the new settlements? It is possible, but extremely improbable. The eorls do not seem to have been numerous in Britain. It would seem that they wore the sword, and that it was usually buried with them; but Mr. Yonge Akerman informs us that in certain Anglo-Saxon villages, whose cemeteries he investigated, the sword-bearers seemed to have been but three or four in number—quite a small percentage. In the time of Edward the Confessor the land-holding thanes of Somerset (and we have none mentioned who did not hold land) were somewhere between 2 and 5 per cent. of the population; and the burghers, some of whom may have been of that rank, were 3 per cent. Again, if the greater part, or a very large part, of the British native population became under their conquerors free churls, and constituted the mass of the nation, how was it that the words Wealh and Wylisc came to mean slave and servile? The word churlish never sank to such signification. This single fact is almost sufficient to show that slavery was, during at least the early stages of the conquest, the common lot of those Britons whose lives were spared. That in some western counties the case was different I am prepared to admit, and even to maintain; there I believe many Britons to have been ulti- mately enrolled among the churls, and the same may have been the case

---

* Læts are met with in Kent, and in Kent alone *eo nomine*. They were of three degrees, and each degree had an appropriate weregyld. They were evidently, says Lappenberg, the lazzi or læti of the Continent. Their existence in Kent furnishes yet another argu- ment against the British origin of the Kentish churls, except perhaps in the Weald.

in many parts of Mercia. Still, even there many were reduced to serf-dom, as appears by the great number of serfs mentioned in the *Domesday* account of Western and Southern Mercia, a number varying from 10 per cent. in Northamptonshire to 17 in Salop and 24 in Gloucestershire.

At this point it is impossible to pass by without notice the researches and arguments of Seebohm as to the status of the actual cultivators in Anglo-Saxon manors. His work deals with questions which are strictly social, and only indirectly have an ethnological bearing; still, he shows pretty distinctly his opinion that the churls, or so-called free cultivators, were from the first fixed to the soil and bound down to labour for the lord of the ham or manor; that this was the case both in England and in Swabia and elsewhere where free Germanic tribes had occupied lands within the old Roman empire; and that these semi-servile tenants were, in England, for the most part either Germanic captives settled on the land at prior dates by the Romans, or the descendants of the Belgo-British population whom Cæsar and Claudius had found already in its occupation.

Elton, on the other hand, holds to the older view, that the bulk of the Saxon settlers had at first a great deal of that freedom of which they long retained at least the name;* but that, with the increase of power of the kings and great nobles and of the church (we may add, with the increase of population and the lessening of that once constant warfare which made fighting men valuable), the descendants of freemen fell under onerous rents and services. And to this view I am disposed to adhere, with some qualification. It is evident, from the examples so carefully given by Seebohm himself, that in the west, at Tidenham in the Forest of Dean for example, the conquerors must have substituted the manorial organisation for that which previously prevailed, and which continued for hundreds of years to prevail on the other side of the Wye. That the Wye was not the national boundary before the Saxon conquest we can hardly doubt; the fact that it was not the ecclesiastical boundary until then makes this pretty clear. If, then, Tidenham was placed under a new system at that time, while some traces of an older one were allowed to remain in places further east, *e.g.*, Cirencester, may not the Saxons have acted similarly in many or most of the manors of England? If, again, the services in different manors, at the time when we begin to learn something definite about their nature, varied greatly in detail, may we not allow the possibility of considerable changes, in the direction perhaps of greater onerousness, between the conquest and the periods in evidence? Again, Cirencester and Tidenham were both con-quered after the invaders had for some generations been familiar with the country and with the various tenures already existing in it.

It is possible that the services on the royal manors, of which Seebohm

---

* "Even the cottier," we are told in the *Rectitudines singularum personarum*, "pays hearthpenny on Holy Thursday, as every *freeman* ought to do." But not long after-wards, in *Domesday*, the liber homo is distinguished from the villan and cottier.

gives one instance even in the very Saxon Hampshire, may have been heavier than the average of manors held by eorls or thanes. If so, the tenantry on the former may have been in larger proportion wealhs. Thus, after the Norman conquest, as has been pointed out to me by Mr. Bazeley, Saxon customary tenants remained on the king's land in larger proportion than elsewhere.

But in truth the system of noble tribesmen living separately in the family hall or dwellings, and plebeian or servile cultivators dwelling together in a village, was already in operation in free Germany, according to Seebohm's reasonable interpretation of Tacitus. In fact it was perhaps older and more widespread than the separation between Germans and Celts.

The fate of the Romano-British cities is involved in the same obscurity that more or less clouds the whole subject. Some of them had certainly been pillaged and desolated by the Picts and Scots; and others were destroyed, and their inhabitants massacred, by the Saxons. Probably Silchester, Wroxeter, and many others, shared the fate of Anderida, where, we are told, there was not one Briton left alive. From others, with the departure of the old civilization and commerce, the population, where not positively enslaved and driven off, would wander away, or gradually perish by famine and disease, as Gildas seems to indicate. Verulam may have been among these: in the tenth century its spacious buildings were a nuisance to the Abbots of St. Albans, being a haunt for bad characters of both sexes; but the history of the city had been forgotten. In a few places in Essex, and in Ozengal in Kent, according to Mr. Wright, there is evidence that the natives and the invaders dwelt together for a while; but in these cases, and in others in which the Saxons occupied and inhabited the ancient sites, the Christian religion died out, and the churches were either destroyed, or were no longer recognised as such; for when Christianity was reintroduced into London, Canterbury, and York, it was necessary to build new churches. In the north of England, we have the evidence of Canon Raine that every Roman station and house bears traces of destruction by fire.

Wright and Coote lay great stress on the strength and population of the towns in the middle and late Saxon periods; but we have very few facts indeed to support the notion that this importance had continued through the *early* Saxon period. The only considerable ones I have met with are, firstly, that Cadwallon was besieged by Osric in York, A.D. 643, and that Bede speaks of the transaction as happening in the municipal town; and secondly, that the burning of Catterick, by Beornred the Mercian, in 769, is recorded as an important occurrence.

The subsequent importance of some cities is of little moment; for though the Saxons were not originally a town-loving people, they in process of time found the convenience of market towns, and even of fortified places, just as their continental kinsmen did during the ravages of the Avars and the Hungarians; and such towns grew up gradually, in new as well as in old sites.* Among them was new Cambridge, which was built close to the site of the old Camboritum, a Roman city which we know to have been a "waste chester." Yet Cambridge had acquired great privileges by the tenth century, and in the eleventh it possessed a thane's guild, evidently, in this instance at least, not a Roman survival.

We cannot, I think, neglect to allow great importance to the constant intercourse which subsisted between England, after its conversion to Christianity, on the one hand, and France and Italy on the other. If the Saxons and Angles were barbarians, they were very capable and receptive barbarians. And whereas the Saxon legal codes and municipal regulations, so much of them as is positively known to us, are of date posterior to that conversion, I should be disposed to refer to introduction from abroad rather than to inheritance from the Romano-Britons most of those regulations and terms which savour of Latin origin. The one with regard to which I feel most difficulty is the Bridge-and-burgh-rate, to which landed property was liable. Taking this separately, it is vastly easier to suppose it a legacy from the Roman occupation.

The clean sweep which the invaders made of Christianity in the eastern portion of the island is surely not consistent with the views of Mr. Coote. If the Romano-Britons had lapsed into heathenism it would have been their own heathenism, not that of the rude Saxons; and except the prohibition of drycraft † (Druidic magic?) by a Saxon law, we have hardly any indication of this in the east. Again, if Christianity had endured in the towns, side by side with the Saxon heathenism of the rural aristocracy, there would surely have been some intercourse with the Christians of the continent; but we hear of none: no second St. Germanus seems to have crossed over to comfort the brethren and retain them in the faith. If any cultivated Romans, or Romanized Celts, remained to carry on the traditions of the municipalities, it is strange that we have no monuments or epitaphs referable to the succeeding centuries. All these are only inferential arguments indeed, but collectively they surely have some force. Mr. Coote finds in the sixhynd-man of Ine's Laws the Romano-British burgess. But we hear of no sixhyndman except the Wealh who has five hydes, i.e., apparently, the Damnonian chieftain who has become subject to the King of Wessex. The English burgess was probably eorl or ceorl, twelfhyndman or twy-hyndman, according to his birth and descent; and we find the landed nobility owning houses, and probably occasionally dwelling in them and exercising the rights of chief burgesses, in York and in other towns, in the time of Edward the Confessor.

The present seems a favourable opportunity for considering a subject that might have been taken earlier, viz., the testimony of the Triads,

---

* "Caistor was a city when Norwich was none,
 And Norwich was built with Caistor stone."—NORFOLK RHYME.

† Pearson, *Early and Middle Ages of England*, pp. 46, 47.

and of alleged Welsh tradition, to the effect that the Lloegrians became Saxon, and that the Coranied treacherously sided with the invaders. Acknowledging my incapacity to test the authenticity of the documents on which these statements are founded, I confess that I regard the poems of Llywarch Hên as genuine, relying as much on the authority of Skene as on the internal evidence. Now Llywarch speaks of " the circularly compact army of Lloegria " as opposed to that of Cyndylan.

I can quite conceive that the Welsh may have, so to speak, served the Romans and the Saxons, successively, heirs to the Lloegrian name, as being possessors of the Lloegrian country. Instances of this kind of misapplication of names are plentiful. Thus Tamerlane, in his journal, speaks of Sultan Bayazid as the Kaiser of Roum; and Cappadocia, long the eastern fringe of the Roman empire, retains the name of Roum under the Ottoman government. Thus, again (and this is still more closely in point), the old Breton ballads speak of the Franks as Gauls. And the Welsh, in later days, called the Normans Saxons, as they had called the Saxons Lloegres.

It may be, however, that the foes of Llywarch and Cyndylan may have included a Lloegrian contingent. The Britons who fought under Ceolric at Wanborough, in 591, may have been the same who had joined in the storming and sacking of Wroxeter eight years before; and I would hazard the conjecture that they may have been the inhabitants of Arden,* that difficult forest region which to this day, as philo-Celtic admirers of Shakspere are fond of telling us, retains indications of a large British element in its population.

But it is only in some such limited sense as this that the statement of the Triads can be true. We know positively that the Lloegrians of the south were reduced only by strenuous warfare, renewed campaign after campaign, and generation after generation, for hundreds of years. So, too, the natives of the north (who, however, do not seem to have been Lloegrians at all, but Brythons or Cymry), protracted their resistance, with various vicissitudes of defeat, subjection, and revolt, from the battle of Cattraeth to that of Dunmailraise. With regard to Essex and Mercia as far west as the Severn, we have so little information that it is quite possible that in certain tracts small British states, or Romano-British towns, may have allied themselves with the invaders, and thus for a time deferred their own destruction, though we cannot positively say that it was so. That anything of the kind occurred in East Anglia, unless on the smallest scale, I entirely disbelieve: the physical characteristics, the local names, the great number and moderate size of the hundreds and parishes, which justify an estimate of the free population at 50,000 or more, and the neighbourhood to the continental homes of the invaders, all tend to show that this region was very densely settled by a population almost exclusively Teutonic. Of Essex I have spoken

---

* The retention of the name Carnavy by the peasantry, as already mentioned, for a district in central Warwickshire should be remembered.

already: its people, except near the coast, are more usually dark-haired, I think, than those of Kent, Norfolk, and Suffolk. That some compact may have been made between the invaders of Mercia and the southern portion of the Coritanian tribe, is rendered less improbable by the marked physical difference, already mentioned as noted by the late Professor Phillips as well as by myself, between the people of Leicestershire and those of the counties to the north, although Leicestershire was very densely colonised by the Scandinavians in later times. Palgrave conjectured that some of the Mercian counties might represent small British states, which, after holding out for a time, might by treaty, or even by royal marriages, have passed under the Saxon yoke. Possibly something of the kind may have happened to Rutland, or to Huntingdonshire (which is probably enough the South Gyrwa of earlier times), but I do not think we can admit the probability of the existence of any considerable British state in Mercia after the sixth century. We may conjecture that Mercia was built up out of a great number of small states or chieftainships, among which no one or two greatly preponderated for a generation or two after the beginning of Teutonic colonisation. The names of the marks, as investigated by Kemble, render it probable that this colonisation was naturally subsequent to that of the kingdoms on the coast, and much less dense, and this last fact is confirmed by certain statements of Bede's and others in the document in Sir Henry Spelman's glossary (article Hida)* as to the number of hydes in a number of districts, whose names are for the most part no longer recognisable with certainty, but some of which certainly, and most of which probably, did ultimately coalesce into the great Mercian kingdom. Thus, while Kent had 15,000 hydes, North and South Mercia had together but 12,000, and Hwicca is said to have contained only 600, only half the number of the Isle of Wight. This last statement is so extraordinary as to arouse one's suspicion; however, Worcestershire contains but five hundreds at the present day, and Staffordshire the same number, while Sussex has 72.†

On the whole, the following is the theory of the early history of Mercia which most commends itself to me. About the close of the fifth century, a number of incoherent British tribes and decaying Romano-British towns, without any recognised head. This state of things first disturbed by the Anglian conquest of Lindisse, and the ravages of Cerdic about Oxfordshire. The country gradually penetrated by Saxon settlers from the already consolidated states of the south-east, and Anglians from East Anglia or Deira, or from the continent, who settle down in small bodies, sometimes enslaving or expelling a previous population, but sometimes peacefully reclaiming land from the waste

---

* Kemble i., 81.

† Sussex is said to have contained 7,000 hydes; if the number of hundreds was about the same as at present, there must have been a hundred hydes to each of them, i.e., probably a hundred free holdings, of, say, 30 acres each, or 60 at most.

or the forest. Wars and alliances take place between the natives and the new-comers, generally on a small scale. In some districts the latter come thus to form merely a military aristocracy, but in the country north of the Trent, as far westwards at least as the Staffordshire and Derbyshire mountains and Cannock Chase, the whole population is destroyed, expelled, or enslaved, either by Ethelfrid Fleisawr of Northumbria, on his march towards Chester, or by an extension up the Trent valley of the Gainas and Lindiswaras. Thus a compact Anglian state, at first dependent on Deira, is formed, which in process of time, by conquest, agreement, or even marriage, absorbs the other Saxon states, and the remaining British ones, if any.

The philological evidence on the subject under discussion may be considered under two heads. The first is that of local names; the second that of current language.

The local names of England have been investigated in detail by Leo and Isaac Taylor; and Kemble has made some very valuable contributions to our knowledge in this department.

Taylor, " in order to exhibit," as he says, " the comparative amount of the Celtic, the Saxon, and the Danish element of population in various portions of Britain," made an analysis of the names of hamlets, hills, woods, valleys, &c., in five counties, with the following result:

PERCENTAGE OF NAMES.

From the	Suffolk.	Surrey.	Devon.	Cornwall.	Monmouth.
Celtic	2	8	32	80	76
Anglo-Saxon	90	91	65	20	24
Norse	8	1	3	0	0

These figures, however, cannot be taken as really exhibiting the proportions of the elements of population; nor do I suppose that Mr. Taylor meant to claim for them anything more than an approximate and comparative value. For example, it is pretty certain that the Saxon element in the blood of Devon is nothing like 65 per cent., if, indeed, it be the half of 65; but it may very well be that the Saxon blood in Cornwall bears to the Saxon blood in Devon some such proportion as 20 to 65. Again, Suffolk has fewer Celtic names than any other county on the list, and we may very fairly conclude that it has also less Celtic blood; but every other line of argument tends to indicate that even in Suffolk the proportion of Celtic blood must be much greater than 2 per cent.

A somewhat similar investigation of the place-names in the south of Scotland yielded me the following results:

PERCENTAGE OF NAMES.

From the	Berwick, Rox., Selk., Peeb.	Lothian.	Dumf., Lank., Stirling.	Renf., Ayr, Galloway.
Celtic	11	24	39	49
Doubtful	17	10	7	10
Saxon or Norse	72	66	54	41

Here the Teutonic element in Galloway and the west is very much overstated, but whether it is much so in the first or Tweeddale group of counties is matter of doubt.

Many circumstances obviously affect the value of this kind of evidence. Thus, objects of great magnitude, or visible from afar, and therefore likely to be named and spoken of in the intercourse of two neighbouring races, such as rivers* and mountains, usually retain their original names through all changes of race and language. When a conquest is gradual, or very limited in extent, so as to be merely a small advance of the frontier, comparatively few names will be changed, because, as a rule, the old names will have already become familiar to the conquerors. But with lapse of time the old names tend to die out, and to be replaced by new ones which are significant in the minds of the people, and which often nearly resemble the old ones in sound. And as all local names are at first significant, *animo imponentis*, all castles, houses and hamlets erected subsequently to the introduction of a new language will almost certainly be named in accordance with it. Suffolk was thoroughly English in speech more than a thousand years ago, but I have no doubt that at that period the proportion of Celtic local names there was very much greater than 2 per cent.

Where the invaders and the invaded are nearly equal in numbers, it may perhaps depend on national peculiarities of character and civilisation whether the former or the latter leave the more numerous traces of their presence in the local names. The Danes and Norsemen, for example, seem to have had a much greater power of giving local names than of transmitting their language. Both in Normandy and in the Hebrides they have left their mark in multitudes of local names; but in the former their speech faded out in a generation or two, and in the latter it was not much more enduring. On the other hand, the colonisation of Ulster by the English and Scotch, though it involved an enormous change in the nationality of the population, and an entire change of language, had very little effect on the local names.

On the whole, the evidence of local names seems to favour the opinion already expressed, that the population in a great part of the East of England (and I may add the South-Eastern Lowlands, from the Cheviots almost to the Forth) have more Saxon than Celtic blood in their veins, and that a great part of the churls must have been Saxons. Of particular districts, in which I have supposed the natives to have remained in large proportion, the Weald and the borders of Romney Marsh retain a number of Celtic or other ancient names, as Lympne, Appledore, Appledram, Glynde, Rusper, Findon, and numerous Combes. The names in the Fenland are mostly modern; but some of the more ancient appear to be Celtic: the most notable is a Gaelic one, Wiskin, *i.e.* water-island. In Cumberland, the nature and distribution of local names support in a markworthy manner the views I shall presently put for-

* Mr. Taylor has judiciously excluded river-names from his table.

ward. Many Celtic names, Gaelic as well as Cymric, remain, especially of natural objects on a large scale, as rivers and mountains; but others have only Norse names, and considerable tracts occur in which the latter exclusively prevail. These facts accord with the hypothesis of the existence of a scanty and scattered British population, among and between whose occupations strong Norse colonies gradually settled down.

The investigation of the evidence of current language and provincial dialects is of considerable importance for our purpose, but that importance has perhaps been overrated by most of those who had entered on the quest. It does, however, tell us much, and would doubtless tell us more if more thoroughly worked out; but the field of labour is wide, and the labour itself difficult, and the fruit often ambiguous. The rude old theory was, that language being the best evidence of national kinship and descent, and the English language being Teutonic, the English people must be Teutonic too. The history of the Cornish language furnishes a sufficient answer to the former of the above premises. The second one has seldom been doubted, until of late some have endeavoured to dispute it, on the ground that Teutonic words do not form half the contents of the English dictionary. There is no doubt, of course, that the current opinion on this point is the correct one. The commonest and most important and necessary of our words, particularly among the verbs, are Teutonic; so are most of our scanty grammatical forms and rules; and even in pronunciation (though this, too, has lately been disputed) those who have had opportunities of hearing Frisians or Schleswigers or Jutlanders in conversation, and who have also listened to Welshmen similarly engaged, will surely agree with me that the English in general follow in intonation and cadence what may be called the paternal rather than the maternal side.

Some of the points urged by philo-Celtic writers are pretty certainly baseless; *e.g.*, the supposed Celtic feminine termination *-ess*, which was really brought from France by the Normans, and was not a Cymric legacy. A genuine remnant of the old British (Lloegrian) pronunciation may be found in a quarter where it might well be looked for, namely, in Devonshire, where, in travelling westwards, we encounter a people long thoroughly Anglicised, but some of whom seem to have spoken Cornish down to Elizabeth's time. Here, or more exactly on this side of the Devonshire border, but beyond the Parret and the Axe, the sound of the French *ü* begins to be heard. The French probably inherit it from the Gauls, whose kindred, the Welsh, retain it, though they do not use it much. I do not think it is known to the Frisians.

Mr. Pike* quotes from William Edwards the statement that, in Mezzofanti's opinion, the extreme irregularity of English pronunciation is traceable to its Welsh (or British) ancestry. There is, however, no peculiar difficulty or variability about the Welsh pronunciation of vowels,

* *Origin of the English Nation.*

and it is to the vowels that this characteristic of the English apper-
tains. I may oppose to Mezzofanti's remark one by a probably better
authority. "The variation of the vowel sounds," says Barnes, in his
Grammar of the Dorset Dialect, "in the speech-forms of the English, as
well as in the other Teutonic languages, are almost endlessly manifold.
In the Vale of Blackmore, *will* is at different times wŏŏll, wull, and wüll,
even in the same mouth; and Mr. Halbertsma, a Frisian, says: "In
the village where I was born, we said indiscriminately *after, efter* and
æfter."

With respect to the English vocabulary, it is unfortunate that few of
the compilers of provincial glossaries have been Celtic scholars: had
they been so, it is probable that our stock of known derivations from
Celtic tongues would have been somewhat increased.

On the whole, the nature of such as have been recognised is very
significant. "The Anglo-Saxons," says Garnett, "found many imple-
ments, processes, and artificial productions of which they previously
knew little or nothing; and what was more likely than that they should
partially adopt the names by which they were designated?" The
explanation applies to some of the terms he quotes, which belong to
agriculture and household service. Thus, the *mattock* seems to have
been known to the Celts (Welsh MATOG) as well as to the Slavonians,
but not to the Teutons, who had no word to express it. *Spear* is claimed
by Garnett, but erroneously: the word exists, according to Skeat, in
several Teutonic speech-forms. As we know, from the contents of their
tombs, that it was a favourite weapon with the invaders, their acceptance
of a new name for it from the natives would have been a strong point in
favour not only of these latter having survived as an element of population, but of their having retained a military—that is, an honourable—
status in Anglo-Saxon society. *Smoke*, again, is unfairly claimed. A
good many of the genuine British derivatives are distinctly feminine, or
what are called spindle-words, and some are servile. Basket, the most
generally known of the whole class, may be either. Dad, Babe, Cradle,
Darn, Hem, Posset, Flummery, are clearly of the feminine class, and
point to the survival, in marriage, concubinage, or slavery, of captive
British women.

The rhyming score, used by shepherds and others for counting up to
twenty, and formed by a corruption of the Welsh numerals, has been
found to be known in Scotland, in Northumberland and Yorkshire, and
in several other counties, mostly, if not all, I think, western or central.
Until it is traced back historically, I am not inclined to attribute much
importance to it as an index of mixture of race, though it was almost
certainly first produced on some race frontier. The attraction of its
jingle and rhyme would tend to spread it when once produced.

The dialect of Craven, supposed to be the Carnoban of the Triads,
still contains a moderate number of words unknown to English. Of
these, some are common to the Welsh Marches, and others to the Low-

lands of Scotland; most of them are derivable from the Cymric, but a few from the Gaelic, which latter enters to a notable extent into the dialect of Lonsdale.* The Lowland Scotch, originally developed in Lothian, and probably identical with the Northumbrian, received its distinctive impress from the reflux of the Gaelic, after the earldom of Bernicia began to yield to the power of the Scottish kings, a reflux which seems to have imposed a few new place-names and introduced new words, without materially affecting the structure and general character of the dialect, which was subsequently reinforced, from the Anglian and Scandinavian side, by the results of the Norman conquest.

A provincial word of some interest, used in Herefordshire and Worcestershire and the neighbouring counties, is *Keffil*, which is derived from the Welsh *ceffyl*, a horse; but it is remarkable that it is always used in a depreciatory sense, so as nearly to correspond to *jade*, or, in modern slang, *screw*. It is often applied to a man as a term of abuse; thus, " You great keffil!" to a clumsy fellow. This word must clearly have been taken into use while the English and Welsh were living in intercourse with each other, but while the former regarded the latter with dislike and contempt.

Another interesting provincialism is mentioned by Palgrave. It is the word *Daymath*, a day's mowing, used in Cheshire to denote a certain quantity of land, but which Palgrave says is employed in the same way by the Frisians. The author of a *Cheshire Glossary* notes the similarity of many of the characteristic words in the speech of Cheshire and of Norfolk, where the intervening counties differ. It is generally supposed (and I do not contest the belief) that there is much Celtic blood in Cheshire; but the facts just mentioned, and the reduction of Chester by Ethelfrith to the condition of a waste Chester, seems to point, in the absence of precise knowledge, to an early and direct, or almost direct, colonisation by Anglo-Frisians of at least some part of the county rather than a mere extension of frontier from the Staffordshire side, analogous to the successive conquests of portions of Somerset by the kings of Wessex.

Mr. Barnes says there are few provincial words, even in Dorset, for which he cannot find a fairly good etymology in some one of the many varieties of Teutonic speech. Yet Dorset is, on the whole, one of our more Celtic counties, and contains districts where the pre-Saxon population was probably little disturbed. Even after making allowance for the great number of cases in which Celtic and Teutonic speech approach so nearly as to allow an almost equally good derivation from either side, one is rather disposed to wonder at the small amount of modification apparently suffered by the English dialects through contact with the Celtic ones than to attach great importance to the new elements taken up. Welsh seems to have taken from the English almost as much as it

* *Peacock's Glossary*, ed. Atkinson.

has given. The whole subject of the relations of these languages would surely well repay the minute attention of a Celtic scholar.*

On the whole, the philological evidence does not seem adverse to the inferences we have drawn from considerations of other kinds. If the Saxons had been in a minority in the districts *first* occupied by them, or if they had brought no women from the Continent, they could hardly have succeeded in establishing their language. Their children would have spoken British, or Romano-British more or less corrupted, as the children of the Normans in Neustria spoke the Picard Romanesque, except about Bayeux and in the Cotentin, which had been already settled by the Saxons. If this reasoning be valid, it applies to several portions of the island; for the language thus established by the conquerors was not uniform, but had already, in its earliest extant specimens, its dialectical differences. Northumbria and Lindsey did not receive their speech-form from Sussex, nor Hampshire from East Anglia. A great part of the churls, or rather of the cultivators, were Saxons, for many of the terms of husbandry are Teutonic. But many women and theows, and perhaps some free cultivators (who became churls), of British blood did remain in the land; otherwise the words of the *Basket* type, which are common to all England and not merely to the west, would not have been introduced into Anglo-Saxon.

But though the language does thus furnish a strong presumption that the colonists were a majority in several parts of the coast-lands of England, it would be quite inadmissible to extend this reasoning to the central or western districts. With respect to these language tells us nothing, except that the Welsh element of population probably increases, more or less, as we travel westwards. For the Anglo-Saxon once fairly established over considerable areas may, as before remarked, have gradually won its way afterwards without any great change of population, very much as we know it to have done at a later date in Cornwall, and in Monmouthshire east of the Usk; but the language alone is incompetent to tell us whether this was or was not the case.

* There is a popular *resumé* of it in Nicholas's *Pedigree of the English People*.

CHAPTER VI.

Germanic Conquests Elsewhere, especially in Switzerland.

IF we seek for countries or districts on the Continent whose ethnological history may throw light, by virtue of analogous conditions,
on the nature of the Anglicising process in Eastern Britain, we
shall probably look first at Flanders, then at the country about Trèves,
and then at Switzerland.

Of these the first was Teutonised as completely as East Anglia or
Sussex, and by tribes identical or nearly allied to their conquerors, *i.e.*,
by Franks, Saxons, and Frisians. In both cases there is a little doubt,
a doubt which, though I do not share it, I cannot ignore, whether a
Germanic people were not already the occupants under the Roman rule.
Setting this aside, we may say that many of the arguments for the
predominatingly British character of the mixed population existing
after the invasion in England would equally apply (reading Gallic or
Belgic for British) to the mediæval or modern Flemings and Brabançons.
On the other hand, as we find in England a Teutonic tongue over-
spreading the land without suffering much admixture or colouring from
the native Celtic one, so was it also in Flanders. I apprehend, though
here I speak under correction, that most of the Latin words which the
English took up during the earlier centuries of its existence were equally
accepted by the Flemish. Be that as it may, there can be no doubt
as to the physical type in Flanders being widely different from that
prevalent in the comparatively un-Teutonised portion of Belgium.
Vanderkindere's statistics, got officially from the schools, are conclusive
on this point; and the beautiful maps by which he has illustrated them
indicate one of the most distinct anthropological frontiers in Europe.*
In the map of arrondissements the division of the Flemish and Walloon
tongues is identical with that of the prevailingly blond and brunet
types respectively; and even in the detailed map of cantons the frontier
remains almost perfectly regular. A better example of the great value
of hair-colour as a test of race could hardly anywhere be found; for
every observer is struck with the difference in physiognomy of the
Walloon-speaking and Flemish-speaking peoples, yet the test of stature
fails, and that of simple head-breadth is by no means trenchant. In

* *Nouvelles Recherches sur l'Ethnologie de la Belgique.*

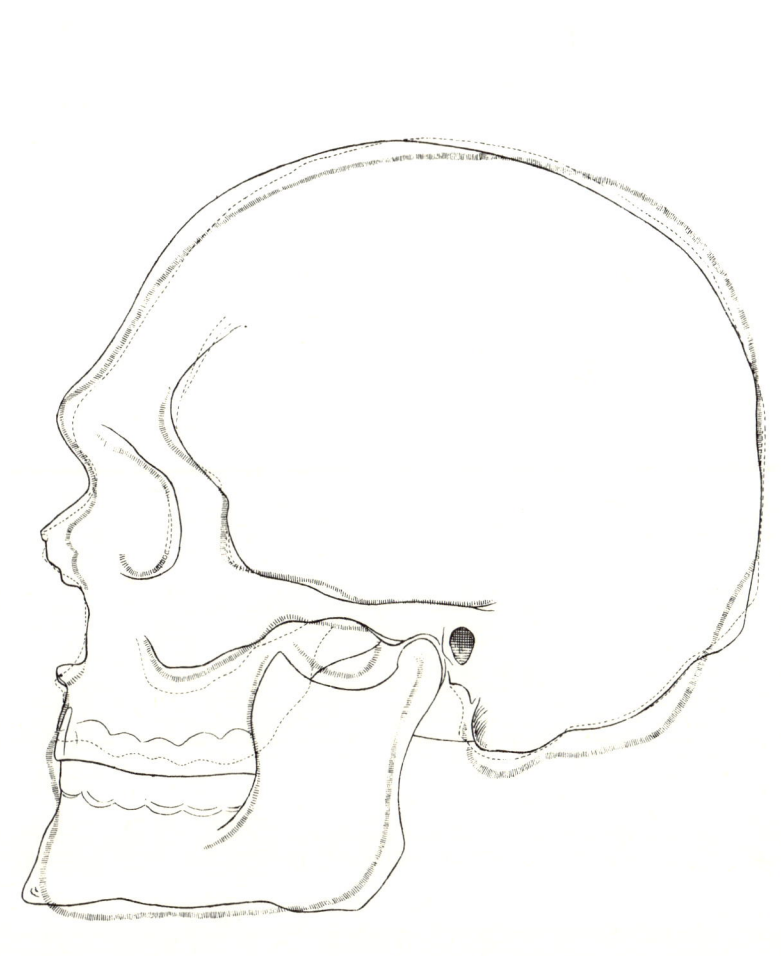

——————— OUTLINES OF BRITISH SKULL FROM BALLIDON MOOR
(ROUND BARROW) FROM CRANIA BRITANNICA.

·············· OUTLINES OF A SWISS SKULL (SION TYPE?) FROM THE
DAVOS BONE-HOUSE, IN THE AUTHOR'S POSSESSION.

▪▪▪▪▪▪▪▪▪ OUTLINES OF A SKULL FROM BORREBY, DENMARK, (STONE
PERIOD) AFTER QUATREFAGES.

both the prevailing race-elements were tall, and the compound remains so ; and though M. Houzé has shown us how the Flemish heads resemble in their rather narrow form that of their Frank and Saxon kindred, while the Walloon heads are somewhat broader, and the mixture of the two in Brussels has produced an intermediate average, these differences are by no means so strongly marked as those of hair-colour, and might not by themselves have helped us to a conclusion, especially as much broader heads prevail in Zealand, a little further north.

Further to demonstrate the value of this colour-test, I have reprinted my own tables of the hair and eyes observed in Holland or Belgium in journeys taken from fifteen to thirty years ago. They have not, of course, the value of Vanderkindere's, which have so extensive a base ; but they have the merits of having been made by one single observer, and made upon adults rather than on children. It will be found that they would corroborate, if corroboration were needed, those of my distinguished friend ; though, as they are taken mainly from urban populations, the contrasts among them are not quite so sharp.

Much of what has been said about Flanders applies also to the district of Trèves. There is the same slight uncertainty as to whether the old inhabitants, the Treviri, may not possibly have been Germans,* though the balance of probability is greatly against the notion. Nowadays Trèves resembles Aix, ethnologically, though the blond Germanic type is less strongly represented ; and, judging by the eye, I should say the head-form was broader on the average, verging probably towards the Lotharingian type, which is broad-headed, though often blond.† There is little that is not English in the general aspect of the modern Treviri ; and, on referring to my colour-tables, it will be found that their index of nigrescence is about that of several towns in the west-central parts of England, though the proportion of dark eyes is a little in excess at Trèves :

	Light Eyes.	Neutral Eyes.	Dark Eyes.	Red Hair.	Fair Hair.	Brown Hair.	Dark Hair.	Black Hair.	Index.
Bristol ...	56·1	12·5	31·4	3·8	14·2	39·4	38·4	4·2	·28·8
Trèves ...	48·4	15·6	36	4·6	15·8	37·4	37·4	4·8	26·6

Passing on to Switzerland, let us first note the points of likeness between the Saxon conquest of England and the Alemannic one of Eastern Switzerland.

In each case the conquerors were pagans ; and the vanquished were a civilised and more or less Romanised people, believed to have been of darker complexion than their conquerors. In each case remains of these people exist ungermanised in remote and comparatively inaccessible localities, of the Rhætians in the Grisons, of the Lloegrian Britons in Cornwall (where we know that the change of language was not due to the change of blood), of the Cymric Britons in Wales ; and in all

---

* See ante, pp. 21, 22.

† Collignon, "Etude des principales Races de France," *Bulletins de la Société d'Anthro. de Paris,* 1883.

these cases these remains are dark-haired folk, as my tables will presently show. In each case the invaders destroyed the Roman civilisation, and within a limited time (how short we do not know) extirpated the pre-existing language from the more accessible districts. They also extirpated or allowed to perish the Christian religion, or any Latin paganism that may have survived alongside of it. Nevertheless, we find in each case that when historical light once more dawns upon the obscured regions, laws and usages of Latin aspect or affinity can be recognised among them, mixed with relics of a barbarian German polity; and that the agrario-social system differs little from the Roman.*

I am aware that I am putting the case as regards England more decidedly, perhaps, than Professor Stubbs would allow; but so much the stronger will be my position in the argument from physical anthropology.

The points wherein we believe the two conquests to have differed are these:

The Saxons and Angles were Germanic tribes who had had much less contact and intercourse with the Romans than the Alemanni; and the latter had already subjugated a Romanised people (the provincials of the Decumates Agri, the modern Swabia), and, though they apparently refrained as much as possible from mixing blood with their subjects, had probably already imposed upon them their own Germanic language. They certainly brought numbers of these with them to the invasion and settlement of Switzerland, which, from this point of view, more resembled, perhaps, that of Worcestershire or Somerset than that of Sussex. Just as the old blond warrior type may have been diluted in the warriors of Ceawlin, or at least in their families and followers, by admixture with the Lloegrians of Hampshire and Berkshire, so may it have been in the mingled swarm of Swabians whom the Alemanni led across the Rhine to repeople the vales of the Aar, the Limmat, and the Reuss.

The history of the Burgundians was curiously different from that of the Alemanni. Later in their arrival on the Roman frontier, they earlier succeeded in breaking through it. Having had less contact with and knowledge of Christians, they were readier to accept Christianity. We know that they crossed the Rhine as pure embodiments of the northern warrior type as were the gesiths of Ælla or of Ida of Bamborough. We hear from Sidonius Apollinaris of the greasy, good-natured giants who lounged in his chambers; and we find in their tombs the long skulls and straight profiles, the weapons and the ornaments, of the Merovingian or the Saxon. The Romanised Celts whom they conquered had, it would seem, already a cross of a northern element among them. If the strong-browed Sion skulls, so like in some respects to those of Borreby and of the British bronze-men, were those of the Helvetii, the Helvetii had also been conquerors from the north. But all this avails us nothing. The Burgundians were Christians; they were

* Seebohm.

apparently not very numerous; a moderate share of the land and the serfs contented them; their language melted away silently and quickly, "like snow off a dyke," or like the Norse tongue in Normandy; and little is left to tell of them except the name of a French province, and the long limbs of a few French grenadiers from the Doubs.

Let us return, therefore, to the Alemanni, and try to find out what legacy of physical characters they have been able to transmit to the modern German-Swiss. They themselves were, as we know from the contents of their graves in Wurtemburg and Baden,* a tall race, with skulls of the long Hohberg or grave-row type. We cannot doubt, moreover, that they were generally blond. Black as well as red hair has been found in Alemannic graves; but the known tendency of corpse-hair to change colour under varying conditions gives this kind of evidence very little value. There is no reason to suppose that in this respect they differed from the rest of the old Germans, the fairest, most xanthous people known to the ancients.

Their serfs in Swabia had short, round heads; † about their complexion we *know* nothing, though we may infer a good deal. The modern Swabians are a mingled people as to colour, and length of head, and stature: long heads and fair complexion seem apt to go together there, as do the opposites of these.‡

Of the physical type of the Rhætians, the most ancient inhabitants of Eastern Switzerland, we also know very little. Some old skulls, supposed to have belonged to them, present the Disentis type—short, very broad, squarish or heart-shaped when viewed from above, singularly square when viewed laterally, from the flattening of the occiput (natural, but perhaps a little exaggerated by the manner of nursing), and the absence of prominence in the brows. It is a variety of the brachycephalic type of Central Europe, and may be said to be nearly or quite identical with the Tyrolese variety, but further removed from the Ligurian, Savoyard, &c. It was pretty surely that of one element in the mysterious Etruscan people. The Etruscans were dark-haired; but we are not entitled to infer anything therefrom as to the Rhætians: there are, however, better grounds for such inferences, as we shall presently see.

A few years ago an investigation was made in Switzerland, instigated, I believe, by Dr. Guillaume and other national anthropologists, into the colour of the hair and eyes of the school-children. The plan adopted was pretty nearly that which Virchow had recommended for Germany: red was, however, distinguished from blond hair in the schedules. Professor Kollmann has published the chief results in a valuable paper. But after carefully studying it, as well as an elaborate and beautifully-mapped paper by Dr. Th. Studer on that portion of the facts which relates to the

---

* See Ecker and Von Hölder, passim.　　　　　　† Von Hölder.

‡ With the Bavarians this does not seem to be the case. See, further on, Ranke's observations.

Canton of Bern, I remain in doubt whether the system of classification adopted brings out all the points that might be valuable.

This system, which is, I believe, that of our great master, Virchow, consists in noting the percentages of A, the pure blond type, blue eyes and fair hair, and of B, the pure brunet type, brown eyes and dark hair, and paying little attention to other combinations, which are regarded as results of crossing. In Switzerland, the number of children with gray eyes and fair hair is returned as very large in many cantons, and the question arises what the observers meant by gray eyes, and whether the distinction from blue can be relied on, or is of much value. Not that I am not ready to admit that pure blue eyes are more common in the Teutonic than in the Slavonic, or perhaps any other race; but that I doubt whether the observers can be trusted to draw so fine a distinction.

Dr. Kollmann's map of the brunet type shows that it is massed together in the east and west, and is comparatively rare across the centre from north to south. But the distribution of the rein-blond (fair blue-eyed) type tells us little or nothing: it is scattered irregularly over the greater part of the country, and Ticino has more of it than Luzern or Unterwalden, which, though a Longbard element is really (*teste meipso*) recognisable in Ticino, will certainly surprise the ordinary observer.

I have, therefore, made trial of another plan, and have constructed tables and a map showing the index of nigrescence for the several cantons, which Professor Kollmann's figures enable me to do. Those of Dr. Studer, unfortunately, do not help me at all, as he has published only those on which he has himself formed conclusions. I regret this, as Bern, with its tripartite division of Alps, Plains, and Jura, and with its Alemannic and Burgundian, its German-speaking and French-speaking districts, is a kind of epitome of Switzerland. It is a pity, too, that some native anthropologist has not extracted and published the statistics relating to the Grisons and Valais, in each of which cantons remarkable local differences would pretty surely come to light.

I have so arranged my map that not only is the index of nigrescence exhibited by a gradation of colour, but any excess of one or other colour of eyes is notified; while the percentages of red and black hair in each canton are denoted by stars, with a number of rays corresponding to those percentages of red and of black hair. There is another possible source of fallacy in the case of red hair. This colour is notoriously unpopular in several countries, while in some others it is much admired; and its status in this respect does not altogether depend on the degree of its frequency. In the German schedules no place is assigned for red hair; but, even allowing for that, it is curious that in the towns of Bavaria but a single case of it is noted. It is strange that the colour which is believed to have specially characterised the old Germanic conquerors should be unpopular among those who claim to be their descendants.

There is less risk of error in the naming of the colours of the iris;

nevertheless, there are many shades which it is difficult to style positively blue, or gray, or brown, but which are probably assigned to gray by most observers where no further option is given. In my scheme such hues are called "neutral." Observers certainly differ much about the limits of blue and light gray; and I feel assured that this is the reason why in Obwalden only 2 per cent. of blue eyes are recorded, and in Nidwalden, formerly a part of the same little State, so many as 18.

In order, however, to be able to derive much information from these official reports, we must allow—as, indeed, I am ready to do—that the ideas respecting colours entertained by the majority of the observers were tolerably uniform, or at least that the errors would, on the doctrine of probabilities, to a great extent counterbalance each other.

There is yet another comment on the method of the investigation which remains to be made: it is one which was worked out long ago, with valuable results, by Dr. Guillaume, of Neufchatel. The gradual darkening of the hair of children with advance in age, and the different proportions of the two classes (those under and those over 11 years) in the several cantons complicate the matter somewhat. Taking all Switzerland together, these two classes differ as follows:

HAIR:	Red.	Fair.	Brown.	Black.	Other.	*Index.
Under 11	2·9	52·9	38·9	4·2	1·1	−8·5
Over 11	2·7	46·4	43·9	5·8	1·2	+6·4
Both together	2·7	50	41·2	4·9	1·2	−1·7

But in Nidwalden, Schwyz, Tessin, Uri, and Geneva, the number of children over 11 years is far too small in proportion, and several of these cantons† accordingly lean unduly toward the blond side. On the other hand, in the Outer Rhodes of Appenzell there are more of the elder than of the younger children, and they overbalance the scale in the opposite direction. I have, therefore, constructed a table exhibiting the colours of the older children separately, but it is hardly worth publishing. The broad results of the enquiry are not, of course, affected by this little flaw.

The results, as exhibited by the method of the Index of Nigrescence, are, on the whole, much like those shown by Professor Kollmann's map of the *brunet* type. Like it, but more distinctly, my map indicates a stream of blond population, radiating from the Rhine between Basel and Schaffhausen, occupying the greater part of central Switzerland, and leaving a large mass of the brunet element to the east, and a smaller and less intense one to the west. There are, however, many differences in detail, not unimportant. Thus, my method excludes Valais from the blond area, as was likely to be the case, on historical and geographical grounds. To this point I will presently return. It

---

* The Swiss schedules, like the German ones, do not distinguish neutral brown (chestnut) from dark brown hair. I am obliged, therefore, to deduce my index thus: Brown + 2 Black − Red − Fair = Index; reckoning all the browns as dark, as most of them doubtless are.　　　　　　　　　　† Not Schwyz, however.

also excludes Zug, whose position is not so easy to explain. Zug exhibits a remarkable excess of gray eyes and of dark hair; but as brown eyes are below the average, it has but a small proportion of Dr. Kollmann's brown type. The numbers are small; and I suspect the peculiarity may be due to errors of nomenclature—to the personal equation, in fact. Baselland, the Bernese Jura, and Schaffhausen, all brown on the map of Professor Kollmann, are all light on mine, having all an excess of light hair, but also of dark eyes. Probably the statistics of Baden and Wurtemberg might illustrate those of Schaffhausen. Dr. Georg Mayr* has demonstrated that in Bavaria the towns have, generally speaking, a population decidedly darker, both in eyes and hair, than the rural districts. This does not hold good in the civic and the rural divisions of Basel, perhaps by reason of the immigration into Basel City from Elsass and Baden.

The position of Geneva is the same in both maps, and is worthy of notice. The prevailing fair complexion of the Genevese is probably correlated with their high stature, which Professor Dunant finds to be 1·674 metre at twenty years, and 1·688 at full growth (= 5 ft. 5·9 inches and 5 ft. 6·4 inches). Both may, with some show of likelihood, be referred to the fact that Geneva was for some time the capital of a Burgundian kingdom, and that a numerous body of that "sesquipedal race," as Sidonius called them, probably located themselves there.

It is much to be regretted that M. Dunant's investigations into the stature of the Swiss, very valuable so far as they went, were not followed up in other than the four cantons to which they extended. The fact that the Alemannic portion of the canton Fribourg yields a lower average than the Burgundian is very striking. The canton Wallis especially would probably repay minute examination of both stature and colour, with due regard to the possible influence of "media" as well as of race. In my map Wallis, as a whole, comes out rather dark, with a remarkable proportion of both red and black hair. A moderate excess of red occurs in all the Burgundian cantons, and of black in three of them, viz., Fribourg, Vaud, and the Bernese Jura. In the absence of apparent ground for any other theory, and in view of the fact that both black and red are common among the " Keltic " peoples of the British Isles, I am disposed to see in this excess a legacy of the Helvetii rather than of the Burgundians.

The mass of the eastern cantons, from Thurgan to Ticino inclusively, is characterised by an excess of brown eyes, an excess of dark but not always of black hair, and a deficiency of red hair. These may be conjectured, then, to be the marks of the Disentis, or, if you will, the Rhætian race, which seems to be at its purest in the more remote valleys of the Grisons, though it is strong, perhaps even predominant, throughout the whole, or almost the whole, of Switzerland, and not only its eastern portion. Dr. Studer points out that the brunet region of the west nearly cor-

* Die Bayerische Jugend, Sep. Abd. des Bayr. stat. Bureau, 1875.

responds with the chief seats of the pile-dwellers; and it seems probable that these pile-dwellers themselves were dark-haired brachycephali.

Observations of my own, unfortunately not very numerous, but embracing a good many towns and districts in Switzerland, have enabled me to construct yet another map, which, with the figures on which it is founded, may serve for mutually testing themselves and the official statistics, and also for comparison with those of the other countries in which my method has been applied. These observations, being restricted to adults, naturally yield much higher indices of nigrescence than those from school-children. These indices are fairly comparable with those met with in various parts of the British Isles; and their range is equally great, though Switzerland is so small a country. The following are notable points:

There is a general correspondence with Professor Kollmann's Brunet Map and with my own one constructed on the basis of his statistics. The blond element would seem to have radiated from the lower Rhine, the canton Argau being its centre; and my own observations would indicate that it pressed in great strength up the valley of the Aar. The greater potency of the brown elements in the adults of Geneva may depend on the recent influx of French and Savoyards into that city, who are gradually swamping the native breed. The Savoyards, as may be seen in my French table, are a very dark people.

Further east, it will be seen that I failed to detect in Nidwalden that singular prevalence of blonds which in the official statistics distinguishes this interesting little canton from all its neighbours, and which, looking to the remarkable history and character of its people, I was quite prepared to find. It is true I saw but few of the peasants. There are, however, two facts which lead me to think my own observations probably correct, at least so far as the town of Stanz is concerned. One is, that the breadth-index of twenty skulls, taken indiscriminately from the bone-house of Stanz, was so great as 83·6; the other, that in the gallery of portraits of the Landammans of Unterwalden the majority are brown or dark-haired. The countenances of the modern people, it must be allowed, are generally fair, and so Germanic or Anglo-Saxon in type that I was a little surprised at finding so large a breadth-index.

The figures got from the Grisons are extremely interesting; they run *pari passu* with the supposed lessening proportions of Alemannic blood. Davos, for example, is more Germanic than most parts of the Grisons; the valley is said to have been colonised by the German-speaking folk of the Upper Wallis. The Prattigau and the valleys below Thusis are somewhat Germanised; but the higher portion of the Vorder-Rheinthal is purely Rhætian, and speaks mostly Romantsch to this day. Accordingly we find at Disentis in the highest degree the combination of dark hair with short, broad skulls. It was not without reason that His and Rutimeyer gave the name of this place to their Rhætian type. I had not time to measure many skulls; but one of the few I got hold of gave me an index of 92 ; and probably this is frequently exceeded. The concurrent depth of colour (usually very dark gray or light brown eyes, with very dark brown, seldom coal-black hair) seems to indicate pretty distinctly the colour-type of the original Rhætian race. There is more of light hair and blue eyes in the upper valleys of Ticino than in the Ober-Rheinthal.

The recognisable race-elements with which we have to deal in Switzerland are therefore as follows :

1st. The Disentis, of undoubted antiquity in the east, if not in the whole of Switzerland.

2nd. The pfeil-bau folk, though some of them, as at Auvernier, may have been long-headed, included also brachycephalic elements, whether of the Disentis or of some other race.

3rd. The Sion type may be assigned with some confidence to the Helvetii, generally supposed to have been a fair race. Persons having the same conformation, in the British Isles, have very frequently blue or gray eyes, with brown or reddish hair.

4th. The Romans hardly need to be brought into the question. Though His and Rutimeyer assigned to them the Hohberg type, I do not think they have any followers in the conjecture ; probably they gave it up long ago. The Romans were comparatively few in number and of mixed blood, and can hardly have transmitted any distinct type to the modern Swiss, though individual cases of atavism may occur.

5th. I pretermit any mention of Cimbric or Scandinavian colonies, supposed to have settled in the Bernese Oberland or in the Forest cantons, not being aware of there being any sufficiently solid grounds for such supposition.

6th. The Burgundians have been already described ; they overlay the Helveto-Romans on the west.

7th. It has been said that the Alemanni, when they finally crossed the Rhine, were no longer a pure Germanic people, unless perhaps in the highest of their social strata. Some of the skulls from Alemannic graves, figured by His and Rutimeyer, fully confirm this view. They were probably, therefore, less uniformly blond or xanthous than the Burgundians. And if any one race is responsible for the frequency of gray eyes in Switzerland (which I very much doubt), their local distribution seems to point to the Alemanni, inasmuch as the excess of gray affects all the central cantons, including the blond Unterwalden, but not, generally speaking, those to the east and west.

The speedy extinction of the Roman speech, except in the Grisons, seems to indicate, what we learn also in other ways, that the Alemanni, with their dependents, were more numerous than the population they subjected ; still the latter were in sufficient numerical strength notably to reinforce the brown short-headed element in the nation. This latter element has probably been gaining ground ever since, during the earlier centuries by, first, the expenditure in warfare of the males of the generally tall and blond military caste, and secondly, the reluctance universal in such castes to allow its surplus of women to intermarry with the servile classes; and during the middle ages, after the admixture of the social strata had become a little more uniform, by reason of the taller stature, and more courageous, restless and adventurous character, which seem generally to concur with the xanthous temperament. As Switzerland, especially its central region, was for ages the great recruiting ground of mercenary soldiers, it is probable that the tall blond long-headed element would emigrate at a more rapid rate than the brown short-headed one. In this way may also be accounted for the apparent decline in the stature of the modern Swiss, who certainly do not, as a rule, now justify the descriptions given of their huge physical development in earlier days, the days of halberds, morgensterns, and two-handed swords.

But if the old Swiss aristocracy has well-nigh become extinct, and the long-headed soldierly race may also be dwindling away, they have imparted their prevailing complexion to a considerable extent to the mixed breed who now occupy the country. The distribution of colours among the central and north-eastern Swiss does not differ very notably from that which obtains among the English. One might be transported from Zurich to London, or *vice versâ*, without noticing anything in the complexions of the people to remind one of the change. Nor are the prevailing features by any means so different from those of the English as is the usual form of head.

At this conclusion I had arrived before reading the recent work of Johannes Ranke, which has thrown a flood of light on the anthropology of the neighbouring Bavarian land. Ranke, in whom has arisen a new and powerful champion of the potency of media, thinks that the greater prevalence of short heads and dark complexions in Southern as compared with Northern Germany must be due in part to the long-continued influence of local circumstances, and not wholly to the greater numbers and persistence of the ancient race of the south. He proves that in at least one district of Bavaria proper the amalgamation of the races is so complete that the blonds are neither taller nor longer-headed than the brunets, and that both have the broad skull (83.2 index) which now rules in that country. The Hohberg (old long warrior-type of skull, which is still common in England) he considers to be well-nigh extinct in Bavaria, so far as the calvarium or braincase is concerned, but the facial skeleton, the physiognomy, remains, as he says, attached to a short and broad braincase.

In Baden, and especially the Brisgau, certainly one of the earlier conquests of the Alemanni, Ecker states the breadth-index in modern times at 83. In Wurtemberg it is evidently as large, or nearly as large; but Von Hölder nowhere, I think, gives the exact figure: he entertains a horror of averages.

In Switzerland, too, we have no trustworthy average. I found one of 83·6 in 20 skulls at Stanz; and one exactly identical in 36 at Davos. In

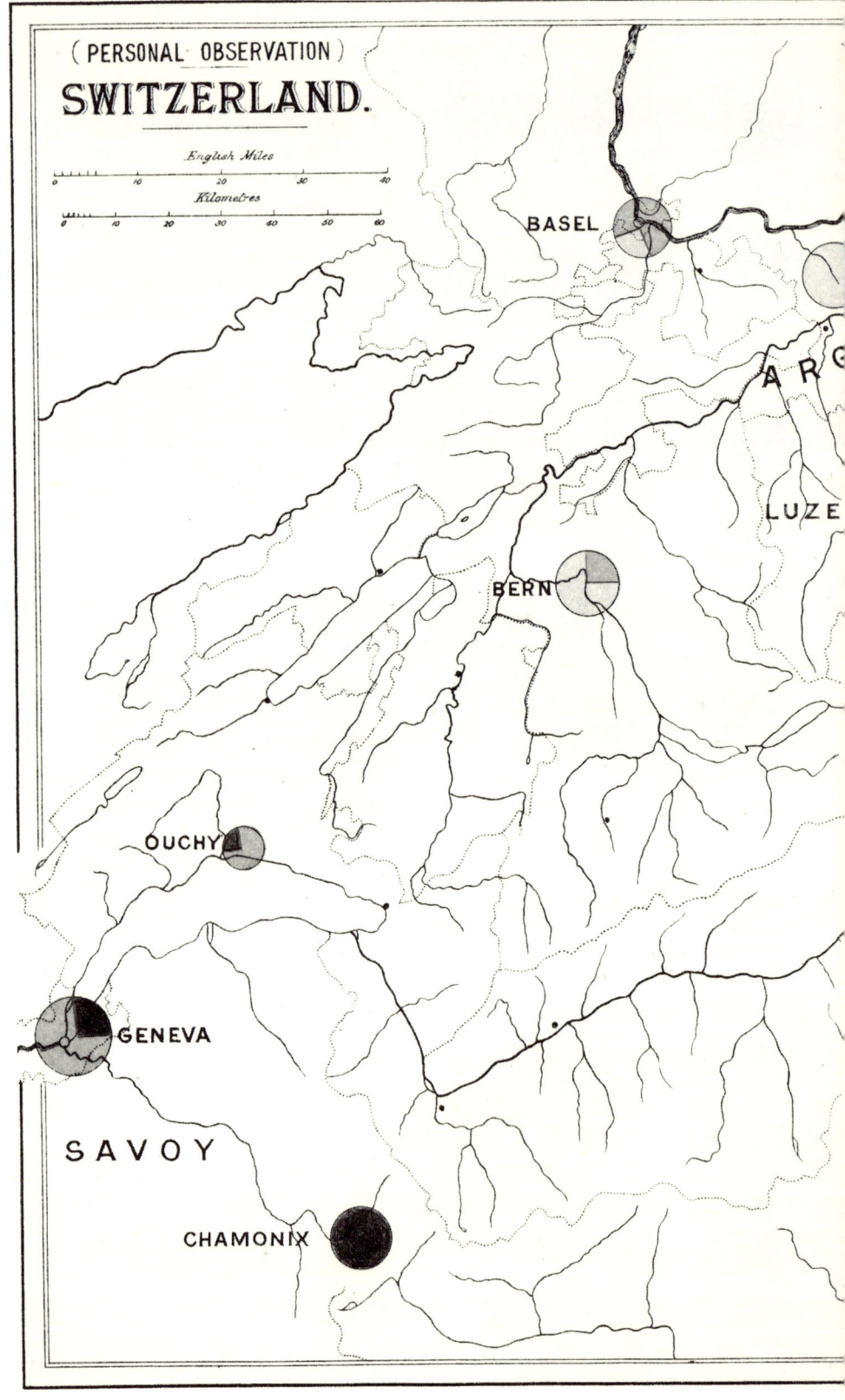

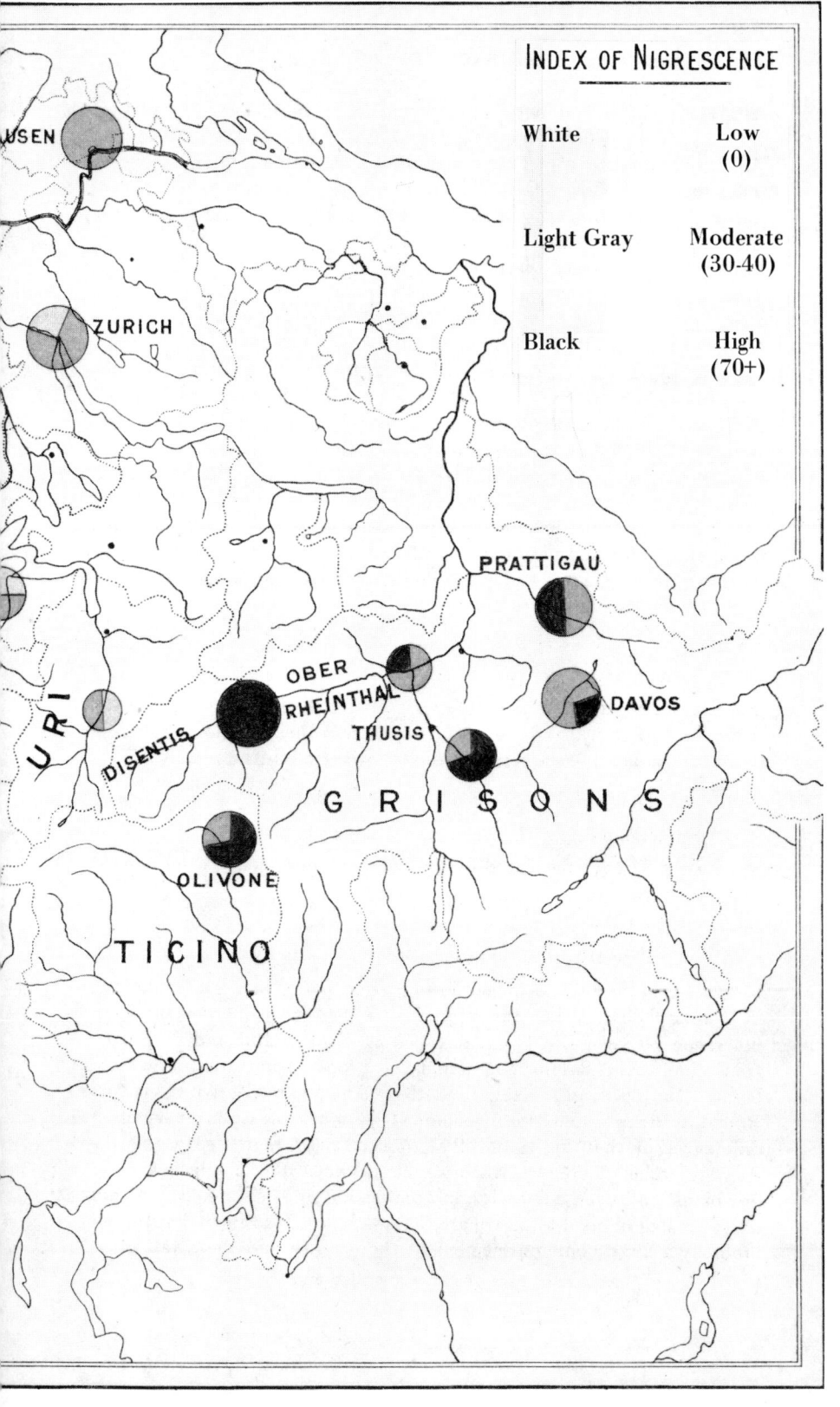

USEN

ZURICH

URI

PRATTIGAU

OBER
RHEINTHAL

DISENTIS

THUSIS

DAVOS

G R I S O N S

OLIVONE

TICINO

a table appended hereto will be found the measurements of 7 of these latter, selected as exhibiting typical varieties; their average index is but 82·8, but the broad round variety is not so fully represented among the 7 as among the entire series of 36. I saw living specimens of the rarer varieties among the 7 in the village, and may append measurements of the living head in one of the Belair and one of the Sion type: the former was a native of the Prattigau, of an ancient noble family.

I feel sure the average breadth is greater about Disentis, in the Oberrheinthal, as it certainly is in Savoy, across the French frontier. On the other hand, judging by the eye, I should say it was less in the Bernese peasantry. Setting one fact against another, then, we may pretty safely affirm that it is not *much* greater in Switzerland generally than in earlier Germanised regions to the north and north-east. If we compare the official statistics of colour, there is also no very great difference between Bavaria and Switzerland, although Bavaria includes a considerable extent of country which was never Roman. In Bavaria 54 per cent. of the scholars are reported to be blond-haired (including the red), 41 brown, and 5 black-haired; while in Switzerland the proportions are 52·7, 41·2, and 4·9. There are, however, more brown eyes in Switzerland, the proportions being:

	Blue Eyes.	Gray Eyes.	Brown Eyes.
Bavaria	29	37	34
Switzerland	16	43	40

and the smaller number of blue eyes makes the difference between the two countries appear too great when tested by the rein-blond and rein-brunet methods. These result in the following figures:

	Pure Blond.	Pure Brown.
Bavaria	20·4	21·1
Switzerland	11·6	25·7

while the difference measured by the index of nigrescence would be:

$$\text{Bavaria} \quad 41 \; +2(5) \; -54 \; = -4$$
$$\text{Switzerland} \quad 41\cdot2 + 2(4\cdot9) - 52\cdot7 = -1\cdot7 *$$

Switzerland darker-haired than Bavaria by .... 2·3

Having added the evidence of statistics, so far as available, to that of ordinary observation and opinion, to show that there is no great difference between the physical types of Switzerland and of Swabia respectively, and having noted that the peoples subjugated and incorporated by the Anglo-Saxons and the Alemanni respectively, viz., the Romano-Britons and the Romano-Rhætians, presented very great differences of that kind, and that, nevertheless, there is to this day a considerable degree of resemblance between the English and the Swabians, and even the Swiss, in complexion and feature, if comparatively seldom in head-form, we are, I think, entitled to infer that there is probably a large common element in the English and the Swabians or

* See note on page 5 on method of deducing this index.

Swiss.* In this point of view, the less Alemannic blood we allow in Switzerland, the less can we afford to minimise the Anglo-Saxon element in England; otherwise, the resemblances can hardly be accounted for.

To sum up, we have in Switzerland, and in the country immediately to the north, evidence that a Pagan Germanic people intruded about the fifth century; that they settled some districts almost exclusively; that they enslaved some portion of the prior population, and in their law of weregylds treated them as serfs; that they uprooted Christianity; that they changed for the most part the local nomenclature; yet that they adopted, or allowed to remain, certain Roman usages connected with land, &c.; and that their descendants exhibit certain changes in physical type, which approximate them somewhat to the original inhabitants, without much obscuring their own primitive type. All this is the exact counterpart of what seems to have happened in England about the same period. The Alemanni were undoubtedly a very numerous people, and probably more numerous in many parts of Switzerland than the survivors of their predecessors. Why may not the Anglo-Saxons in the East of England have been in similar strength, as analogy would indicate? On the other hand, we have in Switzerland districts (in the Grisons chiefly) which the Alemans conquered indeed, but did not colonise, unless in small patches, and into which their blood and language filtered slowly; the former never becoming considerable, the latter prevailing here and there, but not universally. Here we have the analogues of Cornwall, Wales, Herefordshire, &c.

One other inference I hope the reader will derive from this chapter, viz., that the mode of reckoning by the index of nigrescence, even without using any subsidiary means of utilising the proportions of iris-colour, is more apt to represent ethnological truth than that of separating and estimating the pure blond and pure brunet types. No one, I think, will deny or even doubt that the map constructed on the former system, classing together, as it does, the central cantons as most Germanic, and excluding the distant and peripheral ones, such as Valais and Ticino, accords better with our ideas of the history of Germanic invasion than does Professor Kollmann's brunet map, not to speak of his rein-blond one, in which several of the central cantons (Luzern, Nidwalden, Obwalden), notwithstanding the frequency of fair hair, are excluded from the blond area. The fact is, that the latter method virtually, though not at the first blush, bases itself mainly on iris-colour, which, though valuable as an index of race, is certainly less so than hair-colour. The stress now laid on this detail will be found to be justified by the results of the two methods as applied in England, where also the index of nigrescence, especially when supplemented by some indication of the colour of the eyes, will be found to give anthropological results more capable of interpretation, and more in accordance with ethnological probability.

* In speaking thus of the Swiss, I do not, of course, include the Bundners (Grisons) nor the Ticinese.

COLOUR OF HAIR AND EYES IN SWITZERLAND.

	No.	Sex.	Light Eyes — Red	Fair	Brown	Dark	Black	Total Light Eyes	Neutral Eyes — Red	Fair	Brown	Dark	Black	Total Neutral Eyes	Dark Eyes — Red	Fair	Brown	Dark	Black	Total Dark Eyes	Index of Nigrescence — Gross	Per Cent
Basel	133	68/65	4·	17·	22·	11·5	1·5	56	1·	1·5	8·5	10·5	·5	22·	...	3·	16·	31·5	4·5	55·	40·	...
per cent.	...	...	3·	12·7	16·5	8·6	1·1	42·1	·7	1·1	6·4	7·9	·4	16·2	...	2·2	12·	23·6	3·4	41·3	...	30·
Zurich	143	70/73	3·	17·5	41·	13·5	...	75·	...	3·	6·	9·	...	18·	1·5	1·	12·	30·5	5·	50·	41·	...
per cent.	...	...	2·1	12·2	28·7	9·4	...	52·4	...	2·1	4·2	6·3	...	12·6	1·	·7	8·4	21·4	3·5	35·	28·7	28·7
Argau	60	42/18	1·5	14·	13·5	1·5	·5	31·	...	4·	3·5	3·5	...	11·	...	·5	8·	8·5	1·	18·	-4·5	...
per cent.	...	...	2·5	23·3	22·5	2·5	·8	51·6	...	6·6	5·8	5·8	...	18·3	...	·8	13·3	14·1	1·6	30·	...	-7·5
Bern	26	m	1·	4·5	5·5	1·	·8	12·	...	...	...	...	...	...	...	...	3·	10·5	·5	14	7·	...
Total	124	f	5·	24·	26·5	7·5	...	63·	2·	3·5	5·5	4·	...	15·	...	1·	16·5	25	3·5	46	8·	...
Total	150	...	6·	28·5	32	8·5	...	75·	2·	3·5	5·5	4·	...	15·	...	1·	19·5	35·5	4·	60	15·	...
per cent.	...	...	4·	19·	21·3	5·7	...	50·	1·3	2·3	3·6	2·6	...	10·	1·3	·6	13·	23·6	2·6	40·	...	10·
Schaffhausen	40	20/20	2·	5·	10·	1·	...	18·	...	...	1·	2·	1·	4·	...	...	5·	10·5	2·5	18	13·5	33·7
Luzern	50	16/34	...	7·5	11·	3·5	...	22·	...	...	·5	2·	·5	7	·5	1·	7·5	9·	2·	20·	9·5	19
Stanz	90	41/49	2·5	12·5	27·	9·	...	51·	...	1·	6·	6·5	·5	14·	...	1·	5·	18·5	·5	25·	19·	...
per cent.	...	...	2·7	13·9	30·	10·	...	56·6	...	1·1	6·6	7·2	·6	15·5	...	1·1	5·6	20·5	·6	27·8	...	21·1
	1	2	3	4	5	6	7	8	9	10	11	12	13	14	15	16	17	18	19	20	21	22

	1	2	3	4	5	6	7	8	9	10	11	12	13	14	15	16	17	18	19	20	21	22
Uri	28	13/15	1·	2·	10·	2·	·5	15·	...	1·	3·	3·	...	7·	...	...	3·	3·	...	6·	4·	14·3
Prättigau	60	33/27	1·5	3·5	13·	9·5	·8	28·	...	...	2·	3·	...	6·	2·	...	3·5	17·	3·5	26	32·5	...
per cent.	...	...	2·5	5·8	21·6	15·8	·8	46·6	...	...	3·3	5·	1·6	10·	3·3	...	5·8	28·3	5·8	43·3	...	54·2
Davos. Sertig.	50	m	1·	6·	11·5	4·	·5	23·	...	·5	2·5	5·5	·5	9·	...	...	2·	11	·5	18	25·	...
	28	f	·5	4·	7·5	3·	...	15·	...	...	...	2·5	·5	3·	...	...	2·5	7	5	10	11·	...
Total	78	...	1·5	10·	19·	7·	·5	38·	...	·5	2·5	8·	1·	12·	...	...	4·5	18·	5·5	28	36·	46·1
per cent.	...	...	1·9	12·8	24·3	9·	·6	48·7	...	·6	3·2	10·2	1·3	15·4	...	...	5·7	23·1	7·	35·9	...	...
Thusis, Versam. Vollendaz, We-sen; Prot. vills. in Rheinthal	50	25/26	2·	5·5	6·	3·5	1·	18·	...	1·	·5	6·	1·5	9·	...	1·	7·	10·5	4·5	23·	24·5	...
per cent.	...	...	4·	11·	12·	7·	2·	36·	...	2·	1·	12·	3·	18·	...	2·	14·	21·	9·	46·	...	49·
Cathc vills. on Hinter-Rhein ...	31	1⅘	...	2·	8·	5·5	·5	16·	...	...	...	2·	...	2·	...	·5	2·	8·5	2·5	13·	20·	64·5
Ilanz, Truns, and Disentis ...	123	6 1/22	2·5	6·5	19·5	16·5	2·	47·	...	...	3·5	11·	5·5	20·	...	·5	11·5	32·5	11·5	56·	88·5	...
per cent.	...	...	2·	5·3	15·8	13·4	1·6	38·1	...	...	2·8	8·9	4·4	16·2	...	·4	9·3	26·4	9·5	45·5	...	72·
Italian Laborers in Switzerland	25	m	...	2·	5·	5·	1·	13·	...	...	2·	3·	...	5·	1·	...	1·	5·	1·	7·	15·	60·
Olivone, &c.	53	2 4/27	...	3·5	11·	5·5	...	20·	...	...	3·5	2·5	1·	7·	...	...	2·5	17·	5·5	26·	33·5	...
Lukmanierglen, N. of summit ...	7	f	1·	2·	...	...	...	3·	...	...	...	1·	...	1·	...	...	1·	2·	...	3·	0·	...
Biasca	16	7/9	...	...	3·5	2·5	...	6·	...	...	...	1·5	·5	2	...	...	1·	4·	3·	8·	15·	...
Total Ticino and Itals. ...	101	...	1·	7·5	19·5	13·	1·	42·	...	...	5·5	8·	1·5	15·	1·	...	5·5	27·	9·5	43	62·5	61·9
Ouchy	30	2 0/10	...	5·	6·	2·5	·5	14	...	...	2·	3·	...	5·	...	...	1·	7·5	2·5	11·	14·	47
Geneva	100	5 0/50	2·5	8·5	17·	12·	...	40	...	1·	8·	8·	...	17·	1·	1·	6·	28·	7·	43·	48·	...

NOTES.

Except in the Grisons, and perhaps at Stanz, which is a very small town, the numbers observed are more or less insufficient for building on. Still, besides the general results, which seem somewhat valuable, and which are described in the text and map, there come out in the details some curious coincidences with the official statistics, and some additional points of interest. Thus Stanz appears in both with the largest proportion of light and of the smallest of dark eyes. Schaffhausen in both abounds in dark eyes, as seems to be the case (see Dr. Georg Mayr) in some neighbouring Swabian towns. Argau, doubtless the gateway of the Alemanni, yields in both the smallest index of nigrescence, if we exclude Niedwalden. The Lukmanierthal, before the road was made, was probably more open to the Italian than to the Grison side; and the brilliant blonds whom I saw therein did not look like Grisons people. The natives of Geneva are in process of being swamped by dark-complexioned immigrants from France and Savoy; but their comparative fairness is still noticeable in my table.

The apparent difference between Catholic and Protestant villages in the Rheinthal is what might have been expected.

CHAPTER VII.

The Danish Period.

WE have now followed the history of the Saxon conquest of Britain down to the period, about the middle of the ninth century, when the invasions of the vikings, commonly comprehended under the name of Danish, began to be really formidable, and when the westward progress of Anglo-Saxon conquest and colonisation was checked by the necessity of defence against these assailants *à tergo*.

The operations of the Northmen, as they affected the ethnology of England, might be thus distinguished:

A. The great invasions and settlements of the latter part of the ninth century, which resulted in the establishment of the Danelagh.

B. The renewed invasions in the reign of Ethelred II., and the conquest of all England by Sweyn Forkbeard and Knut.

C. The comparatively obscure colonisation by the Norwegians, from Ireland, Man, the Hebrides, &c., of Cumbria and some other parts of the North-west.

D. The gradual infiltration of Northmen, singly or in small bands, as warriors (huscarls), merchants and seamen.

E. The colonisation of Scotland and Ireland may be taken later.

A. We have no certain data whereon to found an estimate of the numbers of the Scandinavian invaders. The rapidity of the movements of their hosts, and the ease with which they obtained horses in number sufficient for their purposes, give us the idea of small bands of buccaneers rather than of important national migrations. Moreover, it is difficult to understand how the denizens of three countries, one of which was small, the second mostly uninhabitable, and the third certainly then, as now, thinly peopled, could have furnished a sufficient number of fighting-men to maintain incessant broils at home, while they were plundering the whole coasts of Europe, peopling Iceland, Shetland, and Orkney, together with cities, provinces, and islands in Great Britain, Ireland, and France, and acquiring a great and sometimes preponderant influence in the politics of all these countries as well as of Russia. All this they did within as short a space of time as may easily be allowed for the Saxon conquest of Lothian and the eastern half of England, a fact which goes far to do away with the argument on the insufficiency of Old Saxony, &c., to furnish a new population to these latter countries.

The numbers of the ships are sometimes given with an exactness that almost demands belief; and as we have some evidence as to their size and complement of men, we feel obliged to acknowledge that some of the invading armies may have included many thousands of warriors. The destruction of life through their means among the English must have been very great, and the Chronicle speaks of the "mortality among cattle and men" during their operations as though it had been much greater than the actual slaughter. We are told that they "divided the lands of Deira," and tilled and sowed them, which latter clause seems to imply that they were too numerous to constitute a mere military aristocracy, and that they must have formed a considerable portion of the population where they permanently settled. Moreover, they in some expeditions brought their wives and children with them, and their thralls also,* which again throws additional light on the probable character of the Anglo-Saxon immigration. It was during this first period of Danish aggression that the counties of York, Lincoln, Notts, Leicester, Norfolk and Suffolk assumed the Scandinavian character, which the first four ever afterwards retained, and which strongly tinctured East Anglia thenceforward. Some other counties, as Derby, Northampton, and Cambridge, received also a considerable military population of Danes.

Northumberland, Durham, and Lothian, though subdued by Halfdan, were little interfered with subsequently, and were generally left under eorls of Anglian descent. The Scandinavian element in Yorkshire must have been greatly strengthened during the early part of the tenth century by the invasions of Ragnald and the two Olafs. Still, it would be difficult to explain the history of the Danelagh during this period without allowing something for the somewhat nearer relation, in language and blood, between the Anglians and Danes, than between the latter and the men of Wessex.

B. The great Danish and Norwegian invasions in the days of Ethelred II., and the rule of the Danish sovereigns subsequently, must have introduced a good deal of fresh northern blood; but there is little indication of the invaders having anywhere settled down in large masses, as in the ninth century. Perhaps the small Danish settlement about Lydford, which Taylor asserts on the evidence of local names, may have taken place about this time. But in the main the effect of these later invasions was not so great from an ethnological as from a political point of view. A good deal of land, however, in Wessex and the West, as well as elsewhere, passed into the hands of Danish holders, the names of whose sons appear in *Domesday*.

C. The colonisation of the western coast by Scandinavians, chiefly Norwegians, from the Hebrides, Man, and the cities of the Ostmen in Ireland (Dublin, Waterford, Wexford, &c.), is, considering its importance and the late period at which it must have taken place, singularly

---

* Note the mention of leysings in Alfred's treaty with Guthrum.

obscure. Respecting the settlement about Milford Haven, we have, I believe, no evidence at all except that of certain local names, as those of Milford, Haverford, Langum (Langholm?), Haroldston, and the islands of Caldy, Skokholm, and Skomer, though the *Annales Cambriæ* and the *Brut-y-Tywysogion* repeatedly, under the tenth century, mention the devastation of Menevia and Dyfed by the " Pagans." The settlement of Cumberland, Westmorland, Furness, and Eastern Dumfriesshire has been studied by Ferguson, who is of opinion that it must have been effected from the Isle of Man. The facts we have to deal with are these:

1. The history of Southern Cumbria, the modern Cumberland and Westmorland, remains very obscure after the seventh century, when we know that it was under Northumbrian sway. Edred, an Anglian, ruled at Carlisle in 918;* but the population may have been still largely British, while the country lay very open to the raids of the Norsemen.

2. A.D. 945, Cumberland and Strathclyde, we are told, were harried with fire and sword by King Edmund, their king Dunmail, Domnhal or Dunwallon, expelled from the former if not from the latter region, and the country granted to the King of the Scots, to be held of the English Crown. We may presume that the land was still sparsely inhabited.

3. A.D. 1000, Ethelred II. invades Cumberland ("ubi Dacorum maxima mentio," says Henry of Huntingdon), and wastes the country.

4. When Malcolm Canmore ravaged Northumbria, and swept away a great part of the remaining population of Yorkshire into slavery, Cumberland and Westmorland were his,† and the Cumbrians doubtless formed part of his army. Moreover, Cumberland was the nearest and safest refuge for the Anglo-Danes of Yorkshire, when they were fleeing from the wrath of William the Bastard.

5. Dolfin, son of Cospatric, was Earl of Cumberland till William Rufus expelled him; but Waltheof, his brother, retained extensive lordships therein. William introduced a colony of Saxons from the south, whom he settled in and about Carlisle.

6. We find the local names of Cumberland, Westmorland, Furness, Lonsdale, Annandale, and Eskdale for the most part Teutonic, and rather Scandinavian than Saxon, rather Norse than Danish. The dialect is strongly tinctured with Norse characteristics; and the people, while bearing a certain degree of resemblance to the modern Strathclydewallians, in stature and feature, approach more nearly, I think, in these respects, to the Norwegians, with whom they also agree in being remarkably fair.

7. Man was in the possession of the Norsemen for several centuries, and they have left their mark on the local names, customs, and laws of the island; but the language and the physical character of the people are "Celtic" to this day, though doubtless somewhat modified.

* Robertson, *Scotland Under her Early Kings*, i., 70, 71.
† At least the parts north of the mountains which divide Lonsdale from Edendale.

Cumberland lies opposite to Man, and is a much more fertile and desirable land. We may suppose, therefore, that a continual stream of Norse colonisation poured, during the tenth and eleventh centuries, into the half-deserted mainland, to which Man may have served as a kind of stepping-stone; while the native Manxmen held strongly to their island home, and there perpetuated their race.

D. The influence of this infiltration may have been considerable in the maritime counties and the principal towns. Indications of it crop up everywhere. Thus in London we have Tooley Street and the Church of St. Olave, and the word *hustings*, which seems to have been taken from the speech of London into the common stock of English; and in the Bristol Channel we have the Steep and the Flat Holm, and Worm's Head. The more Celtic portions of South Britain were perhaps more affected in this way than the remainder; for the Danes and Norwegians frequently took service with the Welsh and Cornish chiefs, during their revolts against the English or their struggles with each other. Icelandic Sagas represent the Norsemen as familiar with the Welsh havens and markets. For example, in the *Njalsaga*, Kol, one of the burners of Njal's house, is accidentally encountered and slain by the avenger Kari, in the market of a Welsh port, where Kol, we are told, was about to marry an heiress of the country.

We may now proceed to examine the evidence of the progress of Saxonisation along the western Marches during the period under review, evidence derived chiefly, but not altogether, from *Domesday*.

The "Ordinance respecting the Dunsetas," in Thorpe's *Ancient Laws*, is here of considerable importance. Palgrave, and Dr. Nicholas following him, read Devnsetas, and suppose the document to be a treaty between the Saxon and the British Devonians; and the latter (misunderstanding Palgrave) fixes its date about fifteen years before the Norman Conquest. It is clear, and shall be presently shown, that at that time the Exe, and even the Tamar, had ceased to be a national boundary in a political sense; but as the treaty first appears in a MS. of the tenth century, it may really date from the time when the Devonians west of the Exe were still half-independent. Thorpe, however, shows that the reading Devnsetas occurs only in Lambarde, and not uniformly even there; and I follow him in thinking that some expressions referring to the Wentsetas, *i.e.* probably the inhabitants of the Forest of Dean (which the Welsh reckoned as the easternmost of three Gwents), are almost conclusive in favour of the treaty being one between the English and Welsh, or rather the people under English and Welsh law respectively on the two sides of the Wye.

Though the West Welsh had for centuries (Palgrave thinks from the time of Geraint II., A.D. 589, but this is doubtful) formed a State which was usually, or at least frequently, vassal to Wessex, and though their frequent struggles for liberty always ended in a further contraction of their frontier, they had still, in Athelstan's day, their native prince

Howel, whose jurisdiction did not, however—at all events after A.D. 938—extend east of the Tamar. It must have been later than this when the Saxons acquired the property of the greater part of the soil of Cornwall, which they clearly had under Edward the Confessor. Of the King's Thanes and mesne tenants enumerated in *Domesday*, both before and after the Conquest, after eliminating the Normans and their Breton allies, the great majority have Saxon names. There are a few Welsh ones in both counties; thus, in Cornwall, Grifin holds Roscarnan, and Jovin (probably a Breton) Trevret; and there are several names, viz., Wallo, Colo, Chenisi, Bretel, Wadhel, Waso, Offels, Blohin, Merken, Jaul (? Saulf), Andreas, Blechu, and Rabel, respecting the nationality of which I am doubtful, but some of which are probably Welsh. In Devonshire, Lachelin (? Llewelyn) holds Withecnolle of Godbold; and the names of Levet, Wordron, Edloudieg, Chenias, Ludo, and Wichin are to me more or less doubtful. There are no other exceptions.

In Kemble, vol. i., Appendix C, are some interesting manumissions from the Book of St. Petroc's, Bodmin, dating from the latter half of the tenth century. In these the priests and freemen have, some Saxon, some Cornish names; but those of the slaves, with hardly an exception, are clearly Cornish. On the whole, it is safe to conclude that at the time of the Norman Conquest the landholders in the whole of West Wales were generally Saxon, but that the bulk of the population was Celtic (Lloegrian), not only in blood but in speech, throughout Cornwall and a great part of South Devon, at the very least. It may be worth consideration whether the high physical and intellectual average of the Cornish people may not be partly due to their having in their veins a double portion of the blood of the old Romano-British chiefs and military class; for it is natural to suppose that as the West-Welsh were driven back step by step, the chiefs and fighting men would abandon their lands and take refuge with their countrymen further back, while the servile class would remain on the soil and accept easily the rule of their new and alien lords.

Domesday yields much valuable information respecting the population of the Welsh Marches. It is evident that Offa had succeeded in rendering the north-estern bank of the Wye, up to near the present frontier, English in a certain sense; but the south-western bank, below the same point, including the district of Archenfield, though subject to the King of England, was to a great extent under Welsh customary law; and the same was the case with certain territories in the eastern part of Monmouthshire, which had been annexed by Harold Godwinson.* The King had 96 free tenants, evidently Welshmen, in Archenfield,† who

* Here the King's bailiffs, mentioned in *Domesday*, have mostly Saxon, but in some instances Welsh, names.

† The men of Archenfield had a right to the van of the military force of Herefordshire, a privilege, no doubt, dating from the period when there was still a national distinction.

held carucates, served in the army, and paid 41 sextaries of honey, and 20 shillings in lieu of sheep.* A few Welshmen are mentioned on the left bank of the Wye: thus, one Grifin had half a hyde in Pyon (near Webley); and in one instance a Welshman holds as under-tenant land formerly belonging to Edward, an Englishman. Evidently the Forest of Dean was still Welsh to some extent. Thus, Morgan held Bickanofre (English, Bicknor) in Edward the Confessor's time; and Madoc, a King's Thane, held and still holds Rudford, a few miles west of Gloucester. It is noteworthy here and in Herefordshire that Welshmen are occasionally found dwelling on or even holding parishes having English names: thus, Saissil holds Stanton (Staunton-on-Wye, above Hereford); also that the English names were in some instances very recent: thus, Brismer held Brismerfrum of Earl Harold, and had evidently given the estate his own name. The same mixture of Welshmen and Englishmen continues all along the western border of Shropshire; and Welsh under-tenants are met with in parishes bearing English names, as Whittington and Osulfston. The Welshmen mentioned as such were probably all freemen; and when we read that in Clun, e.g., 8 villans, 2 Welshmen, and 4 bordars hold 2 carucates among them, we need not conclude that all the villans and bordars were English.

I have quoted these particulars from *Domesday* to show that the ancestors of the population of the Marches were certainly to some extent Welsh even in the eleventh century; although its modern representatives have entirely forgotten the fact, and, while bearing in their features, complexion, and moral character evident marks of their descent, affect sometimes to be English of the English.

The period of the Norse invasions and migrations was as important in Scotch as in English history, and was more protracted; for it may be said to have hardly ceased until the battle of Largs, in 1261, or at the earliest until the establishment of Sumarled as ruler of the Hebrides, about 1150. But there, as in England, the great invasions of the ninth century were, ethnologically, the most important. They made the Norwegians rulers of the Shetlands, the Orkneys, the Hebrides and Man; and from that time forth the coasts of Scotland were vexed by their perpetual raids, while their chiefs at various times subdued and exercised dominion over Caithness and other portions of the mainland. These hostile relations did not prevent frequent intermarriage between the ruling families of Norsemen and Picts, or Scots as they are henceforth called; and probably there was a like admixture of blood among other classes. Shetland, Orkney and Caithness accepted the Norse language, and in Shetland especially very little Pictish blood appears to have remained to blend with that of the conquerors. In the Hebrides the latter were evidently less numerous in proportion, but in many of the islands they were able to take a very large, and in the Lewis the

* Seebohm, *loc. cit.*, on the Celtic land-system and food-rents.

largest, share in fixing the local nomenclature,* though they could not root their language permanently in the speech of the people.   There are also points on the western coast where the Norse element has evidently survived in considerable force.   There was a period—the middle of the eleventh century—when Thorfin, Earl of Orkney, ruled over the eastern coast as far southward as the Tay; but as the local names in Buchan, Angus, and the Mearns are almost all either of Celtic or of modern Scottish type, we must suppose that the undoubtedly strong infusion of Norse blood in those quarters must have been of later introduction, probably coeval with the comparatively peaceful and silent Anglo-Danish and Flemish colonisation which followed the Norman Conquest.

The contemporary history of Ireland, from our point of view, resembled that of Scotland as much as the different geographical conditions would allow.   There, too, Danish and Norwegian raids and invasions began early in the ninth century; there, too, points of vantage were speedily mastered by the invaders; but in the case of Ireland there were no large outlying islands placed conveniently for them, except that of Man; and they accordingly seized on the best harbours and ports, those especially of Dublin, Waterford, Wexford, Cork, and Limerick, and utilised them for their mixed military, piratical, and commercial colonisation.   There, too, their dominion occasionally extended over a great, perhaps the greater, part of the whole country; there, too, their military energy declined with the slackening of the flow of immigration from the north, after the battle of Clontarf, and still more after the defeat and death of Magnus Barefoot, towards the end of the eleventh century.   We have the same evidence of frequent inter-marriage; but the Northmen nowhere perpetuated their language, or, if they did do so in some of the ports, it merged into the English introduced by the Anglo-Norman Conquest of the next century.   They fixed but few local names † beyond those of the harbours they frequented, but they left traces of their personal names ‡ among the people, and, in my opinion, permanently modified the breed of man in certain districts.

* Hector McLean and Captain Thomas.   † Joyce.
‡ *E.g.*, Cotter, McAuliffe, McManus.

CHAPTER VIII.

The Normans.

THE racial character of the immigration which is commonly and for shortness called Norman requires some consideration. The army of the Conqueror was drawn not only from Normandy, but from several other provinces of France. Flanders and Bretagne seem to have been very largely represented therein; and Maine, the Isle of France, Champagne, Anjou, Burgundy, and more remote regions contributed in smaller degree. The Normans, however, William's own subjects, were by far the largest element. This is shown, among other indications, by the small number of tenants *in capite* whom he established in England, who cannot be traced certainly or probably to noble Norman houses. Many of William's foreign mercenaries forsook him during his Northern campaigns; and Breton ballads tell us of the return of the Breton soldiery to their homes. It is noteworthy that the surname of Norman is not common in England nowadays, nor was it common, in the south Midlands at least, when the Hundred Rolls were compiled, though Breton and Le Breton were very frequent, and Franceys and Fleming moderately so, and there was a sprinkling of Picards and Maynards and Champneyses. Moreover, Norman was in use, especially among the English, as a Christian name. There are many Normans mentioned in *Domesday*. Where the word came to be used as a surname, it was usually, I think, a patronymic. The inference seems to be that Norman birth and origin were too common in England after the Conquest to furnish a means of distinguishing individuals, but that this did not apply to the other provinces of Northern France.

The Normans of the Duchy were themselves a mixed breed; and the component elements were the same, or very similar, to those which entered into the English race; but their character, mainly perhaps from their peculiar history, but partly from a mixture of the elements in different proportions, did not much resemble that of the people they subjugated. To form the Norman race, the Scandinavians, the "Saxones Bajocassines," and the native Kymro-Kelts had all contributed; but the part of the Scandinavians in the mixture had been more important than in Southern England, and that of the Saxons less so. The proportions were, I think, nearer to those found in another very forcible combination—I mean the Lowland Scotch.

The following are details of the elements:

I. The Gauls whom the Romans found here belonged partly, at least, to the Belgic confederation, which included the right bank of the Seine, if not more. The Belgæ were, we believe, a tall and rather long-headed race; whether they owed their dolichocephaly entirely to continual immigrations of the blond northern type, or whether the southern or Iberian longheads had left many representatives there, I will not say.* The short round-headed dark race of France, the true Celts of Broca, were doubtless also represented, but chiefly on the left bank of the Seine.

II. The influence of the Roman rulers of the country would be but slight.

III. Large numbers of Saxons were planted in Normandy in the latter days of the empire, or settled there subsequently of their own accord. Bayeux was the capital of the settlement, which probably extended to the Côtentin. About Bayeux they bore so large a proportion to the prior occupants that they were able, as in England, to propagate their language, which endured till the tenth or eleventh century. They were doubtless of the familiar physical types, the tall Grave-row and the more compact Batavian one; their heads generally long, their complexions and hair light.

IV. The Scandinavian Conquerors were partly Norwegian and partly Danish, the former especially numerous about the Seine, where Rollo's companions chiefly settled, the latter in the Côtentin, where Harold Bluetooth's army found lands to their liking. Physically, they must have been among the purest specimens of that restless, roving, adventurous type of man, blond or rufous, with straight profile and elliptical head, which evermore crops up among the people of the West of Europe whenever deeds of adventurous daring have to be done.

Scandinavia seems to have exhausted itself and its race by the swarming efforts of the ninth, tenth, and eleventh centuries. Great part of the old kingly race, the sons of Woden, and of Scyrf and Skiold, and so many other mythical heroes, either emigrated or perished; and kindred, but not identical, breeds of men occupied their ancient seats. The spirit of adventure died out in Norway for generations after Harold Hardrada and Magnus Barefoot, and after Hakon the Good.

Doubtless the Norman leaders were in the main of true Scandinavian blood; but the rank and file must have resembled the Normans of the present day, a crafty, capable, energetic, brave and industrious people, presenting, among numerous variations, two leading physical types. Of these, one prevails to the east of the Seine, and is that described by W. Edwards as Kymric, with little modification: the men are tall, long-faced, aquiline-nosed, with square forehead and usually darkish hair.

---

* It may be hoped that the Anthropological Society of Brussels will soon further investigate the physical type of the darkish-haired people along the coast of Flanders, whose existence Vanderkindere has pointed out.

The other is more abundant about Caen, Bayeux, and Coutances, where the men are very generally fair, and resemble the people of the North of England. At Cherbourg, fine specimens of the Anglo-Danish type are particularly abundant. I have prepared a table of the colours of hair and eyes in several provinces of France, in which Normandy is largely represented. It will be seen that precisely where the history and politics of Normandy show that the Scandinavian and Saxon elements were strong, *i.e.*, along the coast to the west of the Seine, there light colours of hair abound, and that they gradually darken as one travels eastwards or inland; also that on the whole the hair is rather darker than in most parts of England, but lighter than in Wales and the West. Head-measurements are much needed; but Broca* found the index of breadth of 53 skulls from St. Arnould, Calvados, to be 78·77, a proportion larger than is prevalent in any part of Britain, but well within the limits of mesocephaly. That of the Norman aristocracy may probably have been smaller; but the ecclesiastics of Norman or French nationality, who abounded in England for centuries after the conquest, and who, in many cases, rose from the subjugated Celtic layer of population, have left us a good many broad and rounded skulls. Thus the crania of three bishops of Durham (Ralph Flambard, Geoffrey Rufus, and Richard de Kellawe) yield an index of 85·6! while those of eight Anglian canons, dating from before the Conquest, yield one of 74·9.† So far, however, as the actual conquest and armed occupation of England was concerned, the aristocracy and military caste, who were largely of Scandinavian type, came over in much larger proportion than the more Belgic or Keltic lower ranks, insomuch that it has been said that more of the Norman *noblesse* came over to England than were left behind.

Bretons came over in large numbers, as was just now said, and some remained. One would expect to meet with them especially in Richmondshire,‡ or in the great barony of Judicael of Totnes, a Breton lord who had large grants in South Devon, but whose principal tenants bore Norman rather than Breton names. The speech in that district was then, and long after continued to be, Cornish; and an immigration of Bretons would hardly leave lasting traces among a people so nearly identical with themselves in language and not very dissimilar in physical type. The Bretons have been carefully studied by Broca and by Guibert of St. Brieuc, and I have myself made about 800 observations on their colours. The prevailing type in Bretagne is short, sturdy, and swarthy, with dark brown or even black hair, but pretty often with blue

* Quoted by Topinard, *Anthropologie*.
† Rolleston, *Archæologia*, vol. xlv. The following is a summary of his measurements:

		Max. Length.	Max. Breadth.	(Vertical) Height (Absolute)	
Three Bishops	mm. ...	181	155·7	149·3	—
Eight Anglian Canons	mm. ...	190	142·2	146·3	134·8

‡ See Whitaker's *Richmondshire*, passim, and my own *Domesday* map of Richmondshire.

or gray eyes. The heads are short and broad (though less so than in central France), and the face often corresponds, the features being coarse and broad, and sometimes Mongoloid. Everywhere, however, there is a minority with well-marked Kymric features and longer heads; and this minority, who nearly resemble our Cornish folk, are especially numerous in the district of the Leonais, on the northern coast, where the colonists of the fifth century are supposed to have landed from the British Isles. Broca obtained average breadth-indices of 82 and 81·2 from two large series of skulls from the eastern and the north-western part of Bretagne respectively.

Frenchmen—that is, people from the dominion of the King of France, then comparatively small—and Picards, Mainards, Angevins, &c., came over in smaller numbers. The seigneurs of France still at that time retained a good deal of the old Frankish blood; but their followers, the men to whom national surnames would generally be applied, had very little of it. They must have added a little to the Keltic and Kymric elements in the English people.

Flemings, of Franco-Frisian or Belgo-Frisian breed, and therefore on the whole Teutonic in blood as well as in speech, came in in large numbers under William Rufus and Henry I., and settled *en masse* in the southern half of Pembrokeshire, in Gower, and in the low country of Glamorgan, where they consolidated the power of the Norman lords, and easily adopted the English language, so near akin to their own. They are thought to have spread up the Teivy into Emlyn, where the mixed breed is said to be tall and comparatively fair; here the Welsh language has completely prevailed. In those districts where English became and continued the common speech, local names, as Flemingston, Reynoldston, &c., still testify to the settlement of the colony; and some surnames of Flemish type, as Jenkins and Watkins, have gradually spread among the Welsh themselves by intermixture or adoption. The descendants of the colony, somewhat mixed with English and other elements, are said to resemble the English rather than the Welsh in their steadiness, candour, common-sense, and rather common-place turn of mind. In person, also, some differences are yet observable. There is more of light and less of dark hair in South Pembrokeshire and in the coastlands of Glamorgan than elsewhere in South Wales; and the general aspect and features do not differ, in the majority, from ordinary English types. Professor Vanderkindere, after visiting South Pembrokeshire, told me the people looked to him rather English than Flemish.

CHAPTER IX.

The Norman Conquest.

THE main facts of the history of the Norman Conquest may be briefly dismissed: its ethnological details require careful investigation.

Within about four years after the battle of Hastings, the whole of England had been overrun by the Gallo-Norman soldiery, the English aristocracy had been to a great extent cleared away and a new one planted in its stead, and the free population of Yorkshire and Lancashire nearly exterminated. Great gaps had been made by fire and sword in some other counties, but these were such as might probably be soon filled up by expansion from neighbouring districts, which was not the case in the desolated Deira. Cumberland and Westmorland probably received a considerable addition to their population from the fugitives, and the same was the case with the Scottish Lowlands, especially, we may suppose, the Lothians, which received at this time a more Danish colouring than they had had before, the exiles being mostly Anglo-Danes, bearing such names as Thor, Sigmund, Dolphin, Arkill, Orm. The dynastic struggles which followed the death of Malcolm Canmore, and which did not altogether cease until the beginning of the thirteenth century, favoured the gradual introduction of an aristocracy, chiefly Norman, from England, and of an Anglo-Saxon middle class; these, reinforced by settlers from Norway and from Flanders, spread gradually over the whole of the Lowlands, from the south northwards, and from the east westwards. To this movement was due the " Saxonisation" of Fife and the eastern coastlands as far as Nairn, the towns being first settled, and the new language gradually spreading into the rural districts.

The expulsion of a numerous body of Flemings from England, on the accession of Henry II., nearly coinciding in time with the suppression of one of the several Moravian insurrections, gave Malcolm IV. opportunity to introduce a colony of them into "the laigh of Moray," which was in a short time so thoroughly settled that the remains of the Moravians, who were confined to the hill-country, came to look upon it as a land of foreigners, and their own lawful prey. Many Flemings also settled at Aberdeen, where such places as Kirkton and Murcroft are already mentioned in the charters of King David. In the Garioch they were less numerous, for the Gaelic language long continued to preponderate in that quarter. Comparatively few foreign settlers (unless possibly from Norway) arrived in Scotland after the reign of the Fourth Malcolm. At that period the new colonists, who received the general name of Saxons, were in possession of little more than the towns and strongholds in the Lowlands north of the Forth. W. E. Robertson, than whom there is no better authority, thinks there was little introduction of new blood at any time beyond the towns. But the whole of Scotland south of the Forth and the Clyde, except Galloway, Carrick, and the western half of Dumfriesshire, was by this time more Saxon than Celtic; the Strathclyde-Welsh and the Galwegian tongue were giving way very gradually, though the proportion of new blood introduced in that quarter may not have been very large, in spite of the appearance here and there of such place-names as Dolphinton and Symington, the settlements of Dolfin and Sigmund. And from this region, but especially from Lothian, probably now pretty thickly peopled, went on that continual northward movement of the Lowland gentry exemplified in the history of the families of Dunbar, Lindsay, Oliphant, Sinclair, Keith, Gordon, Maule, Menzies, Cumyn, Burnet, Fraser, and many others, and which implies the settlement of many of their south-country vassals and dependents on the lands newly assigned to them, whether previously vacant or newly wrested from their Celtic occupants; for the foreign lords, with dispossessed and wrathful Gaels lowering from behind the neighbouring hills, must have felt the need of support at hand in the shape of henchmen and free tenants. The Gaelic language slowly rolled back before the Saxon tide for fully two hundred years, till, about the close of the thirteenth century, the ambition of Edward I. began those troubles which threw back Scotland more than a century in the march of civilisation.

The Anglo-Norman conquest of South Wales was begun A.D. 1087, when Robert Fitz-hamon wrested the low country of Glamorgan from Jestyn. Brecon and the Vale of Usk were seized soon after; and for about two centuries South Wales was continually being fought over. In what we now call North Wales, the frontier of Salop was first advanced by Baldwin de Montgomery, who built the castle that bears his name, and subdued a large tract of Powysland; but beyond that, little advance was made until the final conquest of the country by Edward I. Very little new blood, therefore, was introduced into North Wales, where even the lords of the land continued to be Welsh, generally speaking. In the south there was a larger infusion of French and English; but even there the effects on language, place-names, and physical type would have been small but for the introduction of solid bodies of Flemings, as mentioned in the last Chapter, into South Pembrokeshire and the coastlands of Glamorgan. These last, mixed with settlers from the West of England, succeeded, as mentioned before, in constituting a kind of small nationality in the "little England beyond Wales."

We have now to enquire what was the effect of the Conquest on the proportion and distribution of race. There exists in *Domesday* a large mass of material bearing on this subject, but which has never hitherto, I think, been specially utilised for this end by those who have written upon it. Nearly two centuries later, when the full effect upon the English race of the intercourse with France, brought about by the Conquest, had been developed and experienced, the *Hundred Rolls*, which for some counties give us the surname and agrarian position of almost every male adult, are of very great value. This value was pointed out by the anonymous author of the volume entitled *The Norman People;* but he did not thoroughly work out the vein of evidence he had discovered, and the inferences he drew from it were more or less unsound.

Domesday furnishes us with the number of separate properties in land held in the time of Edward the Confessor; very generally it adds the name of the owner; it also gives, as a rule, the number of burgesses, or of burgage tenures, in the towns. As we have reason to think that in the rural population almost every man above the rank of a churl, almost every man who was *free*, according to the definition of freedom * which had come into vogue, was a possessor of land, we might thus obtain, but for two hindrances, a pretty close approximation to the number of freemen. These hindrances are, first, that where there were several owners in a manor, they are often described by number only, and not by name; thus, seven (nameless) Thanes are stated to have held the manor of Leeds, and it is impossible to be certain whether some or all of these seven may not have held other and separate estates in the neighbourhood, to which their names may be attached in *Domesday*. The second is the absence of surnames, except a few distinctive nicknames, such as are borne by Ulward Wit and Chepingus † Dives; and very rarely the name of the man's father, as in the case of Oger, the son of Ungomar; or an honourable addition, such as that of Child (Swen Cilt). The Saxon system of nomenclature ‡ was, perhaps, the original Arian one: it closely resembled the Greek, and afforded almost as much opportunity for distinctive variety as a single-name system could; in fact, it surpassed in convenience such a double-name system as the modern Welsh labour under. Still, it is often impossible to know whether in neighbouring manors we have to deal with, say, one, two, or three Siwards, or Alsis, or Godwins.

In the table I have constructed to illustrate this chapter I have, accordingly, distinguished the named from the nameless landowners, and have also separated all repeated names, whether supposed to belong to separate individuals or otherwise. The rough estimate of the actual number of individuals, which follows in the next column, may, no doubt, err widely from the truth; but it is far from being so baseless as may at

---

* The boor, and even the cottar or bordar, had been *styled* free, when the *Rectitudines Sing. Pers.* was compiled; albeit their actual position was what we should call that of serfs.

† Chepingus appears in the First Inquest in the Winton *Domesday*.   ‡ Ferguson.

first sight appear: it is conjectural, but grounded on analogies. In Somerset and Dorset I have made great use of Eyton's laborious and valuable work; in the other counties I have had no such assistance.

It is a trite remark that there was far more of individual freedom in the Danish north than in the Saxon south; that in the north absolute slaves were few or none, in the south-east not many, in the west very numerous; and that the freemen below the rank of Thane, outside the burgs, were almost confined to the north and east, *i.e.* to the Danelagh. There was not, however, very much difference in the proportional number of landowners of the rank of Thane. In estimating this proportion, it must be remembered that the total set down in the last column of the table represents the whole number of male adults enumerated in the survey. To estimate the entire number of male adults we must allow a considerable addition for soldiers, serving-men in towns and castles, inmates of monasteries, &c. In this way Eyton brings his computation for Dorset up to 9,000, correlative to a total population of (say) 35,000 or 40,000. This may fairly enough be taken also for the population in the time of the Confessor, as Dorset had suffered very little from warfare in the interim. But the case had been very different with the northern counties, and particularly with Yorkshire. There the East Riding had fallen off in annual value about three-fourths,* and in population probably almost as much; and Ilbert de Lacy's barony, though not so miserably desolated as most parts of Yorkshire, had lost a full half in value,† and probably nearly as much in population. Briefly, we may conjecture that the free landowning population had varied, in the time of King Edward, from about $1\frac{1}{2}$ per cent. in the East Riding to 3 per cent. in Somerset and Dorset, and 4 to $4\frac{1}{2}$ in the hilly and less fertile districts of Derbyshire and the West Riding. In Kent, too, selected as an English and un-Celtic country, with some peculiarities of tenure, the number of proprietors had been large; in the district analysed it had been 3 per cent., not including the large number of sokemen, who in Kent were generally small freeholders, holding of the King directly, not, as in the north, free tenants holding of a lord, to which latter status the surviving sokemen of Kent were reduced after the Conquest.

These 3 or 4 per cent. of landowning nobles and squires can hardly have been the sole legitimate posterity, in blood and status, of the original Anglo-Saxon invaders. True it is that military aristocracies tend to decline in numbers, owing to their being exposed to the accidents of war,‡ and to their jealousy in circumscribing the marriages of their women. Such deadly feuds as that one we hear of in Wessex, about A.D. 755, which cost the lives of all the comites of two princes, Cynewulf and Cyneheard, would aid the process of reduction materially. But Akerman's remark, already quoted, as to the small percentage of Saxon graves containing the sword, the supposed gnomonic sign of an eorl-

---

* Accurately, from £1,347 2s. to £347 13s.   † From £322 5s. 8d. to £154 9s.
‡ Rara est in nobilitate senectus " was a motto of the Herberts.

cundman, may be trusted, probably, to prove that, then as well as at the date under consideration, this class was a small minority. The table has, therefore, little retrospective bearing.

According to the Anglo-Saxon way of thinking, every man of birth and standing had, or ought to have, land of his own, and the more the better. Owing partly, we may suppose, to "commendation" on the part of small and weak men, partly to greed of land and power on that of the strong and nobly born, we find already enormous estates,* on which, in the South of England at least, no tenant appears who is designated in *Domesday* otherwise than as a villan or bordar. I cannot but think that the condition of these "villans" must have varied greatly on different manors. Seebohm gives instances, taken from the Rhenish lands conquered by the Franks and Alemanni, in which freemen, holders of entire manors as well as holders of small parcels of land, having commended themselves to a lord (usually a spiritual one), seem to have become in some sense villans, but without undertaking the meaner kind of service: they became liable to the food-rent, &c., but not to ordinary agricultural labour. Probably many of the villans on these great estates were, so to speak, *mediatised* thanes; while others were churls who had always, or at least for many generations, been in a more servile position. Certain royal manors wherein Seebohm shows the obligations of the villans to have been very heavy may have had from the first—as Tidenham, one of his examples, certainly had—a Celtic population.

Sometimes several thanes are found holding quite small parcels of lands, which they seemed to have tilled themselves, apparently under no superior lord. Thus the twelve thanes in Dorset who seem to have commended themselves after the Conquest to Ernulf de Hesding, the grantee of their lands, and who reappear as his villans (Eyton), had only about five virgates between them.† Again, we are told that the *thanes* of Ernulf de Hesding have not paid the geld on three hides and four acres of his estate at Ambresbury in Wiltshire (Exon *Domesday*, p. 15). This state of things might naturally arise from division of realty among sons, and again among sons' sons. Nothing is more common than to find two or three Thanes holding a small estate together, and sometimes they are positively stated to be brethren.

Whether the sokemen of Kent—apparently allodial proprietors, occurring in little groups of two, three, five, six, eleven, twelve, and fourteen, sometimes with and sometimes without villans or bordars dependent on them—were of thanish or churlish blood, does not appear; probably they were of the latter. In one case Ulwil Wild, a sokeman, seems to

---

* Not only those of the great ealdormanic families, but those of Merleswain and Brictric, for example.

† Observe the analogy to the two principal kinds of tenure in ancient Ireland, the Saer and the Daer; the latter again agreeing with the base steelbo tenure of Scotland. On this division of the subject see Seebohm, Elton, and E. W. Robertson, passim.

have held a considerable estate, valued at £10 10s. yearly, as allodium; but generally these properties were very small.

In Kent the entire nobility and squirearchy (to use a bit of modern slang which fairly expresses the class) had been dispossessed, with a very few exceptions, mostly on abbey lands. The Bishop of Bayeux held the manors of nearly a hundred English proprietors, the names of none of whom reappear as his grantees, the only new tenants of manors mentioned being Norman; and in a few instances French-named men appear as small tenants, one with a mill, another with a wood worth three shillings and fourpence. Yet there are indications that the actual farmers of the lands were sometimes middlemen, between the lords and the villans; and these were probably native. A singular exception, a genuine udaller, occurs under the manor of Hagelei. " In this manor a freeman *(unus homo)* holds twenty acres of land, worth five shillings yearly. He is called Uluret, and does not belong to the manor, nor could he have any lord except the King." Let us trust that he survived to hound Bishop Odo out of the country!

Thus the Bishop of Rochester holds Stoke himself; and it is said to be worth eight pounds and twenty pence annually, " yet *he who occupies it (qui tenet)* pays thirteen pounds and twenty pence." Again, Anfrid holds Badlesmere of the Bishop of Bayeux, and it is worth four pounds: there is in demesne one carucate, and ten villans have one carucate and a half. " The Abbot of St. Augustin claims it, because he had it temp. Reg. Edw., and the hundred bear witness to him: *the son of the man* affirms that his father could choose his own lord *(se posse vertere ubi volnerit)*; and the monks don't agree to that." Again, Hugo de Port had in his manor of Eisse (held of the Bishop) two homines holding a carucate worth twenty shillings, who in King Edward's time could " ire quolibet sine licentiâ."

Early charters in Dugdale show the natives in a position of well-being and partial independence. Hoo was a great manor of Bishop Odo's, said to have been in his own hands, " yet he who holds it pays £113." It afterwards came under Archbishop Anselm. There seems to have been an English family who took their name from Hoo, and were probably its sub-tenants; for Ægelnoth de Hoo gave to the monastery of Rochester, with his son, when he made him a monk there, a marsh worth fifteen shillings, and Archbishop Anselm confirmed the grant. Osbern of Biliceham also became a monk, and gave the tithes of Lyafrun, wife of Siward de Hoo,* with an estate in the Isle of Grain worth forty shillings yearly, on which Ulfward de Hoo, " cognomine Henricus," resigned his claim. Ulfward, *alias* Henry, afterwards himself became a monk, and gave the monastery all the tithes of Cobham, and his tithes of Hoo, and the third part of his substance after his death, to which gift his wife, and his son Robert, and his brothers Siward and

---

* She probably held land in her own right, for her husband seems to have been living.

Edward, consented. Here we have a notable instance of the way in which the use of Norman christian names crept into fashion among the English, beginning with the richer class. Ægelnoth has only a Saxon name; one of his sons (?) takes a Norman *alias*, and his grandson is christened Robert.

Eadulf de Scærlesfelda gave half his tithe from Elham and Limmings: he seems to have owned land, so far at least as to have power to direct the tithe as he would, in at least two manors; yet there is no sign of him in *Domesday*. Woolmer, a vassal *(homo)* of Arnulf de Hesding's, gave his tithe, worth ten shillings yearly.

If we go on to Essex and Suffolk, *Domesday* and the *Monasticon* continue to yield evidence of the gradual mixture of the races and the adoption of Norman christian names by the descendants of the vanquished. For Colchester we have in *Domesday* a nominal list of the burgesses, which enables us to say positively that the Normans and Frenchmen were only four, or at most six, per cent. For Mendham Priory, Suffolk, founded in the next century, temp. Stephani, we find that the witnesses to the early charters almost all bear names of French form, though *Eilward* and Roger fil. *Alredi* occur; and, later still, Will. fil. *Haroldi*, a notable conjunction. The following is a list of men, seemingly nativi or villans, who were given to the Priory " with their wives, children, tenures and customs ": Wluric, Hodard, Walter, Hulf, Hedrit (Edred ?), Norman, Bond, Richard, Alwin, Richard fil. Hulfi, Godwin Aldewin, Osgod, Robertum de Bosco, Godric de Haliac, Will. fil. Hosketel, Sigar, and Gerold.

Here the majority have still English names, but fashion is gradually driving them out. These men may all be Anglo-Saxons in blood; even Robert de Bosco may be an English Robert à Wood as easily as a French Robert de Bois. But in a similar list at Colchester, where, however, only the lands are specified, and nothing said of the persons or families of the tenants, occurs one Turstin Wiscard, who can hardly be anything but a foreigner. In the Conqueror's reign, Robert Malet, in founding Eye Priory, gives to it the tithes of his French vassals, but the lands of several Saxons, *i.e.*, he transfers them as tenants to the Priory. Here Alfred de Combia occurs as witness to a charter.

In the populous and wealthy county of Norfolk we find the natives generally holding their own under the new lords. One Englishman at least, Godric, retained great power and influence;* and in later days many families of English descent, among them probably that of Howard, came to the front. Thetford and Bromholm monasteries were founded early in Henry I.'s reign by Norman nobles. Bartholomew de Glanvile gave to Bromholm " the land of Toche de Briges, which Toche himself gave in free gift." William de Warenne gave to Thetford, among other large gifts, the services of Algar, son of Godric; also the land held by

---

* See Freeman as to Godric, and for a mine of facts and inferences on the subject in hand.

Egga at Denham, and Edric de Thorp, with all his land and his men in Thorp, or Dumirick, or elsewhere ; and all the land and men of Archeline in Tasburgh, and the church of Tasburgh, and the land of Ulf the priest, and Ulmer of Tasburgh, with all his land, and two men in Stretton. This grant, which is a sample of a good many, raises some interesting questions. Edric de Thorp is given with his land and men ; but when the land and men of Archeline (*probably* a Norman by his name) are given, Archeline himself is not expressly mentioned. Was there any difference in their status? I think not. Edric was evidently a man of wealth, and could hardly be of lower degree than a sokeman or liber homo, a free tenant, all claims on whom were transferred to Thetford Abbey.

Castle-Acre Priory had several very early documents ; it was founded by William de Warenne in the Conqueror's reign. In a charter of the second Earl William it is mentioned that all the francigenæ tenentes of his vassal, Hugh de Wanci, gave their tithes. There were nine of them ; but two bore names that look more English than French, viz., Lietmerus and Brongarus ! In a list of twenty-nine persons who gave their tithes occur, with seventeen names of French type, the following : Bundi and Frotmund, priests ; Alured, son of Godeva ; Burmund, Gotwin, Torfort, Azor, Brixit, Brusnam, Dienulf, Osmund, and Scula. The Earl gives the land of Ulf de la Wella, yielding six shillings, *and a shilling more if he pays more.* Here it would seem as though Ulf remained a vassal of the Earl, and nothing but a money-rent was transferred.

Lincolnshire is notable in *Domesday* for its evident wealth and large population, including a multitude of sokemen ;* also for the number of considerable landowners,† dating from before the Conquest, who had managed to retain or augment their estates. Even here, however, the great majority of the English capital and mesne tenants disappear from the record ; and the valuable list of Lincolnshire landowners temp. Henry I. indicates that those who survived gradually lost their possessions or had to commend themselves to Norman lords.

Meanwhile one or two native families rose into consequence. Thus Haco holds in *Domesday* a small manor at Hainton, under Roger of Poitou ; and only sokemen and villans appear in Multon and Pincebek, holding under Ivo de Tailbois and Wido de Credon. But in 1091, when Croyland Abbey has been burnt, Haco appears as Haco de Multon, sending to the forlorn monks twelve quarters of wheat and twenty hogs ; and in the Lincolnshire survey of Henry I., William, the son of Hacon, is a large holder, partly *in capite*. Hence the baronial family of Multon. One Elsi de Pincebek sends to Croyland one hundred shillings in silver and ten hogs. In Spalding, again, no one above the status of a villan is mentioned in *Domesday ;* yet in 1114 we hear of " Turbrand, a knight of Spalding," as a donor to Croyland, together with ten priests, from

---

* 11,503, out of a census mentioning 25,305 persons.
† Colsuan, Colgrim, Surtebrand, and Ketelbjorn.

Deeping, Grantham, and elsewhere, of whom seven bear English names. Croyland, it is true, remained a very English house throughout: Waltheof, of the line of Cospatric, and Edward of Ramsey were among its abbots in the twelfth century, though already in 1109 many of the monks bore names of French form.*

Returning to the south, we find in Hampshire and Wiltshire two counties, perhaps the only two, which neither suffered in the campaign of 1066 nor joined in the subsequent revolts. Accordingly we find in both of them an uncommonly large number of King's Thanes retaining their lands.

Southampton being the port of Winchester, and Winchester a royal residence, and one of the principal cities of the kingdom, we might naturally look for an immigration of Frenchmen into them. Sixty-five francigenæ and thirty-one Englishmen are mentioned as having become burgesses of Southampton since the Conquest. There had been eighty-four tax-paying citizens previously; but a large number of houses had existed besides, so that the English must have been a very large majority. That Winchester was very English in the Conqueror's day is testified by the details of Waltheof's execution. About fifty years after Hastings, in the First Inquisition in the *Liber Winton*, we find, out of 238 owners holding 288 tenements, 86 or 36·1 per cent. bearing Saxon names, and 5·1 besides whose fathers had had Saxon names; 126 = 52·9 per cent. bore Norman or French names, the latter class holding nearly 60 per cent., the former over 35 per cent. of the tenements, whose actual occupiers were evidently much more English than the owners, while the latter were more English than their names. I shall return to the table of Winchester names presently. Meanwhile, it may be noted that at Wallingford, of 268 tenements (hagæ) remaining from King Edward's time, 22 only were occupied by French burgesses (francigenæ); there were, however, about 200 other houses belonging to individuals, of the tenantry of which we have no means of judging. "In Norwich," says Pearson, "the foreign settlers were only as one in thirty-three." They assuredly were not in less proportion than that; but as the survey was concerned with taxation rather than nationality, it does not furnish us with material for certainty. There may have been as many as eight or ten per cent., though probably not. Shrewsbury is the only other town, except York, in which the number of French-born burgesses is stated.

In Gloucestershire are found, especially on the King's land about Gloucester and Berkeley, a large number of English freemen, apparently military tenants bound to serve against the Welsh, who are called rad-knights. Several considerable families, in the opinion of Mr. Bazeley, arose from among these or from among the King's customary tenants thereabout. He justly remarks that on the King's own lands, as he had

* In 1109 Abbot Joffrid sent out monks to beg for the rebuilding fund: Ægelmer and Nigel to France and Flanders, Fulco and Oger to the North, Swetman and Ulsin to Denmark and Norway, Austin and Osbern to Wales, Cornwall, and Ireland.

not, like many of the great nobles, his own henchmen and dependents to provide for, the old customary tenants, who are seldom mentioned in *Domesday*, would, as a rule, remain.

A good instance occurs in the Forest of Dean of an English landed family disappearing in *Domesday* and reappearing in the twelfth century. Three Thanes—Godric, *Elric*, and Ernwi—had held manors in Dene, T.R.E., by the service of keeping the forest. Subsequently William Fitz-Norman held them of the Conqueror by the same tenure; he also held Bickanofre (Bicknor). His son Hugh was living in 1131. Some time between 1120 and 1133 Henry I. granted to Milo of Gloucester "terram de Bickanovero quæ fuit *Ulurici* de Dena." Milo's son Roger, Earl of Hereford, by a charter undated, gave to the newly-founded Abbey of Dean certain lands called Westadene, which did belong to *Walfric*, and certain lands of Geoffrey, son of the said Walfric. Then, in 1155, Roger granted to William de Dene the keepership of the Forest; he founded a considerable family, which endured in the male line till the fourteenth century, and the names of Geoffry and William occur among his earlier successors, holding the lands which Elric had held under Edward the Confessor.

It has been already indicated that there were some large landowners under the Conqueror who seem to have been particularly favourable to the vanquished, and to have dealt more generously with them than others did with respect to their lands. Of such, Arnulf de Hesding was one, and Robert de Stafford another. Thurkill de Warwick was himself an Englishman, and retained a number of English mesne tenants on his large territory. Ilbert de Lacy, as will be seen from my *Domesday* Table, behaved in a similar manner, and many Anglo-Danish tenants appear on his lands in Nottinghamshire and Lincolnshire, as well as on those he had in the West Riding. Under his manor of Crophill, in Nottinghamshire, occurs a singular and significant entry.

"In Crophill, Ulviet and Godric had four oxgangs of land to be taxed. Land to two ploughs. Ilbert de Laci was possessed of this land; but when Roger of Poitou received his land he seized this manor over Ilbert. The wapentake bear witness that Ilbert was seized; it is now in the King's hand, except a third part, and the Thane who is the chief of the manor, whom Ilbert holds ('et Tainum qui est caput manerii quem tenet Ilbertus'). There is now one plough in the demesne, and four sokemen, having nine oxen in a plough, and six acres of meadow."

What are we to think about this "Thane, the chief of the manor"? Was he Ulvict or Godric, surviving on what had been his own land? If so, was he the headman of the four sokemen, or was he the reeve or bailiff of Ilbert? In any case, he is still recognised as a Thane in rank. Were there many such instances? This one comes out purely through the accident of the disputed ownership of the manor.

Dugdale furnishes us with another set of facts, which I have not hitherto touched upon—the lists of witnesses to early charters. Examination of them shows that in those of great barons, English names are rare, though it is also rare to find a long list without one at least of them. They may be in the proportion of one to six or twelve, or even more, of Norman names, the latter being generally the relations or principal retainers of the grantor. The exceptions are often men whose names do not appear in *Domesday*, yet who must have been of some position. Thus, Alfridus de Guarham witnesses a charter given to Spalding Monastery by Ivo Tailbois; and Algar de Chetelberga one of Stephen's (Count of Bretagne), whose tenant there he probably was; though in Chettlebiriga *(Domesday)* Count Alan had only small free tenants, and no large holder. In the grants of smaller men, or those made to smaller houses, and especially in the grants of Englishmen, English witnesses are numerous, and often preponderate. Thus, when, in 1111, Picot, son of Colswain of Lincoln, became a monk at Spalding, all his relations, like himself, seem to have borne French names, though they were but in the first generation from the Conquest; but several witnesses from Sutton bear such names as Swan, Hesca, Manna, Turburt, Haldan.

Northumbria remains to be examined. We might divide it into its ancient provinces, the fate of which differed in some important particulars; but as the north-western portion of Deira, *i.e.* North Lancashire and South Cumbria, more resembled Bernicia in its fortunes, we will dispose of all the rest before entering on a more particular survey of Yorkshire, whose more purely Anglo-Danish population, and more severe treatment at the hands of the Conqueror, give it a peculiar interest from our point of view.

Not that William's ravages were confined to Yorkshire. He is said to have carried them to the Tyne; but had they been as thorough northward as southward of the Tees, such an insurrection as that which destroyed Bishop Walcher and his company would hardly have been practicable. In Amounderness (between the Ribble and the Wyre) the destruction had been very great: of 60 villages, only 16 continued to be inhabited; but, on the whole, the apparent scantiness of population to the west of the Pennine range was probably rather the continuance of a condition prevalent before the Conquest than a consequence of that event.

In the Bishopric of Durham the ancient aristocracy continued powerful. We are told, indeed, in one account, that Ligulf had removed to Durham in order to avoid the insolence of the Normans; but when, after his murder, the people rose to avenge it, the foreigners were evidently too few and weak to resist. Even after Odo had put down the revolt with much bloodshed, and its leaders had escaped to Scotland, considerable native landowners survived, of whom the ancestors of the families of Lumley and Surtees are conspicuous examples; and Simeon, or a contemporary of Simeon, speaks, in his tract on the genealogy of the Northumbrian earls, of a feud between the Surteeses and another great native family. In the vision of Boso, which he saw in Rufus's time, the natives (distinguished from the francigenæ) appeared fairly well mounted and armed: "equis admodum pinguibus sedentes et longas sicut soliti sunt hastas portantes;" the Frenchmen followed with greater display: "multo majori quam priores superbiâ." Of Northumberland in the narrow sense we have little record: some great Norman families were founded therein; but in the time of Henry II. there appear in the list of military tenants* for Northumberland more English names than in almost any other county; and in a charter of Tynemouth Priory, dated 1129, out of a list of 26 witnesses, the following names pretty certainly belonged to men of native blood: Ranulphus Blaca, Eilaf presb. de Hagulstald, Gamel de Aclet, Melded (Maldred?) de Aclet, Robertus Firberne (Thorbjorn?), Edulf de Salwic, Unspac Clibern, . . . Gancel fil. Edredi, Edmund fil. Aculfi, Mervin de Hethewrth.

Cumberland, Westmorland, Furness, and Lonsdale continued to be a kind of neutral ground, ethnologically as well as politically, pervaded more or less by the family and influence of that singularly clever and "pawky" Anglo-Scot, Earl Cospatric, who, though repeatedly conspicuous among the opponents of the Conqueror, continued, after firmly establishing his predominance in the Lothians, to straddle, as it were, across the Border, and to hold a great capital estate in Yorkshire.

Ranulf de Meschines and his brother William are said to have given to Waltheof Fitz Cospatric the whole barony of Allerdale, and all the lands from the Cocker to the Derwent. These lands Waltheof and his son Alan (observe already the Norman name) distributed liberally among their kinsfolk and countrymen. The following is a list of these grantees: Odard fil. Liulf, Adam fil. Liulph, Gamel fil. Brun, Waltheof fil. Gileminii,† Orm fil. Ketelli, Dolfin fil. Alwardi,‡ Melbeth his physician,§ Ranulph Lyndesay,|| Cospatric fil. Ormi,¶ Ketel, Cospatric (his bastard son), Uctred, Waltheof fil. Dolfin. Clearly, the Northumbrian aristocracy survived in this quarter; and there is further evidence of the fact in charters, were any further evidence necessary.

In Copeland (South Cumberland) and Furness some Norman barons settled, and at Lancaster was the capital of Ivo de Taylbois's great barony; but the subordinate landholders, who are not mentioned in *Domesday*, were probably mostly natives, like Ailward, who held Broughton of the Lancasters by military service. This I gather partly

---

* In the *Liber Niger*.

† Son-in-law of the elder Waltheof. Gillemin was probably an Anglo-Scot, an another son-in-law.

‡ Not the Dolfin whom William Rufus "drove out" of Carlisle, and who was probably the elder brother of Waltheof, but another son-in-law.

§ Another Scot. Several Scots, or Scots at least in name, were scattered through Yorkshire as landholders, temp. Regis Edwardi, when one Gillemichael possessed almost all Kendale.

|| A Norman, son-in-law to Alan Fitz-Waltheof.

¶ His son Thomas founded Shap Abbey, in Westmoreland.

from the names of benefactors to Cockersand Abbey, *e.g.*, Rob. fil. Gospatricii Albi de Clacton, Godith de Wyresdal, Godith, daughter of William, son of Orm de Kellet; also from the long persistence of English christian names, *e.g.*, *Hereward* was abbot in 1235, and Jordan, son of *Torfin*, quitclaimed some land to the Abbey in 1246; and also from the curious and incredible genealogy of the Lancasters, quoted by Whitaker from a document which was in the Abbey of St. Mary's at York. "Ivo Tayleboyse," says this document, "genuit Eltredum; iste Eltredus genuit Ketellum; iste K. genuit Gilbertum dict. filium Ketelli; iste Gilb genuit Will. primum (De Lancaster)." There are here one or two generations chronologically superfluous; and though Ivo married, we know, a Saxon lady, nothing is known of a son with the Saxon name of Eldred. But Ketel was the lord of Lonsdale before the Conquest, and it is likely enough that by some unrecorded marriage the rights of his posterity were transferred to the De Lancasters.

Southern Lancashire was probably much like the northern part of the county in its conditions after the Conquest. Some Frenchmen settled there doubtless, retainers of Roger of Poitou and others. But the native landowners probably survived in force, to be the ancestors of the mediæval knights and squires. Dugdale gives a charter of Richard, son of Warin Bussell, confirming that of his father, who had founded Penwortham Priory, temp. W. Conq. The following is a list of the eighteen witnesses:

> Waltero presb. de Preston,
> Ealwardo pr. de Langetona,
> Gaufrido, Osberno, Radulpho capellanis,
> Roberto diacono,
> Osberno fil. Edmundi,
> Ormo fil. Magni, Warino fil. ejus,
> Lidulf de Crostona,
> Sweni Child,
> Will. fil. Alani,
> Huctredo fil. Sweni,
> Arcturo de Arston,
> Sweni de Penwortham, Ada frater ejus, et Sibilla et Matilda sororibus ejus.

Here the predominance of the Anglo-Danish element among the lay witnesses is distinct, though the younger people have names of Norman form. Of thirteen witnesses to another charter, a generation later, twelve have such names, though there is no reason to suspect any change in the population of the neighbourhood. About 1150, again, Henry de Lacy granted Alvetham, Clayton, and Accrington to Henry, son of Leofwin, evidently an Englishman in blood, though not, like his father, an Englishman in name.

CHAPTER X.

The Normans in Yorkshire.

THE Norman Conquest fell upon Yorkshire, and parts of Lancashire and Durham, with exceptional severity. It would seem that the statement of William of Malmesbury, that the land lay waste for many years through a length of sixty miles, from York to Durham, was hardly, if at all, exaggerated. The thoroughness and the fatal effects of this frightful devastation were due, no doubt, partly to the character of William, who, having once conceived the design, carried it out with almost as much completeness and regularity as ferocity, and partly to the nature of the country, the most populous portion of which was level and devoid of natural fastnesses or refuge; but also, in some degree, to the fact that the Northumbrians had arrived at a stage of material civilisation at which such a mode of warfare would be much more formidable than while they were in a more barbarous condition, always prepared for fire and sword, and living, as it were, from hand to mouth. Long afterwards the Scots told Froissart's informants that they could afford to despise the incursions of the English, who could do them little harm beyond burning their houses, which they could soon build up again with sticks and turf; but the unhappy Northumbrians were already beyond that stage.

In all Yorkshire, excepting Craven, *Domesday*, which was compiled nearly half a generation after the devastation, during which period its results may have begun to be alleviated, numbered only about 500 freemen, and not 10,000 men altogether. Nor was this scanty population at all evenly distributed. The southern part of the West Riding had suffered comparatively little: William de Warenne's great manor of Conisborough had increased in value since Edward the Confessor's day, and contained 120 sokemen, about a fourth of the whole number remaining in the county. Perhaps the previous insurrection had not involved this district, or, more probably, the Conqueror had marched across it before the departure of the Danes and the dispersion of the Northumbrians gave him free liberty to let loose his revengeful fury. Sherburn, which lay directly in the track, was spared, perhaps at the intercession of the Archbishop, to whom it belonged. From York the destroying host appears to have rolled northwards over the great plain extending to the Tees, almost every township in which was swept with the besom of destruction. The compilers of *Domesday* have departed from their usual rule in the case of Allertonshire, by enumerating the former population of this once flourishing district. " Earl Edwin," they say, " had sixty-six villans there, with thirty-five ploughs ; the yearly value was four score pounds." . . . And again, with an awfully direct simplicity, " There were one hundred and sixteen sokemen ; now it is waste."

Some think that the Conqueror marched on to Hexham, and encountered in the neighbouring mountains the difficulties we are told of ; others, with more probability, I think, that after pursuing the fugitives into Cleveland, he returned by a toilsome march over the eastern moorlands to Helmsley and Pickering. The ravages did not slacken. The manor of Whitby was reduced in value from £108 to £3 ; that of Pickering from £88 to £1 0s. 4d. ; and in and around that of Walsgrave (near Scarborough) only seven sokemen survived of one hundred and eight. Still further south, the town of Driffield, where there had been eight mills and two churches, was left void of inhabitants. Beverley was spared for St. John's sake ; Holderness may have suffered from Danish as well as from Norman invaders ; but in all the East Riding no considerable district wholly escaped. Probably comparatively few perished by the sword ; the nine years' famine which followed, and the free or forced emigration to Scotland, accounted for the rest.

There are two possible *criteria* by the application of which we may form a conjecture as to the actual loss of population. The first is the comparison of the ratios of annual value to enumerated population in other counties, and their application to Yorkshire. The valuation of the East and North Ridings, in the Confessor's time, had been as follows : East Riding, £1,347 2s. That of a few manors is omitted, but I do not think their inclusion would raise the total above £1,360. North Riding, Count Alan's land in Richmondshire, £209 14s. 4d. ; remainder, £761 7s. In this, the central and eastern portion of the Riding, the valuation of upwards of a hundred manors is omitted, probably because there was no inhabitant of the neighbourhood remaining who could give the necessary information. These manors were almost all very small ones, and would not, probably, if included, have brought up the total much beyond £790, or £1,000 for the entire North Riding. I will put the total for the two Ridings at £2,360. That of Norfolk had been £2,219 2s. 11d. ;* its entire enumerated population is put by Mackintosh at 22,304.†

Allowing for a considerable increase of population, say 20 per cent., since the Conquest, the valuation was 12 per cent. in pounds of silver on the numbers of a census on the *Domesday* principle : if the increase

---

* Pearson, quoting Munford, who says, however, that it had increased to £4,154 11s. 7d.

† Mackintosh's computations are far from being always accurate, but they are sufficient for our purpose.

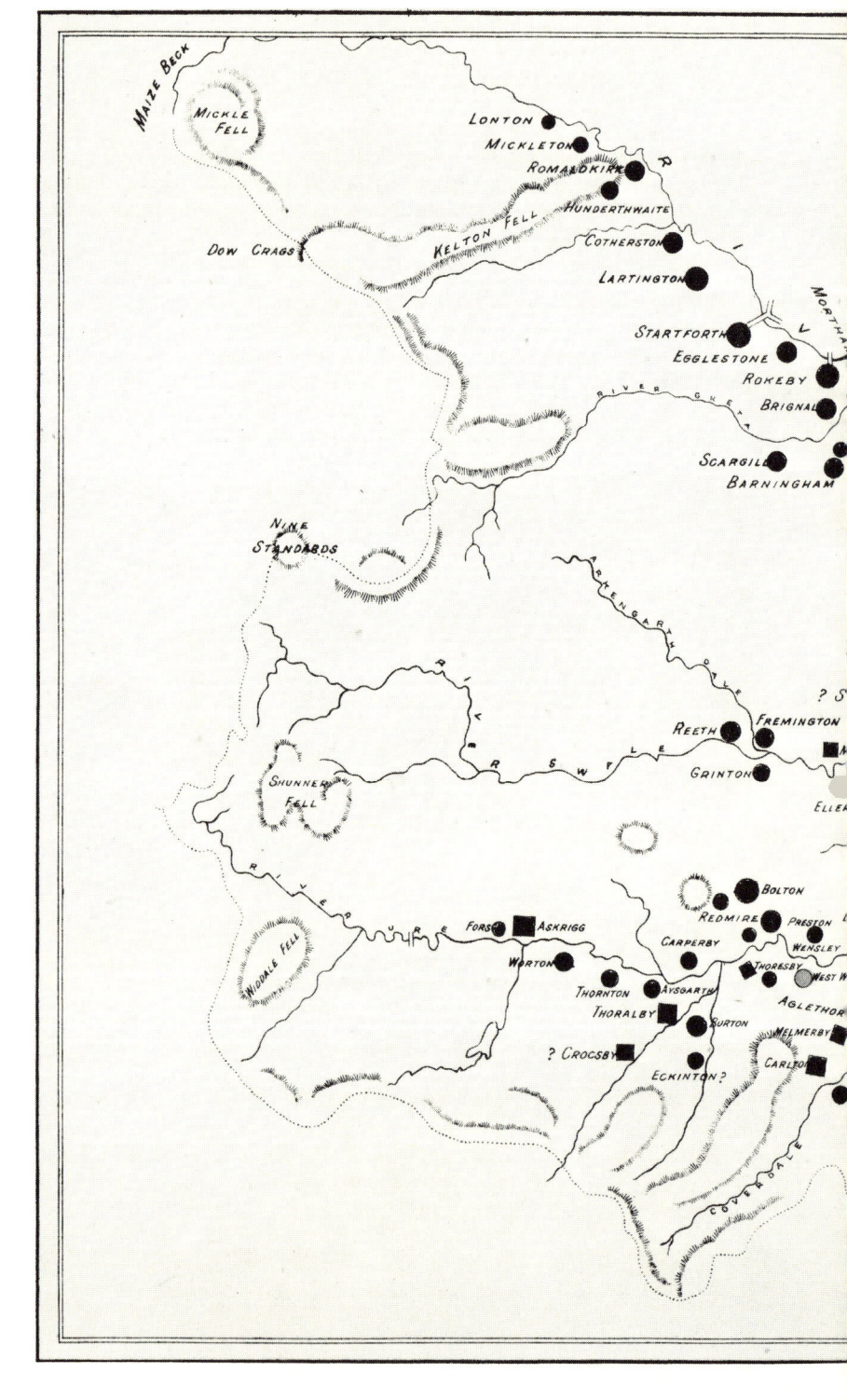

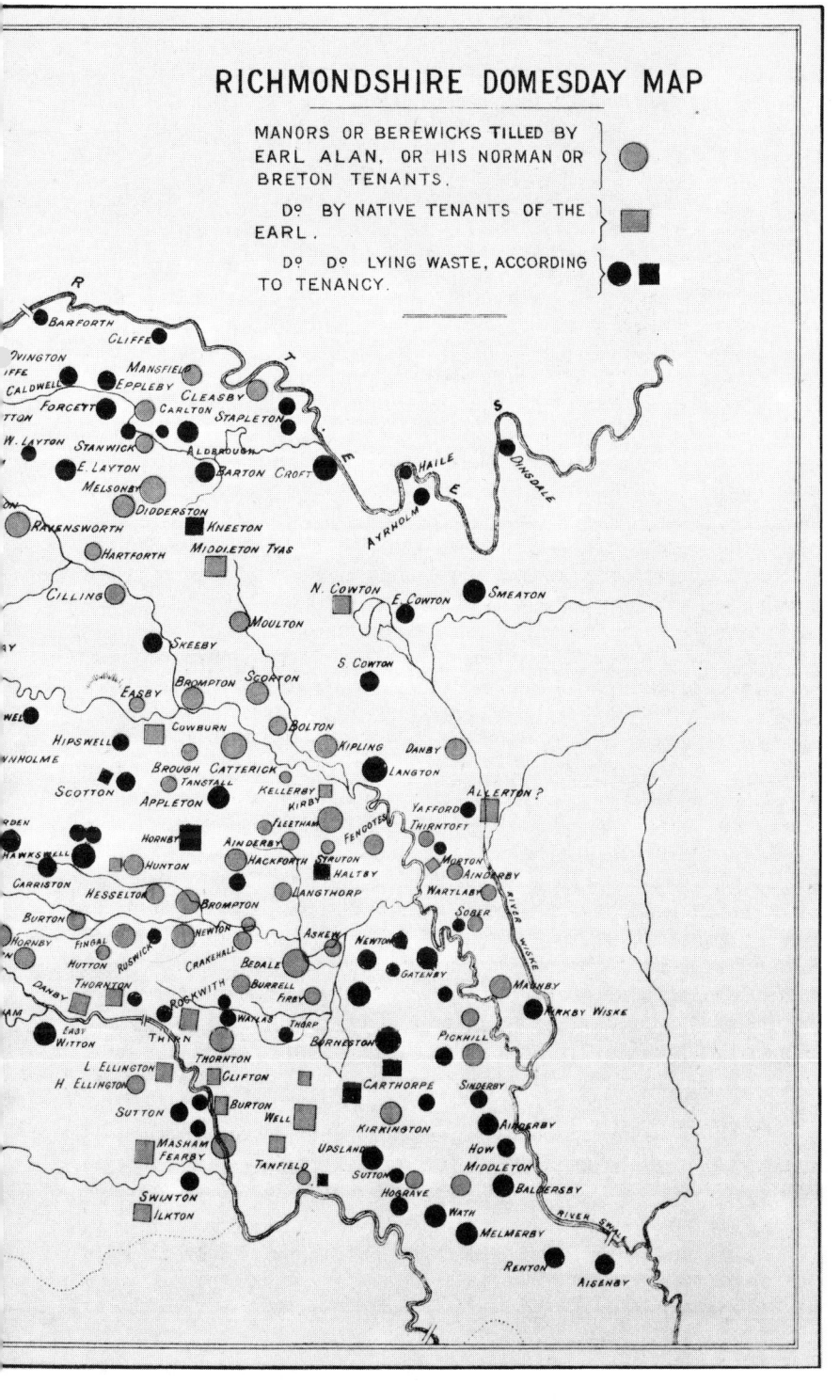

RICHMONDSHIRE DOMESDAY MAP

MANORS OR BEREWICKS TILLED BY
EARL ALAN, OR HIS NORMAN OR
BRETON TENANTS.

Dº BY NATIVE TENANTS OF THE
EARL.

Dº Dº LYING WASTE, ACCORDING
TO TENANCY.

had been 10 per cent., the ratio was about 11 ; while that at the latter date was 18½ per cent. on the actual later census. The mean of these ratios is about 15 ; and this is also the ratio of valuation to census in Derbyshire,* a northern county in several respects analogous to York-shire, but which, though it had suffered a good deal of wasting, was comparatively prosperous, as we may suppose Yorkshire to have been before the invasion.

On this basis the male adult population who would have appeared in such a census as that of *Domesday* may have been about 9,060 + 6,666 = 15,726, and the entire population of all ages and sexes perhaps 75,000. But if we estimate the figures for the two Ridings on the second and simpler criterion, viz., in accordance with the actual ratios of value to census, and of present to former value, we obtain 9,240 + 9,260 = 18,500 for a census in 1068, and a probable population of 90,000 for the two Ridings at that date, against only 20,000 after half a generation of peace. Besides these 20,000 there may have been a few hundreds of people unenumerated, consisting of the garrisons of castles, the hench-men of the new proprietors (though some even of these are mentioned in connexion with the land), a few monks and priests unattached to parishes, a few free artisans, and such of the old aristocracy as farmed lands from the mesne tenants, together with their families.

The small proportion of sokemen in Yorkshire, compared with that found in Lincolnshire, Nottinghamshire, Leicestershire, and East Anglia, is noteworthy. Probably the sokemen furnished the greater part of the Anglo-Danish insurrectionary army ; very many of them may have retired to the north or west, and been joint ancestors of the modern population of the Scottish border. But from the manner in which the remaining ones are distributed, usually in the outlying " sokes," rarely within the manors themselves, and from the great number of the manors, I am led to think that even in the East and North Ridings they had been outnumbered by the villans. In the western parts of the West Riding they certainly were so. This was an Anglian rather than a Scandinavian district : there is a much larger proportion of Anglian names among the local Thanes than in the remainder of Yorkshire ; more Elsis and Ulrics and Lewins, fewer Thorkills and Ravenchils and Gamels. In this respect, as in some others, it resembled Derbyshire, where also sokemen were not numerous. It is not possible to estimate the population and losses of the West as we have done those of the other Ridings, as no particulars are given in *Domesday* of the occupiers and valuation of the extensive district of Craven. The west suffered very much less than the centre, east and north, as may be gathered

---

* The valuation of Derbyshire was, t. R. Edw., £621 5s. 4d. ; and t. R. Will., £456 10s. 8d. It had therefore sunk one-fourth ; while that of the East Riding had fallen three-fourths ; and that of the North Riding, excluding Richmondshire, nearly six-sevenths. The figures are : t. R. W., East Riding, £347 13s. ; Richmondshire, £81 3s. 8d. ; residue of North Riding, £113 3s. 10d.

from the details in the table respecting Ilbert de Lacy's barony, and from its value having been reduced by only a half. Its comparative escape was due probably not so much to its mountainous character, which did not save Eskdale nor Teesdale nor Longdendale in the Peak, as to the direction of the line of march of William's main army.

I have selected Richmondshire, as a well-defined district, the localities in which are mostly easy of identification, for the subject of a map exhibiting the character of the Anglo-Danish settlements therein, and of the gaps caused among them by the devastation. These gaps were not nearly so extensive hereabout as further east, extending in value to about three-fifths only. Count Alan of Bretagne, who had a grant of the entire district, seems to have been a merciful conqueror: several of the former owners retained considerable holdings under him, and became the founders of local families; and within one or two generations Englishmen are found exercising proprietary rights in manors which had been granted to Bretons.*

It is noteworthy that the population had not crept nearly so far up the valleys as it did in subsequent periods. The manorial organisation probably discouraged straggling; and here, as elsewhere in the west, sokemen and liberi homines were few, though the names of the great holders were on the whole rather Scandinavian than Anglian. Agriculture, too, seems to have been more in favour than pastoral husbandry, partly perhaps because the lower valleys enjoy a fairly dry climate. What is more strange is that the upper parts of the three great valleys—Teesdale, Swaledale and Wensleydale—had been entirely cleared of the comparatively few inhabitants they had had. Was it that Count Alan had brought them down to till some of the more valuable, but vacant, manors on the edge of the plain? Was it that they had fled from the wrath of the Conqueror into convenient Westmorland? Or was it that the predatory host of Malcolm Canmore, sweeping over Stainmoor without warning, had driven them off, a portion of a great herd of captives—

> " To weave in *Clydesdale* at another's loom,
> Or bear the water of the *Lugar* home?"

On the eastern side the river Swale and the marshes of the Wiske seem to have afforded some protection, but otherwise the ravages seem to have been impartially distributed over the country.

How were the gaps filled up? The question is an interesting one for archæologists as well as ethnologists; and as such I ventured to commend it to local students, in a presidential address delivered at Bradford several years ago. But I am not aware that any progress has since been made towards answering it.

The strong statements of William of Malmesbury made in the next

---

* Thus Uctred Ulfson gives the church of Middleton Quernhow to St. Mary's of York; it had been part of Enisan's barony. And Donwald gives half a carucate in Ryswick, which he had not had in *Domesday*.

century, and the comparative smallness of the force which the Yorkshire barons could collect to encounter David of Scotland at Northallerton, lead one to suppose that the work of reparation was slow, and must therefore have been due mainly to the natural increase of the native population. In the corner of the county now under consideration it was pretty certainly so. Count Alan and his family settled down and built two or three fine castles; but it may be doubted whether they maintained any considerable force, beyond the retinue of the twelve "milites" mentioned in the survey, who may not all have been Bretons. Intermarriages took place: thus Torfin fitz Robert of Manfield, who held two knights' fees under Earl Conan, derived them through his mother Guthereth from Hermer, a native holder nowhere else mentioned; this family merged ultimately in the Fitzhughs. These latter barons really descended from Bodin, a bastard brother of Count Alan I.; but their accredited pedigree deduced them from Thorkill, a powerful landholder hereabout temp. Reg. Edw.; probably here, also, there may have been a marriage to confirm the title.*

There is a curious document in Whitaker respecting the afforesting of Upper Wensleydale, and the constitution of a village at Bainbridge for the dwelling of the foresters. This was in Earl Conan's time. The names of the first foresters are given: they were Fynehorn, Horm, Astin, Walter Hunsbain, Roger fitz Robert, Roger Porcarius, Uilred Rufus, Meldred, Will. Nobill, Thorphin Calvecape, Hervicius Longus, Walter Wyclous, Richard Schorthose, and Robert Scoryffe. French christian names were coming into vogue, and a little mixture of the language is implied by such a nickname as Calvecape (Baldhead); but in the main these foresters were natives, it would seem, and nowise Breton.

I have already said that the Breton ballads countenance the notion that the Breton soldiery mostly returned home after the invasion. Count Hersart de la Villemarquée, the distinguished Breton archæologist, descends from a Breton family who returned from England in the twelfth century.

The evidence to be gotten from charters in the *Monasticon* as to Yorkshire in general accords in the main with that from *Domesday*. There were many monastic foundations in the county within a century after the Conquest. St. Mary's of York was in great favour among the English; but it is markworthy that these native donors were in large proportion landowners of Cumbria or citizens of Lincoln. Both of these were strongholds of the Anglo-Danes. Ulf Forneson gave to St. Mary's, with other gifts, a carucate of land in Skirpenbeck. Now

---

* Gale (quoted by Whitaker) gives a French pedigree of the Thoresbys and Staveleys, deriving them from Aykfrith (Egfrid), whose existence as a chieftain in Lonsdale is attested by a Runic monument, and who lived about A.D. 1000. One would have little doubt of its correctness were not the clearly Norman Marmions tacked on to it. The Rokebys believed their family to have been "Saxon."

Skirpenbeck had been among the estates of Forne in King Edward's time; but in *Domesday* it forms part of the barony of Odo Balistarius, and no tenant is indicated. Evidently Ulf had held on as tenant of the land which had been his father's.

In the West Riding, as might have been expected, native witnesses and donors are numerous, while in the East they are less so. Thus at Nostel Priory Henry I.'s confirmatory charter mentions, among other benefactors, Swenius fil. Ailrici (a very large holder under the successors of Ilbert de Lacy, whose son Adam gave to Pontefract the church of Silkeston and the tithes of ten townships), Ingulf de Maton, Swenius fil. Edwini, &c., and several Englishmen who gave houses in York.

The city of York has been generally supposed to have been the seat of a considerable French colony, as *Domesday* says that 145 houses were held by "Francigenæ." But 145 is about the total of the mansiones specified as held by the Earl of Mortain and seventeen others, mostly tenants *in capite* of the lands of the county, such as William de Percy and Odo Balistarius, or extensive mesne tenants, such as Richard de Surdeval. The former owners are also specified, and their names are mostly those of the dispossessed Anglo-Danish landowners, whose town-houses they probably were. Thus, for example, Odo Balistarius has, among others, the house of Forne, as well as his lands. But we have seen that Forne's son Ulf had possession of his father's lands, or some part of them, subsequently. Odo was pretty certainly non-resident; and it is likely enough that Ulf Forneson was his tenant in the house as well as in the land.

We are not entitled, therefore, to form any estimate of the numbers of the French colony. Of its existence there is evidence in the list of donors to Whitby Abbey, after its foundation, or rather reconstitution, by William de Percy, which includes a number of French-named and a few English-named persons, each of whom gives one house in York. In one case Arngrim, a native, gives the house of Thomas Lolle, probably a francigena.

Kirklees Nunnery, near Wakefield, is said to have been founded by Rayner the Fleming, as late as Henry II.'s reign. It was a small foundation, by a mesne tenant under William, Earl Warenne. As usual, Rayner's charter has a large proportion (six out of fourteen) of witnesses who bear, or whose fathers had borne, English names; but in the confirmatory one of Earl Warenne no seemingly English name occurs among ten witnesses, though more than half of them *may* have been of native descent, as they have no foreign surname. Wakefield was a royal manor, and some of the signatures to the first charter may be those of the King's customary tenants.

In Cleveland, Wykeham Nunnery was founded about the same time, in 1153. It also was a small foundation, and accordingly five or six of twenty witnesses show signs of Anglicism, and only three have surnames certainly Norman. On the other hand, Rievaulx Abbey, also in the

North Riding, was founded twenty-two years earlier by a great noble, Walter Espec; and, accordingly, we fail to find among the thirty-nine witnesses of his charter, including his family, *homines*, and neighbours, a single English name. There were, however, three early donors with such names, all of whom were on land not ascribed to native tenants in *Domesday*.

The most interesting foundation, however, from our present point of view, was Melsa or Meaux Abbey in the East Riding; and its origin must be discussed, if discussed at all, at some length.

" Capit initium," begins the register of the Abbey, " hoc cœnobium, Melsa Latiné, Meaux Gallicè sive Anglicè a nostris patris nuncupatum. Locus autem ipse a pristinis habitatoribus sortitus est nomen, qui in conquestu Normannorum de quâdam civitate Galliæ Meldis Latinè sed Meaux Gallicè vocatâ exeuntes, post dictum conquestum ipsum locum inhabitantes nomen de Meaux ei imposuerunt, in memoriam suæ pristinæ civitatis * * * * * * * * * * Gamellus filius Ketelli de Melsa avus seu pater dicti Johannis de Melsa, cum Gulielmo Notho rege et conquestore, de prædicto civitate Galliæ, Meaux Gallicè dictâ exiens, cum aliis, in his partibus Holdernessiæ sortem suæ habitationis est assecutus, et ob memoriam civitatis suæ egressionis nomen huic loco quem inhabitabat, ut Meux nuncuparetur, imponebat * * * * Basing de Waghen, Sywardus de Sutton, Franco de Falconburg de Rise, Richard de Scruteville de Rowthe, post guerram Normannorum ut domini profuerunt."

The date of the foundation is not exactly known, but it was early. In a charter of William de Albemarle and Johannes de Melsa, Buring is the only English name out of fifty-three, unless William Chidenoth be accounted another. This rather favours the idea of a French settlement; and the story appears coherent and probable, except that Gamel,[*] son of Ketel, is a most unlikely name and father's name for a Frenchman from Meaux, which was not even a Norman city.[†] The place is called Melse in *Domesday*. The statements about the neighbouring landowners are likely enough.

Waghen was a berewick, or out-farm, of the manor of Aldborough, which Ulf had temp. R. Edw. Drogo de Bevrere had afterwards four knights in the manor and berewicks, whose names are not given. Another portion of Waghen belonged to Beverley. Basinc had a small manor in Sproatley, t. R. E., which Roger had afterwards under Drogo. Gamel, son of Basinc, occurs in the twelfth century. Grimkell held Sutton, t. R. E., and Lambert later; but Ulchil, a King's Thane, had a

---

[*] *Gamel* is Anglo-Danish as a rule, though not invariably. The Normans had not seemingly quite forgotten the name; its meaning I believe to be "Camel," and not "Old," as some think. *Ketel* was, I think, always Anglo-Danish; though the Normans still used the word in composition—thus, Anschitil, Asketil.

[†] The author of *The Norman People* says there was also a place called Mience in the Vexin.

small manor there both before and after the Conquest. Also a francus homo had nine oxgangs and three villans in Sutton (apparently the same place) under St. John of Beverley. Siward had t. R. E. and t. R. W., as a King's Thane, a carucate of land in Kirkby, jointly with Arngrim. Siward had had 9½ carucates in Acklam t. R. E., and land for four ploughs; afterwards two vassals had it of the King. Siward may have been one of them. Amand de Sutton was a landholder under Hawisia of Albemarle, daughter of the founder. Cnut had Rise t. R. E., but afterwards Franco had it under Drogo. Two Francs are mentioned in Holderness previous to the Conquest, but it is more likely that Drogo's tenant was a Fleming.

On the whole, I am inclined to believe in the story and the persons connected with it, except Gamel, son of Ketel. Ketel is probably the shadow of Chetel, an Englishman who had a holding under St. John of Beverley, and who may have been an ancestor of John de Melsa on the mother's side.

We thus have in one and the same narrative indications of the settlement of a small French colony on some vacant lands, and of the survival in its neighbourhood of native landowning families, one of which might have been supposed, from the silence of *Domesday*, to have entirely disappeared. The descendants of Basinc rose to knightly rank, and were great benefactors to Meaux; and the surname of Wawn (Waghen) is not extinct.

The evidence already adduced, and a good deal more of the same kind, leads me to the following conclusions, or rather opinions:

The Norman Conquest did not at once introduce any very large accession to the population.

The mesne tenants mentioned in *Domesday* are, it is true, generally foreigners, and indeed they are so in far greater majority than some writers allow.*

But it is probable that in very many, perhaps the majority of cases, the actual resident superior of a manor was a native unmentioned in *Domesday*.

The foreign colonists consisted chiefly of the capital and mesne tenants, their families and henchmen, the latter more numerous towards the frontiers, *e.g.*, at Shrewsbury. In the East and North Ridings of York their proportion to the natives was larger than elsewhere; in thickly peopled counties, such as Norfolk, it was probably small.

A good deal of intermarriage went on between them and English women, at least in the upper ranks.

* Hallam, quoted by Pearson, says more than half were natives, which is quite incorrect, unless the King's Thanes are included. See Table.

ANALYTICAL TABLE OF POPULATION MENTIONED IN *DOMESDAY BOOK*.

	FORMER OWNERS.				DOMESDAY OWNERS.			DOMESDAY MESNE TENANTS AND OTHERS.															
	Named.	Nameless.	Repetitions of Names.	Conjectural Total.	In cap. excluding King's Thanes	King's Anglo-Thanes.	English Mesne Tenants.	Doubtful ditto.	French ditto.	Milites, ? Nation.	Censorii (farmers).	Burgesses.	Priests or Clerks.	Franci Homines.	Vassals.	Sokemen.	Villans.	Bordars.	Cotters.	Slaves.	Others.	Total Male Population Enumerated.
East Riding of Yorkshire	111	17	89	150?	16	17	4	5	32	24	9	19	42	1	8+	123	1,620	430	...	...	...	2,350
Count Alan's lordship in Richmondshire, North Riding	54	...	129	55?	1	0	8	1	13	12	...	...	5	2	...	3	556	159	...	...	...	759
Entire North Riding	103	25	482	150?	9	8	9	1	21	12	13	...	33	...	4	52	1,384	327	...	...	...	1,873
Ilbert de Lacy's lordship, West Riding ...	66	16	127	90	1	0	25	...	18	.	...	60	20	2	...	19	536+	283	16	...	...	986
Nottinghamshire	142	52	268	200?	28	18	20	4	41	8	2	382	64	8	10	1,661	2,622	1,002	...	15	...	5,885
Derbyshire	111	11	186	140?	13	16	12	...	24	5	42	140	56	2	...	113	2,838	741	...	...	...	3,002
Dorset	111	341	?	300?	38?	38	33	7	60?	8	9	500	5!	...	20	...	2,663	2,827	397	1,165	98	7,868
Somerset	234	274	?	400?	63+	29	60	3	101	13	7	481	5!	...	...	...	4,947	4,377	299	1,565	310	12,260
Kent, five lordships...	30	77*	...	107?	5	0	3	...	19	.	1	...	?	...	...	45	387	411	...	94	...	965

* Sokemen holding allodially, mostly in Romney Marsh.   + Six Smiths.   The material for Dorset and Somerset was drawn from Sir H. Ellis and from Eyton, who frequently disagree; in the other counties and lordships I have relied on my own computation, but many uncertainties remain. As to the difficulties attending the computation, see Ellis, "General Introduction," ii., 421.

CHAPTER XI.

Norman=French Immigration.

WE have now to consider what was the extent and character of the immigration from the Continent which took place after the Conquest, but while the political connexion between France and England continued intimate and friendly.

The most important portion of the evidence available on this subject is that to be derived from the names, and especially the surnames, of the English people during this period. This fact was, I believe, first pointed out by the author of a book called *The Norman People*, who was well qualified for the task he undertook by his industry and his extensive acquaintance with genealogy and heraldry. Unfortunately he chose to remain anonymous, which perhaps lessens the authority of his dicta; but his work is valuable, though rather one-sided. For brevity's sake, I shall quote him as "N. P."

Immediately after the Conquest began a change in the system of nomenclature in use among the English. Hitherto their system had pretty closely resembled that of the ancient Greeks. Every man had a single name, usually compounded of two elements; and the great number of such elements in use gave scope for very great variety in the names. Men might be known to belong to certain families, to be Mannings or Skeldings or Skirvings, and they might be distinguished by soubriquets,* or by the names of their fathers; but surnames as we recognise them were not yet in use. Even the names of the Jewish patriarchs and Christian apostles† had not begun to be admitted into this name-system, in which, however, Thor and his attributes retained the place into which the Northmen had introduced him.

With the Conquest, as has been just said, a notable change began. The subjects adopted the Christian names of their rulers, most of which, after all, had been constructed on the same system as their own, though usually of slightly different elements; while others differed only by having undergone phonetic degradation in the mouths of the Neustrians.

---

* In Winchester, in the Confessor's time, occurred such names as Edwin Wridel, Goda Clenehand, Godwin Penifeder, Ulveva Betteslave. Possibly some of these were already becoming hereditary.

† St. John was almost the only exception, owing to the popularity and renown of St. John of Beverley.

The faculty of construction, of putting together elements so as to form a new name, had, moreover, been lost by the Normans. The priests favoured the use of the names of foreign and of Jewish saints. The new fashions spread, like other fashions, from the upper to the lower, from the free to the servile classes, and from the more central to the more remote districts. There were, it is true, some countervailing eddies of practice. The stubborn conservatism of the people of some southern counties made up for their nearer neighbourhood to the centres of innovation. And vague patriotic recollections may have had something to do with the survival of such names as Godwin, Harold, and Hereward, the last of which endured for many generations, and apparently slipped ultimately into a fitly honourable station, with but little phonetic change, in becoming Howard. Moreover, intermarriages were common; and we know from the case of Ordericus himself that they occurred among the smaller freemen as well as among the nobles. The husband would usually be the Norman. There must have been in England, from the circumstances of the war, a large excess of males among the Normans and of females among the English; and the women of England were renowned for their beauty and their skill in domestic arts. And the mother's wish would often prevail in the matter of the children's names. Thus it was, we know, with Orderic; and thus, too, if the story be true, with Torfrida, the daughter of Hugh of Evermue, and granddaughter of Hereward, who married Richard de Rulos, ancestor of the Rollos.

Matthew Paris has an interesting passage on these intermarriages, and on the settlement of Englishmen in Normandy, in his *Life of Abbot Frederic of St. Albans.* " Quibus tamen (*i.e.*, for the Saxon nobles) Rex Willielmus laqueos multiplices tetendit et muscipulas, sub dolo et specie amicitiæ: ducens aliquos eorum secum tanquam domesticos et speciales amicos in Normanniam, eodem anno quo triumphavit; et ipsos puellis Normanniæ matrimoniali copulâ confæderavit: et Normannos, mulieribus Angliæ generosis copulavit, terras Anglis ultramarinas, et Anglicanas possessiones dans Normannis. Sed et Anglorum castra, maneria et possessiones ut essent ab invicem remotæ, cautè procuravit; ne ex vicinitate roborentur." This account seems extremely probable. We know that William *promised* his daughter to Edwin of Mercia, though he never carried out his engagement; and we know that many names of English form occur in Normandy, in documents dating from A.D. 1180 to A.D. 1200.* Such are Godwin, Farman, Fere, Vitene (Whiting?), De Wailun (Wayland?), and Stanilonda. No less than twenty-eight persons occur called Anglicus or L'Anglais; and there is a curious surname given as Sake espee or Sac espee, which may have been Saxby or even Shakespear, as N. P. suggests. It would have been in keeping, too, with William's policy, to reward his English soldiers with lands in Normandy or Maine.

Burton Abbey, Staffordshire, may furnish us with an example of the

* N. P., passim.

spread of the fashion of French names by the early part of Henry the First's reign. Of three great and forty-three smaller tenants at that time, thirteen had names of French and thirty-three of English form. As the sub-tenants of Robert de Ferrers and William de Sobenhale (two of the greater tenants; the third was Orm, a native) are not mentioned, it is unlikely that more than two or three of the thirteen were really of French extraction; for Burton Abbey was remote, the estate was church land, and the district had apparently been little meddled with.

Three lists of names, very valuable for our present purpose, have come down to us from the twelfth century; and I have thrown their contents, so far as names are concerned, into a tabular form. The first and second are the lists of house-owners in Winchester, from the *Liber Winton*, one dating from about A.D. 1115, the other from 1148, so that about a generation elapsed between the compilation of the first and second. Even in the first, the French-named house-owners considerably outnumber the English-named; and in the second they do so by two to one, not reckoning in either case the instances where one proprietor, usually a Norman noble, has two or more houses. The actual occupants would, without doubt, have shown a larger proportion of English names.

It is curious that the number of persons without surnames (or more accurately without second names, for a great part of those we have were doubtless not transmitted) increased between the first and second survey; for this I cannot account, unless by the conjecture that they were mostly the sons of Englishmen. The increase of trade-names among the French-named may probably be partly due to immigration of the trading class from Normandy. The city was growing fast, and must have been fairly prosperous, in spite of the wars and anarchy of Stephen's reign; and Normandy was overflowing with population in the eleventh and twelfth centuries.* But the point to which I would call attention is the number of French-named persons (5·0 and 4·4 per cent. respectively) whose fathers are proved to have borne English names; while the converse does not occur in the first, and only to the extent of 0·3 per cent. in the second inquest. In some cases the English-named father actually appears in the first list, and his French-named son can be identified in the other.

The third column in the same table is compiled from the list of tenants of the Bishopric of Durham in the *Boldon Book*. Its date is A.D. 1183, or more than a generation later than the second Winchester list; yet the number of English prænomina is very nearly as great as in Winchester, being in the ratio of 24·5 to 25·4. The Bishopric was far remote from France: it was a comparatively rude and backward region, probably not very attractive to colonists from the Continent: the natives, we have seen, continued to be powerful and warlike. The lists of names of benefactors contained in the *Liber Vitæ Dunelmensis* lead one to the

* Palgrave.

inference that names of the old type continued in use, there or there-about,* until well on in the thirteenth century, when they somewhat rapidly waned away and almost disappeared, more rapidly indeed and more completely than in the South of England, where the process began earlier and was more gradual. Possibly this disappearance may have been a little earlier than has just been stated (see Note), or the later names of Anglo-Danish type may be chiefly those of people from kin-dred districts (the Lothians, Cumberland, Man, and the Isles) rather than of the Bishopric; but in any case the statement just made as to the comparative rapidity of the process holds good. Yet it did not depend on a rapid influx of new ethnological elements; there is nothing in the history of the period to suggest anything of the kind.

There is not much to be said on the composition of the list. There are still over 30 per cent. of persons without any semblance of a sur-name or soubriquet. The rarity of noble Norman names, and of trade-names, is just what might have been expected. The prevalence of names of locality continues in that part of England to the present day. On the other hand, patronymics, now so exceedingly common in the North of England, seem to have been comparatively rare: perhaps the rarity was rather in the pen of the writer than in the mouth of the people. One solitary example is given of the old Anglo-Saxon patronymic in ING: " Ulframming (the son of Wolfram) holds land under the Bishop."

In the return of military tenants to Henry II., in the *Liber Niger*, there are very few English names, particularly of tenants-in-chief, except in Northumberland and in the West Riding, and not many even there. We are, however, told by the author of the *Dial. de Scacc.*, in a well-known passage, that by about that time there was much difficulty in distinguishing, among the freemen, between those who were of Norman and those of Saxon descent. This could hardly have been the case if the English of the upper class had in any considerable proportion held to their own names. There *may*, therefore, be many of genuine English descent in the list referred to; but this is rather improbable on other grounds. The effect of every political change, at that period, was to bring over a fresh swarm of adventurers from the Continent; and any lands falling to the King's disposal were almost always granted to them, rather than even to the descendants of the original Norman invaders, now much mixed with English blood.

* It must, however, be allowed that some of the names in the *Liber Vitæ*, and we cannot tell how many, are those of donors dwelling far away from the Bishopric. Thus Dunegal,.son of Sumerled, appears, with his sons, Olaf, Dunechal *(sic)* and Raynald. This is evidently Somarled, Lord of Argyle and the Isles, who fell in battle A.D. 1164. The entry may be taken to have been made in the lifetime of his son Dougal (Dunegal), whom E. W. Robertson believes to have died before the end of the twelfth century. Yet the entry is stated, by the learned Editor of the *Liber Vitæ*, to be in a hand of the thirteenth century. Probably, therefore, either this judgment is erroneous, or the entry has been copied into the book after the time to which it refers. In either case, some doubt is thrown upon the attribution, in point of date, of other names.

	CLASSES OF SURNAMES.	Winton 1st Inquest, 1110—1120.	Winton 2nd Inquest, 1148.	Durham Tenants, 1183.
Norman prænomina, or such as came in with the Normans.	1 None	4·6	18·4	16·2
	2 Noble	7·5	4·1	2·5
	3 Local	9·2	7·1	17·1
	4 Nicknames	7·5	7·6	8
	5 Trades	6·3	10·2	3·4
	6 Qualifications *	8·7	6·4	8·9
	7 Patronymics	9·2	7·9	6·4
	8 Ditto English father	5·1	4·4	4·2
Native English or Danish prænomina.	9 Ditto Norman father	...	·3	·8
	10 Patronymics	5	·8	2·1
	11 None	18·5	14	14·8
	12 Local	1·2	1·3	3
	13 Nicknames	2·1	3	1·7
	14 Trades	2·5	3·7	1·3
	15 Qualifications †	6·7	2·3	·8
	16 Breton	...	·7	Scot. ·8
	17 Jew	...	·4	...
	18 Doubtful	6	6·7	5·5
Total... ...	1 2 3 4 5 6 7 9	52·9	62·5	66·2
Total... ...	8 10 11 12 13 14 15	41·2	29·5	27·9
Total... ...	1—18	100·1	99·8	99·6
	Repetitions of Norman Names ...	18·1	39·2	...
	Ditto of English ditto	2·9	4·9	...
	Ditto doubtful	...	2·0	...
	Number of Individuals	238	856	234

* Such as Clericus, Presbyter, Miles.
† In other Tables styled Offices, &c.

ANALYTICAL TABLE OF ENGLISH SURNAMES IN THE LATTER PART OF THE 13TH CENTURY.

	Woodstock, Oxon, House owners.	Bampton Hun., Oxon, Free Tenants.	Wotton Hun., Oxon, Villans.	Bampton Hun., Oxon, Servi.	Marlow Town, House Tenants.	Bedfordshire, Free Tenants.	Bedfordshire, Villans.	Godmanchester, Tenants.	Cottenham, Cambs, Villans.	E. Suffolk, Landowners and Tenants.	Gillingham, Dorset, Tenants.	Birmingham, Owners, &c.	Malmesbury Abbey, Tenants.	Rothley Soke, Leicestershire, Tenants.	Kent, Wrongdoers and Wronged.	Hunts, Beds, Oxon, Wrongdoers, &c.	Devonshire, Wrongdoers and Wronged.	Norwich, Flegg, Wrongdoers, &c.	Yorkshire, N.E.&C., Wrongdoers, &c.	Yorkshire, South, Wrongdoers, &c.	Average Percentage.
Number	103	150	200	200	100	100	100	359	250	314	110	100	300	200	300	100	100	150	314	102	
1. Norman, doubtless	2	5·3	2·5	4·5	2	3	2	3·3	2·4	6·3	·9	2	·3	·5	·3	3	2	2	3·8	2	2·5
2. " believed	6	7·3	6	4·5	7	11	6	7·7	5·6	4·4	4·5	5	1·7	·5	1·7	3	1	2	5·7	7	4·9
3. " probable	1	3·3	...	2	9	3	...	1·3	2·4	1·3	1·8	1	3·3	2·5	5·3	8	7	6	2·8	3	3·2
4. French nicknames	...	4	5	2	3	11	1	3·3	1·2	1·6	·9	1	1·3	1·5	2·7	2	3	1·3	3·2	...	2·4
5. Latin nicknames	...	...	...	·5	...	...	1	·3	...	...	...	...	...	·5	·7	...	2	·6	·3	...	·30
6. Saxon nicknames	2	3·3	5·5	6	5	1	14	8	10·4	8·9	3·6	1	6·7	8·5	5	7	2	6·6	4·4	4	5·6
7. " nicknames, probable	3	4·6	4·5	7	4	7	5	9·1	10·8	4·1	6·3	3	2·3	6·5	4	6	3	6	6·7	9	5·6
8. English nicknames	8	6	2·5	7	10	3	7	4·7	6·4	3·8	5·4	7	12·7	5	2·7	5	7	10	4·8	5	6·1
9. Local specific	18	24·6	7·5	6·5	11	13	5	6·1	4·8	25·8	23·4	24	15·3	11·5	24·7	18	43	20	36·6	30	18·4
10. " general	11	10	24	14	4	2	9	6·6	9·6	6·3	15·3	13	18·3	6·5	10·3	5	12	8·6	3·2	8	9·8
11. " of county	1	...	...	...	...	...	1	1·1	·4	...	·9	...	...	...	·3	1	...	2	·6	...	·36
	1	2	3	4	5	6	7	8	9	10	11	12	13	14	15	16	17	18	19	20	21

	1	2	3	4	5	6	7	8	9	10	11	12	13	14	15	16	17	18	19	20	21
12. Local of country	...	·7	·5	2·5	3	...	...	1·6	·4	·6	...	2	·7	·5	2	...	...	2	2·5	1	1
13. " of France	...	...	1	3	...	2	...	...	...	...	...	...	·7	·5	1·7	...	1	2	1·3	2	·76
14. Patronymics	5	5·3	7·5	11·5	4	2	9	6·4	6·8	10	10	7	8·3	7	5·3	10	4	2	1·6	1	6·2
15. " in Fils	1	2·6	6·5	·5	...	6	11	7·5	10·8	7·3	1·8	3	1·7	29	5·7	9	1	4·6	5·1	9	6·15
16. Trades, French	13	4	3	1	9	5	6	4·1	3·2	1·9	2·7	5	1·7	...	3	3	1	2	1·3	2	3·6
17. " English	7	·7	...	1	4	1	1	3	1·6	2·2	2·7	6	2·7	·5	1·7	1	2	2	·6	...	2
18. " Latin	5	1·3	2·5	2	7	4	...	2·8	4	1	3·6	2	1·3	2·5	5·7	1	3	1·3	3·2	3	2·8
19. " Rural, French	3	·7	...	...	1	1	2	·3	...	...	...	...	·3	·5	...	1	...	...	...	1	·54
20. " English	2	...	3·5	1·5	...	2	4	1·1	·8	1·3	1·8	3	2·3	...	1·3	1	...	2·6	·6	2	1·54
21. " Latin	1	2	3·5	1	6	1	4	1·6	2·4	...	2·7	...	2·3	2·5	·7	3	1	2	·9	1	1·9
22. Offices, &c., French	4	2·6	2	3	...	3	...	2	1·2	1·3	·9	7	2·3	1·5	·7	2	2	2	·3	...	1·9
23. " English	...	·7	·5	2·5	...	1	1	1·1	2	2·5	·9	2	3·3	·5	·7	2	...	·6	1·3	...	1·13
24. " Latin	1	2	3·5	2	1	2	6	2·8	2·4	1·9	...	...	1·7	6	1·7	3	...	2·6	1·9	5	2·3
25. Miscellaneous	...	...	...	...	...	...	...	1·5	...	·6	...	...	·3	...	1·3	...	...	...	·9	1	·26
26. Doubtful	9	8·7	7·5	13·5	9	17	5	12	10·8	6·7	10	6	8·7	6	10·7	5	3	9·3	6	6	8·5
Total of 1, 2, 3, 4, 13	9	19·9	14·5	16	21	30	9	15·6	11·6	13·6	8·1	9	7·3	5·5	11·7	16	14	13·3	16·8	14	13·8
Total of 1, 2, 3, 4, 13, 16, 19, 22	29	27·2	19·5	20	31	39	17	22	16	16·8	11·7	21	11·6	7·5	15·4	22	17	17·7	18·4	17	19·8

ANALYTICAL TABLE OF MODERN ENGLISH SURNAMES.

	C. B.'s Civil K. C. B.'s	Univ. London College of Physicians	Selsey, &c. Sussex Directory	Bristol Martin's Act	Glo'stershire Magistrates	Essex Quakers	South-Midland Medical	Wilden and Ravensden Bedfordshire Ratepayers	Wakefield Prison	Salop Medical	West Riding, 1821	North York Quakers	Averages
	200	200	200	300	200	250	100	200	200	100	465	250	...
1. Norman, doubtless	7	2·5	1·5	·7	3·5	...	1	4	2	1	·8	...	2
2. " believed	9·5	6	7	6·3	9·5	...	4	4	2	1	2	1·6	4·4
3. " probable...	4·5	5	2	2	2·5	6·8	7	4	3·5	5	5·1	6	4·45
4. French nicknames...	1·5	2·5	3	1	2	·4	4	1	2	2	·2	·8	2
5. Saxon "	3·5	4·5	4	3·3	5	10·4	2	1	3·5	3	1·7	2·8	3·7
6. " " probable...	5	5	5	4	3	1·6	4	1	6·5	4	5·5	4·8	4·1
7. English "	5	5	3	3·3	2	6	3	7	3·5	5	2·6	3·6	4·1
8. Local, specific	15·5	21·5	20	7·7	27	6	12	17	16·5	26	37·5	18·8	18·8
9. " general...	7·5	5·5	5	8·3	6	17·2	9	4·5	9	11	8·6	8·4	8·6
10. " of county	...	1·5	·5	·7	...	...	...	...	·5	...	...	·4	·3
11. " of country	·5	...	...	...	...	·4	...	...	·5	...	·4	...	·15
12. " of France	...	1	2	1	...	...	...	...	...	...	·4	...	·36
13. Patronymics, ordinary ...	9	9·5	14·5	14	9·5	5·2	13	17·5	8·5	6	4·7	6·4	9·8
14. " in SON	7	4	1·5	1·3	2·5	11·6	7	7·5	11	6	10·9	23·2	7·8
	1	2	3	4	5	6	7	8	9	10	11	12	13

	I	2	3	4	5	6	7	8	9	10	11	12	13
15. Patronymics, doubtful Welsh	2·5	4	3·5	6·3	2	2	8	3·5	10	6	·6	2·4	4·2
16. Trades, French	3	4·5	4	2·7	·5	2·4	1	6	3·5	...	1·7	·8	2·5
17. " English	2·5	1·5	1	6·3	5·5	13·6	6	3	5·5	9	3	3·6	5
18. " Latin	...	1	2	1·3	...	...	1	1·5	...	1	...	...	·65
19. " Rural French	·5	·5	...	...	·5	...	3	...	·5	...	·4	...	·45
20. " " English	2	3	2·5	3	3·5	1·6	...	...	1·5	3	1·5	2·4	2
21. " " Latin	...	...	...	1	·5	...	1	3·5	·5	...	·2	...	·55
22. Offices, &c., French	·5	·5	1	1·6	1·5	...	2	1·5	1	1	·6	...	·9
23. " English	1·5	1·5	...	3	1	6·8	2	4	1·5	3	1·5	...	1·9
24. " Latin	1	·5	2	1·3	1	...	4	...	...	3	1·1	2	1·3
25. Doubtful	11	10·5	10	9·3	11	8	6	7·5	7	8	8·4	10·4	8·3
Excluded Welsh	2·5	7	·5	7	6	1·6	6	1	5·5	12	·2	2	4·3
Scotch	31	12·5	1	1	2·5	3·2	13	1	4·5	11	1·7	4	7·2
Irish	4·5	2·5	·5	2·3	1	·8	6	·5	4	4	...	...	1·9
French mod.	4	3	...	...	...	14	...	...	·5	...	·2	...	1·9
German	...	2	...	...	1	...	...	1	·5	...	·2	...	·4
Jewish	1	·5	...	...	...	...	...	...	...	...	...	...	·1
Total of 1, 2, 3, 4, 12 ...	22·5	16	15·5	11	17·5	7·2	16	13	9·5	9	8·5	8·4	13
" 1, 2, 3, 4, 12, 16, 19, 22	26·5	21·5	20·5	15·3	20	9·6	22	20·5	14·5	10	11·2	9·2	16·8

We may now proceed to the evidence supplied by the *Hundred Rolls*, and by some other documents of about the same period, *i.e.*, the beginning of the reign of Edward I. Such evidence is still almost exclusively to be derived from the surnames appearing therein.

The value of the *Hundred Rolls* to the lawyer and the historian can hardly be overrated: we will see whether they may not be of some service to the ethnologist.

They furnish us with lists, for the counties of Oxford, Bedford, Huntingdon, Cambridge and Buckingham, or for a very large portion of them, of all the householders and the tenants of land, large and small, with the nature, extent, and conditions of their tenures, and generally with their names.

By that time every individual, or at least every head of a family, seems to have had a second name; though doubtless it often hung very loosely upon him, and was often purely personal, not hereditary. I have, accordingly, been able to construct an analytical table of the surnames occurring in nine districts in the counties just named. There is considerable variety in the character of the communities selected. I have taken (1) the house-owners of Woodstock, (2) the house-tenants of Marlow, (3) all the tenants of Godmanchester, of both houses and lands; (4) the free tenants of Bampton Hundred, Oxon, and of a district in South Bedfordshire; (5) the villans of Wotton Hundred, Oxon, of South Bedfordshire, and of Cottenham in Cambridgeshire; (6) the Servi, so called, or servile tenants, in Bampton Hundred. To these I have added the tenants, of whatever quality, in Gillingham, Dorset, the only manor in that county for which a similar return exists, and the sokemen and larger tenants (most of the smaller ones are not named) in the Hundred of Lothingland, Suffolk. There are three other columns in the table, the data for which are not taken from the *Hundred Rolls*. One of these is a list of the sokemen (or of 200 of them) of the soke of Rothley in Leicestershire; the data are published by Mr. G. T. Clarke in vol. 47 of the *Archæologia*. Mr. Clarke thinks his document may date some time in Henry III.'s reign, soon after the middle of the thirteenth century: this would bring it within a few years of the *Hundred Rolls*. Another comprises about half a list of the tenants of Malmesbury Abbey, Wiltshire, also from the *Archæologia*.

There is also a list, from Toulmin Smith's *Men and Names in Old Birmingham*, of the first hundred names of land and house-owners and inhabitants that occur in the history of Birmingham: they date from 1285 down to 1431, but are mostly early; among the earlier ones some are probably not abiding surnames. The lower orders of the town are scarcely represented.

There remain six other columns, gotten from the *Hundred Rolls* in the following manner:

Though the lists of landowners and tenants for other counties than those above-mentioned either never existed or have been lost, the

Hundred Rolls contain much valuable matter from all the other counties in England. In particular, they give us, in answer to enquiries as to the evildoings and delinquencies of the King's and lords' bailiffs and others, the names of numbers of persons who had suffered exactions at the hands of the bailiffs, together with those of persons offending in sundry other ways, as by exporting wool, &c. I have taken all the names that occur in these presentments, excepting those of great landholders, sheriffs and bailiffs, for the counties of York and Kent, and of Bedford, Oxford, and Huntingdon, and for the eastern part of Norfolk, hoping thus to get something which might fairly compare, so far as the character of the names was concerned, with the returns of the general population of the five counties first named. The list for Bedford, Oxon, and Hunts may serve as a criterion as to whether those gotten in this second way are really comparable. It is fairly satisfactory.

N. P., basing his opinion on the number of French surnames met with in the *Hundred Rolls*, thinks that " probably not less than a moiety of the free* classes in England continued to be Norman in the reign of Edward I." In another passage, on a consideration of contemporary surnames, he is led to think that the Norman element in England " is from one-fourth to one-third." The discrepancy may be explicable on his lines, but he does not take any notice of it.

These proportions are somewhat startling; but the evidence for their correctness is fairly stated, and candidly laid open to criticism. There is one great preliminary objection which equally affects N. P.'s method and my own, and which it may be well to consider in the first place.

Camden says: " Among the common people, which sway all in names, many surnames have been changed in respect of occupations, and not a few have been changed in respect of masters; for in every place we see the youth very commonly called by the names of their occupations, as John Baker . . . and many by their masters' names, as John Pickering, Thomas Watkins, Nicholas French, whereas they served masters of those names, which often were conveyed to their posterity, and their own surnames altogether forgotten." † Doubtless this practice was common enough among the Scottish Highlanders, where the commonalty in some cases took the surnames of their chiefs, as Grant, Macdonald, ‡ Mackenzie; and it may be that on the English border even, men of small and weak families may sometimes have dropped their surnames for those of more powerful ones, though I know no positive evidence of the fact. In more modern times, in the West Indies and the Southern States of the American Union, freedmen often assumed the surnames of their masters. But the number and distribution of surnames in the

---

* He includes villans, &c., among the free, excluding none but absolute serfs, whose names are not mentioned in the *Rolls*.

† *Remains concerning Britain*, chapter on Surnames.

‡ It is quite incredible, though not physically impossible, that the 30,000 Macdonalds in Scotland, not to speak of the Macdougalls, &c., could all have sprung from Somarled.

South-Midlands, as shown in the *Hundred Rolls*, lead me to think that this kind of adoption of names must have been at least uncommon.

Occasionally, no doubt, noble Norman names appear in low positions. Thus Henry Peverel held at Toft in Cambridgeshire four acres of land, paying fourpence, and John Peverel half an acre and a small house, paying three shillings to the Prior of Barnwell; but they were free tenants, and the former at least had a beneficial tenure. The explanation appears to be that England at that period was growing rapidly in population, and that there was little opening for the expansion of the class who held small landed estates; hence they frequently quartered the cadets on their property, giving them parcels of land at low or nominal rents. Thus at Bidenham, Bedfordshire, Radulfus Passelewe held a knight's fee; Nicholas Passelewe had half the fee under him, and of him Robert Passelewe held one half-virgate for 2s. 6d., and another for 2s., while another (?) Radulfus Passelewe held of Nicholas half a virgate for 3d. and court-service. In the same parish Robert and Ralph Passelewe each held also small portions of church lands, conjointly with other tenants, at equally beneficial rents. The actual value of a virgate held in villenage was twenty shillings or more yearly, besides customary labour, &c. Here the relationship of the Passelewes to one another is not mentioned, but can surely be hardly doubtful; hardly more so, indeed, than where John, Lord of Caldecote, lets to his two brothers respectively, to the one four acres of land for one penny and homage and the King's service, and a house and half an acre for a rose and homage, &c., to the other one acre for a penny and homage, &c.

Alan Vavasur occurs among the villans of William de la Haye in "Schepere," Cambridgeshire: he has four acres of land, and pays two shillings, and "opera" worth 1s. 3d. But he also appears as a free tenant under Ralph fitz Fulk, holding half an acre for a shilling, and under Will. Blunt as a crofter, holding five acres of church-land by deed for a shilling. He followed, evidently, the condition of the land, whether bond or free.[*] Thus it comes to pass that we may find William Frankeleyn among villans, and William Bonde[†] among free tenants. I have found but one instance, which seems to me hardly explicable, as above stated. Robert de Bekeringe held in Catworth "unum coterellum" under Thomas de Bekeringe, for which he paid four shillings. This, in Catworth, was a full rent; and Robert cannot, I think, have been a near relation of his lord and namesake.

On the whole, therefore, I am not disposed to attach much importance to the objection founded on Camden's remark, which, as already stated, strikes at the root of our method of investigation, inasmuch as the master from whom the name was borrowed would have been often, most often, a Norman, and the borrower probably as often a native.

---

[*] In short, he was a villan reguardant.

[†] Bonde may, however, be Bondi, from Bondig, a Saxon personal name.

N. P., however, seems to me to commit two capital errors, which unduly swell his lists of Norman names:

1st. He is probably too ready to admit *identity* of origin in cases of *similarity* of arms. However it was with surnames, there is, I imagine, little doubt that in the early days of heraldry the feudal as well as the family connexions of a great house were apt to adopt their arms with a difference.

2nd. Identical local names are not indefeasible proof of identical descent. It is evident from the *Hundred Rolls* that birth in or origin from a village or manor was extremely often the ground whence a man derived his surname.* Persons bearing local names, usually those of neighbouring parishes or hamlets, literally swarm among the base tenants of Cambridgeshire and the neighbouring counties; while not unfrequently the largest free tenant in a manor, or even one of the largest villan tenants, bears the name of the place. Thus in Keston, Hunts, is a villan of only half a virgate named Geoffrey de Keston;† and in the hamlet of Upthorp,‡ close by, a free tenant of a little more bears the name of Upthorp.

3rd. N. P. claims as " Norman " not only all trade-names of French form, *e.g.*, Le Ferrer, Boulanger, which may fairly be conceded to him, but all those which in the *Hundred Rolls* are Latinised, as Faber, Messor, Pistor, Clericus, Molendinar; and even the English trade-names, because the French article is prefixed, *e.g.*, le Woodwarde, le Foulere. Of course, the probability is that the *Faber* of the notary was in most cases called Smith by his neighbours, and not Le Fevre; and that the *Molendinarius* was called Miller, and so forth.

4th. N. P. claims also all patronymics derived from christian names of French form. This amounts, in fact, to claiming almost all the patronymic surnames which originated in England after the time when French-formed christian names had nearly superseded English-formed ones among the native population. A patronymic surname of English form does furnish some sort of evidence that its possessor's male ancestry was native, because the sons of Francigenæ, as has been shown, rarely bore native names; but the converse certainly does not hold at all. Patronymics were still increasing, at the expense of other classes of surnames, in the thirteenth century, if not later, and almost every new name formed on that plan must have been based on a French christian name.

The application of the criticisms above stated to N. P.'s local lists has a great effect in diminishing the proportion of probable Normans. His examples are taken from six manors in Beds, Bucks, Hunts, and

---

* N. P. would probably claim all Cliffords as of Norman origin. There are large numbers of farmers of this name in the Cotswold country in Gloucestershire, clustering round a parish of Clifford. I have little doubt their forefathers were churls who migrated thence into the surrounding parishes, and their ancestry was probably Saxon or British.

† *Hundred Rolls*, p. 614.   ‡ *Hundred Rolls*, p. 615.

Oxon, from the list of house-owners in Cambridge town, and that of
office-bearers in the City of London.   Of these three lists the first contains 212 names, and in it N. P. finds 113 Normans, or 53 per cent.;
I find 45, or 22 per cent.   In the second list, of 241 names, he finds 106,
or 44 per cent.; I find 77, or 32 per cent.   The third, or London list,
contains 239 names: this also yields to him (105 =) 44 per cent.; and I
think he is entitled to very nearly all of these.

The application of N. P.'s principles to my 200 sokemen of Rothley
would give at least 56 per cent. of Normans, which seems to be a kind
of *reductio ad absurdum*.   In Leicestershire, then as now, the prevailing
name-type was the patronymic in SON, *e.g.* Hodgson, which appears in
the list as Fil Rog., and would be claimed by N. P. as Norman.

Let us now proceed to examine the strong and the weak points of
my own method.

It is probable that the period at which the *Hundred Rolls* were
compiled was about the most favourable for our purpose.   In that generation* the use of surnames had become universal.   The migration
from France which began at the Conquest had practically ceased, and
the foreign ingredient in the population may be said to have nearly
attained its maximum.   So too, probably, had the percentage of foreign
names.   My table of modern surnames will show that whatever changes
of individuals' names have taken place (and in some classes doubtless
they have been very numerous), the proportions of the classes among
themselves have not varied very much.   The class which has most
lessened is that of trade-names, especially French trade-names: these
latter have been translated, or perhaps some of those in the *Hundred
Rolls* were translations from the vernacular.   Saxon patronymics have
also declined, as might have been expected, seeing that scarcely any
new ones could be produced after the reign of Edward I., Saxon prænomina, except those destined to survive to our own times, being then
nearly extinct.   Other patronymics have perhaps increased, owing partly
to the immigration of Welshmen.

Distinctly Norman names (excluding trade-names) have declined but
little: they were mostly of old fixation, and being more or less unintel-
ligible or void of significance to the users, there was no temptation to
change them as they became inapplicable.   Local specific names have
perhaps slightly increased.   This must be owing to the occasional application of new names of this class to persons who migrated, and whose
old surnames were unfamiliar to their new neighbours, or had ceased to
be applicable.

On the whole, the effect of the foregoing considerations is, I think,
favourable to my method; but there are other formidable objections to
it, besides the one already drawn from Camden.   The same author gives

---

* In the Rothley list, which is perhaps twenty years earlier, and comes from a
county rather more remote, 26 persons out of 226 have no second name.   In the
Hundred Rolls single names hardly ever occur.

a list of ten different surnames, all borne by the posterity of William Belward, of Malpas: five of these were of the local class. No doubt many families of Norman blood were entirely absorbed in English local names; still the proportion they bore to the whole population, and even to the whole multitude of local names, was not very large; for, as I have shown above, the greater part of local names was not borne by the owners of manors, but by smaller tenants. A balancing consideration on the other side is, that the immigration from France was largely masculine, and Norman surnames were in the second generation borne by numbers of people of mixed blood. As for French trade-names, such as Taylor, Bullinger, and Hooper, and official or caste-names, such as Spencer and Burgess, they did not invariably and certainly denote a French bearer; for an apparent example to the contrary, I may quote Edmund Boulanger, a citizen of Winchester in one of the Winton inquests. But I should think such cases were rather the exception than the rule. The great abundance of the name Taylor might be thought to throw a doubt on this point; but the tailor was probably chiefly employed by the upper or French-speaking class, who would give him his designation. Moreover, the name Seamer was long used by the natives to express the same idea, and there are several persons of that name in the *Hundred Rolls*.

After all has been said, I must confess that my method is a loose one for the determination of the proportion of Norman or French immigrants to natives; but it is much less liable to objection when used to indicate the relative proportions of the foreign element in the several provinces or counties of England.

It consists, as will be gathered from the tables, in summing up, firstly, surnames which were certainly or probably imported, or, being of French form, were probably first assumed within a moderate time after the Conquest, or which actually imply in themselves foreign blood, as Pickard and Champneys; and secondly, trade and official names of French form; and taking the total to represent the amount of the so-called "Norman" population introduced into England within the two centuries after the Conquest. Any excess under the second head may balance the number of Norman families concealed under local names and patronymics.

The resulting percentages will still, probably, be considered large by most of my readers; but I am satisfied that N. P. is right in maintaining the existence of a flow of migration of the lower class of freemen from Normandy to England during a century or more after the Conquest.

I have already referred to the table of modern surnames. It is not quite so satisfactory as the mediæval table, inasmuch as it contains rather too large a proportion of the upper class. The column gotten from the Bristol offenders against Martin's act is particularly valuable from the mixture of town and country labourers which it contains: the names of these classes, as a rule, do not find their way into printed lists.

The Wakefield prisoners were all of English birth, and in large proportion natives of Yorkshire, Lancashire, and other northern or north-
midland counties. The lists of the Society of Friends, in some respects
convenient, are liable to the objection that they contain too many persons of single names, which are perhaps rare elsewhere. Thus the
bearers of the French Huguenot name of Marriage, and the Anglo-
Saxon one of Barrett, swarm in the county of Essex, and the Richard-
sons in the northern counties. The West Riding list, dated 1821, I owe
to Mr. J. Knowles: it is an upper and middle class list, free from the
effects of the immigrations of later years. The Wilden and Ravensden
list of ratepayers, due to Mr. Mark Sharman's kindness, may indicate
that the ancient excess of Norman blood still remains in Bedfordshire.

The following are the inferences I draw from the tables:

The proportion of Norman or French blood in southern and eastern
England in the time of Edward I. may have equalled 15, or even
approached 20 per cent. It was greater than this in the south-midland
counties, but less in East Anglia, and in the western and northern
counties, especially where free sokemen abounded. It was perhaps
rather small in Kent, taken as a whole, owing to the nature of the land-
tenures there, which gave little opportunity to foreigners to get on the
land. It was greater in Yorkshire, or at least the north and east of
Yorkshire, than in other counties equally remote, owing to the devastation of Deira by the Conqueror having left openings for colonisation.

The Scandinavian patronymic terminating in SON was already the
favourite form of surname in the North of England in the time of
Edward I. I incline to think that it was not confined in its origin to
the Anglo-Danish districts, but extended to some of the Anglian ones.

Migration from the North of England to the South, and *vice versâ*,
except to great manufacturing centres, was very small until our own
times. The absence of patronymics in SON from the rural districts of
the south-west is almost absolute.*

No complete amalgamation of the different social strata, nor even of
the racial elements, has taken place during the past six centuries. In
the thirteenth century the great landowners and the upper class generally were still mainly Norman, though the foreign element had penetrated
to the lowest strata. The villans, the farming communities, the ancestors of the copyholders of later days, were probably the most purely
English class, more purely so than the cottars, labourers, and poorer
class of townsfolk.† Nor do I think that subsequent changes have altogether effaced these distinctions, though they have gone far in that
direction. The small farmers are still, I think, the most Saxon or

---

* Mr. Park Harrison found but 0·7 per cent. among the farmers of the whole of
Dorset. About Bristol the proportion is much the same.

† See W. Hunt, *Norman Britain*, p. 239 *et seq.*, for a good summary of the history of
the villan class.

Anglian part of the population in the south-east and east of England, and the most British or Celtic in the south-west.

Was any permanent change in physical type effected by the results of the Conquest? and if so, where, and in what direction?

The addition of fifteen or twenty per cent. of a foreign element, or, more correctly, the addition of fifteen or twenty of a foreign to eighty-five or eighty of a native one, might be expected to produce a distinct and lasting effect if such new element were homogeneous; but homogeneous it was not. The prevailing types among the Galato-Merovingian military aristocracy of France, as well as among the mostly Scandinavian aristocracy of Normandy, were still, we have reason to believe, blond and long-headed; and the remains of the Anglo-Danish one, with which they certainly mixed to a considerable extent, were a purer breed of the same type, which is still the prevailing one among the upper classes of England.

The bulk of the immigrants, however, especially of the portion of them who filtered in gradually and peacefully in later times, would doubtless more resemble the majority of the modern inhabitants of the north of France; that is to say, they would be in the main a mixture of the square-browed long-faced type which the French ethnologists call Kimric, with the short swarthy round-headed type of Broca's Kelts or Kelto-ligurians. This last, being rather feebly represented here previously, would not easily merge. I think it continues pretty common in the districts where my name-tables lead me to think the most Frenchmen settled. Short, dark, blunt-featured people are commoner, I think, in the South-Midlands than in most other parts; and the small, swarthy, round-faced people whom Phillips* met with so frequently along the Yorkshire Ouse, and who struck him by their contrast to the prevailing Yorkshire types, may as well be traced to this immigration as to any early Iberian or Ugrian strain. I have not, unfortunately, measured many heads from the East of England; but it is a little curious that of 29, 9 who had dark or darkish hair yielded me a breadth-index of 79·85, while 20 with red, fair, or chestnut hair gave one of 78·06 only. Now in the West of England, where my larger experience enables me to speak more positively, the broader heads go on the whole with lighter hair. I am disposed to infer that in the East, where French immigrants were comparatively numerous, they brought in, or at least materially reinforced, the *dark* broad-headed type.

* *Rivers of Yorkshire.*

CHAPTER XII.

Subsequent Migrations.

IN Ireland, after the defeat and death of Magnus Barefoot, the Scandinavians had for ever lost the chance they had once seemed to have of completely subjugating Ireland. With community of religion, and increased frequency of intermarriage, no doubt the citizens of Dublin, Waterford, and the other Danish towns, became more Irish in blood; while the Scandinavian race, on the other hand, diffused itself somewhat in the surrounding districts. It is a question with me whether the tall blond race, which prevails from Wexford and Waterford, across Southern Tipperary, to Limerick, may not owe its peculiarities, physical and moral, in some measure to a Danish cross.* The Golden Vale, as it is called, from its richness and accessibility, must have been a tempting and an easy prize to almost every invader of Ireland; and it may be that even before the Danish epoch, some blond race of conquerors, Galatic or what not, had settled down there, leaving the mountain ranges, south and north, to the swarthy aborigines who still hold them.

The coming of the Anglo-Normans, however, obscured the existence of the Danish or Norse race in the ports of Ireland, as every one of them soon fell into the hands of the new invaders. The same kind of coalescence took place here as in England and Scotland, the Normans taking the lead, while the descendants of the Danes, mixed with new colonists from the West of England, formed the bulk of the burgher communities.

For many centuries after the coming of Strongbow—nay, even down almost to our own times—the invasion of Ireland from Great Britain has continued. It has been a perpetual ebb and flow, the ebbs sometimes considerable and of long duration. For ages the valour of the Ulster men, who even then, as Giraldus tells us, differed by their manly and vigorous character from their soft and treacherous countrymen in the south, defended their country from the intruders, who at one time or other made themselves masters of almost the whole of the other provinces. Notwithstanding the savage and exterminating character the warfare often assumed, no such complete clearance of the natives took place from any extensive district as to admit of a thorough racial change. If there was any exception, it was in the baronies of Forth and Bargy, in the southern peninsula of county Wexford, which were probably peopled from the English or Anglo-Flemish part of Pembrokeshire. After them, and after the immediate neighbourhood of the

* Being struck by the Scandinavian aspect of a Bristol cabman, who, nevertheless, spoke with an Irish accent, I made a guess at his origin. "You are from county Wexford, I suppose?" "Ay sure, sir, jist a mile beyant Enniscorthy."

principal seaports, the counties of Kildare, Carlow, and Kilkenny* were most Anglicised during the Middle Ages.

The wars of Elizabeth, and the plantation of James I., caused considerable changes in Munster and Ulster. In the former, they were attended with so much destruction of life that the moderate number of colonists introduced by the grantees of forfeited land assumed some importance, as a rare element. In most parts of Ulster the change, later in coming, was more complete than in the provinces, owing not so much to extermination as to colonisation—not so much to the lessened number of the natives as to the great number of English and Scotch settlers. But it did not extend, as is sometimes supposed, to the whole of the province. The more mountainous districts, especially Donegal, and even parts of Antrim and Down, were little disturbed. The rebellion and massacres of 1641, which diminished the English and Scottish element, were counterbalanced by the arrival of fresh settlers. The nature of Cromwell's famous transplantation is often misunderstood. It was not the mass of the population (who were mostly of the native race) that he proposed to expel from the three eastern provinces and to settle in Connaught; it was the disaffected landlords, who even at that period must have been mostly of Anglo-Norman or mixed descent. Ethnologically, it was in some counties little more than the substitution of one set of English landlords for another,† with the addition of a partly English element to the hitherto very Gaelic population of Connaught. Connaught, however, continued to be, in spite of this unwilling invasion of the "Saxons," by far the most Gaelic of the provinces. In the following table of surnames the proportion of the exotic element is probably overrated, if anything; the pure native population of the mountainous tracts does not enlist in fair proportion to that of the more civilised districts:

TABLE

Percentages of Surnames in Ireland, taken from 1,336 Recruits.

PROVINCES.	INDIGENOUS NAMES.	EXOTIC NAMES.
Down, Antrim, Derry	37·5	62·5
Dublin	45	55
Rest of Ulster	56·4	43·6
Rest of Leinster	60	40
Munster	67·3	32·7
Connaught	75·8	24·2

* Shortly after visiting Kilkenny, where the features and the small proportion of very dark hair had indicated to me the prevalence of English, or at least of Teutonic blood, I was spending an evening with the late Dr. Petrie. Speaking of the collection he had made of ancient Irish tunes, I asked him whether he had visited Kilkenny with a view to it. "Yes," he said; "and I got some good old tunes, but they were not what I wanted; *they were all old English airs.*"

† Prendergast (*Cromwellian Settlements*, &c.) gives a list of 74 persons transplanted to Connaught from a district in co. Waterford: 21 of the names appear to me English, 46 Celtic, 7 doubtful. But Waterford, except the eastern semi-Danish corner, was and is a very Gaelic county.

The surnames may be much more trusted as evidence of race-proportions in Ireland than in England. No doubt there have been reciprocal changes, as when the Burkes went into rebellion and took the style of MacWilliam, or when a large portion of the clan of O'Sullivan took that of Harrington. But enactments of Parliament, requiring the native Irish to forsake their old names, were, doubtless, scarcely operative outside the English pale, and not permanently even there. There is a twyform difficulty in Ulster: how to distinguish the native Irish from the imported Hebridean names, and how to classify the latter when so distinguished, they being strangers by birth, but scarcely strangers in blood.

These same Hebrideans have, it is true, a considerable share of Scandinavian mixed with their Gaelic or Ibero-Gaelic blood, varying, however, a good deal in the several islands. The Norsemen had great success in the Isles in a matter wherein they failed in Ireland; they to a great extent altered the local names, which to this day are (excluding modern English) in Lewis as 3 or 4 Norse to 1 Gaelic, and in Islay as 1 Norse to 2 Gaelic. Captain F. W. L. Thomas, from whose laborious and valuable papers [*] I take these proportions, seems to think that the Norse vikings had at one time completely exterminated the native Gaels and Picts, but this is scarcely likely: thralls were always needed; it was easier to keep those who were on the spot than to bring others from foreign countries; and the subsequent recovery of the Gaelic tongue is hardly explicable on Thomas's hypothesis; for though the dominion, and to a great extent the chieftainships and rights of property, passed away from the Norsemen to the Scots, through wars, feuds, or marriage, no one supposes that the new lords made a clean sweep of the population; indeed, Captain Thomas himself believes the Macleods, Macaulays, and Morisons, the three old clans of the Lewis, to be of Scandinavian blood; and yet the Gaelic tongue—mixed, it is true, with Norse words—prevails now even in that island.

Shetland and Orkney seem to have been occupied by the Norwegians towards the end of the eighth century, prior to their conquest of the Hebrides. If they anywhere extirpated a Celtic population, it was here. We know that prehistoric folk dwelt in these islands, and yet the old names are pretty purely Scandinavian. Even here, however, such a name as Dunrossness (the southern part of the mainland of Shetland) seems to point to the survival of some Gaelic-speakers into the period of Norse dominion. Else, how came the Shetlanders by the Gaelic appellation Dunross, to which they must have affixed the tautological NESS after the meaning of ROSS had been forgotten? [†]

* *Proceedings of the Society of Scottish Antiquaries.*

† This is the converse of what happened in Sutherland and Ross, and in the Lewis, where, in such names as Strathhalladale and Loch Laxford and Loch Langavat, the meaning of *dale, ford* (firth), and *vat* (water) has been clearly forgotten and supplemented by Gaelic prefixes.

Caithness, too, was largely colonised by the Norsemen, who left permanent memorials of their dominion in the shape of place-names, not only in the level parts of the county still so called, but more scantily along the coasts of Sutherland and Ross. Here, too, the representatives of the ancient occupants recovered possession, after several generations, and the Norse language gave up the partial hold it had obtained (perhaps only among the ruling caste), and receded within the limits of the low country of Caithness. We shall see, however, further on, in the tables and commentary, that Norse blood did not die out with the language.

When, at a still later period, an unredeemed mortgage brought Shetland and Orkney under the Scottish Crown, numerous officials and adventurers flocked thither from the mainland, and largely crossed the blood of the inhabitants, especially in Orkney, where surnames of Scottish type or origin are said to be almost as numerous as native ones. The latter are mostly characterised by the termination in -SON, and sometimes by that in -BISTER.

For centuries past there have been no marked alterations in the distribution of races in Scotland, except those brought about by the imperceptible progress of individual migration and counter-migration. The Highlands and Galloway have become less purely Celtic, and the Teutonic element has been somewhat diminished in the Lowlands. Great cities, too, have grown up in the latter province, containing, of course, a very motley population. The great Irish immigration of late years is not at present, ethnologically, very important ; for the Irish are amongst us, but not of us, and generally intermarry among themselves. Relatively, it is far larger in Scotland than in England : in the former country the persons of Irish birth were, in 1871, 6·18 per cent. of the whole population ; and in 1881, in the presence of a much increased number of natives of Scotland, they were still 5·85. They are mostly concentrated in the large towns and mining villages : in Glasgow they amount to 13·07, or rather more than an eighth ; and in 1871 they were 14·32 per cent.; and in Greenock 16·58. The number of persons of Irish descent is, of course, altogether very much greater. It must be remembered, however, that the Irish in Scotland are mostly immigrants from Ulster, and that many of them are more or less Scottish by blood and origin. Moreover, the connecting link furnished by the Gaelic Highlanders helps to facilitate their admixture with the general mass.

In England also, since the thirteenth century, ethnological changes have not been great. The Celtic languages, it is true, have receded greatly. At the Conquest all Monmouthshire doubtless spoke Welsh ; and so did most, if not all, of Archenfield. The boundary then was the Wye ; now it is falling back even from the Usk. And the greater part of Powysland, from Upper Wye to Upper Severn, is now English in tongue. It is probable, however, that these changes have taken place rather by way of contact than by colonisation.

Certainly the most important immigrations into Britain since then have been those from France and the Low Countries. Most of these have been brought about by religious persecutions at home; but even before the Reformation, Flemings and Frisians had settled about Halifax. Subsequent arrivals were partly from Flanders, partly from the Walloon provinces, partly from Normandy and from Languedoc. At Kendal the colony was Walloon, and Walloons were numerous at Norwich and Canterbury. At Cranbrook, in Sussex, most of the names are said still to be Flemish. The Huguenots, from the south of France, were an almost new element, important by their character and their knowledge of the arts rather than by their numbers.

Somewhat later a body of Germans, who from their previous location were probably of a mixed, rather broad-headed type, were driven hither from the Palatinate by the cruel ravages of Louis XIV. Considerable numbers of them settled in villages in Munster, chiefly in the county Limerick.

During the last two centuries there has been little foreign immigration; what has taken place has been chiefly that of Germans and German Jews, who have settled in a few of the largest towns. The former melt down pretty easily among the English, and in the next generation are hardly recognisable, except by the inquisitive ethnologist. Their number is greater than is generally supposed. The Germans by birth amounted to 35,000 in 1871. Ravenstein * states that there were 5,060 foreigners resident in London in 1580, and that the percentage in that city was actually greater then than it is now.

The migration of both Scotchmen and Irishmen into England is, however, far more important. The Scotch began to drift southwards very early. A good many persons surnamed " Scot " are mentioned in the *Hundred Rolls*, A.D. 1271; and so many lords had held estates in both countries before or up to that time that there need be no surprise at this. Probably there was little more migration of this sort till the accession of James I.; but ever since then it has gone on at a rapid and generally increasing rate. In 1871, 213,000 natives of Scotland were living in England and Wales, while there were 70,000 natives of England in Scotland. Judging from the period of the year at which the census is taken, these must be for the most part residents. There is no county or considerable town in England without an appreciable proportion of Scottish residents, nor in Scotland without the same of English ones. Still, the proportions are far larger near the border than elsewhere, and in two or three of the border counties would at first sight seem to indicate an important process of race-change; but, in truth, the Scottish and the English borderers are, ethnically, very much alike, and they constitute the majority of the migrants.† It is difficult to form any idea

* *Birthplacee of the People*, &c. I have borrowed most of my statistics of this kind from this little storehouse of facts.

† Scotch element in Carlisle, 9½ per cent.; in Newcastle, 7; in rural Northumberland, 5½. English element in Berwickshire, 5½ per cent.

of the proportion of Scottish blood in England. In the upper classes it is very large: thus, whereas the natives of Scotland form but 0·56 per cent. of the population of Bristol (Ravenstein), persons with Scotch surnames form about 4 per cent. of the upper and 2 per cent. of the lower classes. In Yorkshire the Scotch are but ·45 per cent.; but in the list of subscribers to a Yorkshire book of local interest I found 4·4 per cent. of Scottish names. In London these percentages would be much larger. I find 12 per cent. of Scottish surnames in a large London club, but only 1 per cent. of purely Irish, and 5 per cent. of Welsh ones.

The Welsh migration into England is very large, and has been so for centuries. Mr. Ravenstein's little book does not help us with regard to it: Wales is treated in the census as a part of England. By means of lists of surnames we may, however, form some idea of the proportion of Welsh blood in England, always remembering, however, that males have usually been more apt to migrate than females, and that the former only transmit their surnames.

The Welsh, like the Scotch immigration, follows the usual law, and spends itself mostly near the frontier. A considerable portion of Herefordshire, including most of Archenfield* (the country south and west of the Wye), was Welsh at the time of *Domesday*.† Whether any part of it remained so up to the time of the general fixation of surnames may admit of doubt. Be that as it may, the proportion of Welsh names in the districts in question (unless the labouring class differs from those which find their way into the *Directory*) equals or exceeds the half. That all eastern Herefordshire was entirely Anglicised seems to be proven by the fact that Welsh surnames are not more numerous in its more hilly and remote than in its richer and more accessible parishes. I presume, therefore, that all the Joneses, Griffithses, Pughs, &c., there, are Welsh immigrants or their descendants; and it is curious that they amount to over 20 per cent., besides 7 or 8 per cent. more of the doubtful Welsh type (Edwards, Richards, &c.) We have here the usual phenomenon of an afflux of the native race towards the capital and other great centres of industry, accompanied or followed by an influx of the poorer or hardier race of the neighbouring mountains. Taking Herefordshire altogether, the farmers with clearly Welsh names are one-third; and so are the artisans and small shopkeepers; but the upper class, with like names, are not one-sixth. These proportions gradually decrease as one passes into Gloucestershire and North Somerset; but even in the Cotswold region there are still 7 per cent. of Welsh names in the local *Directory*.

Shropshire has been reoccupied by the Welshmen in a similar manner. Of 80 natives of Salop (mostly labourers, recruits, lunatics, and criminals), 15 had names undoubtedly of Welsh origin, and 9 names

* A Celtic name, though very English in appearance.
† *The Celtic Substratum of England*, by Thomas Kerslake.

of the doubtful class, or 19 and 11 per cent. In Cheshire, the proportions seem to be about 4 and 6 per cent.; in Worcestershire, somewhat
strangely, they rise to 12 and 7; while in the Eastern and Northern counties names of these classes are almost confined to the towns, and neither
class often exceeds, even if it equals, 2 per cent.

The Irish-born element in England, though not half so strong,
relatively, as in Scotland, amounted in 1871 to 2½ per cent. of the whole
population. Its distribution less agrees with the ordinary laws of
migration than does that of the Scotch or of the Welsh. The Irish crowd
into the towns, it is true, like other immigrants, but by no means always
into the nearest or most western ones. Lancashire, Cheshire, Surrey,
Cumberland, and Durham are the most Irish counties;* Liverpool (15·5
per cent. in 1171), Middlesboro', Manchester, Merthyr, Newcastle,
Bradford, the most Irish of the large towns.

I have already spoken of the difficulty of forming an idea of the
number of English-born persons of Irish blood. The likeliest criterion
would be furnished by the number of Irish-named persons in a list of
surnames, less the number of Irish-born in the same; but to the result
should be added at least a half more, or perhaps nearly two-thirds, for
the people with English or Anglo-Norman names, whose families have
become nationally Irish by centuries of settlement and mixture of blood.
Of 1,000 lunatics in English county and city asylums, not of Irish birth,
I find 27 with surnames of Irish form. This would imply something
over 4 per cent. of Irish blood in the English population, besides nearly
2½ per cent. of persons of Irish birth : altogether about 6½ per cent., or
something over one million and a half; and if Scotland were included,
perhaps two millions.

In opposition to the current opinion, it would seem that the Welsh
rise most in commerce, the Scotch coming after them, and the Irish
nowhere. The people of Welsh descent and name hold their own fairly
in science; the Scotch do more, the Irish less. But when one looks to
the attainment of military or political distinction, the case is altered.
Here the Scotchmen, and especially the Highlanders, bear away the
palm; the Irish retrieve their position, and the Welsh are little heard of.

* Ravenstein, *ib.*

CHAPTER XIII.

Preface to the Tables and Maps.
Considerations on Methods of Computation, and of Division of Types.

IN the hope of more firmly settling the subject of eye- and hair-colour,
I have put together another set of statistics, which may serve to
control or corroborate those founded on my own personal observations. This second set is based upon about 13,800 entries in the *Hue
and Cry*, relating to deserters from the army, and, to a much smaller
extent, deserters from the navy and absentees from militia drill. I have
elsewhere explained the imperfections in statistics of this sort, which
depend on the personal equation of the observer. These imperfections
necessarily detract from the value of the results of the enquiry into
eye-and-hair colour by the Anthropometric Committee* of the British
Association, which was published in 1883, as a part of the very able and
elaborate report drawn up for that Committee by Sir Rawson Rawson
and Mr. C. Roberts. Nevertheless, these results are the most valuable
hitherto published in relation to the British Isles. In my own opinion,
however, their worth was somewhat lessened by the manner in which
they were grouped and displayed. This was done somewhat, though
not exactly, after the methods of Virchow and Kollmann. I think it has
been shown already that in the case of Switzerland, methods of this
kind (the separation of certain categories to represent the blond and the
brunet types distinctively) do not develop ethnological fact nearly so
well as the exhibition of the index of nigrescence. I hope to demonstrate the same thing with respect to the British Isles.

The military series, with which we are now dealing, is somewhat
larger than that of the Committee; and the medical officers of the
recruiting department are usually good and careful observers, having
much practice in this way, seeing people from different parts of the
country, and not only from limited districts, and paying attention to the
colours with a view to the subsequent identification of the men. The

---

* As originally chairman, and always a member, though an inactive one, of that
body, I am somewhat reluctant to depreciate any part of its work, which, however, is so
extensive and excellent that it may bear to be attacked in a single department.

division of hair-colours which they adopt, into red, fair, brown, dark, and black, is the same as my own, and as that of most of the Committee's contributors. I half regret having made use of the militia reports, as their medical officers have usually less experience in the nomenclature of colour. I was led to do so by the great deficiency of items from the Scottish Highlands and from some parts of Wales, where few of the natives enlist in the army. Care was taken, however, to use only those militia reports whose approximate accuracy was partially guaranteed by the evident employment of the same division of colours as that in use in the army. In order to counteract any evil that might result from eccentricity in the chromatic scale of a single observer, I chose several annual series, not successive, spread over the last 15 years. On the whole, the resulting schedules may be looked upon as valuable and comparatively trustworthy. The material is fairly uniform and comparable, consisting of young men of 21 years of age, with but a very small sprinkling of the upper and migratory class.

Maps have been constructed, based on these military schedules, to exhibit not only those points which I consider most valuable, viz., the index of nigrescence and the proportion of dark eyes, but also those which Sir R. Rawson and Mr. Roberts have preferred, viz., the amount of the mixed blond* and of the mixed brown type,† together with another, which represents compendiously, and more nearly, though nowise exactly, the plans of Virchow, Vanderkindere, and Kollmann.‡

A comparison of the results, as indicated in the summaries and maps, of the three British enquiries, will show where and how much they differ, and where the concurrence of two or three of them establishes a probability of their correctness.

1. Schedules of the Committee.	2. Military Schedules.	3. Personal Observation.
No very clear relation to ethnological history as generally understood.	Accord with ethnological history in exhibiting larger proportion of light-coloured hair in the regions most subject to invasion and colonisation, and of dark-coloured in the far west.	Resemble No. 2 in these respects.

* Blue or gray eyes, with fair or brown (chestnut) hair.

† Brown, hazel, or "black" eyes, with brown (chestnut), dark brown, or black hair.

‡ Virchow's rein-blond type consists in *blue* (not gray) eyes, with fair or red hair; red is even included under blond in the German schedules. Kollmann excludes the red, which in the Swiss schedules has its separate column. Vanderkindere, though he too gives a column to the red, includes both it and gray eyes under his blond type. The results of the three enquiries are, therefore, not comparable *inter se*, nor with those of our Committee. As the German, Swiss, and Belgian enquiries dealt with children, many of their blonds would become chestnut- or brown-haired in adult life. Their blond type, therefore, approaches that of Roberts and Rawson, except, in two cases, as to the gray eyes. Their brown type is much less extensive than his, answering nearly to my pure-brown or pure-dark, *i.e.*, hazel or brown eyes, with dark brown or black hair.

Order of the Four Countries from Light to Dark.		*Order of the Four Countries from Light to Dark.*		*Order of the Four Countries from Light to Dark.*	
EYES.	HAIR.	EYES.	HAIR.	EYES.	HAIR.
Scotland	Ireland	Scotland	Scotland	Scotland ?	Scotland
Ireland	Scotland	Ireland	England	Ireland ?	England
Wales	Wales	England	Wales	England	Ireland
England	England	Wales	Ireland	Wales	Wales

Connaught has less of dark eyes and dark hair than any other province of Ireland, or than any part of Great Britain, except (partially) the Scottish Islands.

In England, there is most of the mixed brown type in Cambridgeshire, Bedfordshire, Leicester, Worcester, Carnarvon, &c., Kent, Hants, Salop.

Connaught ranks second to Ulster as to lightness of eyes; and has more dark hair than any province of Ireland or of Great Britain, except Argyle.

In England, most of the mixed brown type in Dorset, Wilts,* Cornwall, Gloucestershire, the Welsh Marches, South Wales, Bucks, and Herts.

Connaught has a medium position as regards eyes, and has apparently more dark hair than any other province.

No comparison can be fairly made, my division of eyes being threefold; but almost all those counties named under 1 and 2 appear to have an excess of dark eyes.

It is difficult to follow up this comparison, or contrast, with exactness; but I will proceed to more details. Lincolnshire is generally supposed to be a particularly Teutonic county. Whether Lindum Colonia was destroyed by the Angles we do not know: perhaps, as it kept its name and situation, it fared better than most Romano-British towns, and retained more of its ancient population; but certainly Lincolnshire received a large colony of Angles, who divided it into a great number of hundreds, and who were subsequently overlaid by a heavy stratum of Danes, as the place-names testify.† The inhabitants have‡ the tall and bulky frame which is generally believed to be Anglo-Danish, though the nature of the soil and other conditions may have to do with it.

Yet the Committee's maps indicate a paucity of the blond and a superabundance of the brunet type in Lincolnshire.

On the other hand, according to the military schedule, Lincolnshire not only stands third in all England on the blond scale, as tested by my index of nigrescence, but when tested by the method of the Committee yields 56 of the mixed blond, and only 30·5 of the mixed brown type, 48·5 and 33·1 being the averages of England. My own observations, taken in six different parts of the country, and extending to nearly 2,400 individuals, corroborate the military schedule, indicating a moderate proportion of dark eyes and a great deal of light or lightish brown hair, with a low index of nigrescence.

* The discrepancy here is due to a curious local peculiarity. The "Wiltshire eye" is known to recruiting officers. It is a muddy hazel-gray, very prevalent in the county, and common also in the West Riding of Yorkshire. The recruiting surgeons seem to have classified it as hazel; but some would call it gray. I make it neutral.

† Streatfield, *Danes in Lincolnshire.*

‡ The Committee's Report, and my own *Stature and Bulk.*

Take again Cumberland and Westmoreland, to which I have added the district of Furness, or Lancashire north of Morecambe Bay. According to the Committee's schedule, these counties differ little from the averages of England; they have rather fewer dark eyes, but rather more dark hair, the latter being somewhat frequently combined with light eyes.

According to the military returns, they have more of the pure blond type than any other counties in England; they have also but little of the brown type, and stand second in England, and either third or fourth in Britain, when tested by the index of nigrescence. My own observations here, again, agree with the military statistics, placing Cumberland and Westmoreland about the head of the blond scale. Both here and in Lincolnshire the error in the Committee's reports was probably as much local as personal: the observers pitched their standard of darkness low, from being accustomed to live in the midst of a blond population.

Nearly the same may be said of the peninsula of Fife, which looks somewhat dark in the Committee's map, but is placed at the top of the blond scale for the three kingdoms by the military surgeons. The Fife men, who, owing to their geographical position, are less mixed in blood than most communities, are generally reputed to be a fair race. My own observations have been limited to the coast, but would lead me to place them above the mean of Scotland in this respect.

Gloucestershire, on the other hand, appears conspicuous by its whiteness in two out of three of the Committee's maps; while in the military ones it is assimilated, with more semblance of probability, to the neighbouring Welsh Marches. It is a very heterogeneous county with respect to race: the Cotswolds are very much West-Saxon; the Forest is Silurian, the Vale lies between the two; and the physical type follows the race. Assuredly, however, the medium character of the county is nearer to that of the military schedule. In this case the error probably arises out of the system of classification, out of the dividing of the brown or chestnut-haired between the blond and brunet types, in accordance with the colour of the eyes.

This kind of examination could be followed through many other counties, with the result of showing very frequent discrepancies between the Committee's and the military schedules, and a much more general agreement between the latter and my own, which agreement the reader will, I hope, interpret in favour of the majority.

Before quitting this subject, one more example may be presented in which the method of the Committee, without correction, would certainly lead to misconception.

Among my own returns is one from Boston town. The civic population there, though not quite so strikingly fair as the surrounding peasantry, are much more so than in most parts of the islands: they have all the characteristics of almost pure Saxo-Frisians, and are hardly distinguishable from the frequenters of Antwerp market. Their index of nigrescence is the lowest I have met with in any considerable town in Britain. Yet on only one of Mr. Roberts's maps, the supplementary one indicating the proportion of persons who combine light eyes with dark hair, would they appear as a white spot; and on the map of the brown or dark type they would be allotted the medium depth of shade. This would depend on the remarkably large proportion of hazel, generally light hazel, eyes coupled with brown (chestnut) hair. The possessors of this combination, which is frequent in Holland, Westphalia, &c., are usually very fair of skin, are in fact in all other respects of blond aspect and constitution. The Continental anthropologists have avoided this source of misconception. Working with school-children as their material, they exclude from their brown type those with dark eyes and light hair, which latter in after-life darkens into what we English call brown. The most simple plan, however, and decidedly the most fruitful, of utilising the colour of the iris, is to represent it separately, either by taking the percentage of dark eyes, where only two tints have been recognised, or by subtracting the dark from the light, or *vice versâ*, and neglecting the neutral, where a neutral column has been introduced, as in my own schedules, or thirdly, and I think best, by stating the proportion of dark eyes to light, the latter being reckoned at 100.

Probably the most valuable feature in the military schedules is that part of them which relates to the Irish colony in England. It consists entirely of recruits bearing Irish surnames, among which I have included those of Anglo-Norman or English origin which have long been nearly or quite peculiar to Ireland, such as Fitzgerald, Bodkin, and Burke, as well as the purely Celtic ones, such as Dempsey and Macarthy, and the Dano-Irish ones, such as Cottar and MacAuliffe. When in doubt, I have sometimes been decided by the Irish character of the christian name.

No doubt Irishmen desirous of entering the most purely English or Scotch regiments sometimes falsely allege that they are natives of Great Britain; but in the great majority of instances the birthplace is given correctly. And in any case, the components of this special table were enlisted in Great Britain, and examined by the same officers who described the English and Scottish recruits. Thus what may be called the difficulty of the local and personal equation is got rid of: the same officer describes the Londoner or Yorkshireman and the Irishman, and assigns to them their distinctive colours in accordance with the same standard. It may be objected that an Irish surname is insufficient evidence of Irish blood and probable Irish physical type; that an O'Hanlon may be the son of an English mother. But this is very rarely the case: Englishwomen rarely marry Irish, or at least Catholic Irish, men; nor would the question be much affected if it were so.

It will be observed that the Irish by descent are, in colour, "ipsis Hibernis Hiberniores;" that with the same proportion of light eyes they have more dark hair than the natives of Ireland themselves. This may be due partly to local perversion, which leads the observer, stationed in Ireland among a generally dark-haired people, to raise his standard of darkness, and overestimate the blond element; and partly to the fact that persons with Irish surnames are really on the whole the purest Irishmen, and when taken *en masse* present the national characteristics of colour and feature with the greatest intensity. The figures seem sufficient to prove that the Irish are, as a whole, considerably lighter in eye, but yet more considerably darker in hair, than the English as a whole.

The Irish-named natives of Scotland are not so dark-haired as those of England; but in index they approach the men of Ulster, whence the ancestry of most of them was derived. The other variations which they show from the Irish standard may be ascribed to admixture of blood; for the near kindred and common language of the Gaelic Highlanders to some extent bridges over the chasm, and I believe intermarriages between the races are not so rare as in England. Moreover, the Ulstermen are already strongly tinctured with Scottish blood. The number, however (100), is somewhat too scanty for generalisation.

The next table submitted is one referring almost exclusively to the West of England and South Wales. It should combine several advantages; for it is the work of a single observer; the observations were leisurely made; and the birthplaces of its constituent members were all ascertained. Its material was gathered in the course of several years' practice at the Bristol Infirmary and Clifton Dispensary, and it is already in print.* Hospital patients probably furnish a sufficiently good sample of the population for this particular purpose, but by no means a perfect one. Dr. Baxter † has shown that among the light-complexioned recruits of the American army, during the great war, disease of various kinds was more rife than among the dark-complexioned; but whatever may be the explanation of the fact (and more than one possible explanation occurs to me), ‡ I doubt whether the rule holds good in Great Britain. Both in Scotland and in England I have found that the proportion of persons with dark eyes and hair who apply for medical aid is larger than that of such persons among the general population. This may

---

"Testimony of Local Phænomena to Permanence of Anthropological Type," *Anthrop. Memoirs.*

† *Statistics, Medical and Anthropological, of the Provost-Marshal-General's Bureau,* vol. I.

‡ German immigrants appear to suffer much more, in the United States, from several diseases, than do the natives. They are not, however, set down by Dr. Baxter as much lighter in complexion than the natives. It may be that the American climate is more prejudicial to the blond than to the brown European, and that the slight darkening which seems to have occurred in the American race may be due chiefly to a process of natural selection. Or it may be that the moral difference, the difference of temperament, was active in America as it seems to be here, and sent more blond men, sound or unsound, to the bureaux. With us the typical soldier, and especially the typical dragoon, is blond and red-bearded.

depend on moral rather than on physical differences; on the greater courage and cheerfulness, for example, of the sanguine temperament, which generally, though by no means always, coincides with the light complexion. Persons of the melancholic temperament, I am disposed to think, resort to hospitals more frequently than the sanguine, under like circumstances. Accordingly this third, or West of England table, yields slightly higher indices of nigrescence and of iris-darkness, for several districts, than will be found in the first or great table, the material for which was collected in streets and market-places.

Next follows a series of numerical tables, exhibiting the colour of the hair and eyes in France, in Holland and Belgium, in Germany, in Austria, in Italy, in some parts of Asia Minor, and among the Jews scattered over several countries. Most of these details have been published, at one time or another, in the *Transactions* of the British Association, of the Ethnological and Anthropological Societies, or of the Anthropological Institute, or of the Societé d'Anthropologie, or in the *Revue d'Anthropologie*. It seems, however, desirable to collect and republish them, with additions, so as to bring together in a form fit for comparison as much as possible of my work in this department of anthropology.

For the same reason have been added certain small tables on special subjects, such as the colour of eyes in connexion with Virchow's method of estimating race-elements, the effects of conjugal selection, supposed alterations of colour type, and the relation of complexion to disease.

Several other tables contain the results of visits to the (alas! very few) remaining ossuaries of Great Britain; the measurements of a collection of skulls from Davos in Switzerland, to illustrate the eleventh chapter; comparative measurements of the living head, in several countries of Europe and several parts of the British Isles; and particularly a large table of measurements of pure-blooded, or reputed pure-blooded, Scottish Highlanders.

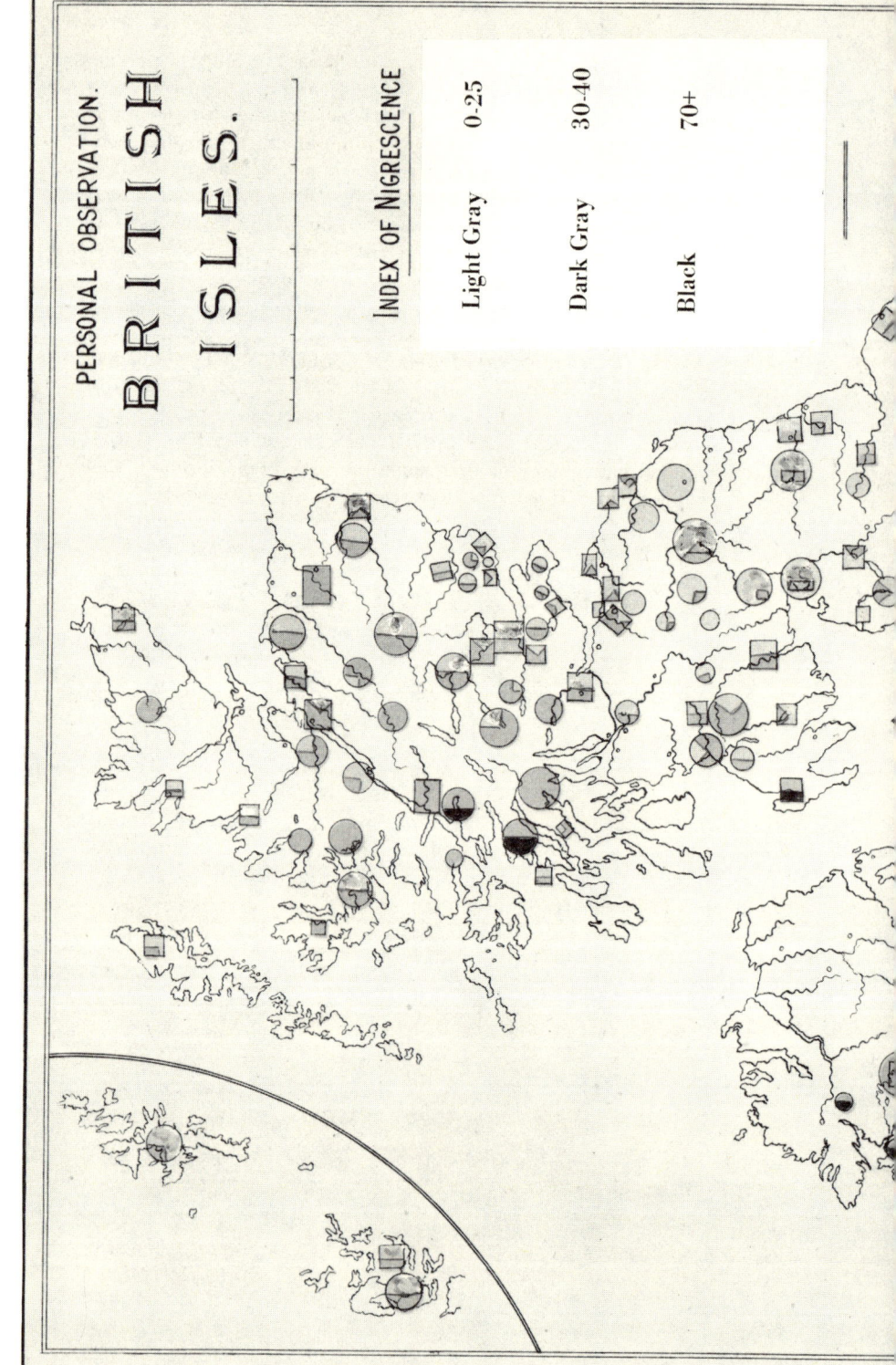

PERSONAL OBSERVATION.

BRITISH ISLES.

INDEX OF NIGRESCENCE

Light Gray	0-25
Dark Gray	30-40
Black	70+

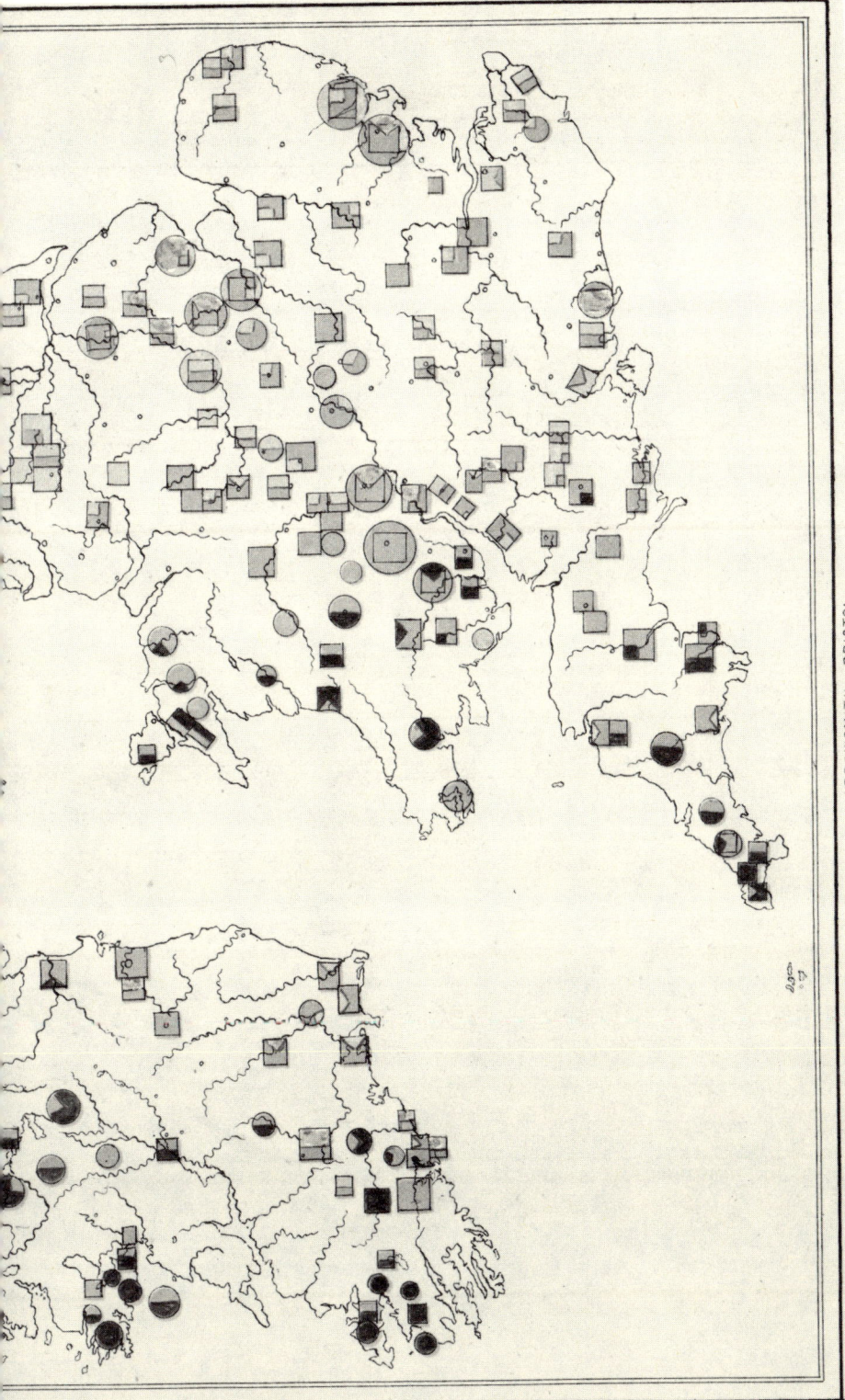

COLOUR OF HAIR AND EYES IN SEVERAL DISTRICTS OF THE UNITED KINGDOM, FROM PERSONAL OBSERVATION.

SCOTLAND.

Colour of Hair	Number	Sex	EYES LIGHT.					Eyes Light.	EYES INTERMEDIATE OR NEUTER.					Eyes Neuter.	EYES DARK.					Eyes Dark.	Indices.	
			Red	Fair	Brown	Dark	Nig.		Red	Fair	Brown	Dark	Nig.		Red	Fair	Brown	Dark	Nig.		Gross.	Per Cent.
THE ISLES.																						
1. Shetland (Lerwick, Scallo-way, Sound, &c.) per cent.	285	both	3·5	21	35·4	11·9	{	71·8	1	1	2·1	3·8	{	7·9	1	·6	3·8	14·3	?	19·7	...	1·9?
2. Kirkwall (Orkney) per cent.	400	both	3	16·2	37·5	13·5	...	69·2	·5	1·7	5·2	6·7	...	14·3	·5	·5	3·2	11·2	?	16·5	...	9 ?
3. Stromness, Stennis, Hoy, Haray, &c., per cent.	168	both	4·7	13·1	41·7	15·5	...	75·3	...	1·2	4·1	6·5	...	11·8	·6	·6	4·7	5·9	?	12·8	...	7·7?
4. Orkney, total, per cent.	568	both	3·5	15·3	38·7	14·1	{	71	·4	1·6	4·9	6·7	{	13·6	·5	·5	3·7	9·7	?	15·4	...	8·7?
5. Stornoway (Lewis), per cent.	125	=	6·8	22·4	21·6	10·8	·8	62·4	...	1·6	5·6	7·2	{	14·2	...	...	9·2	7·6	6·4	23·2	...	9·2
6. Strath, Sconser, Broadford (Skye), per cent.	145	both	4·1	16·5	38·6	13·1	2·1	75·6	·7	...	1·4	5·5	·7	7·7	·7	...	4·8	9	2·7	16·7	...	16·6
7. Portree (Skye), per cent.	70	⅔m.	3·5	21·4	22·8	18·5	·7	67	...	...	1·4	7·1	4·3	13	1·4	...	2·1	11·4	5	20	...	30·7
8. Skye, total, per cent.	215	both	4	18·1	33·5	14·9	1·6	72	·5	...	1·4	6	1·8	9·7	·9	...	4	9·7	3·5	18·1	...	21
9. Seal and Luing (Argyle), per cent.	68	¾m.	1·5	20	31·5	11	2·2	66·2	...	1·5	5·9	7·3	1·5	16·2	1·5	...	4·4	8·7	3	17·6	...	15·9
CAITHNESS.																						
10. Wick, town, per cent.	300	both	5	14	30·6	12	...	61·9	1·3	1·6	7·6	5·3	...	15·8	·6	1	6·6	14·3	...	22·3	...	8·1+
NORTHERN HIGHLANDS.																						
11. Sutherland, N.E., per cent.	35	both	5·7	12·8	34·2	10	...	62·7	...	...	...	...	...	...	...	2·9	2·9	21·4	10	37·2	...	30
12. Ullapool (Ross), per cent.	50	⅔m.	10	16	21	22	1	70	2	...	8	6	2	18	...	...	4	6	2	12	...	16

	I	2	3	4	5	6	7	8	9	10	11	12	13	14	15	16	17	18	19	20	21	22
13. Glenshiel, Kintail, Lochalsh, Strome, per cent.	120	bͻth	2·5	15·4	30·4	23	3	74·3	...	...	2·5	4·1	3·3	10	·8	·8	1·6	10	2·5	15·7	...	35·2
14. Dingwall, Garve, per cent....	50	m	4	18	29	20	3	74	...	...	2	14	2	18	...	2	2	2	2	8	...	26
15. Beauly, Aird, Strathglass, Muir of Ord, market, p. ct.)	170	most m	3·5	14·3	35·9	18·8	1·7	74·2	1·2	1·2	6·4	3·5	2·9	15·2	...	...	1·2	8·8	·6	10·6	...	20·3
16. Inverness, town, per cent. ...	200	bͻth	7	9·7	26	19·7	...	62·5	2·5	·5	2·5	6·5	1	13	·2	·2	6·5	12	5·5	24·5	...	31
17. Nairn, town, per cent....	80	both	2·5	15	42·5	15	...	75	...	1·2	5	5	1·2	12·5	1·2	1·2	1·2	8·7	...	12·5	...	10
18. Inverness, district, total, p.ct.	500	both	5	12·9	32·1	18·7	·9	69·6	1·4	·8	4·2	6	1·8	14·2	·3	·5	3·4	9·4	2·6	16·2	...	23·8
18B. Inverness, town, per cent. ...	50	=	11	9	29	16	1	66	...	...	3	10	3	16	...	...	...	17	3	20	...	37
19. Keith and Huntley, per cent.	200	both	4·5	12·5	31·5	18	1·5	68	·5	...	3	6·5	·5	10·5	·5	·5	4·5	11·5	4·5	21·5	...	30·5
EASTERN LOWLANDS.																						
20. Brodie, flower-show, mid-class	125	⁴⁄₉	5·2	13·2	25·2	11·6	·8	56	2·4	·8	4·8	3·6	·4	12	1·6	1·6	8	17·6	3·2	32	...	16·8
20B. Forres, Elgin, Fochabers (Moray), per cent. ...	210	both	9	11·9	34·2	12·9	·9	68·9	...	1·4	5·7	5·2	...	12·6	...	·5	6·2	10	1·9	18·6	...	9·9
21. Valleys of the Don and Ury, per cent. ...	200	both	6·6	16·3	35·4	15·4	1·1	75	...	·6	4·6	3·7	1·1	10	·3	·3	5·1	7·4	1·7	15	...	10·2
Valley of Lower Dee, per ct.	150																					
22. Aberdeen, city, per cent. ...	600	both	5·8	15	34·2	11·3	·8	77·1	·8	1·5	5·7	2·7	·3	11	·5	·5	7·3	10·3	3·2	21·8	...	8·8
23. Brechin, city ...	100	both	4	15	38	4	1	62	...	...	7	6	...	13	...	...	9	10	6	25	...	15
24. A'rbroth', town, per cent. ...	167	both	6·6	16·8	33·5	9	·6	66·5	1·2	1·2	4·8	4·8	·6	12·6	...	·3	6	11·7	3	21	...	6·9
25. Arbirlot, parish ...	100	both	3	13	37	17	2	72	...	...	3·5	8	1·5	13	1	...	5	9	1	15	...	27
26. Broughty, actual number ...	98	both	5	16·5	31	9·5	1	63	·5	·5	5	7	...	13	...	1·5	7	11·5	1	22	8	8·2
27. Broughty and Easthaven, fishers, actual numbers	26	both	1	6	11	2	...	20	1	...	1	1	...	3	...	...	1	2	...	3	3	10·6
28. Angus, other parts, per cent.	150	both	6	14	39·3	8·6	2	69·9	...	1·3	2	5·3	2	10·6	2	...	4	8·6	4·6	19·2	25	16·6
29. Angus, actual total ...	641	both	33	99·5	232	60·5	8	433	3·5	4·5	27·5	38	5·5	79	4	2	38	65	20	129	83·5	...

Colour of Hair and Eyes in several Districts of the United Kingdom, from Personal Observation.—SCOTLAND, continued.

Colour of Hair	Number	Sex	EYES LIGHT						EYES INTERMEDIATE OR NEUTER						EYES DARK						Indices	
			Red	Fair	Brown	Dark	Nig.	Eyes Light.	Red	Fair	Brown	Dark	Nig.	Eyes Neuter.	Red	Fair	Brown	Dark	Nig.	Eyes Dark.	Gross	Per Cent.
Angus, whole, per cent.	...	...	5·15	15·5	36·2	9·4	1·2	67·5	·5	·7	4·3	5·9	·8	12·2	·6	·3	5·9	10·1	3·1	20	...	13·1
FIFE.																						
30. Kirkcaldy, town, per cent.	300	both	6·3	17	31·7	13	1	69	1	1·3	5	3·7	·7	11·7	1·7	·7	4	11	2	19·3	...	8·1
31. Pathhead, Dysart, Wemyss, Methill, Leven, Largo, Colinsburgh, &c., vill., p.c.	300	both	7	16	31	11·3		65·3	·3	2·3	5·7	3·7	·3	12·3	1·3	1·3	4·7	11·7	3·7	22·6	...	6·5
32. Eastern Fife (Anster, Pittenween, Elie, St. Monance), per cent.	200	both	3	16·5	34	9	1	63·5	·5	1·5	5·5	5	·5	13	1·5	1	7	11	3	23·5	...	10
33. Coast of Fife, total,* p. cent.	800	both	5·75	16·5	32	11·4	·6	66·2	·6	1·75	5·4	3·9	·5	12·1	1·5	1	5	11·2	2·9	21·6	...	7·6
MID-LOWLANDS.																						
34. Stirling, town, per cent.	600	both	3·8	17·5	32·5	11·8	1·7	67·3	·7	1·3	5·3	4·3	·2	11·8	·8	·5	6·7	10·3	2·4	20·7	...	10·3
35. Perth, city, per cent.	665	both	7	15·7	25·9	14·8	·7	64·1	·9	1·3	5	8·5	1·2	16·9	·7	·7	4·1	10·4	2·9	18·8	...	23·3
36. Perth, upper class	30	both	3·5	5	6	2·5		17		1	1	1		3	1		3	6		10	...	0
37. Auchterarder & Dunning, p.c	180	107⁄73	5	18	23·3	15·5		61·8		·5	6·3	7	·5	14·3	·8	·3	3·8	13·6	5·3	23·8	...	23·1
38. Forteviot, agricultl. show, mostly farmers	200	m	14·5	32·5	45	26		118	2	4	6·5	17·5	4	34	1	1·5	13·5	25	7	48	34	17
	100	fem	1·5	13	17·5	7		39	1	3	8·5	8·5	1	22	4	3	12·5	15·5	4	39	...	15·5
Total, per cent.	300	...	5·3	15·2	20·8	11		52·3	2	2·3	5	8·6	1·6	18·6	1·6	1·5	8·6	13·5	3·6	29	...	16
HIGHLANDS.																						
STRATHEARN, &c.																						
39. Comrie, athletic sports	100	49⁄51	9·5	12·5	19·5	17·5		59	2	1	5	9·5	2·5	20	1		4	12·5	3·5	21	...	25·5

* Except Buckhaven.

	I	2	3	4	5	6	7	8	9	10	11	12	13	14	15	16	17	18	19	20		
40. Comrie and St. Fillan's	50	m	3	9	13·5	7·5	1	34	1	...	1	5	2	9	...	...	2	2·5	2·5	7	13	...
" "	50	fem	1·5	5	16	8·5	1	32	1	·5	2	5	·5	9	...	...	1	5·5	2·5	9	19	...
Total	100	...	4·5	14	29·3	16	...	66	2	·5	3	10	2·5	18	...	...	3	8	5	16	...	32
40B. Doune	50	both	2	6	17	9	...	...	...	...	1	3	1	...	...	...	3	7	1	...	...	30
40C. Callander	100	both	2	14	33	24·5	3·5	77	...	...	2	3·5	·5	6	...	1	1	10·5	4·5	17	...	38·5
Callander and Doune, p.cent.	150	both	2·7	13·3	33·3	22·3	2·3	74	...	...	2	4·3	1	7·3	...	·6	2·6	11·6	3·6	18·6	...	35·4
BREADALBANE.																						
41. Killin	57	both	5·5	10·5	8·5	13	1·5	39	...	...	...	5	...	5	1	...	1·5	9	2·5	13	19	...
42. Balquhidder	17	both	...	...	7	4	...	11	...	...	...	1	·5	2	...	...	1	1	1	4	7	...
43. Aberfeldy	43	both	5·5	6·5	6·5	4·5	1	24	...	...	...	5·5	·5	6	...	...	3	7	3	13	14	...
44. Glenlyon	56	both	...	15·5	13·5	8	1	38	...	...	4·5	3	1·5	9	1·5	...	...	4·5	2·5	9	8	...
45. Rannoch	6	both	...	...	·5	1	·5	2	...	...	...	...	...	1	...	...	...	2	1	3	7	...
46. Tyndrum	20	both	1	1	4·5	9	1·5	17	...	...	...	1	...	1	...	...	...	2	...	2	15	...
47. Breadalbane, total	99	m	5·5	14·5	25	20·5	3·5	69	...	...	3·5	10	·5	14	...	·5	3·5	9·5	3	16	34	...
	64	fem	2	11·5	12	11	1·5	38	...	...	2	4·5	1·5	8	2·5	·5	1·5	9	4·5	16	23	...
	36	both	4·5	7·5	3·5	8	·5	24	...	...	...	2	...	2	...	·5	·5	7	2·5	10	11	...
Total	199	...	12	33·5	40·5	39·5	5·5	131	...	...	5·5	16·5	2	24	2·5	·3	5·5	25·5	10	42	68	...
Per cent.	...	...	6	16·8	20·3	19·8	2·8	65·7	...	...	2·8	8·3	1	12·1	1·3	·3	2·8	12·8	5	22·2	...	34·1
ATHOL.																						
48. Blair, Pitlochry, Dunkeld, and Logierait, &c., espy.L.	110	m	8	21·5	29·5	18·5	1	78	1	...	2·5	8·5	1	13	·5	1·5	3	11·5	2·5	19	14	...
	50	fem	4	4	12·5	8·5	...	29	...	...	5	4	1	10	...	...	2·5	8·5	...	11	17	...
49. Dunkeld, alone	50	both	2	5	15	6	...	28	1	...	3	2	1	7	...	1	5	7	2	15	13	26

Colour of Hair and Eyes in several Districts of the United Kingdom, from Personal Observation.—SCOTLAND, continued.

Colour of Hair	Number	Sex	EYES LIGHT						EYES INTERMEDIATE OR NEUTER.						EYES DARK.						Indices	
			Red	Fair	Brown	Dark	Nig.	Eyes Light	Red	Fair	Brown	Dark	Nig.	Eyes Neuter	Red	Fair	Brown	Dark	Nig.	Eyes Dark	Gross	Per Cent.
50. Athol (exc. Dunkeld) ...	80	...	4	12	29	14	1	...	1	...	3	4	...	...	...	...	4	6	2	...	13	16·3
51. Athol, total ...	290	both	18	42·5	86	47	2·5	196	3	...	13·5	18·5	3	38	·5	2·5	13·5	33	6·5	56	56	...
Per cent....	...	...	6·2	14·6	29·4	16·2	·8	67·6	1	...	4·6	6·4	1	13·1	·2	·8	4·6	11·4	2·2	19·3	...	19·2
CENTRAL HIGHLANDS.																						
52. Braemar, Ballater, &c., p. ct.	170	both	10·6	15·3	34·7	11·8	4·1	76·5	·6	...	3·5	4·1	·6	8·8	...	...	3·5	10	1·2	14·7	...	11·2
53. Badenoch (Kingussie and Laggan), per cent. ...	50	49/10	7	13	30	12	2	64	3	...	3	9	4	16	2	...	...	13	5	20	17	34
54. Fort Augustus ...	63	both	5	8	16·5	12·5	2	44	...	...	2	5	2	9	1·5	·5	1	6·5	·5	10	18	28·5
55. Banavie and Canal ...	67	both	4	13	22	14	...	53	...	2	5	2	...	9	...	...	2	2	1	5	1	1·5
56. Glen Moriston and Lochness	70	both	3	14	27	8	2	54	1	...	2	2	...	5	...	1	3	7	...	11	2	2·8
57. Region of the Great Glen, total, per cent. ...	200	...	6	17·5	32·7	17·2	2	75·5	·5	1	4·5	4·5	1	11·5	·7	·7	3	7·7	·7	13	2	10·5
WEST HIGHLANDS.																						
58. Glenelg, Inverness-shire ...	19	both	1	1	10	3	...	15	...	...	1	...	...	0	...	...	1	2	1	4	5	...
59. Glen Nevis ...	33	both	2	6	7	9	1	25	...	...	1	1	1	3	...	...	2	1	2	5	11	33·3
60. Fort William, per cent.	400	both	3·6	12·6	29·4	20·7	3·4	69·7	·5	1	3·2	5·2	2·5	12·5	...	·2	3·6	9·4	4·5	17·7	...	38·2
61. Ardgour ...	70	...	1·5	14·5	15	13	1	45	1	...	4	10	...	16	...	...	6	8·5	1	8	18	...
Per cent. ...	...	...	2·1	20·7	21·4	18·5	1·4	64·3	1·4	...	5·7	14·3	1·4	22·8	...	...	1·4	8·5	1·4	11·4	...	25·7
62. Oonich ...	100	61/39	5	12	21	15·5	1·5	55	...	...	5	16	1	22	3	...	...	13	7	23	23	43·5

	1	2	3	4	5	6	7	8	9	10	11	12	13	14	15	16	17	18	19	20	21	22
63. Ballachulish, per cent.	220	bcth	5·2	13·4	24·7	17	2·7	63	1·3	...	3·4	10·7	2·7	18·1	...	...	2·5	10	6·1	18·6	...	40·8
64. Glencoe & Sth. Ballachulish	60	m	3·5	10·5	14	10	1	39	...	...	3	6	1	10	...	...	2	7·5	1·5	11	16·5	...
	64	fem	2·5	9	14	5·5	...	31	...	1	3·5	8·5	2	15	1	...	1	9·5	6·5	18	27	...
	40	mixed	4	7	9	6	...	26	...	...	2	4	1	7	1	...	1	3	3	7	10	40
Total	164	...	10	26·5	37	21·5	1	96	...	1	8·5	18·5	4	32	1	...	4	20	11	36	53·5	...
Per cent.	...	...	6·1	16·1	22·5	13·1	·6	58·5	...	·6	5·2	11·3	2·4	19·5	·6	...	2·4	12·2	6·7	21·9	...	32·6
65. Tyndrum, Glenorchy	60	both	2	7	22·5	16	4·5	52	...	...	...	2	...	2	...	...	...	6	...	6	24	...
Per cent.	...	...	3·3	11·6	37·5	26·6	7·5	86·6	...	...	...	3·3	...	3·3	1	...	...	10	...	10	...	40
66. Loch Katrine, &c.	30	most m	1	4	16	2	...	23	2·5	1	1	...	...	1	1	...	2	3	1	6	2	6·3
67. Arroquhar, Tarbet, &c.	112	both	6	10	31·5	23	3·5	74	...	...	3·5	11·5	1·5	19	...	...	...	15·5	3·5	19	48·5	...
Per cent.	...	...	5·3	8·9	28·1	20·5	3·1	66	2·2	...	3·1	10·3	1·3	17	...	...	...	13·8	3·1	17	...	43·1
68. Inverary, Glen Aray, Cladich	100	both	6	13	35	14	2	70	...	1	3	8	1	13	...	...	...	14	3	17	...	26
69. Dalmally, &c.	100	both	2	9	38	24	1	74	...	1	4·	3	...	8	...	...	3	10	5	18	...	37
70. Lorn, Sonachan	90	both	4·5	8	21	19·5	3	56	1	...	3·5	6·5	1	12	...	...	2·5	13	6·5	22	46·5	...
Per cent.	...	...	5	8·9	23·3	21·6	3·3	62·2	1·1	...	3·9	7·2	1·1	13·3	...	...	2·8	4·4	7·2	24·4	...	51·6
71. Strachur	21	both	...	...	8	2	...	10	...	...	1	3·5	·5	...	...	...	1	5	...	...	11·5	57
GALLOWAY, CARRICK, &c.																						
72. Ayr, market day, half country folk, per cent.	500	bcth	2·6	16	33·6	16	2·2	70·4	·6	·8	3·6	5·2	·6	10·8	...	·8	3	12·4	2·6	18·8	...	23·6
73. Maybole, Cumnock, Dalmellington, Patna, Kirkmichael, &c., per cent.	250	bcth	3·6	14·4	36·8	14	2	70·8	...	·4	4·8	4	...	9·2	·4	·8	4	12·4	2·4	20	19·6	...
74. Sanquhar, Kells, Dalry, Carsphairn	200	bcth	3	23	68	34	3	131	3	1	7	11	1	23	3	2	10	24	7	46	56	28

Colour of Hair and Eyes in several Districts of the United Kingdom, from Personal Observation.—SCOTLAND, continued.

Colour of Hair	Number	Sex	EYES LIGHT						EYES INTERMEDIATE OR NEUTER						EYES DARK						Indices	
			Red	Fair	Brown	Dark	Nig.	Eyes Light	Red	Fair	Brown	Dark	Nig.	Eyes Neuter	Red	Fair	Brown	Dark	Nig.	Eyes Dark	Gross	Per Cent
75. Castle Douglas, &c.	50	both	4	8	15	7	1	36	...	1	2	2	...	5	...	1	5	3	...	9	0	...
76. Upper Galloway, total	250	both	7	31	84	41	4	167	3	2	9	13	1	28	3	3	15	27	7	55	56	...
Per cent.	...		2·8	12·4	33·6	16·4	1·6	66·8	1·2	·8	3·6	5·2	·4	11·2	1·2	1·2	6	10·8	2·8	22	...	22·4
77. Stranraer	100	m	4·5	11·5	22	22	...	60	...	...	6	9	1	16	...	1	2	15	7	24	...	46
77.	50	fem	1	6·5	6·5	8	1	23	1	2	2·	7	1	13	1	1	2	8·5	1·5	14	18	...
Per cent.	150		3·7	12	19	20	·7	55·4	·7	1·3	5·3	10·7	1·3	19·2	·7	·7	2·7	15·6	5·7	25·3	...	42·6
78. Dumfries, per cent.	200	both	3	14	30·5	13	1	61·5	1	1	7·5	4·5	1	15	·7	·5	9	13	1	23·5	...	17
79. Moffat, vil., & neighbourhood	50	both	2	8	18	4	...	32	...	1	2	1	...	4	2	...	4	6	2	14	2	4
80. Leadhills & Wanlockhead, mining villages, highest in Scotland	50	both	3	9	19	8	...	...	...	...	3	1	...	...	...	...	4	3	2	...	...	...
Per cent.	...		6	18	38	16	...	78	...	...	6	2	...	8	...	...	8	6	...	14	...	0
GLASGOW.																						
81. Glasgow	180	90/90	11	21·5	46	26·5	1	106	2	2·5	12·5	10	...	27	2	1·5	12·5	24	6	46	...	...
Per cent.	...		6·1	12	25·5	14·7	·5	59	1·1	1·4	7	5·5	...	15	1·1	·8	7	13·3	3·3	25·5	...	18·6
EDINBURGH.																						
82. Edinburgh, streets, mixed classes, per cent.	2000	both	5·4	13·8	28·2	11·3	1·3	60	·5	1·7	5·5	5·6	·8	14·1	·8	1	6·4	13·6	4·4	25·8	...	20·3
83. Do., lower classes, per cent.	1000	both	5·3	14·4	26·3	11·6	·6	58·2	·9	1·9	5·1	5·1	·7	13·7	·5	1·2	5·8	15·7	4·4	27·6	...	19·6

	No.	Sex																				
84. Canongate, &c., lower class of Scotch and Irish ...	650	both	27	76	182	88	18	391	3	5	30	31	7	76	4·5	7	46	89	36·5	183	208·5	
Do., per cent.	...	...	4·3	12	28·7	13·9	2·8	61·7	·5	·8	4·7	4·9	1·1	11·7	·7	1·1	7·2	13·9	5·5	28·1		32·1
85. Cowgate, &c., purely Irish, per cent.	300	both	5·7	9·7	30·3	13·3	2·7	61·7	·3	1·3	5	6·7	1·7	15	·3	·3	3·3	12·7	6·7	23·3		37
LOTHIAN.																						
86. Leith, Musselburgh, Dalkeith & Portobello, p.cent.	200	both	2·5	20	38	12	·5		1·5	·5	2	5	1		·5	·7	3	11	2	25		9·5
87. Dalkeith, second visit ...	88	bcth	4	18	20	11	1	54		2	6	4		12		1	7·5	12	1·5	22	7	
Per cent.	...	...	4·5	20·5	22·7	12·5	1·1	61·3		2·2	6·8	4·5		13·5		1·1	8·5	13·6	1·7	24·9		7·9
88. Dunbar	150	...	8	24	60	19		111		1	5	8	1	14		1	11	11	2	25	8	
Per cent.	...	...	5·3	16	40	12·7		74		·7	3·3	5·3		9·3		·7	7·3	7·3	1·3	16·6		5·3
89. Midlothian, farmers, shepherds, hinds, per cent.	300	m	6	26	29·3	12·3	·3	74	2	1	5·3	5	·3	12	·3	·7	4·3	7·7	1	14		-6·1
90. *Fisherfolk* of Newhaven and Fisherrow (Lothian), and St. Monance, in Fife	176	mcst fem	6	39	50	14	3	112	2	3	6	7		18	1	5	13	27		46	-·2	
Per cent.	...	...	3·4	22·1	28·5	8	1·7	63·6	1·1	1·7	3·4	4		10·2	·6	2·8	7·4	15·3		26		-1·1
91. Do. of Buckhaven (Fife) ...	67	mcst fem	2	9	25	9	1	46	1	1	2	1		5		2	6	8		16	+·5	
Per cent.	...	...	3	13·4	37·3	13·4	1·5	68·7	1·5	1·5	3	1·5		7·4		3	9	11·9		23·9		+7·4
THE MERSE.																						
92. Eyemouth fishers, known local descent	30	m	1·5	6·5	11·5	4·5		24		1·5	1·5	1		4				2		2		
93. Do., fishers	95	m	7	15	35	6		63		4·5	6·5	4·5	·5	16		2	3·5	9	1·5	16	-·2	
94. Total	125	m	8·5	21·5	46·5	10·5		87		6	8	5·5	·5	20		2	3·5	11	1·5	18	-·5	
Per cent.	...	...	6·8	17·2	37·2	8·4		69·6		4·8	6·4	4·4	·4	16		1·6	2·8	8·8	1·2	14·4	-·7	-5·6
95. Eyemouth, other than fishers	100	m	5	22	27·5	10·5		65		3·5	3	6·5	2	15	1	1·5	5	10·5	2	20		+·5

Colour of Hair and Eyes in several Districts of the United Kingdom, from Personal Observation.—SCOTLAND, continued.

Colour of Hair	Number	Sex	EYES LIGHT.						EYES INTERMEDIATE OR NEUTER.						EYES DARK.						Indices.	
			Red	Fair	Brown	Dark	Nig.	Eyes Light	Red	Fair	Brown	Dark	Nig.	Eyes Neuter	Red	Fair	Brown	Dark	Nig.	Eyes Dark	Gross	Per Cent.
96. Eyemouth (?)	100	fem	3·5	16	20	6	·5	46	1·5	6	9·5	9	…	26	…	1	9	15	3	28	…	+9
97. Burnmouth fishers	12	m	…	3	2	2	…	…	…	…	…	1	…	…	…	1	1	1·5	·5	…	…	…
98. Dunse, Chirnside, and the Merse, mostly peasants	90	m	5·5	24·5	27	6	…	63	…	2·5	7·5	3·5	·5	14	1	1	4	6	1	13	−16	…
	70	fem	1	12·5	21·5	3	…	38	…	2	5	4	…	11	1	…	9·5	10·5	…	21	+1	…
99. Foulden, &c., ditto, ditto	70	both	4·5	11	22·5	4	1	43	1	1	4	2	…	8	2	1	5	13·5	·5	19	+5	…
100. Total Dunse, &c.	230	both	11	48	71	13	1	144	1	5·5	16·5	9·5	·5	33	…	…	18·5	30	1·5	53	−10	…
Per cent.	…	…	4·8	20·8	30·8	5·6	·4	62·6	·4	2·4	7·2	4·1	·2	14·3	·8	·4	8·3	13	·6	23	…	−4·3
THE BORDERS.																						
101. Selkirk and Darnick	100	both	6	15	42	12	…	75	…	2	4	3	1	10	1	…	6	7	1	15	…	2
102. Selkirk, market, second visit	109	m	7	27	28	12	…	74	…	1·5	7·5	5	…	14	…	…	4·5	13·5	3	21	+1	…
	91	fem	6	19·5	26	7·5	…	59	1	2	3	5	…	11	…	…	5	16	…	21	0	…
Total	200	both	13	46·5	54	19·5	…	133	1	3·5	10·5	10	…	25	…	2	9·5	29·5	3	42	+1	…
Per cent.	…	…	6·5	23·2	27	9·7	…	66·5	·5	1·7	5·2	5	…	12·5	…	…	4·7	14·7	1·5	21	…	+5
103. Yarrow dale (some Ettrick)	60	both	2	12	25	7	…	46	…	1	3	1	…	4	…	2	3	5	1	10	−3	…
104. Moffat dale	40	both	2	9	16	6	…	33	…	1	3	…	…	4	…	…	…	2	1	3	−2	…
104A. Yarrow, &c., total	100	…	4	21	41	13	…	79	…	1	6	1	…	8	…	2	3	7	1	13	…	−5
105. Peebles, per cent.	80	both	3·7	18·7	31·3	11·9	·6	66·2	…	1·2	6·2	3·7	…	11·2	1·2	…	5·6	13·7	1·9	22·5	…	9·4

	1	2	3	4	5	6	7	8	9	10	11	12	13	14	15	16	17	18	19	20	21	22
106. Galashiels, town...	60	both	1	8	18	7	1	...	...	...	2	2	...	...	...	...	6	12	1	...	14	...
Per cent.	...	...	1·6	13·3	30	11·6	1·6	58·3	...	3·3	...	...	...	...	...	...	10	20	1·6	31·6	...	23·2
107. Melrose, village	125	both	5·5	21·5	42	15	...	84	1	1	3	7	1	10	1	·5	6·5	18·5	1·5	28	15	12
Per cent.	...	...	4·4	17·2	34·5	12	...	67·2	·8	·8	2·4	5·6	·8	10·4	·8	·4	5·2	14·8	1·2	22·4	...	12
108. Kelso, town	50	both	3	8	16	7	...	34	...	...	2	3	...	5	1	1	2	7	...	11	4	8
109. Jedburgh, town	150	both	6	24·5	46·5	12	...	80	1	2	7	9	...	19	1	2	11·5	24·5	3	42	15	10
110. Kelso and Jedburgh, total...	200	...	9	32·5	62·5	19	...	123	1	2	9	12	...	24	2	3	13·5	31·5	3	53	19	...
Per cent.	...	...	4·5	16·2	31·2	9·5	...	61·5	·5	1	4·5	6	...	12	1	1·5	6·7	15·7	1·5	26·5	...	9·5
111. Hawick, town	180	both	11	25	46	20	...	102	1	1	18·5	12	...	38	1	3	12	21·5	2·5	40	11	...
Per cent.	...	...	6·1	13·9	25·5	11·1	...	56·6	...	7·5	10·3	6·6	...	21·1	·5	1·6	6·6	12	1·4	22·2	6·1	6·1
112. Hawick, ram sale, farmers and peasants ... ... }	100	m	5	18·5	34	12	...	69·5	1	...	3	3	...	7	...	·5	4·5	15·5	3	23·5	...	11·5
113. Lower Teviotdale	44	both	2	8	14	5	...	29	1	2	3	3	...	9	...	...	1	4	1	6	1	...
114. Upper Teviotdale	48	both	3	5	20	4	3	35	1	...	2	...	...	3	...	...	5	5	...	10	6	...
115. Rulewater, Jedwater, and Up. Liddesdale, peasants }	180	both	7	32	63·5	14·5	1	118	...	3	9·5	10·5	1	24	1	4	10·5	20	2·5	38	7	...
116. Total Teviotdale, &c. ...	272	both	12	45	97·5	23·5	4	...	2	5	14·5	13·5	1	...	...	4	16·5	29	3·5	53	14	...
Do., per cent.	...	...	4·4	16·5	35·6	8·6	1·4	66·5	·7	1·8	5·3	4·9	·4	14·1	...	1·4	6	10·6	1·3	19·4	...	5·1
117. Langholm, town, per cent. ...	200	both	3·2	16	34·5	8·7	·5	63	1·5	1·7	6·2	3·5	...	13	1·5	1·2	7·7	12·2	1·2	24	...	2·7
118. Lower Eskdale & Ewesdale	82	both	3	19	33	6	...	61	1	...	5·5	4·5	...	10	1	...	3	6·5	·5	11	-5	...
119. Longtown, Gretna, Loc- kerbie, Lochmaben ... }	74	both	2	12	24	6	...	44	1	...	11	1	...	13	2	2	5	8	...	17	-4	...
120. Total Eskdale and Lower Annandale ... ... }	156	...	5	31	57	12	...	105	1	...	16·5	5·5	...	23	3	1·3	8	14·5	·5	28	-9	...
Per cent.	...	...	3·2	19·8	36·5	7·7	...	67·2	·6	...	10·6	3·5	...	14·7	1·9	1·3	5·1	9·3	·3	18	...	-5·7

COLOUR OF HAIR AND EYES IN SEVERAL DISTRICTS OF THE UNITED KINGDOM, FROM PERSONAL OBSERVATION.

ENGLAND.

Colour of Hair	Number	Sex	EYES LIGHT Red	Fair	Brown	Dark	Nig.	Eyes Light	EYES INTERMEDIATE OR NEUTER Red	Fair	Brown	Dark	Nig.	Eyes Neuter	EYES DARK Red	Fair	Brown	Dark	Nig.	Eyes Dark	Indices Gross	Per Cent.
BERWICK.																						
121. Berwick-on-Tweed, town. p.c	500	both	4·8	18·8	33·4	8	·2	65·2	·6	1	6·5	4·9	·2	13·2	·4	·7	5·8	13·5	1·2	21·6	...	3·3
122. Do., farmers (50), and country folk	100	65/35	6·5	18	37	8	·5	70	...	1	6	3·5	·5	11	...	·5	8·5	10·5	·5	20	...	–1
NORTHUMBERLAND.																						
123. Glendale, Wark, Ford, Wooler	48	m	2·5	18·5	14	6	...	41	1	...	2·5	·5	...	4	...	·5	1·5	1·5	...	3	–14	...
	39	fem	1·5	6·5	11	4	...	23	...	2	1	3	...	6	·5	·5	1	8	...	10	+4	...
	87	...	4	25	25	10	...	64	1	2	3·5	3·5	·	10	·5	·5	2·5	9·5	...	13	–10	...
124. Per cent....	...	...	4·6	28·7	28·7	11·5	...	73·5	1·1	2·3	4	4	...	11·4	·6	·6	2·9	10·9	...	15	–11·5	...
125. Hexham, farmers	105	m	7	29·5	27	9·5	...	73	1	2·5	5·5	3	...	12	...	...	7	11	2	20	=12·5	...
	20	fem	1	3·5	3·5	4	...	12	...	...	3	...	...	3	...	...	1	3	1	5	+4·5	...
126. Total, per cent. ...	125	...	6·4	26·4	24·8	10·8	...	68	·8	2	6·8	2·4	...	12	...	...	6·4	11·2	2·4	20	...	–6·4
127. Hexham, town pop. ...	70	m	3	12	19	6	...	40	...	·5	6·5	3	1	11	...	...	4	12·5	2·5	19	13	...
	70	fem	2	14	20	8	...	44	...	...	3	5	...	8	1	...	6·5	8·5	2	18	8·5	...
128. Per cent....	140	...	3·5	18·5	28	10	...	60	...	·3	6·8	5·7	·7	13·5	·7	...	7·5	15	3·2	26·4	...	15·5
129. Newcastle-on-Tyne	264	both	10	44	77	30	1	162	...	4	15	12	1	31	1·5	4·5	18	40·5	5·5	70	...	...
	1	2	3	4	5	6	7	8	9	10	11	12	13	14	15	16	17	18	19	20	21	22

	1	2	3	4	5	6	7	8	9	10	11	12	13	14	15	16	17	18	19	20	21	22
130. City, per cent.	...	...	3·8	16·7	29·2	11·4	·4	61·5	...	1·5	5·6	4·5	·4	12	·5	1·7	6·8	15·3	2·1	26·4	...	12·8
CUMBRIA.																						
131. Carlisle, city	342	both	16·5	46·5	120	38	2	223	3	4	9	18	2	33	2	7	28·5	36	9·5	83	40	...
132. Per cent.... ...	...	...	4·8	13·6	35·1	11·1	·6	65·2	·9	1·2	2·6	5·3	·6	10·6	·6	2	8·3	10·5	2·8	24·2	...	11·8
133. Carlisle fair, farmers ...	100	m	4	22	34	11	1	72		2	3	3		8	1	2	5	10	2	20	...	-1
134. Do., peasants	400	both	4·9	20	36·1	12·3		73·3	·2	1·9	6	4·2		12·3	·3	·6	4·4	8	1·1	14·4	-·5	-1·2
135. Cockermouth, town ...	184	both	8	37	59	17·5	·5	...		1	7·5	6·5		...	3	3·5	15·5	23	2	...	-·5	...
136. Per cent.... ...	...	...	4·3	20·1	32·1	9·5	·3	66·3		·5	4·1	3·5		8·1	1·6	1·9	8·4	12·5	1·1	25·5	...	-·2
137. Keswick, town	134	both	7	20	50·5	9·5		87		2	7·5	7·5		17	...	2	7	19·5	1·5	30	8·5	...
138. Per cent.... ...	...	...	5·2	14·9	37·7	7·1		64·9		1·5	5·6	5·6		12·7		1·5	5·2	14·6	1·1	22·4	...	6·4
139. Penrith, town	130	both	4	23	42	13		...		4	3·5	8·5		...	1	...	13	15	3	··	10·5	...
140. Per cent.... ...	...	...	3·1	17·7	31·9	10		62·7	1	3·2	2·7	6·5		12·4	·7	...	10	11·5	2·3	24·5	...	7·9
141. Peasantry of the Cumberland Dales: (a) Borrowdale, &c. ...	50	both	3	6	17·5	4·5		31	1	...	3	1·5		6·5		...	3·5	8	1	12·5	+·5	...
(b) Round Keswick and Lorton	63	both	4	12	22	4		42	1	2	2	1		6	1	...	6·5	7	·5	15	-·7	...
(c) Threlkeld, Greystoke, Langwathby, &c.	157	both	9·5	23·5	59·5	16	1·5	110		2	5	7·5	·5	15		1	7·5	23·5	...	32	+15	...
Total...	270	...	16·5	41·5	99	24·5	1·5	183	2	5	10	10	·5	27·5	1	1	17·5	38·5	1·5	59·5	+13	...
142. Per cent.	...	...	6·1	15·3	36·6	9·1	·5	67·7	·7	1·8	3·7	3·7	·2	10·2	·4	·4	6·5	14·2	·5	22	...	4·7
143. Kendal, town, per cent. ...	150	both	4	13·3	35·3	8·7		61·3		2	9·3	6		17·3		·7	6·6	13·3	·7	21·3	...	9·4
144. Do., country, per cent. ...	150	both	5·3	16·7	38	4·7	·7	65·3	·7	·7	6·7	8·7		16·7			4·7	12	1·3	18		6
LONSDALE.																						
145. Kirby Lonsdale (37), Ingleton (43)	54	m	3·5	13·5	19·5	5·5		42		4	4	2		6			1	5	...	6	-4·5	...

Colour of Hair and Eyes in several Districts of the United Kingdom, from Personal Observation.—ENGLAND, continued.

Colour of Hair	Number	Sex	EYES LIGHT						EYES INTERMEDIATE OR NEUTER						EYES DARK						Indices	
			Red	Fair	Brown	Dark	Nig.	Eyes Light	Red	Fair	Brown	Dark	Nig.	Eyes Neuter	Red	Fair	Brown	Dark	Nig.	Eyes Dark	Gross	Per Cent.
145. Kirby Lonsdale (37), Ingleton (43)	26	fem	·5	6	7	1·5	...	15	...	...	2·5	2·5	...	5	1	...	1·5	3	·5	6	− ·5	...
Total...	80	both	4	19·5	26·5	7	...	...	...	...	6·5	4·5	...	...	1	...	2·5	8	·5	...	− ·4	...
Per cent. ...	...	...	5	24·4	33·1	8·7	...	71·2	...	...	8·1	5·6	...	13·7	1·2	...	3·1	10	·6	15	...	·5
DURHAM.																						
146. Durham, city	154	m	7·5	34·5	40	11	1	94	3	1	9	10·5	1·5	25	...	...	7	22·5	5·5	35	14	...
	96	fem	5·5	19·5	16	10	...	51	1	2·5	5·5	7	...	15	...	2	6·5	17·5	3	29	10	...
Per cent. ...	250	both	5·2	21·6	22·4	8·4	·4	58	1·6	1·4	5·8	7	·6	16·4	...	·8	5·4	16	3·4	25·6	...	9·6
147. Barnard Castle, some Darlington and country	138	both	3·5	28·5	41	17	1	...	...	1·5	8	8·5	1	...	·5	2·5	4	19	2	...	16	...
Per cent. ...	...	...	2·5	20·6	29·7	12·3	·7	65·9	...	1·1	5·8	6·1	·7	13·7	·3	1·8	2·9	13·8	1·4	20·2	...	11·6
148. Higher Teesdale, both banks	48	m	3	21	7	2	...	33	...	1·5	4·5	4	...	10	...	...	3	2	...	5	−17·5	...
	24	fem	...	7	4·5	3·5	...	15	...	...	2·5	1·5	...	4	...	...	·5	4·5	...	5	+2·5	...
Total...	72	both	3	28	11·5	5·5	...	48	...	1·5	7	5·5	...	14	...	...	3·5	6·5	...	10	−15	...
Per cent. ...	...	...	4·1	39	16	7·6	...	66·7	...	2	9·7	7·6	...	19·3	...	...	4·8	9	...	14·1	...	20·8
LANCASHIRE.																						
149. Lancaster, town and country	400	both	5·7	18	31·2	8·2	...	63·1	·2	1·9	7	4·2	·6	14	·7	·6	6·7	11	3·9	22·9	...	5·3
150. Manchester ...	289	m	11·5	42	68	31·5	2	155	4	3	16·5	17·5	1	42	2	5	24	47	14	92	62·5	21·3
	186	fem	9	21	52	17·5	·5	100	2	5·5	10	11·5	2	31	·5	1·5	15	33	5	55	37·5	20·1

	1	2	3	4	5	6	7	8	9	10	11	12	13	14	15	16	17	18	19	20	21	22
Total...	475	both	0·5	63	12·0	49	2·5	255	6	8·5	26·5	29	3	73	2·5	6·5	39	80	19	147	100	...
Per cent. ...	...	...	4·3	13·3	25·2	10·3	·5	53·6	1·2	1·8	5·6	6·1	·6	15·3	·5	1·4	8·3	16·8	4	31	...	21
YORKSHIRE.																						
151. Settle, Gigglesdwich (112), Upper Ribblesdale (42), Malham (26)	124	m	5·5	17·5	41	8	...	72	·5	2	13·5	12	...	28	1	...	9·5	12·5	1	24	8	...
	61	fem	2	8·5	11·5	5	...	27	...	1	4	7	...	12	...	...	4·5	14	3·5	22	21·5	...
Total...	185	both	7·5	26	52·5	13	...	98	·5	3	17·5	19	...	40	1	...	14	26·5	4·5	46	29·5	16
Per cent. ...	...	...	4	14	28·4	7	...	53·4	·3	1·6	9·5	10·3	...	21·7	·5	...	7·6	14·3	2·4	24·8	...	...
152. Skipton-in-Craven	233	both	8	35·5	65	22·5	2	133	2	6	12	16·5	2·5	39	3·5	2	23·5	24·5	7·5	61	30·5	...
Per cent. ...	...	...	3·4	15·2	27·9	9·6	·8	57	·8	2·6	5·1	7·2	1·1	16·8	1·5	·8	10·1	10·5	3·2	26·1	...	13·2
153. Haworth	105	66/39	6·5	20·5	18	6	...	51	2	2·5	14·5	9	...	28	1	1·5	8	13·5	2	26	-1·5	...
Per cent. ...	...	...	6·3	19·5	17·1	5·7	...	48·6	1·9	2·4	13·8	8·5	...	26·6	1	1·4	7·6	12·8	1·9	24·7	...	-1·4
154. Keighley	118	m	7·5	29	29·5	10·5	·5	77	2	3·5	5·5	5	...	16	2	·5	7	14	1·5	25	-11	...
	82	fem	2·5	13	13	6	·5	36	2·5	6·5	5·5	4·5	...	19	·5	1·5	8	14·5	2·5	28	+4·5	...
Total...	200	...	10	42	42·5	16·5	1	113	4·5	10	11	9·5	...	35	2·5	2	15	29·5	4	52	-6·5	...
Per cent. ...	...	...	5	21	21·2	8·2	·5	56·5	2·2	·5	5·5	4·7	...	17·5	1·2	1	7·5	14·2	2	26	...	-3·2
155. Keighley, agricult. show, mostly farmers ...	50	few f	·5	10·5	12	2	...	25	1	1	6	...	...	8	1	2	8	6	...	17	-8	-16
156. Farnley ironworks (100), Gildersome (50) ...	150	most men	3·5	30	36	9	·5	79	1·5	3·5	13	8	...	26	1	5	12	23·5	3·5	45	4·	...
Per cent. ...	...	...	2·3	20	24	6	·3	52·6	1	2·3	8·6	5·3	...	17·3	·6	3·3	8	15·6	2·3	30	...	2·6
157. Farnley wool mill, young women ...	50	fem	1	8	17·5	1	·5	28	·5	2·5	5	1	...	9	·5	2	5·5	5	...	13	-6·5	-13
158. Bradford	1400	both	56	195	412	117	6	786	13	31	110	70	7	231	10	25	116	200	32	383	147	...
Per cent. ...	...	...	4	13·9	29·4	8·4	·4	56·1	·9	2·2	7·9	5	·5	16·5	·7	1·8	8·3	14·3	2·3	27·4	...	10·5

Colour of Hair and Eyes in several Districts of the United Kingdom, from Personal Observation.—ENGLAND, continued.

Column groups: **EYES LIGHT** (Red, Fair, Brown, Dark, Nig., Eyes Light); **EYES INTERMEDIATE OR NEUTER** (Red, Fair, Brown, Dark, Nig., Eyes Neuter); **EYES DARK** (Red, Fair, Brown, Dark, Nig., Eyes Dark); **Indices** (Gross, Per Cent.).

Colour of Hair	Number	Sex	Red	Fair	Brown	Dark	Nig.	Eyes Light	Red	Fair	Brown	Dark	Nig.	Eyes Neuter	Red	Fair	Brown	Dark	Nig.	Eyes Dark	Gross	Per Cent.
159. Leeds	333	both	10	55	86	25	...	176	4	8	26	13·5	·5	52	1·5	8·5	28	58	9	105	28·5	...
Per cent.	...	...	3	16·5	25·8	7·5	...	52·8	1·2	2·4	7·8	4	·1	15·6	·4	2·5	8·4	17·4	2·7	31·5	...	8·5
160. Ripon, chiefly excursionists	130	both	6·5	26·5	31	15·5	·5	80	1	2	9	14·5	·5	27	2	1·5	9·5	29	1	43	23·5	...
Per cent.	...	...	4·3	17·6	20·6	10·3	·3	53·3	·6	1·3	6	9·6	·3	18	1·3	1	6·3	19·3	·6	28·6	...	15·6
161. Ripon, city	120	both	8	20	26	13	...	67	1	4	6·5	1·5	1	14	2·5	3·5	12	16·5	4·5	39	3	...
Per cent.	...	...	6·6	16·6	21·6	10·8	...	55·8	·8	3·3	5·4	1·2	·8	11·6	2·1	2·9	10	13·7	3·7	32·5	...	2·5
162. Thirsk (market), mostly country folk	150	m	12	34	27·5	13·5	...	87	·8	4	9·5	10·5	1	25	1	1	8·5	22	5·5	38	7	...
	110	fem	4	22·5	23·5	10·5	·5	61	...	2	5·5	4·5	1	13	2	2	7·5	21·5	3	36	13	...
Total...	260	...	16	56·5	51	24	·5	148	...	6	15	15	2	38	3	3	16	43·5	8·5	74	20	...
Per cent.	...	...	6·1	21·7	19·6	9·2	·2	56·9	...	2·3	5·7	5·7	·7	14·6	1·1	1·1	6·1	16·7	3·2	28·4	...	7·7
163. Whitby, fishers	33	m	1	6·5	14·5	4	...	26	...	...	...	1	...	1	...	...	4·5	1·5	...	6	−1	−3
Others ...	107	m	7	19	38·5	8	·5	73	...	...	6·5	4	·5	11	...	...	6	12·5	4·5	23	9·5	...
	105	fem	2	13	34·5	12·5	...	62	...	1	7	3	...	11	...	1	10	19·5	1·5	32	21	...
Total...	245	...	10	38·5	87·5	24·5	·5	161	...	1	13·5	8	·5	23	...	1	20·5	33·5	6	61	20·5	...
Per cent.	...	...	4·1	15·7	35·7	10	·2	65·7	...	·4	5·5	3·3	·2	9·4	...	·4	8·4	13·7	2·4	24·9	...	12
164. Bridlington Quay	100	84/16	7·5	11	35·5	6	...	60	...	1	11·5	4·5	1	18	...	...	3	18	1	22	...	13
165. Bridlington, town	100	80/20	5	17	39	9	...	70	...	...	7	5	...	12	1	1	4·5	12·5	...	18	...	3·5

	1	2	3	4	5	6	7	8	9	10	11	12	13	14	15	16	17	18	19	20	21	22
166. Beverley, market	166	145/5	5·5	28·5	55	18·5	·5	108	1	1	8	7	…	17	1	…	14	21·5	4·5	41	20	…
Per cent.	…	…	3·3	17·2	33·1	11·1	·3	65	·6	·6	4·8	4·2	…	10·2	·6	…	8·4	13	2·7	24·7	…	12
167. Hull	200	120/80	5·5	21·5	70·5	17	1·5	116	…	3·5	10	9·5	1	24	1·2	2	18·5	30	7	60	40·5	20·2
Per cent.	…	…	2·7	10·7	35·2	8·5	·7	58	…	1·7	5	4·7	·5	12	…	1	9·2	15	3·5	30	…	20
168. Malton	50	4/6	2	6·5	17	4·5	…	30	…	…	2·5	3·5	…	6	3·5	…	4	6·5	·5	11	10	20
169. York, city	225	both	9	36	52·5	17	·5	115	4	7	15·5	16	·5	43	3·5	4	14·5	42	3	67	19·5	8·6
Per cent.	…	…	4	16	23·3	7·5	·2	51	1·8	3·1	6·9	7·1	·2	19·1	1·5	1·8	6·4	18·6	1·3	29·7	…	…
LINCOLNSHIRE.																						
170. Gainsborough, farmers, &c.	190	¾ m	6·5	34·5	63·5	26·5	…	131	…	4	8·5	13·5	1	27	1·5	1	5	20·5	4	32	23	…
Per cent.	…	…	3·4	18·2	33·4	13·8	…	68·9	…	2·1	4·5	7·1	·5	14·2	·8	·5	2·6	10·8	2·1	16·8	…	12·1
171. Do., townsfolk	150	m & f =	3	13	42·5	16	·5	75	1	1	13·5	13·5	…	20	2	·5	14·5	24·5	4·5	46	43·5	…
Per cent.	…	…	2	8·6	28·3	10·6	·3	50	·6	·6	9	9	…	19·3	1·3	·3	9·6	16·3	3	30·6	…	29
172. Market Rasen	100	¾ m	3	15·5	25·5	10	…	54	…	4·5	6·5	7	…	18	…	1	7·5	17·5	2	28	…	14·5
173. Lincoln (city), some country folk	500	both	10	75	175·5	42·5	1	304	2	6	26	22	1	57	4·5	6·5	40·5	79	8·5	139	60·5	…
Per cent.	…	…	2	15	35·2	8·5	·2	60·8	·4	1·2	5·2	4·4	·2	11·4	·9	1·3	8·1	15·8	1·7	27·8	…	12·1
174. Boston, town	158	m	4	31	55	12	…	102	…	3	9	5	…	17	1	3	13·5	19	2·5	30	−1	…
	182	fem	12	27	39·5	11·5	…	90	·5	1	14	8·5	…	24	3	1	7·5	34·5	2	68	+14	…
Total...	340	both	16	58	94·5	23·5	…	192	·5	4	23	13·5	…	41	4	4	21	53·5	4·5	107	+13	…
Per cent.	…	…	4·7	17	27·8	6·9	…	56·5	·1	1·2	6·8	4	…	12	1·2	1·2	…	15·7	1·3	31·4	…	3·8
175. Boston, country folk	80	m	2·5	24·5	31	3	…	61	…	3	2·5	1·5	…	7	1·5	2·5	6	6·5	…	12	…	…
	50	fem	2	7·5	16·5	4	…	30	…	…	4	1	…	5	…	·5	1·5	8	·5	15	…	…
Total...	130	both	4·5	32	47·5	7	…	91	…	…	6·5	2·5	…	12	1·5	3	7·5	14·5	·5	27	−19	…
Per cent.	…	…	3·4	24·6	36·5	5·4	…	70	…	2·3	5	1·9	…	9·2	1·1	2·3	5·8	11·1	·4	20·7	…	−14·6

Colour of Hair and Eyes in several Districts of the United Kingdom, from Personal Observation.—ENGLAND, continued.

Colour of Hair	Number	Sex	EYES LIGHT						EYES INTERMEDIATE OR NEUTER						EYES DARK						Indices	
			Red	Fair	Brown	Dark	Nig.	Eyes Light.	Red	Fair	Brown	Dark	Nig.	Eyes Neuter.	Red	Fair	Brown	Dark	Nig.	Eyes Dark.	Gross.	Per Cent.
176. Grantham, town, per cent...	300	both	2·7	12·1	34·6	10·3	·7	60·4	·3	1	6	5·3	...	12·6	·4	1·3	8	15	2·4	27	...	19
177. Barrowby, Harlaxton, Manthorpe, &c.; round Grantham ...	300	both	2·7	13·7	35·3	11·5	·5	63·7	1	·7	7·7	6	·3	15·6	...	1·3	5·2	12·1	2	20·6	...	15·8
178. Stamford, town, per cent...	200	¾ fem	4	11·5	30	9	...	54·5	...	·7	7·2	6	...	14	2	1	5	20·5	3	31·5	...	22·3
Do., peasants ...	175	=	5	34	61·5	16·5	...	117	...	...	10·5	10	·5	21	...	·5	7·5	24	5	37	22	12·5
Per cent. ...	...	...	2·9	19·4	35·1	9·4	...	66·8	...	...	6	5·7	·3	12	...	·3	4·3	13·7	2·8	21·1	...	...
LINCOLNSHIRE—Total 2385, per cent.	...	...	3	15·2	32·6	8·6	·2	59·4	·3	1·1	6·3	5·4	·1	13·4	·8	1	7·3	15·7	2	26	...	12·6
NOTTINGHAMSHIRE.																						
179. Newark, per cent.	300	both	2	13	40·7	10·3	·7	66·7	·7	1·7	5	5	...	12·3	...	1	6	11	3	21	...	15·3
180. Nottingham ...	700	about =	26	107	172·5	69·5	2	...	7	13	43	35·5	·5	...	8	10	63	127·5	15·5	...	...	...
Per cent. ...	...	...	3·7	15·3	24·6	9·9	·3	53·8	1	1·8	6·1	5·1	·1	14·1	1·1	1·4	9	18·2	2·2	32	...	14·1
181. Do., farmers...	100	m	2	20	25·5	11	·5	59	·5	2·5	7	5	...	15	...	3	9	11·5	2·5	26	...	5·5
DERBYSHIRE.																						
182. Derby, town	100	both	1·5	18·5	39·5	6·5	1	...	1	2	7·5	·5	...	...	2	...	5·5	13	1·5	...	...	0
183. Castleton, Chapel-en-le-Frith ...	40	both	1	11·5	8	6·5	...	...	...	...	2	2	...	...	1	·5	3	4·5	...	...	−1	...
Per cent. ...	...	...	2·5	28·7	20	16·2	...	...	...	...	5	5	...	...	2·5	1·2	7·5	11·2	...	...	...	−2·5

| 1 | 2 | 3 | 4 | 5 | 6 | 7 | 8 | 9 | 10 | 11 | 12 | 13 | 14 | 15 | 16 | 17 | 18 | 19 | 20 | 21 | 22 |

LEICESTERSHIRE.																						
184. Leicester, town	284	m	9	42	76	19·5	·5	147	2·5	6	16	20	·5	45	·5	5	22	51	13·5	92	54·5	...
	256	fem	7·5	33	67·5	19	...	127	2	2·5	20	17	·5	42	1·5	2	20·5	56·5	6·5	87	58	...
Total...	540	both	16·5	75	143·5	38·5	·5	274	4·5	8·5	36	37	1	87	2	7	42·5	107·5	20	179	...	...
Per cent.	...	...	3	13·9	26·6	7·1	·1	50·7	·8	1·6	6·6	6·8	·2	16·1	·4	1·3	7·8	19·9	3·7	33·1	...	20·8
185. Leicester, country folk ...	30	$\frac{25}{5}$	1·5	3·5	10	5	...	20	...	1	1	1	...	3	...	...	1	6	...	7	6	20
186. Rutland (Uppingham, Belton, Seaton, &c.), country folk	70	$\frac{54}{16}$	2·5	11·5	23	9	...	46	...	...	5	3·5	·5	9	...	...	2	10·5	2·5	15	15	...
Per cent.	...	...	3·5	16·4	32·8	12·8	...	65·7	...	...	7·1	5	·7	12·8	...	...	2·8	15	3·5	21·4	...	21·4
STAFFORDSHIRE.																						
187. Leek	120	both	2·5	9	41·5	24	1·5	...	...	1	5	6	...	...	1	...	6	19·5	2·5	...	...	...
Per cent.	...	...	2·1	7·5	38·6	20	1·2	69·4	...	·8	4·2	5	...	10	·8	...	5	15·8	2·1	23·7	...	36·2
188. Stoke-on-Trent	100	m	2	12·5	25·5	13	...	53	...	1	9·5	6	·5	17	...	1·5	9·5	15·5	3·5	30	...	25·5
	100	fem	3·5	12	29·5	7·5	·5	53	...	1·5	8·5	7	...	17	...	2	10	16	2	30	...	16·5
189. Hanley, per cent.	194	$\frac{94}{100}$	2·5	10	23·9	14·8	2·5	53·7	1·5	1	4·4	7·2	·7	14·8	1·5	1	6·7	17	5·1	31·3	...	38·1
190. Potteries, total, per cent. ...	400	=	2·7	11·1	25·7	12·5	1·4	53·4	·8	1·1	6·7	6·8	·5	15·9	·8	1·4	8·1	16·4	3·9	30·6	...	29·5
191. Market folk at Hanley, and other country folk ...	143	$\frac{68}{75}$	4	20	41	18·5	·5	84	...	1	7	9·5	1·5	19	...	1	8	26·5	4·5	40	41·5	...
Per cent.	...	...	2·8	14	28·7	13	·4	58·7	...	·7	4·9	6·9	1·1	13·3	...	·7	5·8	18·5	3·1	28	...	29·1
192. Biddulph Moor	31	$\frac{13}{18}$	1	1	14	6	1	23	...	...	1	...	...	1	...	...	·5	4	2·5	7	15	48·5
193. Moorlands above Leek ...	19	$\frac{5}{14}$	...	1	9·5	2·5	...	13	...	...	1	1	...	2	...	...	...	4	...	4	6·5	35
194. Stafford...	70	$\frac{42}{28}$	1·5	10	15·5	8	...	35	...	1	5·5	4·5	...	11	1	2	5	12	4	24	17	...
Per cent.	...	...	2·1	14·3	22·1	11·4	...	50	...	1·4	7·8	6·4	...	15·7	1·4	2·8	7·2	17·1	5·7	34·3	...	24·3

Colour of Hair and Eyes in several Districts of the United Kingdom, from Personal Observation.—ENGLAND, continued.

Colour of Hair	Number	Sex	EYES LIGHT.						EYES INTERMEDIATE OR NEUTER.						EYES DARK.						Indices.	
			Red	Fair	Brown	Dark	Nig.	Eyes Light	Red	Fair	Brown	Dark	Nig.	Eyes Neuter	Red	Fair	Brown	Dark	Nig.	Eyes Dark	Gross.	Per Cent.
195. Burton-on-Trent...	258	m	6	44	71	35·5	·5	157	...	6	13·5	11·5	3	34	2·5	1	12·5	40	11	67	46·5	...
	102	fem	3	12	34	10·5	1·5	61	...	...	4	5	...	9	1	1	10	18	2	32	23·5	...
Total...	360	...	9	56	105	46	2	218	...	6	17·5	16·5	3	43	3·5	2	22·5	58	13	99	70	...
Per cent. ...	...	...	2·5	15·5	29·2	12·8	·5	60·5	...	1·6	4·8	4·8	·8	11·9	·9	·5	6·2	16·1	3·6	27·5	...	19·4
196. Tamworth (cattle market), mostly farmers ...	200	167/33	7·5	31	75	30·5	...	144	...	...	10	8	...	18	·5	1	8·5	24·5	3·5	38	...	...
Per cent. ...	...	...	3·7	15·5	37·5	15·2	...	72	...	...	5	4	...	9	·2	·5	4·2	12·2	1·8	19	...	15
197. Wolverhampton ...	309	both	4	40	99	32·5	2	186	2	8·5	10·5	18	...	39	1	3·5	24	49·5	6	84	...	...
Per cent. ...	...	...	...	...	...	10·5	·6	63·2	·6	2·8	3·4	5·8	...	12·6	·3	1·1	7·7	16	2·1	27·2	...	15·9
SALOP.																						
198. Shrewsbury, town ...	132	m	3	14·5	34·5	19·5	2·5	74	...	1	5	8·5	·5	15	1	...	6	24·5	10·5	43	59	...
	150	fem	9	17·5	41	15·5	...	83	·5	2·5	3	6·5	·5	13	2	·5	9	37·5	5	54	38·5	...
Total...	282	...	12	32	75·5	35	2·5	157	·5	3·5	8	15	1	28	3	1·5	15	62	15·5	97	97·5	...
Per cent. ...	...	...	4·6	11·3	26·8	12·4	·9	55·7	·2	1·2	2·8	5·3	·3	9·9	1	·5	5·3	22	5·4	34·4	...	34·6
199. Shrewsbury (48), Church Stretton (14), country folk	62	=	1	6	16	9	...	32	...	...	2	6	...	8	1	...	3	15	3	22	28	...
Per cent. ...	...	...	1·6	9·6	26	14·5	...	51·6	...	...	3·2	9·6	...	12·0	1·6	...	4·8	24·2	4·8	35·5	...	45
200. Cleobury, South Salop ...	100	both	2	11·5	31·5	21·5	1·5	68	...	...	3	6	...	9	...	...	4	16·5	3·5	24	...	40·5

HEREFORDSHIRE.

	No.	Sex																					
201. Hereford, city	133	m	8	12·5	36	20·5	4	82	...	1·	5	10	1	17	·5	·5	3	22·5	8·5	35	...	...
	142	fem	6	17	39·5	17·5	...	80	...	1	7	6·5	·5	15	1·5	1·5	10	29	6	47	...	...
Total...	275	...	14	29·5	75·5	38	4	161	...	2	12	16·5	1·5	32	·5	2	13	51·5	14·5	82	97·5	...
Per cent...	...	...	5·1	10·7	27·4	13·8	1·4	58·5	...	·7	4·3	6	·5	11·6	·7	·3	4·7	18·7	5·3	29·8	...	35
202. Do., farmers and peasants	68	m	1·5	7·5	20	14	1	44	...	1	2	6·5	1·5	11	...	1	6	5·5	1·5	13	24	...
	150	fem	5	9·5	40	22	1·5	78	...	1·5	12·5	7	2	25	...	1	9	33·5	3·5	47	57·5	...
Total...	218	...	6·5	17	60	36	2·5	122	2	2·5	14·5	13·5	3·5	36	...	1	15	39	5	60	81·5	...
Per cent...	...	...	3	7·8	27·5	16·5	1·1	55·0	2	1·1	6·6	6·2	1·6	16·5	...	·4	6·9	17·9	2·3	27·5	...	37·4
203. Kington and neighbourhood (Welsh border)	70	both	3	3·5	23	12	·5	42	·9	...	1	5	...	6	...	...	1	16	5	22	37·5	...
Per cent...	...	...	4·3	5	33	17·1	·7	60	...	...	1·4	7·1	...	8·5	...	...	1·4	23	7	31·4	...	53·5
204. Leominster and country, thence eastward	50	30/20	2	2·5	10·5	8	1	24	...	...	3	6	...	9	...	...	3	11	3	17	...	...
Per cent...	...	...	4	5	21	16	2	48	...	...	6	12	...	18	...	...	6	22	6	34	...	57

WORCESTERSHIRE.

	No.	Sex																					
205. Worcester, city	150	m	2	19	46	20	1	88	1	1·5	7·5	9	2	21	...	...	11	24·5	5·5	41	47	...
	150	fem	8	17	39·5	19	·5	84	...	2	9	12	...	23	...	1·5	8	29	4·5	43	41·5	...
	700	both	16	76	238	86·5	6·5	423	5	6·5	33	34·5	1	80	2	4	39	134·5	17·5	197	196	...
Total, per cent.	1000	both	2·6	11·2	323	12·5	·8	59·5	·6	1	4·9	5·5	·3	12·4	·2	·5	5·8	18·8	2·7	28·1	...	28·4
206. Kidderminster	373	both	12	39·5	124	57	4·5	237	...	6	24	18·5	·5	49	1·5	3·5	18·5	56·5	7	87	93·5	...
Per cent...	...	...	3·2	10·6	33·2	15·3	1·2	63·5	...	1·6	6·4	4·9	·1	13·1	·4	·9	4·9	15·1	1·8	23·3	...	25
207. Stourport	100	both	4	12·5	41	8·5	...	66	1	1	5·5	5·5	...	13	...	...	4·5	15	1·5	21	...	13·5

Colour of Hair and Eyes in several Districts of the United Kingdom, from Personal Observation.—ENGLAND, continued.

Colour of Hair	Number	Sex	Red	Fair	Brown	Dark	Nig.	Eyes Light	Red	Fair	Brown	Dark	Nig.	Eyes Neuter	Red	Fair	Brown	Dark	Nig.	Eyes Dark	Gross	Per Cent.
			EYES LIGHT.						EYES INTERMEDIATE OR NEUTER.						EYES DARK.						Indices.	
208. Bewdley	500	both	17·5	38·5	171·5	62	2·5	292	1	2	20	25	2	50	2	4·5	33	102·5	16	158	165	...
Per cent.	...		3·5	7·7	34·3	12·4	·5	58·4	·2	·4	4	5	·4	10	·4	·9	6·6	20·5	3·2	31·6	...	33
209. Worcestershire, central, rural	700	both	19	92	243·5	133	1·5	489	2	2	23	31	2	60	4	5	27·5	100·5	14	151	175·5	...
Per cent.	...		2·7	13·1	34·8	19	·2	69·8	·3	·3	3·3	4·4	·3	8·5	·6	·7	3·9	14·3	2	21·5	...	25·1
210. Worcestershire, N. W., forest and rural district	500	both	11·5	42·5	164	82·5	5·5	306	3	1	29	24	4	61	1	4	33·5	82·5	12	153	...	...
Per cent.	...		2·3	8·5	32·8	16·5	1·1	61·1	·6	·2	5·8	4·8	·8	12·2	·2	·8	6·7	16·5	2·4	...	...	33·7
WARWICKSHIRE.																						
211. Birmingham	310	m	7·5	42·5	76	42·5	2·5	171	2·5	6·5	18·5	18	1·5	47	...	4·5	21·5	57	9	...	...	...
	357	fem	19·5	55	94·5	40·5	·5	...	...	6	16	17	...	...	2·5	5	26	65	9·5	...	...	...
Total...	667	both	27	97·5	170·5	83	3	...	2·5	12·5	34·5	35	1·5	...	2·5	9·5	47·5	122	18·5	...	134·5	...
Per cent.	...		4	14·6	25·6	12·4	·4	57	·4	1·8	5·2	5·2	·2	12·8	·4	1·4	7·1	18·3	2·8	30	...	20·1
212. Stratford - on - Avon fair, mostly country folk	125	m	4·5	17	32	17·5	1	72	...	2	5	7	...	14	...	...	6	26·5	6·5	39	41·5	...
	175	fem	3	26	41	24	...	94	1	1	10	9	...	21	2	2·5	15·5	35	5	60	42·5	...
Total...	300	both	7·5	43	73	41·5	1	166	1	3	15	16	...	35	2	2·5	21·5	61·5	11·5	99	84	...
Per cent.	...		2·5	143	24·3	13·8	·3	55·3	·3	1	5	5·3	...	15	·7	·8	7·2	20·5	3·8	29·3	...	28·2
213. Rugby	53	49/13	2	4	12·5	7	1·5	27	...	...	3	7·5	1·5	12	·5	·5	2	9	2	14	...	...
Per cent.	...		3·8	7·5	23·6	13·2	2·8	51	...	...	5·6	14·1	2·8	22·6	·9	·9	3·8	17	3·8	26·4	...	50

NORTHAMPTONSHIRE.

	No.	Sex																				
214. Heyford, Flure, Stowe, Bugbrook, Weedon (Sth. West Northamptonshire)	119	m	3·5	16	38·5	16	...	74	...	1	4	4·5	·5	10	1·5	·5	6·5	23	3·5	35	29	...
	61	fem	2	4·5	18	18	...	31	...	...	2	4	...	6	1	...	4	18	1	24	24	...
Total...	180	...	5·5	20·5	56·5	22·5	...	105	...	1	6	8·5	·5	16	2·5	·5	10·5	41	4·5	59	...	...
Per cent.	...	...	3	11·4	31·4	12·5	...	58·3	...	·5	3·3	4·7	·3	8·8	1·4	·3	5·8	22·8	2·5	32·8	...	30
215. Northampton	155	m	4	13·5	59·5	22·5	·5	100	1	1	1·5	8·5	...	12	...	·5	5·5	29	9	44	...	...
	145	fem	5	16	47·5	17·5	2	88	...	1	9	5	...	15	1	1	10·5	27	2·5	42	...	...
Total...	300	...	9	29·5	107	40	2·5	188	1	2	10·5	13·5	...	27	1	1·5	16	56	11·5	86	...	...
Per cent.	...	...	3	9·8	35·6	13·3	·8	62·6	·3	·7	3·5	4·5	...	9	·3	·5	5·3	18·7	3·8	28·6	...	31·1
216. Peterborough	113	6/30	...	18·5	34·5	12·5	·5	66	1·5	·5	6	4	1	13	...	...	10·5	21·5	2	34	...	...
Per cent.	...	...	...	16·4	30·5	11·1	·4	58·4	1·3	·4	5·3	3·5	·9	11·5	...	...	9·3	19	1·8	30	...	21·7
OXFORDSHIRE.																						
217. Oxford, city ...	720	both	31	85	246	80	3·5	446	4·5	9	37	35·5	1	86	5	6	51·5	111	14·5	188	...	...
Per cent.	...	...	4·3	11·8	34·2	11·1	·5	62	·6	1·2	5·1	4·9	...	11·9	·7	·8	7·1	15·4	2	26·1	...	17
218. Oxfordshire, militia	66	m	2	9	24	4	...	39	...	...	6	1	...	7	...	2	8	10	...	20	2	3
219. Do., peasants	30	most m	·5	5·5	11	4	...	21	...	...	...	2	...	2	...	...	4	3	...	7	3	10
BUCKS.																						
220. Aylesbury ...	100	6/30	4·5	20	25·5	9	...	59	3	2	4·5	7·5	...	18	...	1	4	15	3	23	...	9
BEDFORDSHIRE.																						
221. Dunstable ...	112	m	2·5	16	32	14·5	1	66	...	1	4	5·5	·5	11	1	...	6·5	26·5	3·5	35	...	...
	128	fem	5·5	17	32·5	20	...	75	...	1	6	6	...	13	...	1	4	30	2·5	40	...	...
Total...	240	both	8	33	64·5	34·5	1	141	...	2	10	11·5	·5	24	1	1	10·5	56·5	6	75	73	...
Per cent.	...	...	3·3	13·7	26·9	14·4	·4	58·7	...	·8	4·2	4·8	·2	10	·4	·4	4·4	23·5	2·5	31·2	...	30·4

Colour of Hair and Eyes in several Districts of the United Kingdom, from Personal Observation.—ENGLAND, continued.

Colour of Hair	Number	Sex	EYES LIGHT.					Eyes Light.	EYES INTERMEDIATE OR NEUTER.					Eyes Neuter.	EYES DARK.					Eyes Dark.	Indices.	
			Red	Fair	Brown	Dark	Nig.		Red	Fair	Brown	Dark	Nig.		Red	Fair	Brown	Dark	Nig.		Gross.	Per Cent.
CAMBRIDGESHIRE.																						
222. Ely, city	108	7⁄8	1·5	18·5	41	12·	1	74	...	1	5	4	...	10	...	...	3	17	4	24	22	...
Per cent.			1·4	17·1	37·9	11·1	·9	68·4	...	·9	4·6	3·7	...	9·2	...	...	2·8	15·7	3·7	22·2	...	20·3
223. Cambridge, town ...	130	m	1	15	39	10·5	...	66	...	3	9·5	7	·5	20	·5	2	13	25·5	3	44	...	...
	70	fem	...	8·5	21	7·5	...	37	...	1	6·5	1·5	...	9	...	1·5	5·5	14·5	2·5	24	...	...
Total...	200	...	1	24	60	18	...	103	...	4	16	8·5	...	29	·5	3·5	18·5	40	5·5	68	...	...
Per cent.	...	...	·5	14	30	9	...	51·5	...	2	8	4·2	·2	14·5	·2	1·7	9·2	20	2·7	34	...	22·7
EAST ANGLIA.																						
224. Norwich, assizes and market	130	m	6·5	21·5	36·5	10·5	...	75	·5	2·5	8	5	...	16	1	2	14	20	2	39	5·5	...
	160	fem	8	18·5	44	14·5	...	85	...	·9	20·5	5·5	...	27	1	·5	14·5	31	1	48	24	...
Total...	290	...	14·5	40	80·5	25	...	160	·5	3·5	28·5	10·5	...	43	2	2·5	28·5	51	3	87	29·5	...
Per cent.	...	...	5	13·8	27·7	8·6	...	55·2	·2	1·2	9·8	3·6	...	14·8	·7	·8	9·8	17·6	1	30	...	10·2
225. Yarmouth, regatta day ...	175	m	5·5	22·5	45·5	15·5	1	90	·5	3	13·5	10	1	28	...	1	12·5	38·5	5	57	...	...
	275	fem	7·5	28·5	81·5	20·5	2	140	2	2	16·5	14·5	...	35	...	1	17·5	78·5	3	100	...	...
Total...	450	both	13	51	127	36	3	230	2·5	5	30	24·5	1	63	...	2	30	117	8	157	...	...
Per cent.	...	...	2·9	1·3	28·2	8	·6	51·1	·5	1·1	6·6	5·4	·2	14	...	·4	6·6	26	1·8	34·9	...	28·4
226. Do., sailors and fishermen..	100	m	1	29	34	8·5	·5	64	...	1	9	3	2	15	...	1	5	12	3	21	...	11·5

	No.	Sex																					
227. Ipswich, market, farmers and drovers...	150	m	2·5	28·5	42·5	16·5	…	90	…	…	18	…	6	8·5	3·5	…	2	…	15	20	5	42	16	…
Per cent.	…	…	1·7	19	28·3	11	…	60	…	…	12	…	4	5·7	2·3	…	1·3	…	10	13·3	3·3	28	…	10·6
228. Ipswich, town	150	m	1	25	43·5	16·5	…	86	…	1·5	20	1·5	8·5	8	1	1	·5	…	15·5	20	8	44	35·5	…
	100	fem	4	9	40	12·5	…	66	…	…	10	…	4	5	1	…	…	…	5	18	1	24	23·5	…
Total	250	both	5	34	83·5	29	…	152	…	1·5	30	1·5	12·5	13	2	1	·5	…	20·5	38	9	68	9	…
Per cent.	…	…	2	13·6	33·4	11·6	·5	60·8	·5	·6	12	·6	5	5·2	·8	·4	·2	…	8·2	15·2	3·6	27·2	…	23·6
ESSEX.																							
229. Colchester, town...	66	m	2·5	8·5	21	9	…	41	…	1	9	1	7	1	…	…	1·5	2	10·5	16	2·5	16	21·5	…
	47	fem	1	3	14	6	…	24	…	…	5	…	1	3	1	…	6·5	10·5	18	1	18	14·5	…
Total...	113	…	3·5	11·5	35	15	…	65	…	1	14	1	8	4	1	…	8·5	21	34	3·5	34	36	…
Per cent.	…	…	3·1	10·2	31	13·2	1	57·5	…	·9	12·4	·9	7·1	3·5	·9	…	7·5	18·5	29·1	3·1	29·1	…	31·8
230. Colchester, farmers	180	m	5·5	29	59	14·5	1	109	…	1	20	1	8	9	1	1	10	30·5	51	7	51	31	…
	30	fem	1	6	8	7	…	22	…	1	6	1	2	2·5	1·5	1	1	1	2	…	2	1·5	…
Total...	210	…	6·5	35	67	21·5	1	…	1	…	…	…	10	11·5	2·5	·5	11	31·5	…	7	…	32·5	…
Per cent.	…	…	3·1	16·6	31·9	10·2	…	62·4	…	·5	12·4	·5	4·7	5·5	1·2	·9	5·2	15	25·2	3·3	25·2	32·5	…	15·5
231. Braintree, town ...	83	6·6/2·3	1	14·5	19·5	6·5	…	42	…	·5	11	…	8·5	2·5	…	…	4	20	30	6	30	32·5	…
Per cent.	…	…	1·2	17·4	23·5	7·8	·6	50·6	…	·6	13·2	…	10·2	3	…	…	4·8	24·1	36·1	7·2	36·1	…	39·1
232. Do., country folk	40	2·4/1·4	1·5	6	11·5	6·5	·5	26	…	1	3	…	…	2	1	…	2	7	11	1	11	…	…
Per cent.	…	…	3·7	15	28·7	16·2	1·2	65	…	2·5	7·5	·5	5·5	5	2·5	…	5	17·5	27·5	2·5	27·5	…	17·2
233. Brentwood, town & country	70	4·9/2·1	…	6	18·5	4·5	…	29	…	…	12	…	…	3	3	…	8	17·5	29	3	29	…	…
Per cent.	…	…	…	8·5	26·4	6·4	…	41·4	…	…	17·1	…	7·9	4·3	4·3	…	11·4	25	41·4	4·3	41·4	…	34·4

Colour of Hair and Eyes in several Districts of the United Kingdom, from Personal Observation.—ENGLAND, continued.

Colour of Hair	Number	Sex	EYES LIGHT						EYES INTERMEDIATE OR NEUTER						EYES DARK						Indices	
			Red	Fair	Brown	Dark	Nig.	Eyes Light	Red	Fair	Brown	Dark	Nig.	Eyes Neuter	Red	Fair	Brown	Dark	Nig.	Eyes Dark	Gross	Per Cent
LONDON. 234. Various parts of City and West End, lower classes	1000	m	28·5	105	300	133	6·5	57·3	4·5	15·5	62	49·5	2	13·3	4	9·5	65·5	183·5	32·5	29·5	...	28·1
	1000	fem	34	82	270	106	3	49·5	6·5	19	72·5	59·5	3·5	16·1	7·5	15·5	80	214	28	345	...	28·4
	900	m	29·5	115·5	254	100	4	503	4·5	17	50	37	6·5	115	6	11·5	62·5	165	37	282	213	...
Per cent.			3·3	12·8	28·2	11·1	·4	55·8	·5	1·9	5·5	4·1	·7	12·8	·6	1·3	6·9	18·3	4·1	31·3	...	23·5
	2500	fem	79	205·5	682	299	9·5	1275	17·5	40·5	160·5	148	5·5	372	13	19·5	190	539·5	81	843	803·5	...
Per cent.			3·16	8·21	27·28	11·96	·38	51	·70	1·62	6·4	5·92	·22	14·88	·52	·78	7·6	21·58	3·24	33·72	...	32·15
Ditto	250	both	9	29	81·5	28·5	2	150	2	1	14	15	1	33	1·5	2·5	13	41·5	8·5	67	63	...
Per cent.			3·6	11·6	32·6	11·4	·8	60	·8	·4	5·6	6	·4	13·2	·6	1	5·2	16·6	3·4	26·8	...	26·2
235. Clerkenwell (200), and Rotherhithe (50)	250	both	9·5	22	69	28	2·5	131	1	4	9·5	11	1·5	27	1·5	1	19	56	14	92	91·5	...
Per cent.			3·8	8·8	27·4	11·2	1	52·4	·4	1·6	3·8	4·4	·6	10·8	·6	·6	7·6	22·4	5·6	36·8	...	36·6
236. London, general average of lower classes, p. cent.	6000	⅔ fem	3·2	9·5	28·1	11·7	·5	53	·6	1·6	6·2	5·4	·3	14·1	·6	1	7·3	20·3	3·6	32·8	...	29·7
237. London, upper class, per cent.	500	m	4·1	14·9	30	14·3	·5	63·8	·3	·5	3·4	5·2	·4	9·8	·4	·4	5·5	17·1	3	26·2	...	23·8
Ditto	323	fem	13	58·5	80	35·5	...	187	2	3·5	18·5	16	...	40	3	2·5	20	59·5	11	96	50·5	...
Per cent.			4	18·1	24·7	11·1	...	57·9	·6	1·1	5·7	4·9	...	12·3	·9	·8	6·2	18·4	3·4	29·7	...	15·6
KENT. 238. Greenhithe	100	both	1·5	15	40	8·5	...	65	1	...	8	4	...	13	1	1	6·5	10·5	3	22	...	9·5

No. & Place	No.	Sex																						Index
239. Canterbury	175	both	4	18	68·5	17·5	…	108	…	…	22	…	12	8	2	2·5	1	2·5	11	28·5	2	45	30·5	…
Per cent.	…	…	2·3	10·3	39·1	10	…	61·7	…	…	12·6	…	6·8	4·5	1·1	1·4	·6	1·1	6·3	16·3	1·1	25·7	…	17·4
240. Dover, townsfolk	325	both	7·5	42	119	24·5	…	194	1	…	42	1	16·5	17·5	7	1	1	33	51·5	2·5	89	44	…	
Per cent.	…	…	2·3	12·9	36·6	7·5	…	59·7	·3	…	12·9	…	5·1	5·4	2·1	…	…	10·1	15·8	·8	27·3	…	13·5	
240A. Dover, boatmen	60	m	2	11	25·5	7·5	1	47	…	5	5	…	3	2	…	…	…	3	5	…	8	3·5	…	
Per cent.	…	…	3·3	18·3	42·5	12·5	1·6	78·3	…	…	8·3	…	5	3·3	…	…	…	5	8·3	…	13·3	…	5·7	
241. Ashford, market, farmers	150	¹⁰⁹⁄₄₁	4·5	18·5	43	17·5	·5	84	·5	20	20	·5	8	9·5	1	8	…	13·5	27	3	46	34·5	…	
Do., labourers, some townsfolk	70	…	2·5	12	12·5	12	…	39	…	14	14	…	5	5·5	1·5	5	2	4·5	11·5	1	17	13	…	
Total	220	…	7	30·5	55·5	29·5	·5	123	…	34	34	…	15	15	2·5	13	3	18	38·5	4	63	47·5	…	
Per cent.	…	…	3·2	13·8	25·2	13·4	·2	55·9	·2	15·4	15·4	·2	6·8	5·9	1·1	5·9	1·3	8·2	17·5	1·8	28·6	…	21·6	

SUSSEX.

No. & Place	No.	Sex																						Index
242. Horsham, market, town and country folk	167	m	6	24·5	60	19·5	…	110	…	20	20	2	10	7	1	1	…	10	21	5·5	37	33·5	…	
	45	fem	…	4·5	12	8·5	…	25	…	4	4	…	1	2	…	…	1	6·5	8	5·5	16	10·5	…	
Total	212	both	6	29	72	28	…	135	…	24	24	2	11	9	1	1	1	16·5	29	…	53	44	…	
Per cent.	…	…	2·8	13·7	33·9	13·2	…	63·6	…	11·3	11·3	·9	5·2	4·2	·5	·5	·5	7·8	13·7	2·6	25·1	…	20·7	
243. Battle	33	²⁸⁄₅	…	5·5	12	2·5	…	…	…	6	6	…	2·5	1·5	…	…	…	2	6·5	·5	…	·7	21·2	
Per cent.	…	…	…	…	…	…	…	…	…	…	…	…	…	…	…	…	…	…	…	…	…	…		
244. Chichester, city	70	m	1	10·5	21	4	·5	37	…	3	3	…	1	4	…	…	…	7·5	12·5	2·5	27	+6·5	…	
	23	fem	1	5	10	1	…	16	…	3	3	…	1·5	·5	…	…	…	…	4	…	4	+5	…	
Total	93	…	1	15·5	31	5	·5	53	·5	9	9	3	2·5	4·5	2	1	…	7·5	16·5	2·5	31	7	…	
Per cent.	…	…	1·1	16·6	33·3	5·4	·5	56·9	·5	9·6	9·6	2·1	2·7	4·8	2·1	1·5	…	8	17·7	2·7	33·2	+6·5	…	
245. Do., farmers	79	m	5·5	21	…	3·5	…	48	·5	8	8	…	5	1·5	1·5	…	…	13	8·5	13	1·5	23	+1	7·6

Colour of Hair and Eyes in several Districts of the United Kingdom, from Personal Observation.—ENGLAND, continued.

Colour of Hair	Number	Sex	EYES LIGHT					Eyes Light	EYES INTERMEDIATE OR NEUTER					Eyes Neuter	EYES DARK					Eyes Dark	Indices	
			Red	Fair	Brown	Dark	Nig.		Red	Fair	Brown	Dark	Nig.		Red	Fair	Brown	Dark	Nig.		Gross	Per Cent.
246. Other country folk	66	m	1·5	15·5	16	5	...	38	...	3	3	3	...	9	...	...	6·5	10·5	2	19	+2·5	...
	22	fem	...	4	9·5	3	·5	17	...	1	2	...	...	3	...	...	1	1	...	2	0	...
Total, country	167	...	7	37	46·5	11·5	1	103	...	5·5	6·5	8	...	20	...	...	16	24·5	3·5	44	+3·5	...
Per cent. ...	...	...	4·2	22·1	27·8	6·9	·6	61·6	...	3·3	3·9	4·8	...	12	...	...	9·6	14·7	2·1	26·4	...	2·1
BERKSHIRE.																						
247. Reading, town and country	200	both	4	23·5	78·5	11	...	117	1	·5	18	4·5	...	24	·5	1·5	23	27·5	6·5	59	25	...
248. Pangbourne...	40	both	...	7	11·5	3·5	...	22	...	...	5	2	...	7	...	·5	4·5	6	...	11	4	...
Total...	240	both	4	30·5	90	14·5	...	139	1	·5	23	6·5	...	31	·5	2	27·5	33·5	6·5	70	29	...
Per cent. ...	...	...	1·7	12·7	37·5	6	...	57·9	·4	·2	9·6	2·7	...	12·9	·2	·8	11·5	14	2·7	29·2	...	12·1
249. Berkshire, peasants	20	=	...	3	10	2	...	15	...	...	...	1	...	1	...	...	2	2	...	4	2	10
HAMPSHIRE.																						
250. Southampton	193	m	3·5	38	66·5	16·5	·5	125	3	3	9·5	5·5	...	21	1	2	15	25·5	3·5	47	...	...
	207	fem	10	30	68·5	22	·5	131	1	2	7·5	6·5	...	17	4	·5	15·5	36	3	59	...	...
Total...	400	both	13·5	68	135	38·5	1	256	4	5	17	12	...	38	5	2·5	30·5	61·5	6·5	106	...	...
Per cent. ...	...	...	3·4	17	33·7	9·6	·2	64	1	1·2	4·2	3	...	9·5	1·2	·6	7·6	15·4	1·6	26·5	...	7·2
251. Fareham, town	136	$\frac{35}{33}$	6·5	21	49	12·5	...	89	...	2	5·5	6·5	...	15	...	·5	5	23·5	3	32	20·5	14·3
Do., country	39	$\frac{26}{13}$	...	7	20	3	...	30	...	...	1	1	1	2	...	...	1	5·5	·5	7	3·5	9

Locality	n	ind																				
Total...	175	...	...	24	39	3·5	29	6	·5	...	17	1	7·5	6·5	2	...	119	...	15·5	69	28	6·5
Per cent. ...		...	13·7	...	22·3	2	16·5	3·4	·3	...	9·7	·6	4·3	3·7	1·1	...	68	...	8·8	39·4	16	3·7
252. Farnborough ...	25	m	10	2·5	3	...	2	1	...	...	2	...	·5	1·5	...	...	20	...	3	14	3	...
WILTSHIRE.																						
253. Salisbury ...	220	bcth	...	...	63	3	43·5	13·5	3	...	32	...	18	14·5	4·5	1	125	...	20	68·5	31	4·5
Per cent. ...		...	13·7	3·5	28·6	1·4	19·8	6·1	1·4	...	14·5	...	5·9	6·6	2	·4	56·8	...	9·1	31·1	14·1	2
254A. Wilton ...	67	bcth	...	2·5	17	1	8·5	6·5	·5	1	11	...	3	5·5	1·5	...	39	...	5·5	17·5	14	2
B. Heytesbury, &c. ...	50	36/14	...	...	17	1	6	1	...	...	...	...	3	3	1	...	...	...	4·5	6·5	10	1
C. Warminster ...	50	50/0	11·5	2·5	...	2	6	4	1·5	...	...	1	5	2	...	...	...	...	4	13·5	11	2·5
Total, Wiley valley..	167	...																				
Per cent. ...		...	6·9	11·5	23·9	1·2	14·9	6·9	·9	...	15	·6	6·6	6·3	1·5	...	56·1	...	8·4	22·4	20·9	3·3
Including females	34	fem	30·9	10·5	11	1	8	1·5	·5	...	8	...	5	2	1	·5	15	...	2	8	4	1
255. Devizes, town	100	m	...	10	25	2·5	14·5	6	2	...	19	...	7·5	9	2	...	56	...	8·5	26·5	16	5
Including females	50	fem	22·5	22·5	19	3	13·5	2·5	2	1·4	9	...	4	5	...	·5	22	...	4	13	5	...
Total...	150	100/0	32·5	...	44	5·5	28	8·5	2	1	28	...	11·5	14	2	·5	78	...	12·5	39·5	21	5
Per cent. ...		...	21·6	...	29·3	3·6	18·6	5·6	1·3	1·4	18·6	...	7·6	9·3	1·3	·3	52	...	8·3	26·3	14	3·3
256. Calne ...	70	50/20	27·8	19·5	16	3	10	2	...		8		6	1			46	2	11·5	17·5	13·5	1·5
Per cent. ...		...	27·8	...	22·8	4·3	14·3	2·8	·5	1	11·4	...	8·6	1·4	·5	...	65·7	2·8	16·4	25	19·3	2·1
257. Malmesbury...	143	both	...	34	37	2·5	24	10·5	...	1	26	...	8·6	16	·3	·7	80	1	15	45	16	3
Per cent. ...		...	23·8	...	25·9	17·5	16·8	7·3	...	·7	18·2	...	8·5	11·2	...	1	56	·7	10·5	31·5	11·2	2·1
258. Chippenham and neighbourhood	650	both	88·5	88·5	148	6·5	88	49	3	1·5	140	2	35	92·5	9·5	1	362	2·5	51·5	215	81·5	11·5
Per cent. ...		...	13·6	22·7	22·7	1	13·5	7·5	·4	·2	21·5	·3	5·4	14·2	1·4	·1	55·7	·4	7·9	33·1	12·5	1·8

Colour of Hair and Eyes in several Districts of the United Kingdom, from Personal Observation.—ENGLAND, continued.

Colour of Hair	Number	Sex	EYES LIGHT						EYES INTERMEDIATE OR NEUTER.						EYES DARK.						Indices.	
			Red	Fair	Brown	Dark	Nig.	Eyes Light.	Red	Fair	Brown	Dark	Nig.	Eyes Neuter.	Red	Fair	Brown	Dark	Nig.	Eyes Dark.	Gross.	Per Cent.
259. Corsham (75), Laycock, Hardenhuish, &c. (100)	175	both	7·5	25·5	53	14·5	·5	101	...	4	17	12	...	33	·5	·5	17	21·5	1·5	41	14	...
Per cent.	...	...	4·3	14·6	30·3	8·3	·3	57·7	...	2·3	9·7	6·8	...	18·8	·3	·3	9·7	12·3	·8	23·4	...	8
DORSET.																						
260. Dorchester, town ...	100	49/51	2	12·5	27·5	12	...	54	...	1·5	7	6·5	...	15	1	1	5·5	21	2·5	31	...	26·5
261. Wareham, town ...	50	38/12	·5	7	13·5	5	...	26	1	1	2	3	...	7	...	...	3	12·5	1·5	17	14	...
Per cent.	...	...	1	14	27	10	...	52	2	2	4	6	...	14	...	...	6	25	3	34	...	28
262. Gillingham, village ...	33	21/12	·5	3·5	8	8	...	20	...	·5	2	2·5	...	5	...	...	1	5	2	8	15	45·4
DEVON.																						
263. Exeter	361	m	7	35·5	86	84	3·5	216	·5	2·5	10	20·5	3·5	37	1	2	17·5	69·5	18	108	...	...
	439	fem	11·5	43	121	89·5	6	271	...	3·5	14	30	3·5	51	2	2·5	12	83	17·5	117	...	...
Total... ...	800	...	18·5	88·5	207	173·5	9·5	487	·5	6	24	50·5	7	88	3	4·5	29·5	152·5	35·5	225	...	44·8
Per cent.	...	...	2·3	11	25·8	21·7	1·2	60·8	·6	·7	3	6·3	·8	11	·4	·5	3·7	19	4·4	28·1	...	...
264. Bovey, &c.	30	11/19	2	2	8	3	...	15	...	...	1	2	...	3	1	...	1·5	9·5	...	12	9·5	31·7
265. Paignton, Totnes, and neighbourhood ...	200	m	8·5	24	36	31·5	4	104	...	2	8·5	23·5	5	39	...	...	7·5	32	17·5	57	105·5	...
	160	fem	4·5	12·5	33	35·5	5·5	91	...	2	7·5	15·5	2	27	...	1	4·5	27	9·5	42	92	...
Total... ...	360	...	13	36·5	69	67	9·5	195	...	4	16	39	7	66	...	1	12	59	27	99	...	...
Per cent.	...	...	3·6	10·1	19·1	18·6	2·6	54·1	...	1·1	4·4	10·8	1·9	18·3	·3	·3	3·3	16·4	7·5	27·5	...	54·7

	1	2	3	4	5	6	7	8	9	10	11	12	13	14	15	16	17	18	19	20	21	22
266. Ashburton and Vale of Dart	55	2¾/3¾	2·5	3·5	9·5	12·5	…	28	…	…	1	8	…	9	…	…	4	11	3	18	31·5	57·2
267. Brixham	200	both	5	23·5	51·5	40	4	124	…	1	5	18	3	27	2	1	6·5	29	10·5	49	89·5	…
Per cent.			2·5	11·7	25·7	20	2	62	…	·5	2·5	9	1·5	13·5	1	·5	3·2	14·5	5·2	24·5	…	44·7
268. Dartmouth	200	8·3/11·7	5	18	47·5	42·5	5	118	…	…	5·5	14	1·5	21	…	·5	6	40	9·5	56	105	52·5
Per cent.			2·5	9	23·7	21·2	2·5	59	1	…	2·7	7	·7	10·5	…	·2	3	20	4·7	28	…	52·5
269. Holsworthy	100	7·3/2·7	2	8	28·5	21·5	2	62	…	2	3	9·5	3·5	19	…	·5	1·5	10	7	19	52·5	45·4
270. Thence to Bideford	33	1·2/1	2	2	10	6	2	22	2	…	2·5	·5	·5	3	…	…	1	5·5	1·5	8	15	…
271. Bideford, town	175	10·5/7·0	4·5	20	52·5	20	…	97	1·1	2	10	16·5	·3	31	…	…	12	28	7	47	51	29·1
Per cent.			2·6	11·4	30	11·4	…	55·4	…	1·1	5·7	9·4	…	17·7	…	…	6·8	16	4	26·8	…	…
272. Plymouth, town and country	110	m	4·5	16·5	39·5	10·5	·5	71	1	2	6	9	1	17	…	…	5	13	4	22	17·5	…
	70	fem	2	3	13	10·5	·5	29	1	…	6·5	9·5	…	18	…	…	2·5	18·5	2	23	39·5	…
Total..	180		6·5	19·5	52·5	21	·3	100	·5	2	12·5	18·5	1	35	…	…	7·5	31·5	6	45	57	31·6
Per cent.			3·6	10·8	29·1	11·6	1·5	55·5	1	1·1	7	10·3	·5	19·4	…	…	4·1	17·5	3·3	25	…	51·5
273. Tavistock, Milton Abbot, Launceston	100	6·1/3·9	5	13	16·5	25	…	…	…	…	1	4	2	…	…	…	2	21·5	7·5	…	…	…
CORNWALL.																						
274. St. Austell, flower show, country folk	300	m	10	30	70	52	12	174	2	·5	8·5	20	9	40	1	1	9	53	22	86	166·5	55·5
	550	fem	19	51	113	110	9	302	3	7	20	48	3	81	2	2	22	109	32	167	271	49·2
Total..	850		29	81	183	162	21	476	5	7·5	28·5	68	12	121	3	3	31	162	54	253	437·5	…
Per cent.			3·4	9·5	21·5	19	2·5	56	·6	·9	3·3	8	1·4	14·2	·3	·3	3·6	19	6·3	29·7	…	51·4

Colour of Hair and Eyes in several Districts of the United Kingdom, from Personal Observation.—ENGLAND, continued.

Colour of Hair	Number	Sex	EYES LIGHT.						EYES INTERMEDIATE OR NEUTER.						EYES DARK.						Indices.	
			Red	Fair	Brown	Dark	Nig.	Eyes Light.	Red	Fair	Brown	Dark	Nig.	Eyes Neuter.	Red	Fair	Brown	Dark	Nig.	Eyes Dark.	Gross.	Per Cent.
275. Truro, city	250	m	8	34	51·5	44·5	4	142	2	1	4·5	17·5	7	32	2·5	1·5	10·5	46·5	15	76	111·5	...
	250	fem	8	23·5	62	46·5	2	142	2	2·5	12·5	16	1	34	...	1·5	10	48	14·5	74	108	...
Total...	500	...	16	57·5	113·5	91	6	284	4	3·5	17	33·5	8	66	2·5	3	20·5	94·5	29·5	150	219·5	...
Per cent.	...	...	3·2	11·5	22·7	18·2	12	56·8	·8	·7	3·4	6·7	1·6	13·2	·5	·6	4·1	18·9	5·9	30	...	43·9
276. Truro, country folk ...	81	m	1	9	19	16·5	4·5	50	...	...	2	6	1	9	...	1·5	2	10·5	8	22	48·5	...
	142	fem	4·5	12·5	29·5	21	2·5	70	1	...	4	7·5	6·5	19	...	...	10	32·5	10·5	53	82	...
Total...	223	...	5·5	21·5	48·5	37·5	7	120	1	...	6	13·5	7·5	28	...	1·5	12	43	18·5	75	130·5	...
Per cent.	...	...	2·5	9·6	21·7	16·8	3·1	53·8	·4	...	2·7	6	3·3	12·4	...	·7	5·4	19·3	8·3	33·7	...	58·5
277. Falmouth	200	m	7	24	45·5	32·5	5	114	2	...	9	17	5	33	2	·5	5·5	26	19	53	98	...
	150	fem	5	11·5	26	25	4·5	72	1	2·5	6·5	17·5	3·5	31	1	...	7	27·5	11·5	47	88	...
Total...	350	...	12	35·5	71·5	57·5	9·5	186	3	2·5	15·5	34·5	8·5	64	3	·5	12·5	53·5	30·5	100	186	...
Per cent.	...	...	3·4	10·1	20·4	16·4	2·7	53·1	·8	·7	4·4	9·8	2·4	18·3	·8	·1	3·5	15·3	8·7	28·5	...	53·1
278. Redruth	200	m	6·5	7·5	42	42	7	105	1·5	1·5	7	12·5	4·5	27	...	2	10	31·5	24·5	68	139	...
	200	fem	3	16	36	45	2	102	3	1	5	21	4	34	2	·5	10·5	34·5	16·5	64	120	...
Total...	400	...	9·5	23·5	78	87	9	207	4·5	2·5	12	33·5	8·5	61	2	2·5	20·5	66	41	132	259	...
Per cent.	...	...	2·4	5·9	19·5	21·7	2·2	51·7	1·1	·6	3	8·4	2·1	15·2	·5	·6	5·1	16·5	10·2	33	...	64·7

279. Penzance	125	m	3	12	23	18	4	60	1	1	2·5	9	4·5	18	...	·5	5·5	24	17	47	84·5	...
	125	fem	1·5	10	21·5	22·5	3·5	59	1	1	8·5	15	3·5	29	1	1	8	18	9	37	72	...
Total...	250	...	4·5	22	44·5	40·5	7·5	119	2	2	11	24	8	47	1	1·5	13·5	42	26	84	156·5	...
Per cent.	...	...	1·8	8·8	17·8	16·2	3	47·6	·8	·8	4·4	9·2	3·2	18·8	·4	·6	5·2	16·8	10·4	33·6	...	62·6
280. Newlyn and Mousehole, fishing villages	65	m	2	6	15·5	8	1·5	33	1	1	1	6·5	1·5	11	...	1	2	14	4	21	31·5	...
	79	fem	5·5	7	19	12·5	2	46	...	1	4·5	3·5	1	10	...	1	3	14·5	4·5	23	31	...
Total...	144	...	7·5	13	34·5	20·5	3·5	79	1	2	5·5	10	2·5	21	...	2	5	28·5	8·5	44	62·5	...
Per cent.	...	...	5·2	9	24	14·2	2·4	54·8	·7	1·4	3·8	7	1·7	14·6	...	1·4	3·5	19·8	5·9	30·5	...	43·4
SOMERSET.																						
281. Taunton	100	both	2	11	25	20·5	·5	59	...	...	7·5	5·5	1	14	...	...	6	20	1	27	...	38
282. Wellington	180	both	6	21	46·5	26·5	1	101	1	2·5	11·5	11	1	27	1	1	6	34	10	52	63	...
Per cent.	...	...	3·3	11·6	25·8	14·7	·5	56·1	·5	1·4	6·4	6·1	·5	15	·5	·5	3·3	18·9	5·5	28·8	...	35
283. Yeovil	63	m	...	11	19·5	6·5	...	37	...	1	5	2	...	7	...	...	2	14·5	1·5	18	14	...
	80	fem	..	11	22	6	1	40	...	...	3·5	8·5	...	12	...	...	4·5	23	·5	28	29·5	...
Total...	143	...	...	22	41·5	12·5	1	...	...	1	8·5	10·5	...	...	...	...	6·5	37·5	2	...	43·5	...
Per cent.	...	...	...	15·4	29	8·7	·7	53·9	...	·7	6	7·3	...	14	...	...	4·5	26·2	1·4	32·1	...	30·4
284. Wells	100	60/40	2	14	26	13	1	56	...	·5	4·5	7	1	13	2	...	4	18·5	6·5	31	...	37
285. Cheddar and Axbridge ...	55	35/20	·5	9	15	12	1·5	...	...	...	2	7	...	...	1	...	2	5	...	...	16·5	30
286. North Somerset, Avon to Mendip, country folk...	79	m	3·5	7	17·5	11·5	·5	...	...	2	5	7	...	...	...	...	6	15	4	...	...	...
	54	fem	1	5	17·5	10	·5	...	1	...	·5	6	·5	...	..	...	3·5	6·5	2	...	...	...
Total...	133	...	4·5	12	35	21·5	1	...	1	2	5·5	13	·5	...	...	...	9·5	21·5	6	...	...	...
Per cent.	...	...	3·4	9	26·2	16·1	·7	55·5	·7	1·5	4·1	9·8	·4	16·5	...	...	7·1	16·1	4·5	27·7	...	38·6

Colour of Hair and Eyes in several Districts of the United Kingdom, from Personal Observation.—ENGLAND, continued.

Colour of Hair	Number	Sex	EYES LIGHT.					Eyes Light.	EYES INTERMEDIATE OR NEUTER.					Eyes Neuter.	EYES DARK.					Eyes Dark.	Indices.	
			Red	Fair	Brown	Dark	Nig.		Red	Fair	Brown	Dark	Nig.		Red	Fair	Brown	Dark	Nig.		Gross.	Per Cent.
BRISTOL.																						
287. Bristol, market, peasants	50	both	3	4	17	8·5	·5	66	...	...	2	4	...	12	...	...	1·5	8·5	1	22	...	34
288. Bristol, city	1000	both	1·95	10·8	29·7	13·1	·6	56·1	·5	1·3	5·1	5	·1	12·1	·9	·5	6·6	20·2	3·3	31·6	...	32·1
Do.	1000	m	3·1	12·5	28·4	13·3	·7	58·1	·4	1	4·3	5	1	11·7	·4	·7	6·1	19·4	3·4	30·2	...	30
Do.	1000	fem	2·1	12·2	27·8	11·9	·4	54·6	·6	1·7	5·1	6·4	·5	14	·9	1·1	6·8	20·4	2·1	31·3	...	25·1
Do.	1000	m	2·4	12·9	29·4	11·7	·4	56·9	·3	1·3	4·3	4·4	·5	10·9	·6	·9	6·4	20·2	3·9	32·1	...	27·5
Do.	1000	fem	2·7	12	25·4	13·3	·7	54·2	·5	·9	5	6·7	·5	13·7	1·2	·7	6	20·8	3·3	32	...	31·8
Average of	5000	both	2·5	12·1	28·2	12·7	·6	56·1	·5	1·3	4·8	5·5	·4	12·5	·8	·8	6·4	20·2	3·2	31·4	...	28·8
289. Bristol, Whit-Monday, young people numerous	500	both	14·5	61·5	140·5	71	·5	288	3	5·5	30·5	28·5	1·5	69	2	4·5	37·5	86·5	12·5	143	123	...
Per cent.	...	...	2·9	12·3	28·1	14·2	·1	57·6	·6	1·1	6·1	5·6	·3	13·8	·4	·9	7·5	17·3	2·5	28·6	...	24·6
290. Bristol, mid. class, per cent.	300	m	3·1	11·3	29	10·5	·6	54·5	·5	1·6	6·8	5·8	·5	15·2	·3	·6	6·8	17·6	4·5	29·8	...	27·6
Do., per cent.	300	fem	2·5	15·6	30·1	15	...	63·2	...	1	4·1	3·5	...	8·6	·3	·6	5	20	2	27·9	...	22·5
291. Bristol, Clifton, and Bath, upper class, per cent.	200	m	3·7	13·5	29·7	12·5	·5	60	·5	2·2	3·7	6	·7	13·1	·5	·5	6	17·2	2·7	26·9	...	22·7
Do., per cent.	400	fem	3·4	14	27·4	11·9	...	56·7	·5	1	5·7	5·6	·1	12·9	·6	1·1	5·4	21	2·2	30·3	...	22·1
GLOUCESTERSHIRE.																						
292. Marshfield, Iron Acton	40	both	...	3·5	18	4·5	...	26	...	...	2	1	...	3	...	...	3	8	...	11	10	25

Locality	No.	Sex																							
293. Stroud (70), Berkeley and neighbourhood (30) ...	100	5∕27	16	4·5	33·5	9·5	·5	64	…	2	…	5	5	…	12	…	1	1	1	4	13·5	4·5	24	…	13·5
294. Dursley...	100	5∕5	15·5	2	27·5	13	…	58	…	…	1	3	6	1	11	1	…	1	1	7	18	4	31	…	23·5
295. Gloucester, city, a few country folk	139	m	20	4	34	16	…	74	…	3	1	6·5	8·5	2·5	19	1	·5	2·5	2·5	10	26	5·5	46	34·5	…
	134	fem	25	4	21·5	10	1·5	62	…	2	1·5	12·5	4	2	20	1·5	·5	2	1	13	30·5	5·5	52	36	…
	227	both	23·5	10	63	32	·5	129	1	2·5	…	13	8·5	2·5	·25	…	2	2	1	15	44·5	10·5	73	71·5	…
Total...	500	…	68·5	18	118·5/58	58	2	265	1	7·5	2·5	32	21	7·5	64	4	5	5	4	38	101	23	171	142	28·4
Per cent.	…	…	13·7	3·6	23·7	11·6	·4	53	…	1·5	·5	6·4	4·2	1·5	12·8	·5	1	·8	·8	7·6	20·2	4·6	34·2	…	…
296. Gloucester, market, country folk...	66	both most f	7·5	1·5	15·5	11	·5	36	…	1	1	4	3	1	8	…	1	1	4·5	4·5	14·5	1	22	20·5	31
Per cent.	…	…	11·3	2·3	24·4	16·6	·7	54·5	…	1·5	1·5	6	4·5	1·5	12·1	…	1·5	1·5	6·8	6·8	22	1·5	33·3	…	…
297. Tewkesbury...	100	12∕17	12	6	30·5	10	·5	59	·5	1·5	1·5	6	3	1·5	11	…	…	…	6	6	22·5	1·5	30	20·5	23·5
298. Micheldean, in Forest of Dean	36	46∕26	1	1	11	6·5	·5	20	…	·5	·5	2	·5	…	4	1	…	…	3	3	6·5	2·5	12	103	56·9
299. Chepstow	200	both	17	4·5	46·5	38	2	108	…	1	7	13·5	7	2·5	24	…	2	…	10	10	45	11	68	20·5	…
Per cent.	…	…	8·5	2·2	23·2	19	1	54	…	·5	·5	6·7	3·5	1·2	12	…	1	…	5	5	22·5	5·7	34	…	51·5

WALES.

SOUTH WALES.

Locality	No.	Sex																							
300. Newport	133	16∕18	7	2	35	24·5	2·5	71	1	…	2	11	2	2	16	2	2	·7	1	9·5	26	7·5	46	72·5	…
Per cent.	…	…	5·2	1·5	26·2	18·4	1·9	53·2	·7	…	1·5	8·2	1·5	1·5	12	1·5	1·5	…	·7	7·1	19·5	5·6	34·5	…	54·4
301. Llandaff	33	17∕16	·5	2·5	8·5	1·5	…	13	…	…	2	4	2	…	7	1	…	…	…	…	9·5	3·5	13	21	63·6

Colour of Hair and Eyes in several Districts of the United Kingdom, from Personal Observation.—WALES, continued.

Colour of Hair	Number	Sex	EYES LIGHT						EYES INTERMEDIATE OR NEUTER						EYES DARK						Indices	
			Red	Fair	Brown	Dark	Nig.	Eyes Light	Red	Fair	Brown	Dark	Nig.	Eyes Neuter	Red	Fair	Brown	Dark	Nig.	Eyes Dark	Gross	Per Cent.
302. Abergavenny, town ...	50	m	1	4·5	9·5	6	1	22	1	...	3	2	1	7	...	...	3·5	14·5	3	21	26	...
	50	fem	4	2·5	15·5	6	...	28	1	...	2	4	...	7	...	...	2	10·5	2·5	15	18	...
Total...	100	...	5	7	25	12	1	50	2	...	5	6	1	14	...	...	5·5	25	5·5	36	...	...
303. Do., market, country folk...	110	m	4	12·5	29·5	24·5	·5	71	...	...	4	7·5	3·5	15	1	1	4·5	9·5	8	24	47	...
	90	fem	2	8·5	23·5	12	...	46	...	1	7	6	...	14	1·5	·5	6·5	17·5	4	30	30	...
Total...	200	...	6	21	53	36·5	·5	...	...	1	11	13·5	3·5	...	2·5	1·5	11	27	12	...	...	...
Per cent.	...	...	3	10·5	26·5	18·2	·2	58·5	...	·5	5·5	6·7	1·7	14·5	1·2	·7	5·5	13·5	6	27	38·5	38·5
304. Crickhowel and neighbourhood	80	m/m	3	6·5	22·5	15·5	1·5	49	...	...	1·5	4·5	1	7	1	...	2·5	16	4·5	24	39·5	...
Per cent.	...	...	3·7	8·2	29·1	19·4	1·9	61·2	...	...	1·9	5·6	1·2	8·7	1·2	...	3·1	20	5·6	30	...	49·4
305. Brecon, town	50	m	2	6	10	11·5	·5	30	...	...	...	3	2	5	1	...	1	12·5	·5	15	24	...
	50	fem	3	3	9	9	1	25	...	...	1	3	1	6	...	...	3	16	...	19	25	...
Total...	100	...	5	9	19	20·5	1·5	55	...	...	1	6	3	11	1	...	4	28·5	·5	34	...	49
306. Merthyr, Pant, Taff Vale ...	93	m	2·5	6·5	28·5	11·5	1	50	...	3	4	4·5	·5	12	3	...	7·5	18	4·5	31	37	...
	67	fem	2	2	20·5	14	·5	39	...	...	...	3·5	2·5	7	3	...	3	11	4	21	34·5	...
Total...	160	...	4·5	8·5	49	25·5	1·5	89	1	3	4	8	3	19	3	1	10·5	29	8·5	52	71·5	...
Per cent.	...	...	2·8	5·3	30·6	15·9	1	55·6	·6	1·9	2·5	5	1·9	11·9	1·9	·6	6·2	18·1	5·3	32·5	...	44·5

306A. Pembroke and South Pembrokeshire	90	6/30	3	10·5	22	13	·5	49	...	...	5·5	9·5	1	16	...	·5	6	14·5	4	25	34·5	...
Per cent.	...	...	3·3	11·6	24·4	14·4	·5	54·4	...	...	6·1	10·5	1·1	17·8	...	·5	6·6	16·1	4·4	27·8	...	38·3
307. Caermarthen, eisteddfod, chiefly from neighbourhood of C. but not wholly so	375	m	22	26	52	61	6	167	4	2·5	10	36·5	17	70	2·5	5	19	67·5	47	138	246	...
	325	fem	12	19·5	52	42	2	127	4	2	13	30	4	53	2	5	19·5	82·5	36·5	145	195·5	...
Total	700	·34	.34	45·5	103·5	103	8	294	8	4·5	23	66·5	21	123	4·5	3·5	38·5	150	83·5	283	441·5	...
Per cent.	...	...	4·8	6·6	14·8	14·7	1·1	42	1·1	·6	3·3	9·4	3	17·5	·6	·5	5·5	21·4	11·9	40·4	...	63·1
308. Congregation at Welsh preaching in Bristol	100	46/54	2	6·5	17·5	12	...	38	1	...	6	4·5	1·5	13	1	1·5	13	30	4	49	...	49
309. Radnor	80	both	5	5	19	21	3	53	1	1	13	5·5	...	8	1	...	1	14	4	19	42·5	...
Per cent.	...	...	6·2	6·2	23·7	26·2	3·7	66·2	1·2	1·2	·6	6·9	...	10	1·2	...	1·2	17·5	5	23·7	...	53·1
310. Rhaidr-gwy	50	both	3	1	13·5	14·5	3	35	...	·5	1	2·5	·5	4	·5	·5	·5	6	4·5	11	34·5	...
Per cent.	...	...	6	2	27	29	6	70	...	1	1	5	1	8	1	...	1	12	9	22	...	69
311. Aberystwith, Goginan, Llangurig	100	both	5·5	5	20	19·5	2	52	...	...	4·5	6	3·5	14	...	·5	5·5	21·5	6·5	34	...	60
312. Central Wales, total including Kington, p. cent.	300	both	5·5	4·8	25·2	22·3	2·8	60·6	·3	·3	2·2	6·3	1·3	10·6	·3	·2	2·6	19·1	6·7	28·6	...	58·1
NORTH WALES.																						
313. Dinas Mawddwy, Cemmaes	50	32/18	1·5	1·5	8	6	...	17	1	...	3·5	6·5	...	11	...	...	3	17	2	22	29·5	...
Per cent.	...	...	3	3	16	12	...	34	2	...	7	13	...	22	...	...	6	34	4	44	...	59
314. Welshpool, Montgomery, Newtown	50	30/20	1·5	4	9·5	5	...	20	...	·5	5·5	7	...	13	...	1	5·5	8	2·5	17	18	...
Per cent.	...	...	3	8	19	10	...	40	...	1	11	14	...	26	...	2	11	16	5	34	...	36
315. Llanidloes	12	m	...	1	3	5	1	10	...	1	1	...	·5	2	1	...	...	...	...	...	5	42
316. Ruthin, eisteddfod	150	120/30	6·5	14·5	25·5	29	·5	76	2·5	1·5	7	11	3	25	1	1	7·5	31	9·5	49	71	...
Per cent.	...	...	4·3	9·7	17	19·3	·3	50·6	1·7	1	4·7	7·3	2	16·6	·7	...	5	20·7	6·3	32·6	...	47·3

Colour of Hair and Eyes in several Districts of the United Kingdom, from Personal Observation.—WALES, continued.

Colour of Hair	Number	Sex	EYES LIGHT						EYES INTERMEDIATE OR NEUTER						EYES DARK						Indices	
			Red	Fair	Brown	Dark	Nig.	Eyes Light	Red	Fair	Brown	Dark	Nig.	Eyes Neuter	Red	Fair	Brown	Dark	Nig.	Eyes Dark	Gross	Per Cent.
317. Holyhead	41	15/26	2·5	2·5	9·5	6·5	...	21	...	...	·5	3	·5	4	...	...	2·5	10	3·5	16	22·5	54·9
318. Carnarvon and a few Holyhead	278	115/163	6·5	25·5	55·5	39	5·5	132	1	2	12	25·5	5·5	46	2	1·5	12·5	64	20	100	152	...
Per cent.	...		2·3	9·1	20	14	2	47·5	·3	·7	4·3	9·2	2	16·5	·7	·5	4·5	23	7·2	36	...	54·6
319. Bangor	121	58/63	3·5	7	26·5	23	2	62	1	...	4	11	2	18	2	...	7·5	23	6	41	66	...
Per cent.	...		2·9	5·8	21·9	19	1·6	51·2	·8	...	3·3	9·1	1·6	14·9	1·6	...	6·2	21·1	5	33·9	...	54·5
320. Beddgelert and neighbourhood, Snowdon	68	48/20	1	3·5	13	14·5	2	34	...	...	5	5	4	14	2	...	2·5	12·5	3	20	43·5	...
Per cent.	...		1·5	5·1	29·1	21·3	3	50	...	...	7·3	7·3	5·9	20·6	3	...	3·7	18·4	4·4	29·4	...	64
321. Bettws-y-coed	36		2	1	10	5	...	18	·5	...	1·5	1·5	1·5	5	...	...	3·5	7·5	2	13	17·5	48·6
322. Llanwrst, religious meeting	100	46/55	5	7	18·5	14·5	1	46	3	1	4·5	10	2·5	21	2	...	8	19	4	33	...	40·5
NORTH WALES, TOTALS.																						
323. Total males	467	m	15	36·5	93	92·5	9	246	3·5	2	24·5	37	14	81	4	1	23	90·5	21·5	140	247	...
Per cent.	...		3·2	7·8	19·9	19·8	1·9	52·7	·7	·4	5·2	7·9	3	17·3	·8	·2	4·9	19·4	4·6	30	...	52·9
324. Total females	439	fem	31	31	86	55	3	190	5·5	4	20	43·5	5	78	6	·5	29·5	104	31	171	218·5	...
Per cent.	...		3·4	7	19·6	12·3	·7	43·3	1·2	·9	4·5	9·9	1·1	17·7	1·4	·1	6·7	23·7	7	38·9	...	49·8
325. Total both sexes	906		30	67·5	179	147·5	12	436	9	6	44·5	80·5	19	159	10	1·5	52·5	194·5	52·5	311	465·5	...
Per cent.	...		3·3	7·4	19·8	16·3	1·3	48·1	1	·6	4·9	8·9	2·1	17·5	1·1	1·6	5·8	21·4	5·8	34·3	...	51·2

IRELAND.

Colour of Hair	Number	Sex	EYES LIGHT						EYES INTERMEDIATE OR NEUTER						EYES DARK						Index of Nigrescence
			Red	Fair	Brown	Dark	Nig.	Eyes Light	Red	Fair	Brown	Dark	Nig.	Eyes Neuter	Red	Fair	Brown	Dark	Nig.	Eyes Dark	
1. Dublin, upper class	450	both	4	16·1	33·8	12·2	·8	66·9	·2	·5	4·9	4·3	·4	10·3	...	·7	7	13·3	1·7	22·7	14
2. Charleville, co. Limerick	32	both	...	23·5	32·8	18·8	...	75·1	...	...	3·1	15·6	...	18·7	...	...	3·1	3·1	...	6·2	14
3. Cashel and Cahir, Tipperary	236	both	7·2	12·7	35·1	19·9	·8	75·8	1·3	1·3	3·1	5·9	·2	11·8	...	...	1·5	9·1	1·7	12·3	18
4. Geileen, fishing village, co. Cork	33	both	4·5	22·7	24·2	10·6	1·5	63·5	3	...	6·1	6·1	6·1	21·3	...	...	...	12·1	3	15·1	19·8
5. Youghal, co. Cork	120	both	3·3	17·5	35·8	23	·4	80	...	...	2·5	6·1	·4	9	...	...	·8	10	...	10·8	19·9
6. Cork, upper class	250	both	5·6	15	26	14·8	·2	61·6	·4	1·2	3·4	6	·2	11·2	...	1·2	6·6	15·6	3·8	27·2	21·4
7. Wexford, New Ross, Waterford,&c.	800	both	5·2	14·9	32·5	18·4	1·4	72·4	·2	·4	4	5·4	1·4	11·4	·4	·1	3·3	10	2·2	16	22·4
8. Enniskillen	267	both	4·5	12·9	33	14·1	1·5	66	...	1·1	4·1	4·3	·9	11·1	·4	·2	5·1	15·2	2·8	23·7	24·9
9. Forth and Bargy, co. Wexford	80	both	3·7	10·6	30·6	21·2	1·2	67·5	...	2·5	6·2	6·2	...	15	·7	...	4·4	11·2	1·9	17·5	28
10. Kilkenny	220	both	7	6·8	33·9	16·2	1·1	65	·2	1·1	4·5	5·4	...	11·2	...	...	6	14·1	3	23·8	28·1
11. Cloyne, co. Cork	300	both	2·7	14·2	32·3	21	1·5	71·7	1·1	1	3·3	7·5	1·3	14·2	...	...	2·2	9·2	2·7	14·1	29·6
12. West Cavan, hill country	50	both	2	8	40	23	1	74	2	...	9	6	1	18	...	...	2	3	3	8	30
13. Cong, Joyce co. Mamturk, co. Galway	75	both	4	13·3	30	24·7	.	72	·4	·8	4·7	4·7	4	13·4	1·3	1·3	·7	7·3	4	14·6	32·3
14. Cork, lower class	1800	both	5·6	12·2	29·7	19·2	1·9	68	·4	...	3·2	7	1·7	13·1	·5	·3	2·7	9·8	4·8	18·1	33
15. Kildare	68	both	8·8	11·8	25	22	1·5	69·1	...	...	2·9	7·3	1·5	11·7	...	...	3·7	12·5	2·9	19·1	33
16. Ahadda and Whitegate, co. Cork	73	both	2·9	12·6	37·4	17	1	70·9	...	1	1·9	5·3	1·4	9·6	1	...	1·4	10·2	6·8	19·4	33·4
17. Dublin, lower class	1800	both	4·3	11·3	28	17·1	1·3	62	·3	1·1	4·8	7·5	1·2	14·9	·6	·5	3·5	14·3	4·2	23·1	34·2
18. Claddagh, Galway	170	both	4·7	12·7	32	20·6	3·5	73·5	...	1·2	1·8	7·3	2·1	12·4	...	...	2·4	7	4·1	14·1	35·3

Colour of Hair and Eyes in several Districts of the United Kingdom, from Personal Observation.—IRELAND, continued.

Colour of Hair	Number	Sex	EYES LIGHT.						EYES INTERMEDIATE OR NEUTER.						EYES DARK.						Index of Nigrescence.
			Red	Fair	Brown	Dark	Nig.	Eyes Light	Red	Fair	Brown	Dark	Nig.	Eyes Neuter	Red	Fair	Brown	Dark	Nig.	Eyes Dark	
19. Fermanagh, county	166	both	2·1	11·1	28	22·6	2·4	66·2	·6	·6	3·6	7·2	1·2	13·2	·6	·6	6	10·5	2·7	20·4	37·3
20. Strokestown, &c., co. Roscommon	79	both	5·1	12	26·6	22·1	1·2	67	…	…	1·9	11·4	3·1	16·4	…	…	4·4	10·1	1·9	16·4	39
21. Drogheda	169	both	1·8	10·9	34·3	18·9	3·2	69	…	…	3·3	6·8	1·2	11·3	1·2	…	3·7	10	4·7	19·6	40
22. Killarney, Kerry	75	both	4	10·7	34	18·6	4·7	72	…	…	…	8	…	8	…	…	2·7	14·6	2·7	20	41·3
23. Kiltskin holy well, co. Cork	191	both	6	12	22·8	25·4	2·9	69·1	…	·5	2·1	11·8	2·3	16·7	…	…	1·6	8·1	4·4	14·1	46
24. Collooney, Milkhaven,&c., co. Sligo	124	both	2·4	10·9	32·6	27·4	4	77·3	…	·4	·4	8·9	1·6	11·5	…	…	2·4	6·4	2·4	11·2	47
25. Aran Isle, Galway Bay	90	both	3·9	11·1	25·6	30·6	4·4	75·6	…	…	3·3	10	3·3	16·6	…	…	…	5	2·8	7·8	51·6
26. Pettigo, Donegal	53	both	1·9	8·5	33	13·2	…	56·6	1·9	…	…	7·5	1·9	11·3	…	…	1·9	18·9	11·3	32·1	53·7
27. Galway, town	300	both	4·3	9·2	23	26·7	3·2	66·4	·2	·2	3·2	8·6	1·7	13·9	·3	…	2·3	10·5	6·5	19·6	54·4
28. Sligo, town	295	both	3·9	6·3	25·9	24·1	2·9	63·1	1	·5	2·7	9·3	2	15·5	·7	…	3·4	9·1	7·7	21·2	55
29. Boyle, Roscommon	125	both	3·6	6	30	20·4	3·2	63·2	…	…	2·8	8·4	2·4	13·6	…	·3	2·8	13·6	6·8	23·2	57·6
30. Thurles, North Tipperary	31	both	…	9·7	32·2	21	4·8	67·7	…	…	3·2	8·1	1·6	12·9	…	…	…	12·9	6·5	19·4	58·1
31. Manor Hamilton, Leitrim	105	both	4·8	3·8	30·5	26·7	1·9	57·7	·9	…	2·9	5·2	3·3	12·3	…	…	2·4	11·4	6·2	20	58·6
32. Athlone	125	both	5·2	3·6	30	25·2	1·6	65·6	…	…	3·2	8	3·2	14·4	…	…	2·8	9·2	8	20	59·2
33. Longford and Ballymahon	131	both	2·3	5·3	26·7	30·5	2·3	67·1	1·5	…	2·7	10·3	2·3	16·8	…	…	1·5	9·5	5	16	60·4
34. Oughterard, &c., co. Galway	95	both	…	9	28·4	30·5	2·6	70·5	…	…	2·6	6·8	4·2	13·6	…	…	…	12·1	3·7	15·8	61·4
35. Dingle, Kerry	133	both	2·6	9·8	24·8	21	4·9	63·1	…	·5	2·6	8·3	4·9	15·8	·7	…	3	8·2	9	20·9	62
	1	2	3	4	5	6	7	8	9	10	11	12	13	14	15	16	17	18	19	20	21

	1	2	3	4	5	6	7	8	9	10	11	12	13	14	15	16	17	18	19	20	21
36. Eastern Connemara, co. Galway...	100	both	3	9	24·5	25·5	3	65	...	...	...	8·5	3·5	12	1	...	2·5	11	8·5	23	62
37. Cappoquin, co. Waterford ...	55	both	1·8	5·5	30	24·5	...	61·8	...	...	1·8	12·7	5·4	19·9	...	...	...	14·6	3·6	18·2	62·5
38. Valentia, Kerry	36	both	11·1	7	12·5	12·5	9·7	52·8	...	...	5·5	9·7	7	22·2	2·8	...	2·8	7	12·5	25·1	66·7
39. Carrick-on-Shannon, Leitrim ...	85	both	2·3	4·1	31·8	30·6	2·9	71·7	...	...	1·2	12·4	2·9	16·5	...	...	...	4·7	7·1	11·8	67
40. Iar-Connaught, co. Galway ...	95	both	1·6	8·4	22·6	26·3	6·3	65·2	1	...	3·7	7·9	4·2	16·8	...	...	1·1	7·9	9	18	70·1
41. Cahirciveen, Kerry...	258	both	6·8	5·8	18·4	18·4	3·7	53·1	·4	...	2·7	11·1	7·5	21·7	·4	...	2·5	11·5	10·5	24·9	71
42. Miltown, Killorglin, and peninsula about Cahirciveen ...	234	both	4·5	7·7	18·8	22·4	5·5	58·9	·9	·4	2·3	10·2	7·9	21·7	·9	...	1·1	7·2	10	19·2	72·2
43. Moytura, &c., co. Sligo... ...	103	both	6·3	2·4	20·8	18	5·8	53·3	...	·5	2·4	10·7	2·9	16·5	...	...	1	19·4	9·7	30·1	75·7
44. Ventry, &c., Kerry...	100	both	2	6	25	25·5	3·5	62	...	...	...	8·5	4·5	13	...	...	2	9·5	13·5	25	78·5
45. Mallow, co. Cork	93	both	2·1	7·5	16·1	25·8	9·7	61·2	1·1	...	2·1	14	2·1	19·3	...	...	...	8·6	10·7	19·3	80·6
46. Castlemaine, &c., Kerry ...	150	both	4·7	4·7	17	32·3	7·3	66	·7	...	·7	10	5·3	16·7	...	...	1	8·3	8	17·3	81·7
47. Clifden, co. Galway	111	both	3·1	·9	21·6	26·5	8·1	60·2	...	...	2·2	8·5	10	20·7	·9	...	·9	10·8	6·3	18·9	89·5
Total	9956																				

Note.—The persons observed were those met with at the places or in the districts indicated, and, of course, were not all natives, though in most cases, no doubt, the immense majority were so. The return of Dublin upper class, for example, must include some English strangers. In some places, the number of instances is too small to be relied on as yielding any approach to the true proportions of the several colours; but I have not thought it advisable to exclude the results. For example, the fairness of the Charleville people, and the darker colours of the people of Thurles, are confirmed by what other information I can gather respecting the natives of the county of Limerick and of Northern Tipperary respectively. The people of Clare, whence I have no observations worth publication, are, I believe, comparatively fair towards the east, near Limerick, but very dark in the western part of the county. Geileen, a small fishing village, is probably correctly represented, as 33 constitute a large portion of the adult population.

MILITARY STATISTICS.—From the *Hue and Cry*.

	Index of Nigrescence	Pure Blond Type, with Red	Mixed Blond Type	Mixed Brown Type	Pure Brown Type	Number of Observations	EYES BLUE, GRAY, OR LIGHT. HAIR — Red	Fair, or Light Brown	Brown	Dark, or Dark Brown	Black	Total	Per Cent.	EYES HAZEL, BROWN, OR DARK. HAIR — Red	Fair, or Light Brown	Brown	Dark, or Dark Brown	Black	Total	Per Cent.
Northumberland, includ. some Newcastle	4·7	19·2	49	30·1	12·6	150	7	22	47	24	...	100	66·6	1	6	25	17	1	50	33·3
Newcastle and Gateshead	8·5	25·3	48	30	14·6	150	6	32	34	26	2	100	66·6	...	5	23	18	4	50	33·3
Durham, with Middlesbro'	3	23	54	23·5	11	200	8	38	62	29	5	142	71	...	11	25	20	2	58	29
Cumberland, Westmoreland and Furness	-6·5	34·5	53	22·5	13	200	11	58	37	32	4	142	71	4	9	19	23	3	58	29
North and East Riding	-7·4	25·2	58·6	24	8·6	150	10	28	50	15	...	103	68·6	5	6	23	11	2	47	31·3
West Riding	+5·1	22·3	48	33·4	17·1	600	15	119	154	68	7	363	60·5	8	28	98	87	16	237	39·5
Lancashire	8·5	21·2	48·6	31·7	14·5	800	22	148	219	104	15	508	63·5	10	28	138	91	25	292	36·5
Lincolnshire	-4·7	28	56	30·5	13·9	150	6	36	42	13	2	99	66	1	4	25	19	2	51	34
Nottinghamshire	-1	25	53·5	29	14·5	200	2	48	57	21	1	129	64·5	3	10	29	20	9	71	35·5
Derbyshire	-3·6	26·4	52·4	30·6	9·6	167	7	37	44	22	1	111	66·5	1	4	35	13	3	56	33·5
Staffordshire	+7	21·5	49·5	38	18·5	200	7	36	56	14	4	117	58·5	...	7	39	32	5	83	41·5
Leicestershire	8·6	16·2	43·7	32·4	10	80	3	10	22	11	2	48	60	4	2	18	5	3	32	40
Cambridge	7·5	22·5	62·5	27·5	15	40	1	8	16	4	...	29	72·5	...	...	5	4	2	11	27·5
East Anglia (rest)	-1·6	24·4	43·4	37·2	17·2	250	6	55	48	29	...	138	55·2	2	17	50	39	4	112	44·8
Essex (extramet)	+4·5	19·5	46	37·5	19·5	200	5	34	53	19	...	111	55·5	2	12	36	35	4	89	44·5
Middlesex (extramet)	1·5	19·5	58·5	34·5	10·5	67	...	13	26	3	1	43	64·2	...	1	16	4	3	24	35·8
London	7·3	16·5	48·4	35·5	15·2	1250	29	178	399	130	9	745	59·6	6	55	254	160	30	505	40·4
	1	2	3	4	5	6	7	8	9	10	11	12	13	14	15	16	17	18	19	20

	1	2	3	4	5	6	7	8	9	10	11	12	13	14	15	16	17	18	19	20
Kent (extramet)	2·3	23·7	48·5	32·5	17·1	350	5	78	87	42	1	213	60·8	5	18	54	50	10	137	39
Surrey (extramet)	4·6	22·6	52·6	29·3	18	150	4	30	45	17	…	96	64	4	6	17	20	7	54	36
Sussex	3	27	40·3	36	16·5	200	6	48	27	34	1	116	58	…	12	39	30	3	84	42
Brighton	8	12	56	28	14	50	…	6	22	3	1	32	64	1	3	7	5	2	18	36
Berkshire	3·9	24·1	48	32·7	16	175	4	38	42	21	2	107	61·1	2	9	29	21	7	68	38·9
Hampshire	1·5	23·5	48	32	13	200	3	44	48	20	7	122	61	4	10	38	22	4	78	39
Portsmouth	5·3	20	42·6	34·6	14·6	75	…	15	17	10	…	42	56	…	7	15	6	5	33	44
Wiltshire	8	19	35	44	23	100	1	18	16	10	1	46	46	2	8	21	21	2	54	54
Dorset	11·3	23·7	38·7	51·2	25	80	1	18	12	6	…	37	46·2	…	2	38	16	4	43	53·7
Devon	10·8	23·6	46·8	33·6	18·4	250	6	53	58	32	4	153	61·2	2	11	38	33	13	97	38·8
Cornwall	20·6	18·6	42	44·6	24·6	150	1	27	35	15	2	80	53·3	…	3	30	29	8	70	46·6
Somerset	5·5	18·5	59·5	27·5	13·5	200	6	31	82	21	…	140	70	…	5	28	22	5	60	30
Bristol	14	16	49	33	15	100	1	15	33	13	2	64	64	…	3	18	14	1	34	34
Gloucestershire	12	19·3	47·3	39·3	20	150	3	26	42	14	2	87	58	1	3	29	27	3	63	42
Oxfordshire	·4	26·4	45·6	31·2	13·6	125	1	32	24	18	2	77	63·6	…	9	22	16	1	48	38·4
Bucks and Herts	17	12·5	45	38·5	20	200	1	24	65	22	1	113	56·5	1	9	37	35	5	87	43·5
Northamptonshire, Rutland, Beds., Hunts	10·6	19·3	45·3	35·3	21·3	150	2	27	39	18	…	86	57·3	…	11	21	26	6	64	42·6
Leicestershire	8·6	16·2	43·7	32·5	10	80	3	10	22	11	2	48	60	4	2	18	5	3	32	40
Warwickshire	6	20	39	36	21	100	4	16	19	14	…	53	53	4	7	15	19	2	47	47
Birmingham	10·5	19·5	47·5	37	17·5	200	5	34	56	23	3	121	60·5	2	3	39	32	3	79	39·5
Worcestershire	8	26	51	34	16	100	3	23	25	12	1	64	64	…	2	18	10	6	36	36

MILITARY SCHEDULES

INDEX OF NIGRESCENCE
= Dark + 2 Black
− Red − Fair

Minus
0 to 5
Over 5
Over 10
Over 15
Over 20

IRISH NAMED PERSONS
BORN IN YORKSHIRE
OR LANCASHIRE

IRISH NAMED PERSONS
BORN IN LONDON

IRISH NAMED
PERSONS BORN
IN SCOTLAND

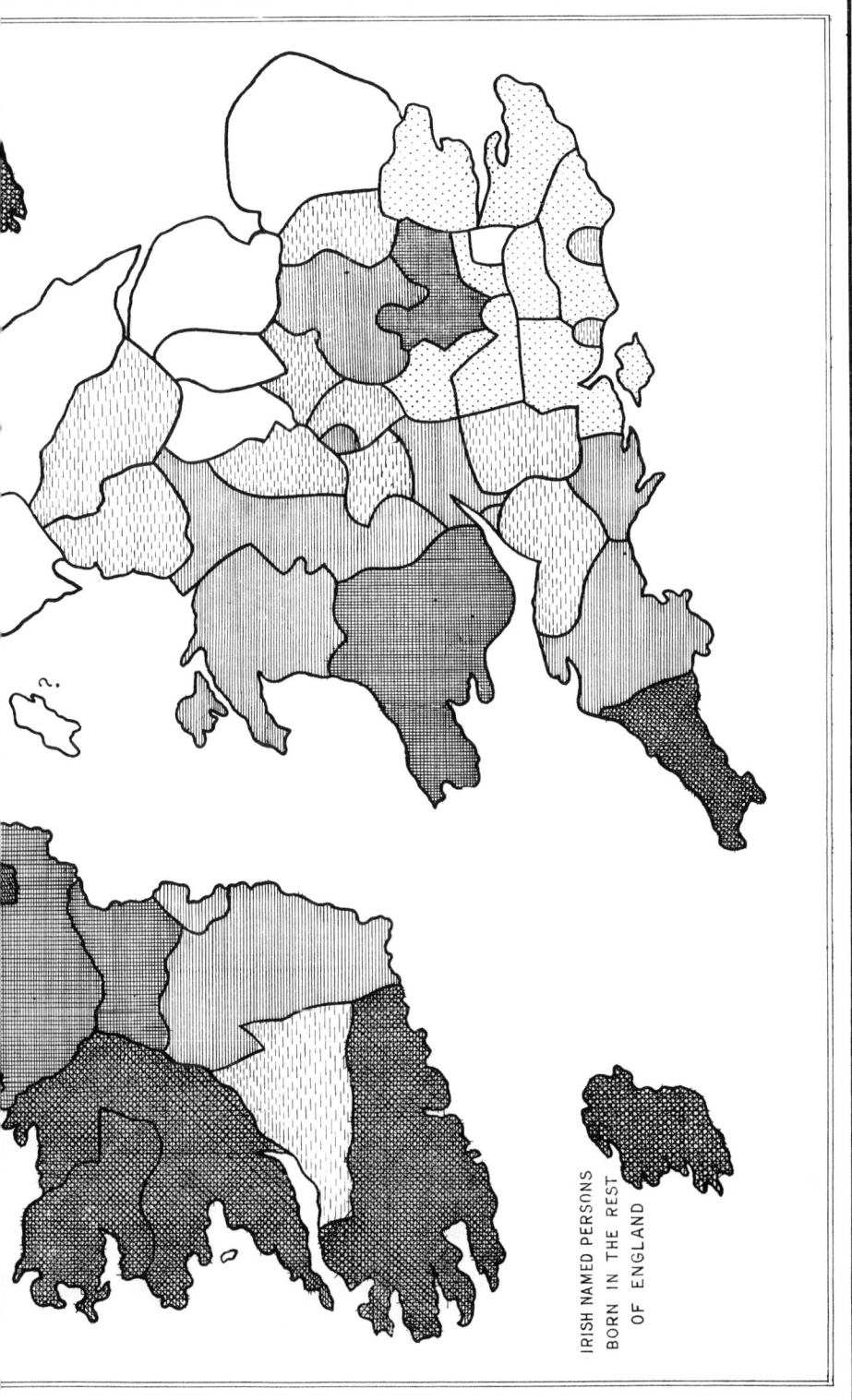

IRISH NAMED PERSONS
BORN IN THE REST
OF ENGLAND

ARROWSMITH BRISTOL.

MILITARY SCHEDULES

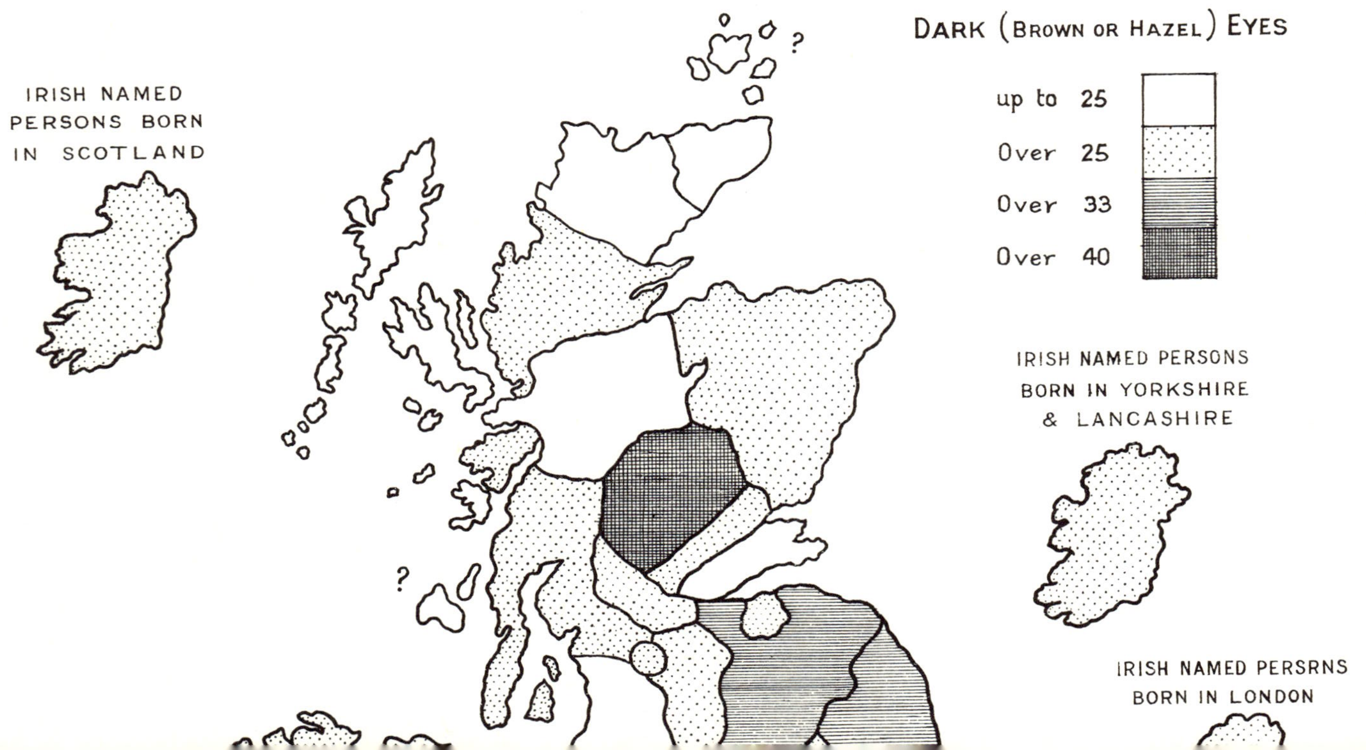

DARK (BROWN OR HAZEL) EYES

up to 25
Over 25
Over 33
Over 40

IRISH NAMED PERSONS
BORN IN YORKSHIRE
& LANCASHIRE

IRISH NAMED PERSRNS
BORN IN LONDON

IRISH NAMED
PERSONS BORN
IN SCOTLAND

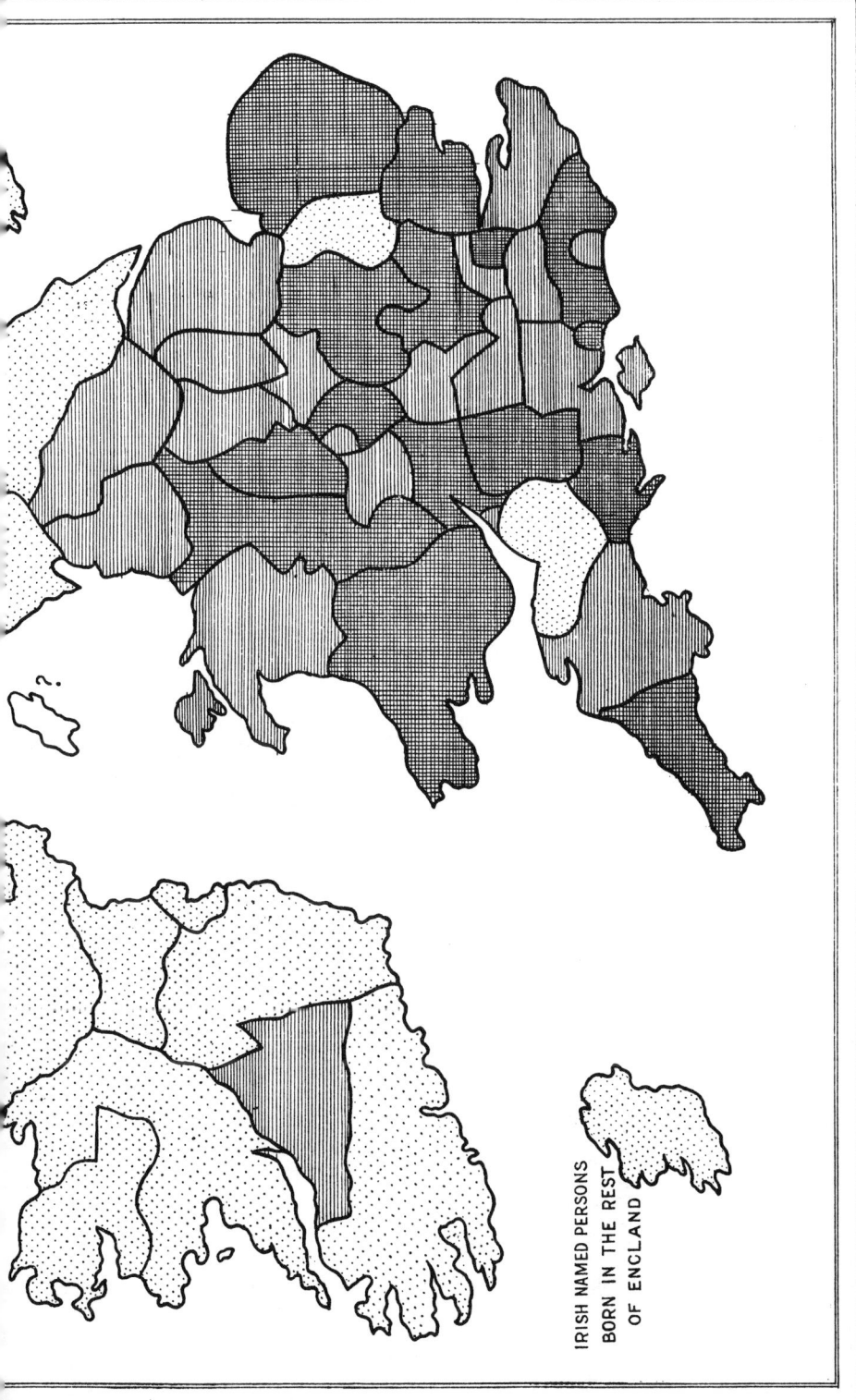

IRISH NAMED PERSONS
BORN IN THE REST
OF ENGLAND

ARROWSMITH   BRISTOL.

MILITARY SCHEDULES

Excess of pure Blond over pure Dark Type.

Over 15
Over 10
Over 5
up to 5
5 to =
up to −5

IRISH NAMED PERSONS BORN IN YORKSHIRE OR LANCASHIRE

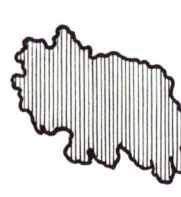

IRISH NAMED PERSONS BORN IN LONDON

IRISH NAMED PERSONS BORN IN SCOTLAND

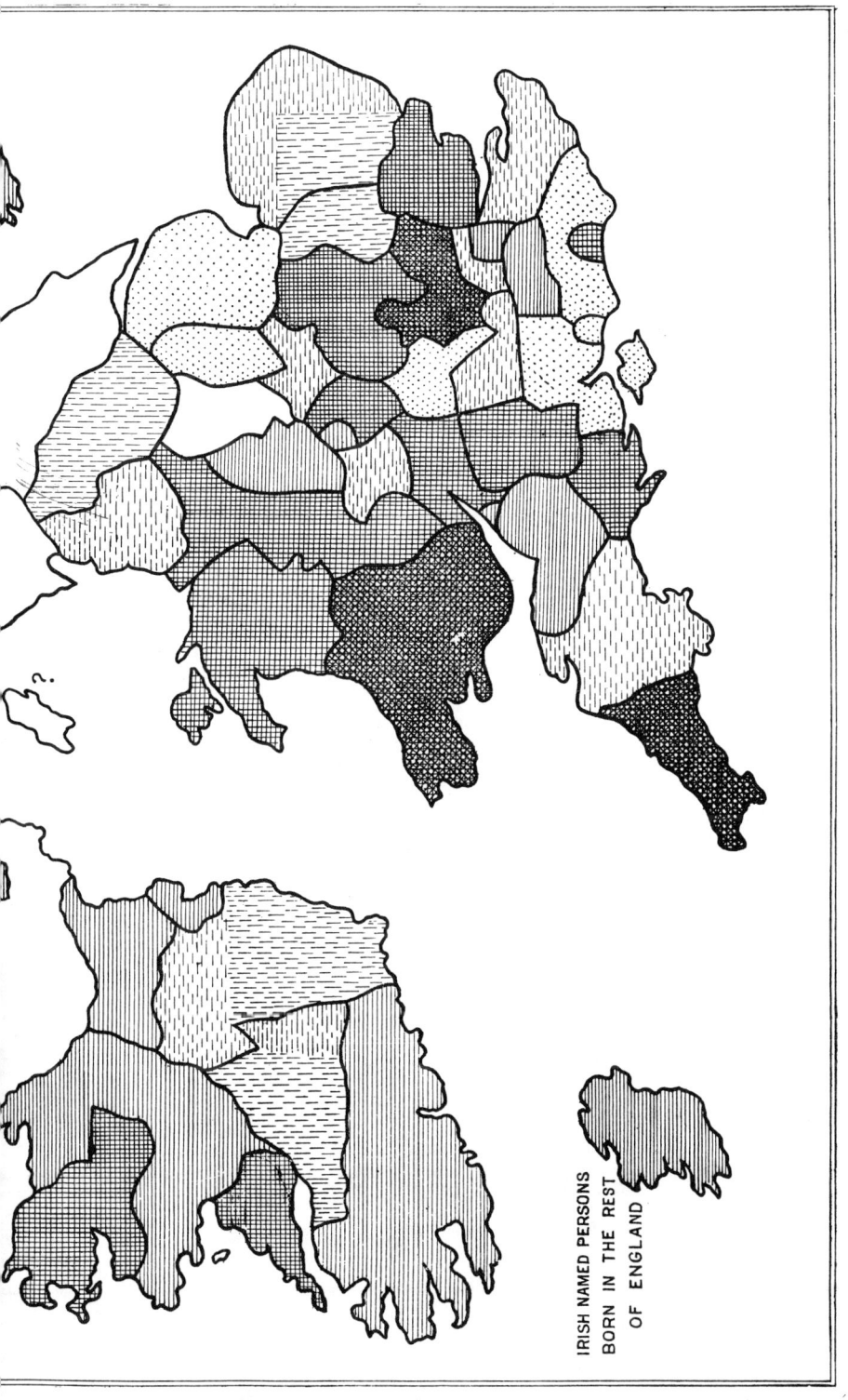

IRISH NAMED PERSONS
BORN IN THE REST
OF ENGLAND

ARROWSMITH   BRISTOL.

MILITARY SCHEDULES

MIXED BLOND TYPE

of the Aathropometric Committee
Blue or Grey Eyes with Red, Fair, or Brown Hair.

Over 55

Over 50

Over 45

up to 45

IRISH NAMED
PERSONS BORN
IN SCOTLAND

IRISH NAMED PERSONS
BORN IN YORKSHIRE
OR LANCASHIRE

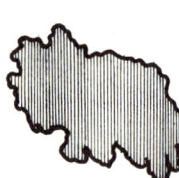

IRISH NAMED PERSONS
BORN IN LONDON

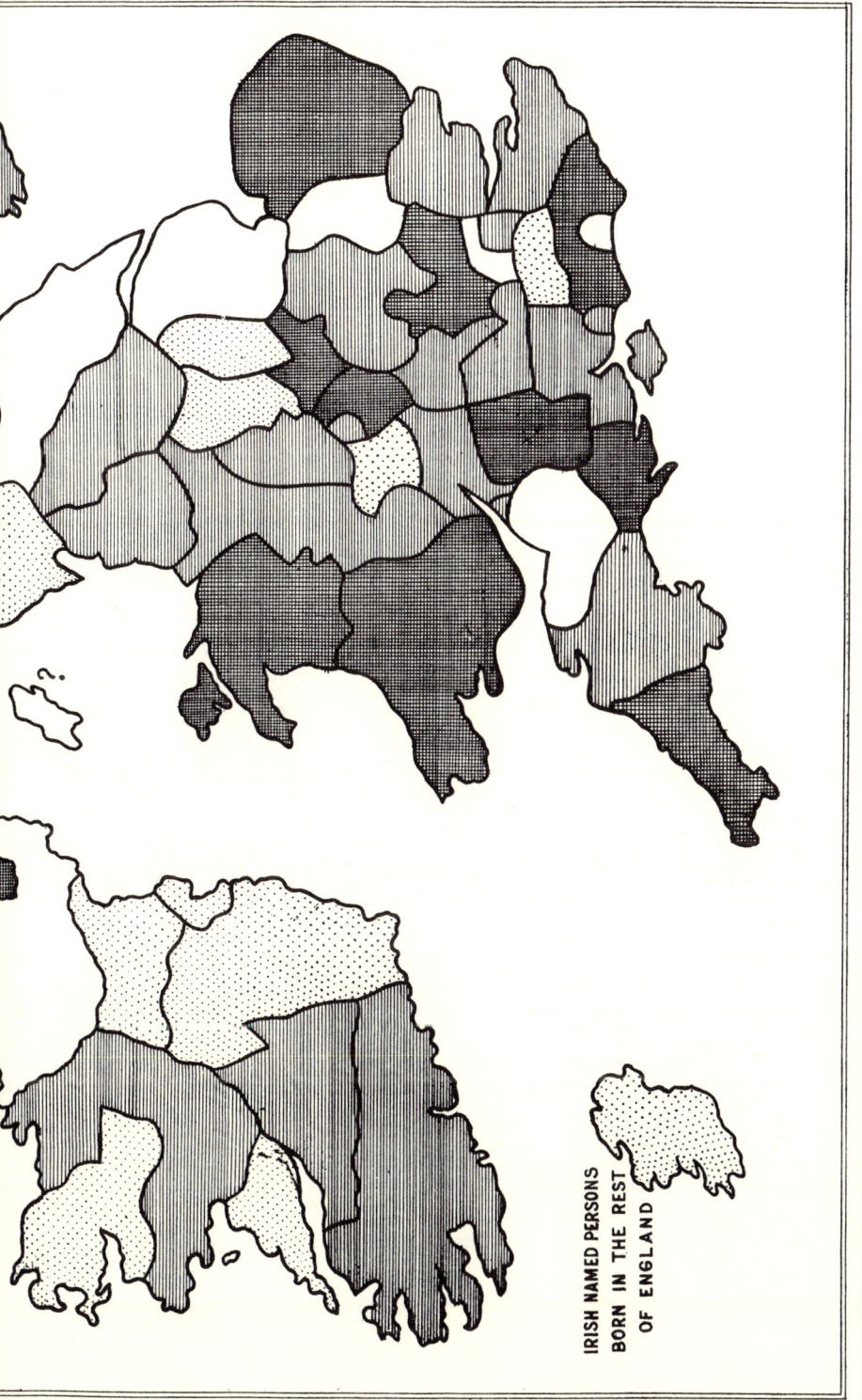

IRISH NAMED PERSONS
BORN IN THE REST
OF ENGLAND

ARROWSMITH. BRISTOL.

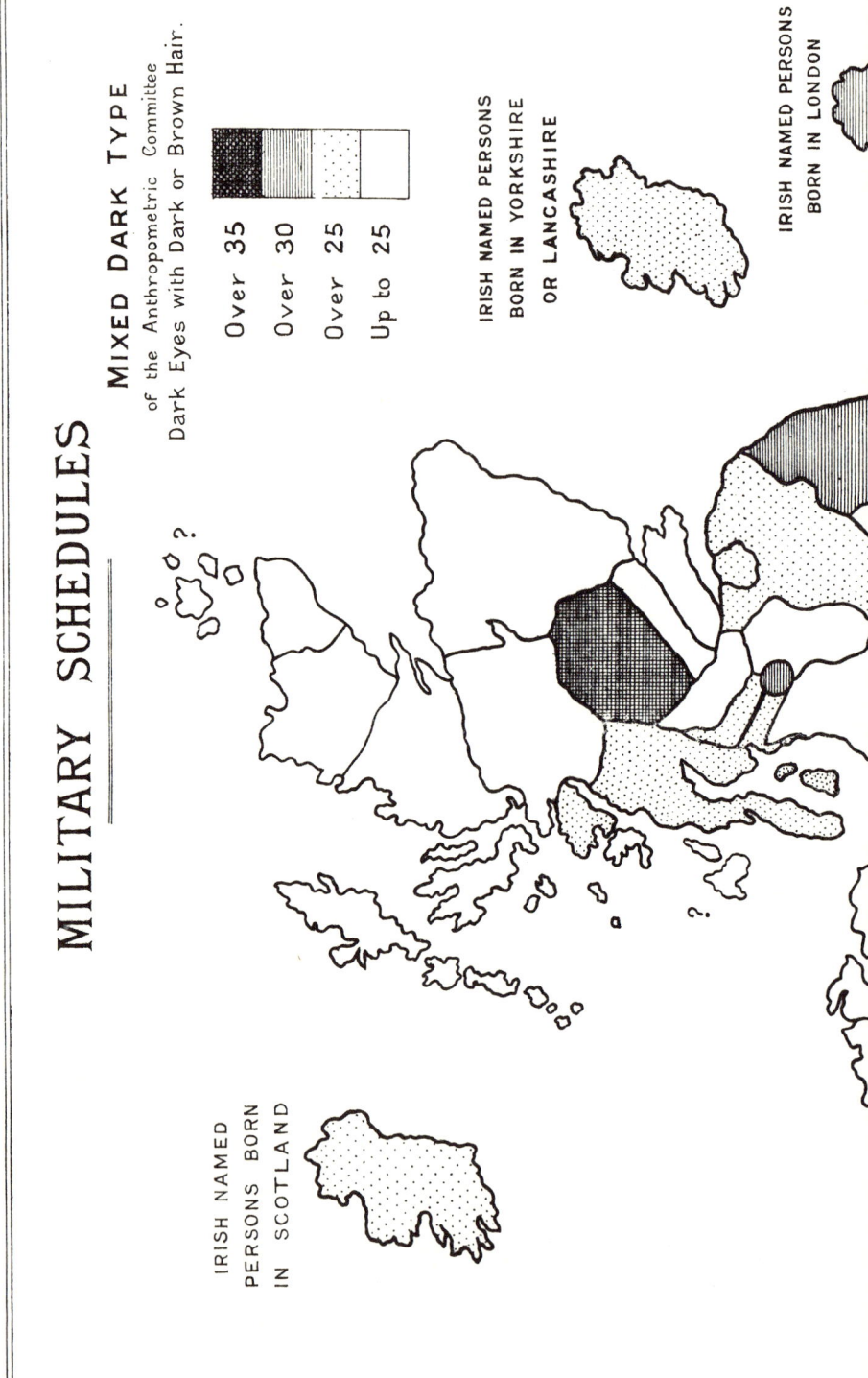

MILITARY SCHEDULES

MIXED DARK TYPE

of the Anthropometric Committee
Dark Eyes with Dark or Brown Hair.

Over 35

Over 30

Over 25

Up to 25

IRISH NAMED PERSONS
BORN IN YORKSHIRE
OR LANCASHIRE

IRISH NAMED PERSONS
BORN IN LONDON

IRISH NAMED
PERSONS BORN
IN SCOTLAND

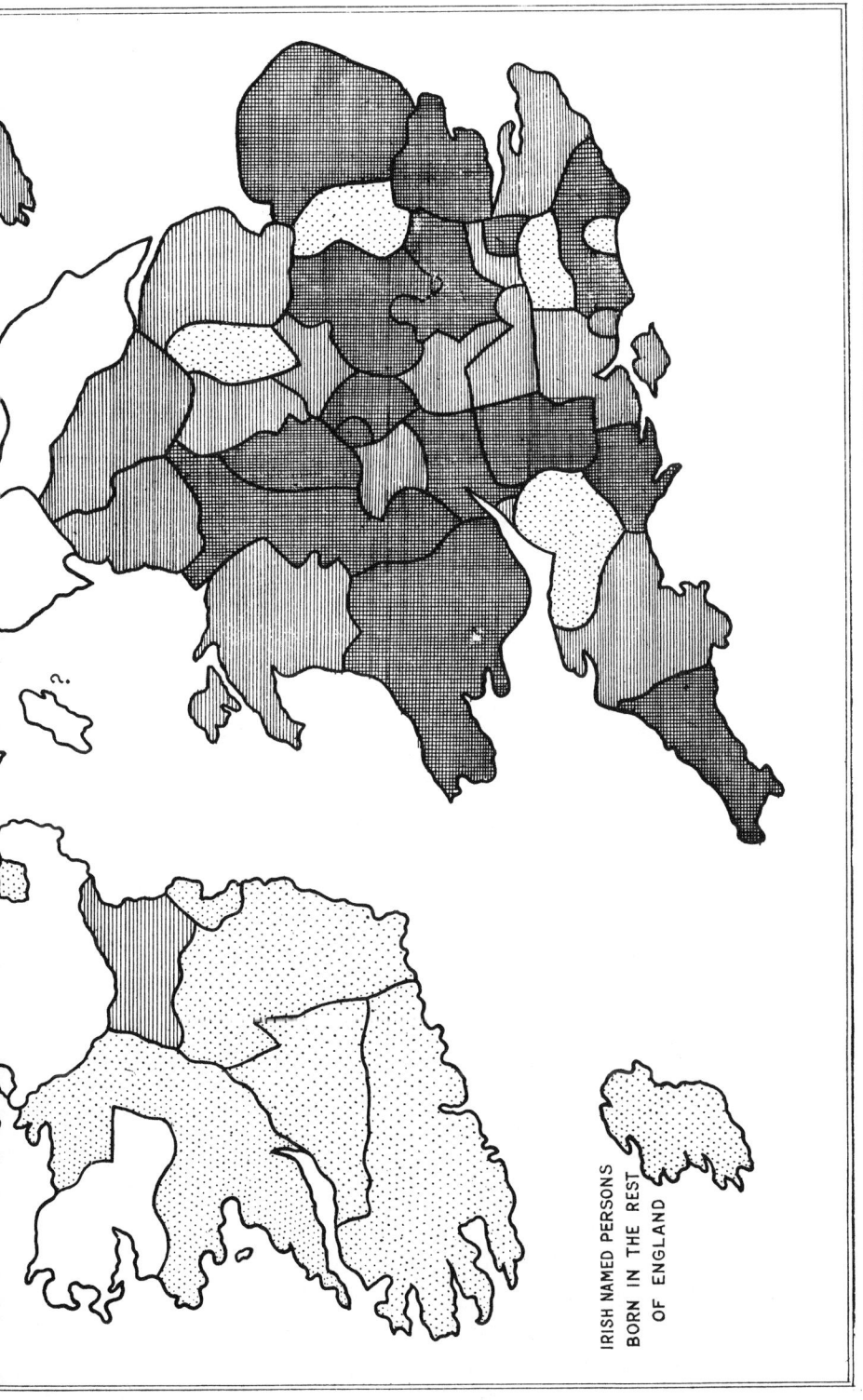

IRISH NAMED PERSONS
BORN IN THE REST
OF ENGLAND

ARROWSMITH BRISTOL.

	1	2	3	4	5	6	7	8	9	10	11	12	13	14	15	16	17	18	19	20
Inverness-shire and N...	21	28·5	45	21	15	67	2	17	11	21	...	51	76·1	1	1	4	6	4	16	23·8
Ross...	-4·3	32·8	49·8	18·5	11·4	70	2	21	12	15	1	51	72·8	1	5	5	7	1	19	27·1
Sutherland and Caithness	-7·5	31·2	61	21	12	67	3	18	20	8	2	51	76·1	...	2	6	8	...	16	23·8
Hebrides...	0	36	58·6	16	10·6	75	1	26	17	12	4	60	80	1	2	4	6	2	15	20
Scotland, total	3·1	25·9	53·4	23·8	14·3	1733	67	383	476	294	31	1251	72·2	15	54	164	195	54	482	27·8
Belfast	26	17	45	26	16	100	5	12	28	18	5	68	68	1	5	10	11	5	32	32
Donegal	24	14	48	24	16	75	1	13	22	11	5	52	69·3	1	4	6	8	4	23	30·6
Rest of Ulster...	17·2	28·8	55·4	22·8	12·8	500	16	104	133	99	15	367	73·4	2	17	50	42	22	133	26·6
Dublin...	15	19·5	53·5	28·5	16·5	200	8	31	68	27	2	136	68	...	7	24	21	12	64	32
Meath (M., W.M., L. and L.)	18·2	25·6	52·8	30·4	21·6	125	7	25	34	18	2	86	68·8	1	...	11	20	7	39	31·2
Rest of Leinster...	13·6	21·7	50·4	25·2	15·7	400	17	70	115	62	15	279	69·7	4	16	38	48	15	121	30·2
Limerick and Tipperary	9·5	26	49·5	29	18	200	9	43	47	32	2	133	66·5	6	3	22	28	8	67	33·5
South Munster (Desmond)...	23·6	18	45·2	26·2	16·4	250	8	37	68	47	12	172	68·8	2	12	23	35	6	78	31·2
Clare...	25	17·5	55	27·5	17·5	...	...	...	...	...	...	...	...	...	...	...	...	...	...	...
Mayo...	31·2	13·6	52·8	24·8	18·4	125	2	15	49	24	2	92	73·6	...	2	8	16	7	33	26·4
Rest of Connaught	25·2	20	46·6	26	16	300	10	50	80	63	9	212	70·6	3	7	30	31	17	88	29·3
Ireland, total	18·8	21·2	49·5	25·7	15·9	2275	83	400	644	401	69	1597	70·2	20	73	222	260	103	673	29·8
Persons with Irish surnames, natives of Scotland	19	23	46	26	18	100	6	17	23	21	2	69	69	...	5	8	14	4	31	31
Do., Yorkshire and Lancashire...	27·3	17·1	49	28	16	333	11	46	106	58	11	232	69·7	3	5	40	39	14	101	30·3
Do., London...	22·4	19·2	48	30·4	18·4	125	4	20	36	23	1	84	67·2	2	1	15	16	7	41	32·8
Do., rest of England	30·9	18·6	50·6	26·2	18·2	175	6	27	56	25	13	127	72·5	1	1	14	26	6	48	27·4
Total Irishmen, natives of Great Britain	24·9	18·1	48·8	27·7	17·2	733	27	110	221	127	27	512	69·8	6	12	77	95	31	221	30·1

COLOUR OF HAIR AND EYES IN THE WEST OF ENGLAND, CHIEFLY FROM OBSERVATIONS MADE IN THE BRISTOL ROYAL INFIRMARY.

ACTUAL NUMBERS OBSERVED.

Natives of	Eyes Light R	F	B	D	N	Total	Eyes Neutral R	F	B	D	N	Total	Eyes Dark R	F	B	D	N	Total	Grand Total	Of whom Males
Bristol	47	183·5	401·5	226·5	4·5	863	8	19·5	91·5	122·5	10·5	252	13	14·5	125	335	54·5	542	1657	562
Clifton	1·5	8	13	6	1	29	1·5	15	6	5·5	·5	11	1·5	1·5	6·5	13·5	3·5	26	66	31
Bedminster		8	14	7·5	1	29		1·5	2·5	5·5	1	11	1·5	1	18	13	3·5	26	66	24
St. George's	8·5	18·5	44·5	17·5	1	90	4	4	15·5	8·5	1	29	1·5	1	18	31	5	55	174	65
Suburbs of Bristol		2	8·5	4·5		15	·5		6	4		4		2	9	6·5	·9	9	28	3
Pill	4	2	13·5	15	1·5	41			6	4·5		12		9·5	13·5	6·5	5	30	83	36
Bath	3·5	10	23	15	1·5	53		·5	4·5	4·5	1	10		4	9	11·5	5	17	75	21
London	2·5	27·5	47·5	27	2	106	1·5	1·5	14	8·5	2	26		4	23·5	22·5	11·5	44	176	44
Somerset, towns	10·5	42·5	103·5	65·5		224	1·5	2·5	12·5	30	2·5	49	4	5	23·5	94·5	15	143	416	147
Ditto, country, east.	·5	4·5	6·5	8·5		18			1	3·5		4	1		5	20·5	4·5	31	120	60
" south	·5	6·5	34	28		69		·5	7·5	11	1·5	20	1		5	20·5	2·5	31	120	60
" west	14·5	9	29	12	1	52			6·5	6·5	1·5	15	2·5	3	23·5	16·5	2·5	27	94	24
" total		44	101		·5	207	5·5	·5	27	31·5		76·5			405	82	10·5	121·5	405	120
Glo'stershire, towns		1				4			3	5		5			2	6·5	2·5	10	18	24
Ditto, country	·5	7·5	17·5	9		36		2·5	10·5	3		14		·5	4·5	6·5	·5	16	84	29
Forest of Dean	5	6·5	35·5	10·5		54		1·5	4	7·5		14			5·5	9·5		19	84	29
Wilts, towns	5	6·5	23	18·5	1	53		1·5	7	5·5		16		1	5·5	26	5·5	38	107	31
Ditto, country	1·5	6·5	30·5	14·5		54		1·5	4·5	11	2	19		1·5	4	21·5	4	28	101	45
Whole of Wilts	1	4·5	4·5	5		15			1	2		3	1		4	10·5	·5	12	30	12
Devon, towns	1	3·5	6·5	4		15		·5	1·5	2·5	·5	5		·5	4	4	3	12	30	10
Ditto, country	4·5	13	20	16·5	1	54		·5	1·5	7		9	1		10	19·5	3·5	34	97	19
Dorset	3	3·5	15·5	10		32		·5	5·5	8		15		7	22	6	35	82	22
Cornwall				4	·5	27			4	5		9				4·5	1·5	6	19	6
Hereford, Cheshire, Salop, Staffordsh., Worcestershire, Warwickshire	3·5	8·5	14	6	1	33		·5	1	4·5	1·5	9		1	·5	12·5	5	18	60	38
East of England to the Welland	2·5	9·5	26·5	9		48		·5	6	3·5	·5	12		4	12·5	1·5	19	79	33
North of England	2	10·5	12·5	2		27			4·5	2·5		7		10·5	5·5	2	19	79	33
Ulster, Dublin, and Wexford	2·5	4	9	5·5		21		·5	1	7		9			2	2		2	32	7
Cork, Waterford, and Kerry	8·5	4·5	26·5	34	1·5	70	·5	·5	6	13	2	22	·5	1	12·5	2	15	107	50
Tipperary, Limerick	2·5	3·5	7·5	5	·5	20			·5	3·5		4			·5	7	·5	7	31	15
Rest of Ireland		1	6	2	·5	8		·5	1·5	1		3			1	1		2	14	3
Scotland		4·5	4·5	5·5		11														9
Total			1199	899	78	3775			1055	990		987				992		1219		1344

PERCENTAGES.

Natives of	Eyes Light R	F	B	D	N	Total	Eyes Neutral R	F	B	D	N	Total	Eyes Dark R	F	B	D	N	Total	Index of Nigrescence	Index of Iris
Bristol	·3	2·8	11·9	21·3	3	52·1	·5	1·2	5·5	7·4	·6	15·2	·8	·9	7·5	20·3	2·8	32·7	33·6	62·7
Clifton													·8		7·5	23·3		31	33·3	
Bedminster													·5	1·1					21·8	
St. George's						49·3		2·6	8	5·3	·7	16·7	·5		9·2	19·1	4	34	22·4	53·9
Suburbs of Bristol		3·3	11·2	10·3															26·6	
Bath					49·3					14·6					6·5	13·5	3·5	36·1	24·1	73·2
London		3	8·5	15·3		70·6		·5	6	6·6				2	6·5	12·8	3·1	22	31·3	31
Somerset, towns	1·5	15·4	13·5			80·2	1·5	1·5	14	8·5	1	11·8	·8	·5	5·1	12·8	6·5	33·4	29	41·5
Ditto, country, east.		6·5	4·8			53·8	1·5	2·5	12·5	30	3·5	16·6	·8					34	39·1	
" total	1·9	9·3	25·7	18·2		55·5	·4	6·5	7·5	7·3		16·6	·9	9·5	20·9	9·3	3·5	25·8	52·9	56·4
Ditto, country	3·9	9·6	30·8	12·7		55·3		·5	7·5	7		15		·6	17·5	26·3	3·1	31·4	42·4	51·9
Forest of Dean	1·3	10·8	24·9	11·7		51·1	2·5	4·5	31·5	8	·8		·6	5·8	20·2	2·6	28·7	31·4	58·7
Wilts, towns						52·2			3	10·5	·3	20·3						25·8	26·5	
Ditto, country		10·8	34	12·7		63·3		2·5	10·4	7·5		16·6		6·5	15·7	21·7	3	27·5	26·1	52·7
Devon, towns	·3	10·8	34	12·7		58·8		1·9	9·5	6·5		18·3	·9		15·7	15·7		19	20·5	30
Ditto, country	1·5	4·7	6·1	17·3		49·5		1·4	6·5	1·9		16		6·5	15·7	29·2	3·5	32·7	23·2	38
Dorset	1	1·5	6·4	17·3	·5	47·6		1·5	4·5	10·2	·9	18·5	·9	5·1	24·3	17·3	3·3	47·6	50	71·7
Cornwall	1	3·8	30	14·3	1	53·5		1·5	2·5	1	2	18·8		1·5	21·3	13·9	27·7	27·5	51·8
South Wales and Monmouth, coast.						55·7			1	7	·5	9·3			10	19·5	3·5	35	33·5	63
Ditto, interior	4·5	13	20	16·5	1	39		·5	6	8		18·3	1	7	22	28·3	5·9	28·3	57·3	109·5
Pembrokeshire	3	3·5	15·5	4					4	5									26·5	
Wales, total		3·8	8·3	17·9		45·4		2	5·5	5·1	1	10·6	·5		8·6	23·2	2·5	37·9	48·5	
Warwickshire		8·5	26·5	6	1			·5	1	4·5	1·5			·5	12·5				40	
East of England to the Welland																				
North of England		9·5	26·5	9	·5			·5	6	3·3				1	4	12·5	1·5		19	
Ulster, Dublin, and Wexford									4·5	2·5					10·5	5·5	2		3·4	
Cork, Waterford, and Kerry		4	9	5·5		65·4		·5	1	7		20·5		2·5	2		14		57·5	21·4
Tipperary, Limerick																				
Total		4715	1190	899	18	3975·9			1055	990		90			960·5	992	5154	1219		

COLOUR OF HAIR AND EYES, FROM PERSONAL OBSERVATION. FRANCE.

Colour of Hair	Number	Sex	EYES LIGHT.					Eyes Light.	EYES INTERMEDIATE OR NEUTER.					Eyes Neuter.	EYES DARK.					Eyes Dark.	Index of Nigrescence.	
			Red	Blond	Chest-nut	Brown	Black		Red	Blond	Chest-nut	Brown	Black		Red	Blond	Chest-nut	Brown	Black		Gross.	Per Cent.
1. Calais and neighbourhood	35	both	2	3	8	3	…	16	…	…	3	2	…	5	…	…	5	7·5	1·5	14	14·5	41·4
2. Amiens	30	m	…	1·5	8·5	3	…	13	…	…	·5	2·5	…	3	…	…	1	9·5	3·5	14	20·5	68
	30	fem	…	3	7	4	…	14	·5	·5	·5	·5	…	2	…	1	·5	9	3·5	14	15·5	51
Total…	60	…	…	4·5	15·5	7	…	27	·5	·5	1	3	…	5	…	1	1·5	18·5	7	28	36	…
Per cent.	…	…	…	7·5	24·8	11·6	…	45	·8	·8	1·6	5	…	8·3	…	1·6	2·5	30·8	11·6	46·6	6	60
3. Dieppe, fishers	50	m	1	6	14·5	9·5	·5	31	…	…	3	2	…	5	…	1	3	7·5	2·5	·4	16	32
Do., others	50	m	…	4	12·5	9	…	26	…	…	2	4	…	7	…	1	3	9·5	3·5	17	24·5	49
Total	100	fem	2	5	20·5	6	·5	34	…	1	10	10·5	1·5	25	3	1	7·5	28	1·5	41	·26	36
Per cent	200	…	3·5	15	47·5	24·5	·5	91	…	3	15	16·5	1·5	37	3	3	13·5	45	7·5	72	76·5	…
4. Havre	60	fem	1·7	7·5	23·7	12·2	·2	45·5	…	4	7·5	8·2	·7	18·5	1·5	·5	6·7	22·5	3·7	36	…	38·2
Per cent.	…	…	1·5	7·5	10·5	9·5	…	29	…	2	1	8·5	1·5	12	…	·7	1·5	15	2	19	29·5	…
5. Rouen	67	m	2·2	12·5	17·5	15·8	…	48·3	…	1	1·6	11·3	2·5	20	…	·7	2·5	25	3·3	31·6	…	49·2
	133	fem	2	11	18	7	…	…	…	1	2	2·5	·5	…	…	…	1·5	14	7·5	…	…	…
6. Do., second visit	100	both	1	14·5	28	12·5	1	…	…	1	4	13	1	…	1·5	1	9·5	36·5	6	…	…	…
Total…	300	…	1	12	21·5	14·5	1	145	…	1	6·5	5	·5	38	1	·5	6	24	21·5	117	131·5	…
Per cent.	…	…	1·3	12·5	22·5	11·3	1·3	…	…	1	4·1	6·8	·6	…	·8	·5	5·6	24·8	7·1	…	…	43·8

Colour of Hair and Eyes, from Personal Observation.—FRANCE, continued.

Colour of Hair	Number	Sex	EYES LIGHT						EYES INTERMEDIATE OR NEUTER						EYES DARK						Index of Nigrescence	
			Red	Blond	Chest-nut	Brown	Black	Eyes Light	Red	Blond	Chest-nut	Brown	Black	Eyes Neuter	Red	Blond	Chest-nut	Brown	Black	Eyes Dark	Gross	Per Cent
7. Lisieux …	80	m	1	10	16	7	…	…	…	1·5	3	9	·5	…	…	…	9	19	4	…	…	…
…	120	fem	3	13	23·5	7·5	…	…	…	1·5	9	8	·5	…	…	4	12·5	34	3·5	…	…	…
Total…	200	…	4	23	39·5	14·5	…	81	…	3	12	17	1	33	…	4	21·5	53	7·5	86	67·5	…
Per cent. …	…	…	2	11·5	19·7	7·2	…	40·5	…	1·5	6	8·5	·5	16·5	…	2	10·7	26·5	3·7	43	…	33·7
8. Bernay …	56	m	1	7·5	12·5	11	1	…	·5	…	3	5	…	…	…	…	…	9	6	…	…	…
…	69	fem	1	5	12	7·5	·5	…	·5	·2	6·5	6	…	…	…	…	6·5	17·5	4	…	…	…
Total…	125	…	2	12·5	24·5	18·5	1·5	57	·5	2	9·5	11	…	23	…	…	6·5	26·5	10	45	62	…
Per cent. …	…	…	1·6	10	19·8	14·8	1·2	45·6	·4	1·6	7·6	8·8	…	18·4	…	…	5·2	21·2	8	36	…	49·6
9. Caen …	133	…	1·5	14	38·5	15·3	1·5	…	…	1	8	7	2	…	2	·5	6	29	6·5	…	…	…
…	206	fem	2	35	58·5	11·5	…	…	1	4·5	13	10	2·5	…	…	·5	15	47·5	5	…	…	…
Total…	339	…	3·5	49	97	27	1·5	178	1	5·5	21	17	4·5	49	2	1	21	76·5	11·5	112	93·5	…
Per cent. …	…	…	1	14·4	28·6	8	·4	52·4	·3	1·6	6·2	5	1·3	14·4	·6	·3	6·2	22·5	3·4	33	…	27·6
10. Bayeux …	114	m	…	9·5	33	15	·5	58	…	·5	10·5	8·5	1·5	21	…	…	5	22·5	6·5	33	…	…
…	141	fem	1·5	10·5	43	14	…	69	…	3·5	10	11·5	…	25	…	…	13·5	23·5	1·5	35	…	…
Total…	255	…	1·5	20	76	29	·5	127	…	4	20·5	20	1·5	46	…	…	18·5	32	8	47	99	…
Per cent. …	…	…	·6	7·8	29·8	11·4	·2	49·8	…	1·6	8	7·8	·6	18	…	…	7·2	55·5	3·1	82	…	38·8
11. Caen and Bayeux (country)..	27	m	1·5	5·5	9	…	…	…	…	…	1	5	…	…	…	…	1·5	21·8	…	32·1	…	…
	33	fem	1·5	3·5	9·5	5	·5	…	…	…	5	1	…	…	…	…	2	3·5	…	…	…	…

	No.	Sex																	
Total...	60	⋮	18·5	·5	36	⋮	⋮	6	6	⋮	12	⋮	⋮	3·5	8·5	⋮	12	8·5	⋮
Per cent.	⋮	⋮	30·8	·8	60	⋮	⋮	10	10	⋮	20	⋮	⋮	5·8	14·1	⋮	20	⋮	14·1
12. Cherbourg	150	m	36·5	⋮	94	⋮	⋮	9·5	9·5	⋮	20	·5	·5	5·5	24·5	5	36	27·5	⋮
Per cent.	⋮	⋮	24·3	⋮	62·6	⋮	⋮	6·3	6·3	⋮	13·3	·3	·3	3·7	16·3	3·3	24	44	18·3
13. Cherbourg	290	fem	63·5	·5	135	3	6	25·5	21·5	2	58	2	2·5	33·5	53	6	97	⋮	⋮
Per cent.	⋮	⋮	21·9	·2	46·5	1	2	8·8	7·4	·7	20	·7	·8	11·5	18·2	2	33·2	-·2	15·1
14. Cherbourg, peasants and fishers ...	100	fem	22·5	⋮	49	2·5	5·5	9	11	⋮	28	1·5	3	6·5	12	⋮	23	⋮	-·2
Total...	540	⋮	122·5	⋮	⋮	5·5	12·5	44	42	2	⋮	4	6	45·5	89·5	11	⋮	68·5	⋮
Per cent.	⋮	⋮	22·7	⋮	51·4	1	2·3	8·1	7·8	·3	19·5	·7	1·1	8·4	16·5	2	28·7	⋮	12·7
15. Morlaix ...	70	m	16	3	⋮	⋮	⋮	1	8	4	⋮	⋮	⋮	1	14	9	⋮	⋮	⋮
	63	fem	10	⋮	⋮	⋮	1	3·5	5·5	⋮	⋮	1	⋮	5	16·5	6·5	⋮	⋮	⋮
Total...	133	⋮	26	3	⋮	⋮	1	4·5	13·5	4	⋮	1	⋮	6	30·5	15·5	⋮	105·5	⋮
Per cent.	⋮	⋮	19·5	2·25	42·7	⋮	·8	3·4	10·1	3	17·3	·8	⋮	4·5	22·9	11·6	39·8	⋮	79
16. St. Malo...	37	m	6	⋮	⋮	⋮	⋮	3·5	3·5	1	⋮	⋮	⋮	2·5	5·5	4	⋮	⋮	⋮
	63	fem	7·5	1	⋮	⋮	1	1	5	⋮	⋮	⋮	1	3	21·5	9·5	47	⋮	⋮
Total...	100	⋮	13·5	1	38	⋮	1	4·5	8·5	1	15	⋮	1	5·5	27	13·5	⋮	⋮	68
Per cent.	⋮	⋮	12	2·5	⋮	⋮	⋮	3	6	3	⋮	⋮	⋮	3	10·5	7·5	46	⋮	⋮
17. Dinan and the roads to Dinard	80	m	20	2·5	⋮	⋮	2·5	4·5	6	2·5	34	⋮	2	4	13	6	46	112	⋮
	110	fem	25·5	2·5	⋮	⋮	2·5	7·5	12·5	5·5	17·8	⋮	2·5	7	23·5	13·5	24·1	⋮	⋮
Total...	190	⋮	37·5	5	110	2·6	2·5	7·5	18·5	5·5	⋮	⋮	2·5	3·7	12·3	7·1	17	55·5	58·8
Per cent.	⋮	⋮	19·7	⋮	57·8	⋮	1·3	3·9	9·7	2·7	⋮	⋮	1·3	⋮	⋮	⋮	24·1	⋮	⋮
18. Quimperlé ...	50	m	6·5	1	15	1	⋮	3	6	9	18	·5	⋮	1	6·5	9	⋮	⋮	111

Colour of Hair and Eyes, from Personal Observation.—FRANCE, continued.

Colour of Hair	Number	Sex	EYES LIGHT						EYES INTERMEDIATE OR NEUTER						EYES DARK						Index of Nigrescence	
			Red	Blond	Chest-nut	Brown	Black	Eyes Light	Red	Blond	Chest-nut	Brown	Black	Eyes Neuter	Red	Blond	Chest-nut	Brown	Black	Eyes Dark	Gross	Per Cent.
19. Quimper, town	30	m	·5	·5	5	10	1	…	…	…	1	3	…	…	…	…	2·5	2	4·5	…	74	…
	56	fem	1	2	7	5·5	·5	…	1	…	2·5	4	1·5	…	1	…	4	13	13	…		
20. Quimper, peasants	89	m	3	1	9·5	14·5	5	…	1	…	1	7	5	…	·5	…	2·5	18	21	…	103·5	…
	15	fem	…	1	3	6	…	…	…	…	2	1·5	·5	…	…	…	1	6	…	…		
21. Total, Quimper and Quimperlé …	240	…	5	4	31·5	37	7·5	85	2	…	9·5	21·5	16	49	2	…	11	45·5	47·5	106	233	
Per cent. …	…	…	2·1	1·6	13·1	15·4	3·1	35·3	·8	…	4	8·9	6·6	20·3	·8	…	4·6	18·9	19·8	44·1		97
22. Auray, Carnac, and Lok-mariaker …	63	m	1·5	4·5	6	8·5	·5	…	…	…	3	6·5	8·5	…	…	…	1	14	9	…		
…	65	fem	…	5·5	11	6·5	1	…	…	…	1·5	6·5	1	…	…	…	4	15·5	12·5	…		
Total…	128	…	1·5	10	17	15	1·5	…	…	…	4·5	13	9·5	21	…	…	5	29·5	21·5	44·4	92	
Per cent. …	…	…	1·2	7·8	13·3	11·7	1·2	35·2	…	…	3·5	10·1	7·4	…	…	·5	3·9	23·8	16·7	…		87·2
23. Reims …	131	m	1	10	19	17·5	2·5	50	1	…	…	15·5	1·5	22	…	·5	8·5	34·5	14·5	59	65·5	
…	119	fem	3	12	20·5	24·5	1	61	1	…	5	9·5	2·5	18	…	·2	5	29·5	5·5	40		
Total…	250	…	4	22	39·5	42	3·5	111	…	…	10	25	4	40	1	…	13·5	64	20	99	157·5	
Per cent. …	…	…	1·6	8·8	15·8	16·8	1·4	44·4	·4	…	4	10	1·6	16	1·4	…	5·4	25·6	8	39·6		63
24. Epernay …	27	m	…	1·5	7	7·5	…	…	…	…	1	3·5	·5	…	…	…	1	2	2	…		
…	23	fem	…	1·5	6·5	6	…	…	…	…	2	1	…	…	…	…	1·5	3·5	1	…		
Total…	50	…	1	3	13·5	13·5	…	31	…	…	4	4·5	1·5	8	…	…	2·5	5·5	3	11	114	
Per cent. …	…	…	2	6	27	27	…	62	…	…	4	9	3	16	…	…	5	11	6	22		57

Locality		No.	1	2	3	4	5	6	7	8	9	10	11	12	13	14	15	16	17	18	19
25. Charleville and Givet	m	27	5	3	5	…	…	…	…	1	2·5	·5	…	…	…	1·5	5·5	3	…	…	…
	fem	53	4	10	4	…	…	…	…	2·5	6·5	1	…	…	…	6	14·5	4·5	…	…	…
Total…		80	9	13	9	…	31	…	…	3·5	9	1·5	14	…	…	7·5	20	7·5	35	47	58·8
Per cent. …		…	11·2	16·2	11·2	…	38·7	…	…	4·4	11·2	1·9	17·5	…	…	9·4	25	9·4	43·8	…	…
26. Bourges, market day	m	150	7·5	21·5	18·5	3·5	48	…	…	2	12·5	4·5	19	…	…	6·5	48·5	28	83	138	92
	fem	270	18	37·5	19	1	77	…	5·5	21	14·5	3	44	3	1	22·5	88	34·5	149	169·5	62·7
Total…		420	25·5	59	37·5	1·5	125	…	5·5	23	27	7·5	63	3	1	29	136·5	62·5	232	307·5	73·2
Per cent. …		…	6·1	14	8·9	·3	29·7	…	1·3	5·5	6·4	1·8	15	·7	·2	6·9	32·5	14·9	55·2	…	…
27. Clermont-Ferrand	m	65	3	11	6·5	1·5	…	…	…	2	6	1	…	…	…	4·5	14·5	14	…	…	…
	fem	108	3·5	13·5	8	…	…	…	…	3	10	2	…	…	1	9·5	37·5	20	…	…	…
Total…		173	6·5	24·5	14·5	1·5	48	…	…	5	16	3	24	…	1	14	52	34	101	151	87
Per cent. …		…	3·7	13·1	8·4	·8	27·6	…	…	2·9	9·2	1·7	13·8	…	·6	8·1	30	19·6	58·3	…	…
28. Clermont-Ferrand, peasants	m	50	2	8·5	6	2·5	20	…	…	…	3·5	1·5	5	…	…	1·5	15	8·5	25	46·5	…
	fem	18	…	1	2	…	3	…	…	…	1·5	·5	2	…	…	1·5	9	2·5	13	18·5	…
Total…		68	2	9·5	8	2·5	23	…	…	…	5	2	7	…	…	3	24	11	38	65	95·5
29. Puy de Dôme, highlanders…	m	37	2·5	7	8·5	2	…	…	…	·5	5·5	…	…	…	…	…	5·5	4·5	…	…	…
	fem	33	2	4	4	…	…	…	…	…	2·5	·5	12	…	1	1	10	5	…	…	…
Total…		70	4·5	11	12·5	2	31	…	…	2·5	8	·5	12	…	1	1	15·5	9·5	27	52·5	75
30. Mont Dore	m	32	…	3	3	1	…	…	…	…	3·5	1·5	…	1	…	1·5	10	7·5	…	…	…
	fem	18	1	3	…	…	…	…	…	…	1	…	…	1	…	…	8·5	2·5	…	…	…
Total…		50	1	6	3	1	12	…	…	…	4·5	1·5	7	…	…	1·5	18·5	10	31	47	94

Colour of Hair and Eyes, from Personal Observation.—FRANCE, continued.

Colour of Hair	Number	Sex	EYES LIGHT						EYES INTERMEDIATE OR NEUTER						EYES DARK						Index of Nigrescence	
			Red	Blond	Chest-nut	Brown	Black	Eyes Light	Red	Blond	Chest-nut	Brown	Black	Eyes Neuter	Red	Blond	Chest-nut	Brown	Black	Eyes Dark	Gross	Per Cent
31. St. Nectaire, &c. ...	20	m	·5	·5	2	3·5	·5	...	...	...	...	3	1	...	...	...	1	3·5	4·5	...	...	...
	30	fem	...	1·5	2·5	...	...	...	...	...	2	3	...	...	...	...	2·5	6·5	12	...	...	...
Total... ...	50	...	·5	2	4·5	3·5	·5	11	...	...	2	6	1	9	...	...	3·5	10	16·5	30	53	106
32. Total Mont Dore, town, and St. Nectaire... ...	100	...	1·5	3	10·5	6·5	1·5	23	...	1	2	10·5	2·5	16	1	...	5	28·5	26·5	61	...	100
33. Brioude	16	m	...	1	3	2	1	...	...	...	1	1	1	...	...	...	·5	2·5	3	...	...	...
	34	fem	...	1	4	2·5	·5	...	...	1	2	2	...	...	...	...	3	13·5	4·5	...	...	...
Total... ...	50	...	...	2	7	4·5	1·5	15	...	1	3	3	1	8	...	...	3·5	16	7·5	27	40·5	81
34. Le Puy	32	m	...	...	1	4·5	·5	...	...	...	2	3	2	...	...	...	2	10	7	...	...	...
	68	fem	...	3	7	6	...	...	...	2	2	3·5	1·5	...	1	...	3·5	23	15·5	...	...	...
Per cent		...	...	3	8	10·5	·5	22	...	2	4	6·5	3·5	16	1	...	5·5	33	22·5	62	97	97
35. Monastier ...	18	m	...	1	·5	4	·5	...	...	...	1	1	2	...	...	...	1	5	2	...	...	...
	32	fem	...	3	2·5	3·5	...	...	...	...	1·5	2·5	...	...	...	...	2	13·5	3·5	...	...	...
Total... ...	50	...	...	4	3	7·5	·5	15	...	...	2·5	3·5	2	8	...	...	3	18·5	5·5	27	41·5	...
Per cent		...	...	8	6	15	1	30	...	...	5	7	4	16	...	...	6	37	11	54	...	83
36. La Beage, &c., Mont Mezene	15	m	...	...	1	1	...	...	...	...	...	3·5	1·5	...	...	...	...	2·5	5·5	...	...	...
	10	fem	...	1	1	1	...	...	...	...	1	1	1	...	...	...	1	2·5	·5	...	...	...
Total... ...	25	...	...	1	2	2	...	5	...	...	1	4·5	2·5	8	...	...	1	5	6	12	27·5	110

	No.	Sex	1	2	3	4	5	6	7	8	9	10	11	12	13	14	15	16	17	18	19	20
37. Privas and Coiron	60	m & f		5·5	8	4	·5	18	10	1	5	3	1				2·5	15·5	14	32	49·5	82·6
38. Vals, village	30	n		1	2·5	3	1·5	8	7	2·5	3·5		·5	·5			1	8·5	5·5	15		
	40	fem		2·5	6	2·5	1	12	4	1·5	2·5				1·5	·5	2	9·5	10·5	24		
Total..	70			3·5	8·5	5·5	2·5	20	11	4	6		·5	·5	1·5	·5	3	18	16	39	68	97
39. La Baume	15	m			1·5	2·5				1	1						1	6	2			
	40	fem		3·5	6	5·5				1·5	1·5	2				·5	3	9·5	7			
Total..	55			3·5	7·5	8		19		2·5	2·5	2				·5	4	15·5	9	29	45	82
40. Janjac, Antraigues, and Vals, peasants	52	m	1	3	5·5	9·5	1			2	6	2·5	·5	1		1	1	9	10			
	78	fem	2	7	8·5	2·5	1			·5	4·5	3	2	2	1·5	1·5	10·5	21·5	11·5			
Total..	130		3	10	14	12	2	40	24	2·5	10·5	5·5	2·5	3		2·5	11·5	30·5	21·5	66	82	63
Per cent.			2·3	7·7	10·7	9·2		30·7	18·3	1·9	8	4·2	1·9	2·3		1·9	8·8	23·4	16·5	50·6		76·4
41. Total of Ardèche, valley	255		3	17	30	25·5	·8			9	19	7·5	3	3·5	1·5	3·5	18·5	64	46·5		195	
42. Total Ardèche, with Privas.	315		3	22·5	38	29·5	4	97	52	10	24	10·5	4	3·5	1·5	3·5	21	79·5	60·5	166	244	77·4
Per cent.			·9	7·2	12	9·3	1·2	30·6	16·4	3·2	7·6	3·3	1·2	1·1	·5	1·1	6·6	25·2	19·2	52·6		
43. Arles	55	both		1	7·5	6·5		15	8		4	4				·5	5·5	18	8	32	43	78·2
Per cent.				1·8	13·6	11·8		27·2	14·5		7·2	7·2				·9	10	32·7	14·5			
44. Savoy, between Geneva and Chamonix	118	m	2	5	15·5	8·5	2	33	23	3	14·5	5·5			1	·5	4	36·5	20	62	101	
	48	fem	1	6·5	6·5			14	6	·5	4	1·5				1	3	19	5	28	25·5	
Total..	166		3	11·5	22	8·5	2	47	29	3·5	18·5	7			1	1·5	7	55·5	25	90	126·5	76
Per cent.			1·8	6·9	13·2	5·1	1·2	28	17	2·1	11·1	4·2			·6	·9	4·2	33·4	15	54		

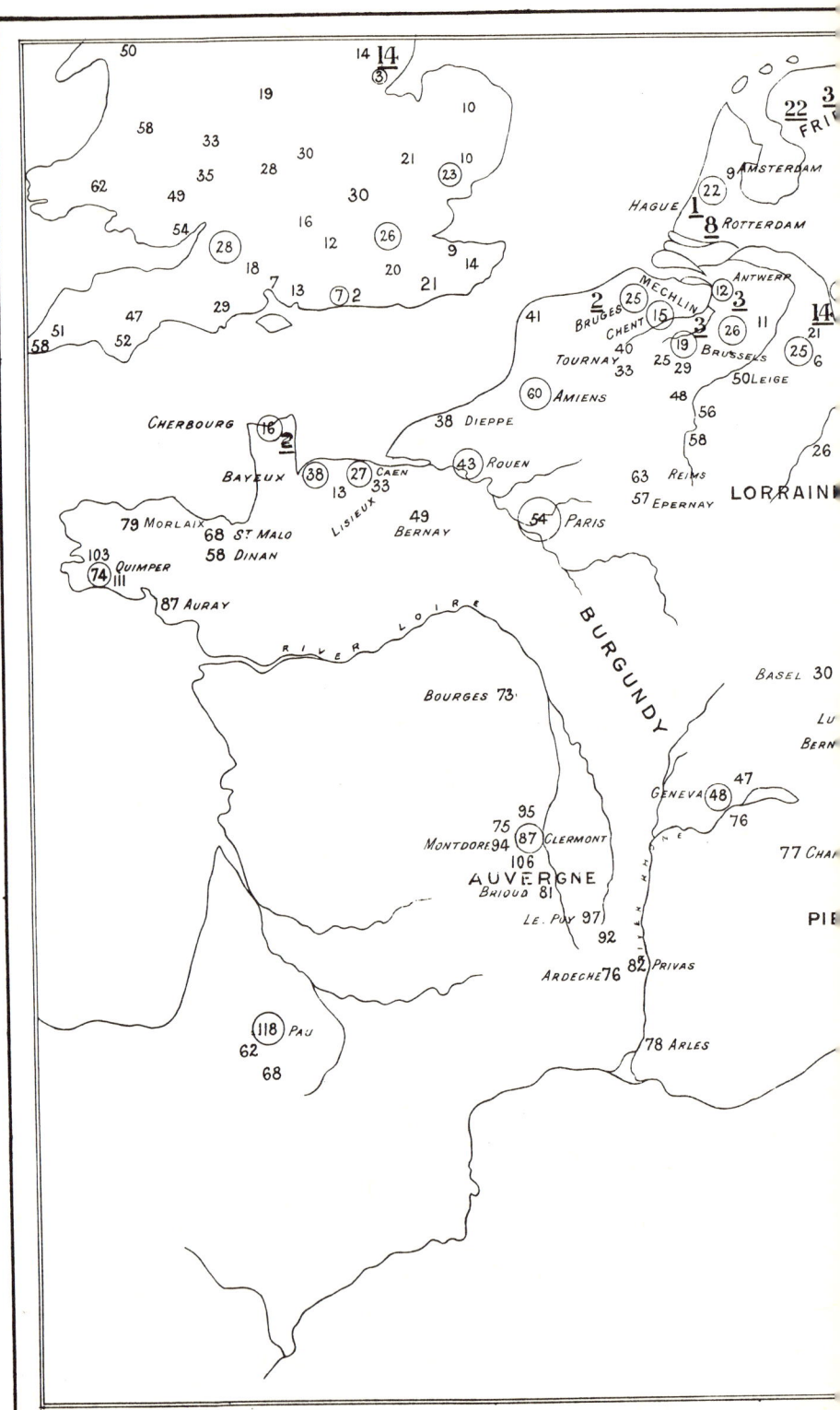

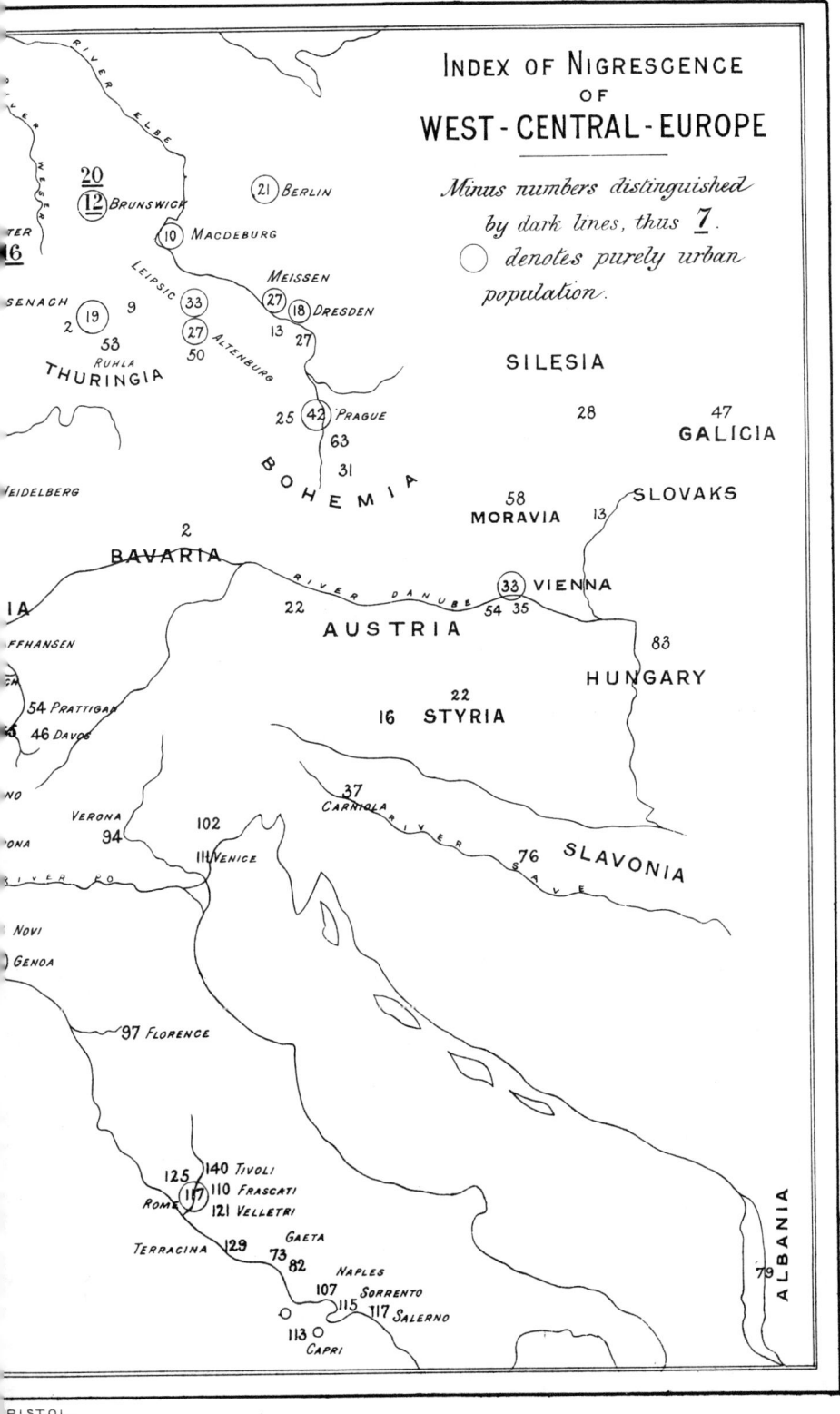

INDEX OF NIGRESCENCE
OF
WEST-CENTRAL-EUROPE

*Minus numbers distinguished
by dark lines, thus ⎯7.
○ denotes purely urban
population.*

RIVER ELBE

RIVER WESER

20
(12) BRUNSWICK

(21) BERLIN

(10) MACDEBURG

MEISSEN

SENACH   (19)   9   (33)   (27)(18) DRESDEN

2   53   LEIPSIC   27   13   27

RUHLA   (27)   ALTENBURG

THURINGIA   50

SILESIA

25 (42) PRAGUE   28   47

63   GALICIA

31

B O H E M I A   58   SLOVAKS

EIDELBERG   MORAVIA   13

2   BAVARIA   RIVER DANUBE   (33) VIENNA

22   54 35

IA   AUSTRIA   83

FFHANSEN   HUNGARY

54 PRATTIGAN   22

46 DAVOS   16   STYRIA

NO   37

VERONA   CARNIOLA RIVER

ONA   94   102

III VENICE   76   SLAVONIA

RIVER PO   SAVE

NOVI

GENOA

97 FLORENCE

125)140 TIVOLI   ALBANIA

117) 110 FRASCATI

ROME   121 VELLETRI

TERRACINA 129   GAETA

73 82

107   NAPLES

115   SORRENTO

117 SALERNO

113 ○

CAPRI

79

Colour of Hair and Eyes, from Personal Observation.—FRANCE, continued.

Colour of Hair	Number	Sex	EYES LIGHT						EYES INTERMEDIATE OR NEUTER						EYES DARK						Index of Nigrescence	
			Red	Blond	Chest-nut	Brown	Black	Eyes Light	Red	Blond	Chest-nut	Brown	Black	Eyes Neuter	Red	Blond	Chest-nut	Brown	Black	Eyes Dark	Gross	Per Cent.
45. Chamonix	67	m	2	4	10	7	2	25	...	...	2·5	7	3·5	13	1	...	4·5	15·5	8	29	49·5	...
	33	fem	...	...	4	5	...	9	...	...	·5	4	·5	5	...	...	5	10	4	19	28	...
Total and per cent...	100		2	4	14	12	2	34	...	...	3	11	4	18	1	...	9·5	15·5	12	48	...	77·5
46. Paris, ouvriers	100	m	1·5	9	19	11	·5	41	1	...	1·5	8·5	4	11	1	...	9	27	11	48	...	57
	100	fem	2·5	7	17	7·5	...	34	1	3	6	8·5	2·5	21	1	...	5	32	7	45	...	52·5
47. Do., second visit	200	both	6	17	28	19	...	70	3	2	10	11	3	29	...	1	15	69	16	101	108	54
Total...	400		10	33	64	36·5	·5	145	5	5	17·5	28	5·5	67	2	1	29	128	34	194	...	...
Per cent.			2·5	8·2	16	9·1	·1	36·2	1·2	1·2	4·4	7	1·4	15·2	·5	·2	7·2	32	8·5	48·5	...	54·4

Notes on Table for France.—See a paper of mine on this subject, with discussion, in the *Bulletins de la Société d'Anthropologie* for 1882.

The custom among the men of cropping the hair close to the roots, makes it difficult to distinguish black from dark brown. In many cases the number of observations is insufficient, *e.g.*, at Amiens and Arles.

Dr. Christison, who is accustomed to my method of working, observed for me the colour of the *hair* at Pau, and in some villages in the Pyrenees (Cauterets, Luz, and Gavarnie). His results were as follow:—

		Hair					Index	
		Red.	Blond.	Chestnut.	Dk. Brown.	Black.	Gross.	Per cent.
Cauterets, &c.	88	2	4	26	46	10	60	68
Pau, women	71	—	—	16	26	29	84	118
Do., male peasants	71	—	5	31	21	14	44	62

The following points are noteworthy:—The influence of latitude is certainly not conspicuous. Putting aside Dr. C.'s observations at Pau, the maximum of nigrescence is obtained in Finistère, at Quimperlé; the minimum among the fisherpeople and peasants of Cherbourg, where the type is in other respects also Scandinavian or Saxon. The blond element decreases, in both Normandy and Bretagne, as the distance from the sea increases. In Central France elevation of site does not appear to tell much, if at all, upon colouration. If the highlanders of the Puy de Dôme yield a lowish index, those about Mont Dore and Mont Mezene yield a higher one than the dalesmen of Janjac and Antraigues, or the citizens of Arles in the hot

COLOUR OF HAIR AND EYES.—HOLLAND and BELGIUM.

Colour of Hair	Number	Sex	EYES LIGHT						EYES INTERMEDIATE OR NEUTER						EYES DARK						Index of Nigrescence	
			Red	Fair	Brown	Dark	Black	Eyes Light	Red	Fair	Brown	Dark	Black	Eyes Neuter	Red	Fair	Brown	Dark	Black	Eyes Dark	Gross	Per cent.
HOLLAND.																						
1. Rotterdam	250	both	5	67	80·5	20	·5	173	…	2·5	16	4	·5	23	1	5	15·5	30·5	2	54	-20	…
Per cent.	…	…	2	26·8	32·2	8	·2	69·2	…	1	6·4	1·6	·2	9·2	·4	2	6·2	12·2	·8	21·6	…	-·8
2. The Hague	250	both	4	49	90	22	…	165	…	8	16·5	4·5	·5	30	…	2	22	30·5	·5	55	-4·5	…
Per cent.	…	…	1·6	19·6	36	8·8	…	66	…	3·2	6·6	1·8	·2	12	…	·8	8·8	12·2	·2	22	…	-1·8
3. Amsterdam	250	both	3	37	94	25	…	161	…	5·5	15·5	13·5	·5	35	1	1	20	31·5	·5	54	24·5	…
Per cent.	…	…	1·2	14·8	37·6	10	…	64·4	…	2·2	6·2	5·4	·2	14	·4	·4	8	12·6	·2	21·6	…	+9·8
4. Leyden	137	both	1	12·5	51	7·5	…	72	1	1	10	5	…	17	…	1	15·5	28·5	3	48	30·5	…
Per cent.	…	…	·7	9·1	37·2	5·5	…	52·5	·7	·7	7·3	3·6	…	12·4	…	·7	11·3	20·8	2·2	35	…	22·3
5. Scheveningen, fishers	17	both	…	5	8	2	…	15	…	…	1	…	…	1	…	…	1	…	…	1	-3	-17·4
6. Lemmer (20), Leewarden (80)	100	both	…	30	46·5	4·5	…	81	…	2	5	…	…	7	…	1	5	6	…	12	…	-22·5
7. Frisian peasants	27	most m	…	6·5	15	·5	…	22	…	…	3	…	…	3	…	1	…	1	…	2	11	-22·2
8. Gröningen	40	both	·5	15	14	·5	…	30	…	·5	2·5	…	…	3	…	…	2·5	4·5	…	7	…	-27·5
9. Do., peasants...	60	both	1	26·5	20·5	3·5	·5	52	…	…	2	1	…	3	1	…	1·5	2·5	…	5	…	-34
Total	100	both	1·5	41·5	34·5	4	…	82	…	·5	4·5	1	…	6	…	…	4	7	…	12	20·5	-31·5
BELGIUM.																						
1. Ostend, many peasants	108	most m	2	17	42	5	…	66	…	…	9·5	4·5	…	14	…	3	15·5	9·5	…	28	-2·5	…
Per cent.	…	…	1·8	15·7	38·8	5·1	…	61	…	…	8·8	4·1	…	13	…	2·7	14·3	8·8	…	26	…	-2·2

Colour of Hair and Eyes, from Personal Observation.—BELGIUM, continued.

Colour of Hair	Number	Sex	EYES LIGHT						EYES INTERMEDIATE OR NEUTER						EYES DARK						Index of Nigrescence	
			Red	Fair	Brown	Dark	Black	Eyes Light	Red	Fair	Brown	Dark	Black	Eyes Neuter	Red	Fair	Brown	Dark	Black	Eyes Dark	Gross	Per Cent.
2. Bruges	500	both	2	46·5	163	29·5	1	242	1·5	5	37	25·5	1	70	...	2·5	65·5	115	5	188	126·5	...
Per cent.	...	...	·4	9·3	32·6	5·9	·2	48·4	·3	1	7·4	5·1	·2	14	...	·5	13·1	23	1	37·6	...	25·3
3. Ghent	500	both	11	62·5	144	37·5	...	255	2	9	34·5	22	·5	68	2	6	64·5	100	4·5	177	77	...
Per cent.	...	...	2·1	12·5	28·8	7·5	...	51	·4	1·8	6·9	4·4	·1	13·6	·4	1·2	12·9	20	·9	35·4	...	15·4
4. Mechlin	100	both	3·5	20·5	31·5	7·5	...	63	...	1	8	4	...	13	...	1·5	11	11	·5	24	...	...
Per cent.	...	...	...	...	...	...	...	...	...	...	...	...	...	...	...	...	...	...	...	...	...	-3·5
5. Antwerp	700	both	8	87	254	45	...	394	...	10	52	23	...	85	1	10	83	118	9	221	88	...
Per cent.	...	...	1·1	12·4	36·3	6·4	...	56·3	...	1·4	7·4	3·3	...	12·1	·1	1·4	11·8	16·8	1·3	31·6	...	12·6
6. Do., market, peasants	...	most fem	3·5	35	65	9	·5	113	...	5·5	22·5	8	...	36	...	4	24	22	1	51	-6	...
Per cent.	...	...	1·7	17·5	32·5	4·5	·2	56·5	...	2·7	11·2	4	...	18	...	2	12	11	·5	25·5	...	-·3
7. Brussels	1000	both	21	131	274	74	1	501	3	15	70	54	3	145	2	45	102	193	12	354	...	...
Per cent.	...	...	2·1	13·1	27·4	7·4	·1	50·1	·3	1·5	7	5·4	·3	14·2	·2	4·5	10·2	19·3	1·2	35·4	...	19·9
8. Louvain	365	=	5	48	96	33·5	·5	183	1	5·5	22	19·5	1	49	2	4	33·5	81·5	12	133	96	...
Per cent.	...	...	1·3	13·1	26·3	9·1	...	50·5	·3	1·5	6	5·3	·3	13·4	·5	1·1	9·1	22·3	3·3	36·4	...	26·3
9. Löwen, peasants	47	both	1·5	7·5	17·5	4·5	...	31	...	...	3	1	...	4	...	...	3·5	8·5	...	12	5·5	11·6
10. Brussels, peasants	78	both	3	13·5	22·5	6	...	45	...	2	6	4	...	12	...	2	8·5	7	3·5	21	3·5	4·5
Total peasants	125	both	4·5	21	40	10·5	...	76	...	2	9	5	...	16	...	2	12	15·5	3·5	33	9	...
Per cent.	...	...	3·6	16·8	32	8·4	...	60·8	...	1·6	7·2	3·6	...	12·8	...	1·6	9·6	12·4	2·8	26·4	...	7·2
11. Waterloo, Soignies, &c. peasants	150	both	1	15	59	20	...	95	...	1	6·5	5·5	1	14	...	1	9·5	26	4·5	41	44·5	...
Per cent.	...	...	·6	10	39·3	13·3	...	63·3	...	·6	4·3	3·7	·6	9·3	...	·6	6·3	8·6	3	27·3	...	29·7
	I	2	3	4	5	6	7	8	9	10	11	12	13	14	15	16	17	18	19	20	21	22

	1	2	3	4	5	6	7	8	9	10	11	12	13	14	15	16	17	18	19	20	21	22
12. Charleroi, &c.	158	both	6·5	19	49·5	21·5	·5	97	...	...	10·5	5·5	2	18	1·5	2·5	8	24·5	6·5	43	40	...
Per cent.	...	·	4·1	12	31·3	13·6	·3	61·4	...	...	6·6	3·5	1·2	11·4	1	1·6	5	15·5	4·1	27·2	...	25·3
13. Tournay...	140	both	1·5	8·5	40	19	...	69	1	...	11	8	1	21	...	...	14	33	3	50	57	...
Per cent.	...		1	6	28·5	13·5	...	49·3	·7	...	7·8	5·7	·7	15	...	...	10	23·5	2·1	35·6	...	40·7
14. Do., peasants...	45	both	...	3	15	3	...	21	...	...	3	3	...	6	1	·5	5·5	8·5	2·5	18	15	...
Per cent.	...		...	6·6	33	6·6	...	46·6	...	...	6·6	6·6	...	13·3	2·2	1·1	12·2	18·8	5·5	40	...	33
15. Liege, city	350	both	4	30	95·5	42	4·5	176	...	5	23	23	4	55	...	2	24·5	78	14·5	119	146	41·7
16. Do., market, peasants...	100	both	...	6	28	11·5	·5	46	...	2	6	5·5	·5	14	...	2	9	23·5	5·5	40	...	43·5
17. Do., second visit, some peasants ...	200	$\frac{8\cdot9}{7\cdot11}$	4	25·5	35·5	23·5	·5	89	1	1·5	4	13	·5	20	1	3	14·5	59	13·5	91	88·5	44·2
Total...	650	...	8	61·5	159	77	5·5	311	1	8·5	33	41·5	5	89	1	7	48	160·5,33·5	5·1	384	280	...
Per cent.	...	...	1·2	9·4	24·4	11·8	·8	47·8	·1	1·3	5·1	6·4	·7	13·7	·1	1·1	7·4	24·7	5·1	38·4	...	43·1
18. Huy, town	162	$\frac{53}{105}$	4	13	32·5	18·5	2	70	1	1	5	13·5	·5	20	1·5	3	6	46·5	15	72	91	...
19. Do., peasants...	88	$\frac{2\cdot2}{8\cdot8}$	1	11	12·5	12·5	...	37	1	1·5	6·5	9·5	·5	14	2	1	10·5	18	5·5	37	34·5	...
Total...	250	both	5	24	45	31	2	107	1	2·5	23	23	1	34	3·5	4	16·5	64·5	20·5	109	125·5	...
Per cent.	...	...	2	9·6	18	12·4	·8	42·8	·4	1	2·6	9·2	·4	13·6	1·4	1·6	6·6	25·8	8·2	43·6	...	50·2
20. Namur, city	55	$\frac{3\cdot5}{2\cdot0}$	3	4	13·5	6	·5	27	1	2	2	1	...	4	...	1	4	12	7	24	25	...
21. Do., peasants...	45	$\frac{2\cdot2}{2\cdot3}$	2	2	7	4	...	14	1	2	3	3·5	·5	8	...	...	1	15·5	6·5	23	36	...
22. Namur to Huy, various	50	both	...	6	20	4	...	30	2	...	...	3	·5	5	...	...	5	8	2	15	11	...
Total Namur	150	...	3	12	40·5	14	1·5	71	2	2	5	7·5	·5	17	...	1	10	35·5	15·5	62	72	48
Per cent.	...	m	2	8	27	9·3	1	47·3	1·3	1·3	3·3	5	·3	11·3	...	·6	6·6	23·7	10·3	41·3	...	...
23. Dinant, town...	179	m	3	15·5	42·5	25·5	1·5	88	...	...	5·5	10	2·5	18	...	...	10·5	49	12·5	73	98	...
	81	fem	1·5	8	15	10·5	1	36	...	...	4·5	8	1·5	14	...	...	2	19	10	31	53	...

Colour of Hair and Eyes, from Personal Observation.—BELGIUM, continued.

| Colour of Hair | Number | Sex | EYES LIGHT. | | | | | | EYES INTERMEDIATE OR NEUTER. | | | | | | EYES DARK. | | | | | | Index of Nigrescence | |
			Red	Fair	Brown	Dark	Black	Eyes Light.	Red	Fair	Brown	Dark	Black	Eyes Neuter.	Red	Fair	Brown	Dark	Black	Eyes Dark.	Gross.	Per Cent.
24. Furfooz, &c., peasants...	40	20/20	1	3·5	11·5	4·5	1·5	22	...	...	4	3	...	7	...	...	1	7	3	11	19	...
Total Dinant district	300	188/112	5·5	27	69	40·5	4	146	...	...	14	21	4	39	1	...	13·5	75	25·5	115	170	...
Per cent.	...	...	1·8	9	23	13·5	1·3	48·6	...	...	4·7	7	1·3	13	·3	...	4·5	25	8·5	38·3	...	56·6
25. Peasants, near Verriers ...	20	both	...	1·5	2·5	3·5	·5	8	...	...	1	1	1	3	...	...	2	4	3	9	16	80
26. Landen & Tirlemont stations	30	both	...	10	10·5	2·5	...	23	...	...	1	2	...	3	...	...	2	2	...	4	3·5	11·6

Notes on the Tables for Holland and Belgium.—The numbers for the Dutch towns are, perhaps, nearly sufficient, unless in the case of Leyden, where my figures may perhaps be explained by the affluence of foreign students to the University during several centuries. Elsewhere the Dutch type of colour comes out distinctly—the hair light brown, flaxen, or yellow, rather than red; the eyes more apt to be hazel than the colour of the hair would lead one to expect.

Gröningen is not considered Frisian, but the breed of man there seems to be the same as in West Friesland.

In my tables, as in the official statistics of Professor Vanderkindere, a distinct line of separation between the Flemings and Walloons may easily be drawn. Contrasts equally great may be found in the British Isles, or in France, but nowhere within so small a distance of each other. Ostend, Bruges, Ghent, Brussels, Louvain, as well as Antwerp and Mechlin, lie north of the line; Tournay, Namur, Dinant, Huy, Liege and Verriers, to the south of it. Charleroi, on the south, is the only town which in my tables departs from its ethnological position, which should be on the dark side of Louvain, instead of being one per cent. lighter. There is no warrant for this in Vanderkindere's figures.

Bruges and Louvain both come out rather dark. The population of the former is commonly said to have a Spanish element; the latter is a decayed old University and manufacturing town. Both are combined officially with large agricultural cantons.

Vanderkindere remarks that no German province shows in the official statistics so high a proportion of blonds as many Flemish cantons (or even arrondissements). This he is apparently disposed to ascribe to the greater extent of the German provinces, in which consequently local distinctions would be somewhat rubbed down. He adds, however, that the brown type is in most parts of Germany much less numerous than in any canton even of Flanders. He wrote this before the German statistics were published, and owed his knowledge of them to a communication from Professor Virchow. In truth, the discrepancy was connected with the different nomenclature of the two enquiries. Vanderkindere, like myself, groups the blue and (light) grey eyes together; Virchow separates them, and his pure blond type *must have blue* eyes. The actual proportion of blond hair (putting aside all question of eyes) is far greater in North-Western Germany than in Flanders and Brabant, and greater even in Swabia than in the Walloon country.

COLOUR OF HAIR AND EYES.—GERMANY.

Colour of Hair	Number	Sex	Eyes Light: Red	Fair	Brown	Dark	Black	Eyes Light	Intermediate: Red	Fair	Brown	Dark	Black	Eyes Neuter	Eyes Dark: Red	Fair	Brown	Dark	Black	Eyes Dark	Index Gross	Index Per Cent
1. E. Friesland, Leer, town and country	250	both	5	83	100·5	15	·5	204	3	2	7	4	…	16	1	2	15·5	11·5	…	30	-64·5	…
2. Stick and Ihrhove, peasants	50	both	…	21	14	2	…	37	…	1	1	1	…	3	…	·5	6·5	3	…	10	-16·5	…
Total...	300	…	5	104	114·5	17	·5	241	3	3	8	5	…	19	1	2·5	22	14·5	…	40	-81	…
Per cent.	…	…	1·6	34·6	38·1	5·6	·1	80·3	1	1	2·6	1·6	…	6·3	·3	·8	7·3	4·8	…	13·3	…	-·27
3. Saterland	30	both	…	8	10·5	2·5	…	21	·5	·5	1	…	…	2	…	…	4	3	…	7	-3·5	…
Per cent.	…	…	…	26·6	35	8·3	…	70	1·6	1·6	3·3	…	…	6·6	…	…	13·3	10	…	23·3	…	-11·6
4. Münster, citizens	150	both	2·5	34	45	9·5	…	91	1	6	11·5	3·5	…	22	…	2	17·5	16	1·5	37	13·5	…
Per cent.	…	…	1·6	22·6	30	6·3	…	60·6	·6	4	7·6	2·3	…	14·6	…	1·3	11·6	10·6	1	24·6	…	-·9
5. Do, peasants	150	both	4·5	46	48·5	9	…	108	·5	6·5	6	3	…	16	1	2	10·5	12	·5	26	-35·5	…
Per cent.	…	…	3	30·6	32·3	6	…	72	·3	4·3	4	2	…	10·6	·6	1·3	7	8	·3	17·3	…	-23·6
6. Söst, Westphalia, citizens and peasants	64	both	2	11	20	3·5	·5	37	…	2·5	3·5	4	…	10	…	…	10	6	1	17	+1	…
Per cent.	…	…	3·1	17·2	31·2	5·4	·8	58	…	3·9	5·4	6·2	…	15·5	…	…	15·6	9·4	1·5	26·5	…	+1·5
7. Westphalia, peasants	60	both	3	15	21·5	3	·5	43	…	2	2	2	…	6	…	…	7·5	3	·5	11	-10	…
Per cent.	…	…	5	25	35·8	5	·8	71·6	…	3·3	3·3	3·3	…	10	…	…	12·5	5	·8	18·3	…	-16·6
8. Brunswick, citizens	130	both	4	27	37·5	8·5	…	77	2	5	13	2·5	·5	23	1	3	12·5	13·5	…	30	-16·5	…
Per cent.	…	…	3·1	20·7	28·8	6·5	…	59·2	1·5	3·8	10	1·9	·4	17·7	·7	2·3	9·6	10·4	…	23	…	-12·7

Colour of Hair and Eyes, from Personal Observation.—GERMANY, continued.

Colour of Hair	Number	Sex	EYES LIGHT						EYES INTERMEDIATE OR NEUTER						EYES DARK						Index of Nigrescence	
			Red	Fair	Brown	Dark	Black	Eyes Light	Red	Fair	Brown	Dark	Black	Eyes Neuter	Red	Fair	Brown	Dark	Black	Eyes Dark	Gross	Per Cent
9. Brunswick, peasants			5	37·5	43·5	6·5	·5	93		3	9	3		15		1	11	10		22	-26	
Per cent.			3·8	28·8	33·4	5	·4	71·5		2·3	6·9	2·3		11·5		·7	8·4	7·7		17		-20
10. Magdeburg, citizens	50		3	7	14·5	1·5		26	·5	1	2·5	3		7	1		5	9·5	1·5	17		+9
11. Eisenach, town	133		2	17·5	46·5	16·5	·5	83	2	2	9	9		22		1	6·5	17	3·5	28	+26	
Per cent.			1·5	13·1	34·9	12·3	·4	62·2	1·5	1·5	6·7	6·7		16·5		·6	4·9	12·7	2·6	21		+19·5
12. Do., peasants	150		8·5	28·5	46	15	1	99	2	2	11	9		24	·5	1·5	8·5	12·5	4	27	+3·5	
Per cent.			5·6	19	30·6	10	·6	66	1·3	1·3	7·3	6		16	·3	1	5·6	8·3	2·7	18		+2·3
13. Thuringia, and the Saale, various	77	both	2	10	34	5		51		1·5	5·5	3		10			5	9·5	1·5	16	7	
Per cent.			2·5	13	44·1	6·5		66·2		2	7·1	3·9		13			6·5	12·3	1·9	20·8		9
14. Rühla, Thuringia	95	both		3·5	23·5	12		39			9	8	1	18	1		7·5	26	3·5	38	50·5	
Per cent.				3·6	24·7	12·6		41			9·5	8·4	1	19	1		7·9	27·3	3·7	40		53·1
15. Heidelberg	33	m	1	6·5	5·5	4		17		1	1	2		4			1·5	8	2·5	12	10·5	
	82	fem	2	11	10	5		28		3	5	6		14	1	1	13	23	2	40	20	
Total	115		3	17·5	15·5	9		45		4	6	8		18	1	1	14·5	31	4·5	52	30·5	
Per cent.			2·6	15·2	13·5	7·8		39		3·5	5·2	7·7		16	·8	·8	12·6	27	3·9	45		26·5
16. Mainz	75	33⁄42		9	13	6·5	·5	29		4	2	4		10	·5	2·5	11	17·5	4·5	36	22	
Per cent.				12	17·3	8·7	·7	39		5·3	2·6	5·3		13	·7	3·3	14·6	23·3	6	48		29·3
1	2	2	3	4	5	6	7	8	9	10	11	12	13	14	15	16	17	18	19	20	21	22

	1	2	3	4	5	6	7	8	9	10	11	12	13	14	15	16	17	18	19	20	21	22
17. Boppart, peasant pilgrims...	34	m	1	9	4·5	1·5	...	16	...	2	3	1	...	6	1	1	4	5·5	·5	12	−5	...
	66	fem	4	19	12·5	·5	...	36	...	6·5	9·5	2	...	12	3	4	9	13·5	·5	18	−23	...
Total and per cent..	...	...	5	28	17	2	...	52	...	8·5	12·5	3	...	18	4	5	13	19	1	30	...	−28
18. Köln, city	300	both	13	40·5	86·5	21	1	162	...	·5	14	17	2·5	34	1	2·5	23·5	62·5	14·5	104	+79	+26·3
Per cent...	...	...	4·3	13·5	28·8	7	·3	54	...	·2	4·6	5·6	1·6	11·3	·3	·8	7·8	20·8	4·8	34·6	...	+26·3
19. Do., market, peasants ...	171	both	10	41·5	44	11	1·5	108	2	7	5	4	...	18	...	3	18·5	23	·5	45	−21·5	...
20. Dusseldorf, market, peasants	28	both	2	10	8	2	...	22	2	...	2	...	...	2	...	...	3	2	...	5	−8	...
Total...	200	...	12	51·5	52	13	1·5	130	2	7	7	4	...	20	...	3	21·5	25	·5	50	−29·5	...
Per cent.	...	...	6	25·7	26	6·5	·7	65	1	3·5	3·5	2	...	10	...	1·5	10·7	12·5	·2	25	...	−14·7
21. Do., town	45	bcth	3	7	9	4	...	23	...	1	2·5	3·5	1	8	...	...	7	5	2	14	7·5	...
22. Railway stations between Aix, Köln, Dusseldorf	100	bcth	3	15·5	30·5	11	2	62	2	1	5	4·5	·5	11	...	5	7	14	3	24	...	+21
23. Aix-la-Chapelle, city ...	300	bcth	11	40	73·5	36	4·5	165	2	5	16·5	10·5	3	37	...	5	26·5	53	12·5	98	75·5	...
Per cent... ...	...	...	3·7	13·3	24·5	12	1·5	55	·6	1·6	5·5	3·5	1	12·3	·3	1·6	8·8	17·6	4·1	32·6	...	25·2
24. Do., market, peasants... ...	250	bcth	9·5	46	73	14	·5	143	1	3	14·5	12·5	...	31	...	3·5	26·5	36	8·5	76	+16	...
Per cent.	...	...	3·8	18·4	29·2	5·6	·2	57·2	·4	1·2	5·8	5	...	12·4	...	1·4	10·6	14·4	3·4	30·4	...	+6·4
25. Treves, city, some peasants	70	m	2·5	7·5	14	11·5	·5	36	...	2·5	4	1·5	...	8	...	·5	3	16·5	4·5	26	25	...
	180	fem	4·5	23·5	42	14·5	·5	85	2	2	13·5	11	2·5	31	2·5	2·5	17	38·5	4	64	41·5	...
Total...	250	...	7	31	56	26	1	121	2	4·5	17·5	12·5	2·5	39	2·5	4	20	55	8·5	90	66·5	...
Per cent.	...	...	2·8	12·4	22·4	10·4	·4	48·4	·8	1·8	7	5	1	15·6	1	1·6	8	22	3·4	36	...	26·6

Colour of Hair and Eyes, from Personal Observation.—GERMANY, continued.

Colour of Hair	Number	Sex	EYES LIGHT.						EYES INTERMEDIATE OR NEUTER.						EYES DARK.						Index of Nigrescence	
			Red	Fair	Brown	Dark	Black	Eyes Light	Red	Fair	Brown	Dark	Black	Eyes Neuter	Red	Fair	Brown	Dark	Black	Eyes Dark	Gross.	Per Cent.
26. Leipzig, city	150	both	3	12·5	42	16	1·5	75	·5	3	11·5	13	...	28	...	1·5	11	30	4·5	47	50·5	...
Per cent.	...	...	2	8·3	28	10·6	1	50	·3	2	7·6	8·6	...	18·6	...	1	7·3	20	3	31·3	...	33·6
27. Do., peasants... ...	22	both	...	3·5	5·5	4	...	13	...	...	...	1	...	1	...	1	2	4	1	8	6·5	29·5
28. Altenburg, town	125	both	4·5	12·5	47	17·5	·5	82	...	...	...	10	...	13	...	1	10	14	5	30	34·5	...
Per cent.	...	...	3·6	10	37·6	14	·4	65·6	...	...	2·4	8	...	10·4	...	·8	8	11·2	4	24	...	27·6
29. Do., peasants in Wendich dress	8	...	...	1·5	3·5	...	...	5	...	...	...	...	1	1	...	·8	1	·5	·5	2	1	50
30. Do., do., in German dress ...	22	...	...	2	6·5	4	·5	13	...	...	1	1	...	3	...	...	...	4	2	6	14	
31. Berlin	500	both	7	60·5	169·5	51·5	1·5	290	1	7	40	26·5	1·5	76	2	8	35·5	70·5	18	134	105	...
Per cent.	...	...	1·4	12·1	33·9	10·3	·3	58	·2	1·4	8	5·3	·3	15·2	·4	1·6	7·1	14·1	3·6	26·8	...	21
32. Dresden	250	both	6	35	77	19	...	137	·5	4·5	17	14	...	36	...	·5	22	48·5	6	77	47	...
Per cent.	...	...	2·4	14	30·8	7·6	...	54·8	·2	1·8	6·8	5·6	...	14·4	...	·2	8·8	19·4	2·4	30·8	...	18·8
33. Meissen, citizens ...	125	both	3	16·5	35	13·5	1	72	...	·5	9	12	·5	22	...	...	9	21	1	31	34·5	...
Per cent.	...	...	2·4	13·2	28	13·2	·8	57·6	...	·4	7·2	9·6	·4	17·6	...	...	7·2	16·8	·8	24·8	...	27·6
34. Dresden & Meissen, peasants	200	both	1	23·5	66	20	·5	112	...	9	13·5	6·5	...	29	...	4	20	33	2	59	26	...
Per cent.	...	...	·5	11·7	33	10	·2	56	...	4·5	6·7	3·2	...	14·5	...	2	10	16·5	1	29·5	...	13
35. Konigstein, and peasants ...	50	both	...	5	20	4	1	30	·5	·5	2	1	...	4	1	...	3·5	9·5	2	16	13·5	...
Per cent.	...	...	1	10	40	8	2	...	1	1	4	2	...	8	2	19	7	19	4	32	...	27

	1	2	3	4	5	6	7	8	9	10	11	12	13	14	15	16	17	18	19	20	21	22
36. Swedes	33	n	2	13·5	9·5	3	...	28	...	...	3·5	·5	...	4	...	...	...	1	...	1	11	...
37. Norwegians	11	n	1·5	4	3·5	1	...	10	...	...	3·5	...	...	1	...	...	...	1	...	1	3·5	...
38. Danes	30	m	1	17	8·5	·5	...	27	...	1	...	...	...	1	...	1	...	1	...	2	18·5	...
39. Finns	11	m	...	3·5	3·5	...	...	7	...	1	1	...	...	2	...	...	1	1	...	2	3·5	...

Notes on the Tables for Germany.—Several points of interest arise out of the German tables. I hardly need repeat that most of their material was collected long before the great national enquiry in the German schools was begun, under the auspices of Virchow. After that it would have seemed hardly worth the trouble. Nevertheless, my statistics retain two points of advantage: they are based on the colours of adults, and they are the observations of a single individual.

I am acquainted with the official statistics only in a general way, except so far as Virchow, for the north-west, and Mayr, for Bavaria, have published the details. My own have a general accordance with them, but, I think, show more distinctly the greater predominance of the blond type in the Saxo-Frisian area, i.e. from the Rhine to the Trave, and from the sea to the Harz.

Among the points which my own tables develop are the following:—

1. The pure Frisians of the Saterland do not come out so fair as the neighbouring populations. This may be an affair of insufficient number, or may be due to a residue of prehistoric folk remaining in the midst of the marshes. My observations in the Saterland were cut short by the setting in of heavy rain, which drove me from a district where I might have been beleaguered by floods.

2. In the cities of the Rhineland, whether from the survival of the old Romanised population, or from the operation of natural selection in close unwholesome towns, in favour of the brunet element, the people are very much darker, in both eye and hair, than the peasants of the surrounding country. It seems much to be desired that some craniologist would ascertain whether any, and what, differences exist between the citizens' and peasants' skulls.

3. In the pure or mixed Frisian area, along the coast, from Ostend to the Elbe, red hair seems to be uncommon: and it is again somewhat uncommon in the semi-Sclavish land east of the Elbe and the Saale, and among the partly pre-Germanic folk of Thuringia; but there is plenty, apparently, in Westphalia and the Rhineland. It is a yellowish or golden red, unlike the strong orange red of the Scottish highlander, and its prevalence to some extent coincides with that of light hazel eyes, as in the pilgrim-peasants from near Boppart. It may be said, provisionally, to belong especially to the descendants of the Ripuarian Franks.

4. Rühla, in the Thüringerwald, is a small town, in a mountain-valley, devoted to the manufacture of tobacco-pipes, and celebrated for the dark style of beauty of its female population. I could hear of no foreign colony there, and suppose the people to be pre-Germanic.

5. The mixture of Sclavish blood, in Brandenburg and in the kingdom of Saxony, is concurrent with a notable darkening of both eyes and hair, but it is curious that this is not more distinctly marked at Altenburg, where the Wendish tongue and costume are not yet extinct, than at Leipzig or Meissen.

6. I have appended here a few observations on sailors, from Sweden, Norway, Finland and Denmark. They are almost all very fair; but the numbers are too small for building upon.

COLOUR OF HAIR AND EYES, FROM PERSONAL OBSERVATION.—AUSTRIA.

Colour of Hair	Number	Sex	EYES LIGHT						EYES INTERMEDIATE OR NEUTER						EYES DARK						Index of Nigrescence	
			Red	Fair	Brown	Dark	Black	Eyes Light	Red	Fair	Brown	Dark	Black	Eyes Neuter	Red	Fair	Brown	Dark	Black	Eyes Dark	Gross	Per Cent.
*1. Vienna	1700	both	28·5	179	407·5	182	8	865	8	19·5	120	100	4·5	252	5	13·5	120	372·5	72	583	570	…
Per cent.			1·7	10·5	27·5	10·7	·5	50·8	·5	1·1	7	5·8	·2	14·8	·3	·8	7	21·9	4·2	34·3	…	33·5
*2. Prague	250	both	1·5	16	70·5	30·5	·5	119	2	1·5	24	16·5	1	45	1	·5	17·5	55·5	11·5	86	106	…
Per cent.			·6	6·4	28·2	12·2	·2	47·6	·8	·6	9·6	6·6	·4	18	·4	·2	7	22·2	4·6	34·4	…	42·4
*3. Do., peasants	200	both	3·5	24	65	19·5	1·5	113·5	1	2	17·5	12·5	…	33	…	·5	14	32	7	53·5	50	…
Per cent.			1·7	12	32·5	9·7	·7	56·7	·5	1	8·7	6·2	…	16·5	…	·2	3·5	16	3·5	26·7	…	25
*4. Atzgersdorf, Mödling, &c., Lower Austria	100	both	2·5	15	24	11·5	1	54	·5	1	4	11·5	·5	17	…	·2	4·5	21·5	3	29	…	35
*5. Styria, German part	150	both	4·5	25	50	18	1·5	99	…	…	5·5	14·5	…	20	…	…	8	18·5	4·5	31	33·5	…
Per cent.			3	16·6	33·3	12	1	66	…	…	3·6	9·6	…	13·3	…	…	5·3	12·3	3	20·6	…	22·3
*6. Carniola, Laybach, &c.	134	both	1·5	11·5	48	14	1	76	…	2	5·5	8·5	…	16	…	…	6·5	30	5·5	42	50·5	…
Per cent.			1·1	8·5	35·8	10·4	·7	56·7	…	1·5	4·1	6·3	…	11·9	…	…	4·8	22·4	4·1	31·3	…	37·7
†7. Vienna	100	both	2·5	11·5	22	14	…	50	…	2	7·5	6·5	…	16	…	…	6·5	21	6·5	34	…	38·5
†8. Lower Austria	150	both	…	13	33	6	1	53	1	1·5	12·5	16·5	3·5	35	…	…	9·5	41·5	12	63	81·5	…
Per cent.			…	8·6	22	4	·6	35·3	·6	1	8·3	11	2·3	23·3	…	…	6·3	27·6	8	42	…	54·3
†9. Vienna, peasants	25	both	…	4	12	3	…	19	…	…	1	2	…	3	…	…	1	1·5	1·5	4	5·5	22
†10. Upper Austria	42	both	…	9	7·5	2	·5	19	…	1	3	5·5	·5	10	…	…	5	6	2	13	9·5	…
Per cent.			…	21·4	17·8	4·8	1·2	45	…	2·4	7·1	13·1	1·2	23·8	…	…	11·9	14·3	4·7	31	…	22·6
†11. Styria, and a few Carinthia	80	both	2·5	11	31	9·5	…	54	1	1	1·5	3·5	…	6	…	…	6·5	12	1·5	20	13·5	…
Per cent.			3·1	13·7	38·7	11·8	…	67·5	…	1·2	1·8	4·3	…	7·5	…	…	8·1	15	1·8	25	…	16·8

* Material collected in the usual manner, in streets and markets.   † Nationality ascertained.   Chiefly patients in military or other hospitals; far more males than females.

	1	2	3	4	5	6	7	8	9	10	11	12	13	14	15	16	17	18	19	20	21	22
†12. Bohemia, Prague hospital, Czechs	50	bcth	...	2	12	5	...	19	...	2	3	5	1	11	...	...	3	10·5	6·5	20	31·5	63
†13. Do. at Vienna, do.	110	bcth	1	14·5	32	13	·5	54	1	2	7	8	...	18	...	1	4	20	6	31	34·5	31
†14. Moravia, do., Czechs	58	bcth	...	8	11·5	5·5	2	27	1	...	1	1	2	5	...	...	4	15·5	6·5	26	34	58·6
†15. Czechs, total	218	..	1	24·5	55·5	23·5	2·5	107	2	4	11	14	3	34	...	1	11	46	19	77	100	...
Per cent.			·4	11·2	25·4	10·8	1·1	49·1	·9	1·8	5	6·4	1·3	15·6	...	·4	5	21·1	8·7	3·5	...	45·8
†16. Bohemia & Moravia, German	54	both	...	9·5	9·5	10	...	29	...	1	2·5	4·5	...	8	...	...	6·5	8	2·5	17	17	31·5
†17. Silesia, do.	28	both	...	5	5	4	...	14	...	1	2	1	...	4	...	...	4	3	3	10	8	28·5
†18. Hungary, do.	20	both	...	3	9	...	...	12	...	2	2	...	...	2	...	...	1	4	1	6	3	15
Total	102	..	...	17·5	23·5	14	...	55	...	...	6·5	5·5	...	14	...	...	11·5	15	6·5	33	28	27·4
†19. Magyars	46	both	...	1	10	7	2	20	...	...	2	5	1	8	...	·5	1·5	10	6	18	38·5	83·7
†20. Slovaks, mostly Trentsiners	30	both	...	8	4·5	4·5	1	18	...	1	3	...	...	4	...	...	1·5	6·5	...	8	4	13·3
†21. Galicia, and Poland	63	both	...	5	14	8	2	29	...	2	6·5	6·5	...	15	1	...	4·5	7·5	6	19	30	...
Per cent.			...	8	22·2	12·7	3·1	46	...	3·1	10·3	10·3	...	23·8	1·6	...	7·1	11·9	9·5	30·1	...	47·6
†22. Southern Sclaves	23	bcth	...	3	3	3	...	6	...	1	1	4	...	6	...	...	2·5	5·5	3	11	17·5	76
†23. Bavaria, a few Wurtemberg	36	bcth	1	8	11·5	·5	...	21	...	...	3	4	...	7	...	...	4	3	1	8	·5	2·7

† Nationality ascertained. Chiefly patients in military or other hospitals; far more males than females.

Notes on Tables for Austria.—The Austrian tables were the fruit of observations made in 1856-7, and a great part of them differ from the bulk of my statistics, in that they relate to persons whose birthplace and reputed nationality were ascertained, usually by actual enquiry, but occasionally by costume only. Upper Austria and Styria indicate by the prevailing colours, as well as by the physiognomy, a considerable admixture of Germanic blood. The Styrians seemed to me to include a good proportion of long-heads, but I do not know whether this has ever been put to the proof. Vienna, too, is, or was, largely Germanic; but the peasantry of Lower Austria do not appear to be so. They are in large proportion swarthy, with dark grey eyes and dark brown hair, and their features often suggest a strain of the Avar or the Hun, Germanized in little except language.

With regard to the Czechs of Bohemia and Moravia, the figures indicate, if anything, a somewhat heterogeneous people. About the 10th century a Jewish traveller, quoted by Virchow (I cannot find the reference), described the Bohemians as black-haired: there must surely have been something very distinctive in this blackness, or it would hardly have been noted. At present, if my figures can be trusted, there are many black-haired people among the Czechs, especially in Moravia; but there is also a strong blond element, not assimilated. Perhaps the history of Bohemia, from the 15th to the 17th century, is sufficient to account for this. The black Czechs do not, however, resemble, to my eye, other Northern Sclaves; the Trentsiner Slovaks, for example, who have a distinct type of their own, are very generally round-faced and flaxen-haired.

COLOUR OF HAIR AND EYES, FROM PERSONAL OBSERVATION.—ITALY.

Colour of Hair	Number	Sex	EYES LIGHT						EYES INTERMEDIATE OR NEUTER						EYES DARK						Index of Nigrescence	
			Red	Fair	Brown	Dark	Black	Eyes Light	Red	Fair	Brown	Dark	Black	Eyes Neuter	Red	Fair	Brown	Dark	Black	Eyes Dark	Gross	Per Cent.
	1	2	3	4	5	6	7	8	9	10	11	12	13	14	15	16	17	18	19	20	21	22
1. Venice and Padua	100	both	…	3	9	6·5	3·5	22	1	1	2	4	1	9	…	·5	8	24	36·5	69	…	111
2. Verona, a few of Brescia, Milan, Monza	160	both	2	3	30·5	24	9·5	69	…	…	3	13	4	20	1	…	7·5	32·5	30	71	150·5	…
Per cent.	…	…	1·3	1·9	19·1	15	5·9	43·1	…	…	1·9	8·1	2·5	12·5	·6	…	4·7	20·3	18·7	44·4	…	94
3. Lombardo - Venetians, at Vienna	47	m	·	3·5	11·5	4·5	…	16	1	1	1	2	2	5	…	…	4	13·5	12·5	26	48	102·1
4. Lavino and Arona	80	both	·5	4·4	15	10·5	1·5	31	1·2	1·2	3·7	4·5	3·1	12	…	…	4	23	10	37	60	…
Per cent.	…	…	·6	…	18·7	13·1	1·9	38·7	…	…	…	5·6	…	15	…	…	5	28·7	12·5	46·2	…	75
5. Sardinian Army	60	m	…	3	13·5	18	2·5	37	…	…	2	1	1	4	…	…	5	12·5	6·5	19	48·5	…
Per cent.	…	…	…	5	22·5	30	4·1	61·6	…	…	3·3	1·6	1·6	6·6	…	…	8·3	20·8	10·8	31·6	…	80·8
6. Novi	44	both	…	…	3	7	…	10	…	·5	1·5	4·5	1·5	8	…	…	3	14·5	8·5	26	45·5	…
Per cent.	…	…	…	…	…	…	…	…	…	…	…	…	…	…	…	…	…	…	…	…	…	103·4
7. Ligurian peasants	24	both	…	…	2	6	3	11	…	…	1	1	2	4	…	…	…	4·5	4·5	9	30·5	127
8. Genoa	450	both	2	9·5	54·5	60	5	131	1	·5	9·5	39	8	58	1	1	23	151·5	84·5	261	430·5	…
Per cent.	…	…	·2	2·1	12·1	13·3	1·1	29	·2	·1	2·1	8·7	1·8	12·9	·2	·2	5·1	33·7	18·8	58	…	95·7
9. Florence	134	both	1	4	13	11	1	30	…	1	3	12	2	18	1	…	6·5	48	30·5	86	131	…
Per cent.	…	…	·7	3	9·7	8·2	·7	22·4	…	·7	2·3	9	1·5	13·4	·7	…	4·9	35·8	22·8	64·2	…	97·7
10. Rome, citizens	70	both	…	…	8	7·5	·5	16	…	…	1	2	1	4	…	…	3	24	23	50	82·5	…
Per cent.	…	…	…	…	11·4	10·7	·7	22·8	…	…	1·4	2·9	1·4	5·7	…	…	4·3	34·3	32·9	71·4	…	117·8
11. Do. peasants	62	both	…	3	3	5·5	1·5	13	…	…	1	5	3	9	…	…	3	15·5	21·5	40	75	…
Per cent.	…	…	…	4·8	4·8	8·9	2·4	21	…	…	1·6	8·1	4·8	14·5	…	…	4·8	25	34·7	64·5	…	125

	1	2	3	4	5	6	7	8	9	10	11	12	13	14	15	16	17	18	19	20	21	22
12. Albano and Velletri	117	both	1	1	6	8	3	19	…	·5	3·5	10·5	5·5	20	·5	2	4·5	31	40	78	141·5	…
Per cent.	…	…	·8	·8	5·1	6·8	2·5	16·2	…	·4	3	9	4·7	17·1	·4	1·7	3·8	26·5	34·2	66·6	…	121
13. Tivoli	140	both	1	1·5	6	11·5	3	23	…	…	2	11	5	18	…	1	2	42·5	52·5	98	182·5	…
Per cent.	…	…	·7	1·1	4·3	8·2	2·1	16·4	…	…	1·4	7·9	3·6	12·8	…	·7	1·4	30·4	37·5	71	…	140
14. Frascati	126	both	…	2	8·5	16·5	4	31	…	…	2·5	10·5	4	17	…	2	4·5	42·5	29	78	139·5	…
Per cent.	…	…	…	1·6	6·7	13·1	3·2	24·6	…	…	2	8·3	3·2	13·5	…	1·6	3·6	33·7	23	61·9	…	110·7
15. Terracina	65	both	…	3	4	4	…	11	…	…	…	4	1	5	…	…	3	18	28	49	81	…
Per cent.	…	…	…	4·6	6·2	6·2	…	17	…	…	…	6·2	1·5	7·7	…	…	4·6	27·6	43	75·2	…	129
16. Mola di Gaeta	150	both	·5	9·5	25·5	18	·5	54	1	…	4·5	11·5	1	18	1	…	8	49	20	78	109·5	…
Per cent.	…	…	·3	6·3	17	12	·3	36	·6	…	3	7·6	·6	12	·6	…	5·3	32·6	13·3	52	…	73
17. Between Terracina and Naples, excluding Mola	280	both	2	13	39	40	7	101	1	2	8·5	24	6·5	42	…	2	15	81	39	137	230	…
Per cent.	…	…	·7	4·6	13·9	14·3	2·5	36	·3	·7	3	8·6	2·3	15	…	·7	5·3	29	13·9	48·9	…	82·1
18. Naples	181	both	1·5	5·5	22·5	15	3·5	48	…	…	5	8·5	6·5	20	2	…	5·5	50·5	55	113	195	…
Per cent.	…	…	·8	3·1	12·4	8·3	1·9	26·5	…	…	2·8	4·7	3·6	11	1·1	…	3	27·9	30·4	62·4	…	107·9
19. Sorrento and Castellamare	96	both	…	1·5	9	12	4·5	27	…	…	4	6	2	12	…	…	6·5	20	30·5	57	110·5	…
Per cent.	…	…	…	1·6	9·4	12·5	4·7	28·1	…	…	4·2	6·2	2·1	12·5	…	…	6·8	20·8	31·7	59·4	…	115
20. Capri	19	both	…	1	…	2	4·5	3	…	…	…	2	…	2	…	·5	·5	7	6	14	21·5	…
Per cent.	…	…	…	…	…	…	4·7	…	…	…	…	…	…	…	…	…	…	…	…	14	…	113
21. Salerno and Pesto	254	both	1·5	7·5	20·5	32	5·5	67	…	…	4	18·5	6·5	29	…	…	5	74·5	78·5	158	297	…
Per cent.	…	…	·6	2·9	8·1	12·6	2·1	26·4	…	…	1·5	7·3	2·5	11·4	…	…	2	29·6	30·9	62·2	…	117
22. Malta	130	both	1	2	9	6	2	20	…	…	4	8	2	14	…	…	4	18	74	96	185	…
Per cent.	…	…	·8	1·5	7	4·5	1·5	15·3	…	…	3	6·2	1·5	10·7	…	…	3	14	57	74	…	142·3

Notes on Tables for Italy.—The material for these tables was mostly gotten in 1857. The chief indications are these: The Italians are everywhere a dark-haired, and, except in two small lists from the old kingdom of Sardinia, a mainly dark-eyed people. But there are two centres of comparative fairness: one of these being apparently in the north-western part of the valley of the Po, perhaps the most Gallic region; the other, more mysterious, centring about Mola di Gaeta, and extending through Fondi, Itri, and most of the tract between Terracina and Naples. There is no doubt about the existence of this latter blond area: many travellers have been struck with the evidences of it; but I have never heard of any hypothesis to account for it.

Mr. Symonds informs me that the gondoliers of Venice, a distinct class, have almost always very light eyes, though generally dark-haired. My numbers for Venetia are too small.

COLOUR OF HAIR AND EYES, FROM PERSONAL OBSERVATION.—THE LEVANT.

Colour of Hair	Number	Sex	EYES LIGHT						EYES INTERMEDIATE OR NEUTER						EYES DARK						Index of Nigrescence	
			Red	Fair	Brown	Dark	Black	Eyes Light	Red	Fair	Brown	Dark	Black	Eyes Neuter	Red	Fair	Brown	Dark	Black	Eyes Dark	Gross	Per Cent.
1. Arnaut Bashibazuks	140	m	...	14·5	13·5	6	...	34	...	2	8	12	2	24	·5	2·5	8	34	37	82	110·5	...
Per cent.			...	10·3	9·7	4·3	...	24·3	...	1·4	5·7	8·6	1·4	17·1	·3	1·8	5·7	24·3	25	58·5	...	79
2. Turkish soldiers at Constantinople	200	m	1	2	10	8·5	1·5	23	1	2	6	14	4	27	...	...	9·5	68	72·5	150	240·5	...
Per cent.			·5	1	5	4·2	·7	11·5	·5	1	3	7	2	13·5	...	...	4·7	34	36·2	75	...	120·2
3. Osmanli—Constantinople, Brusa, &c.	150	m	...	4·5	7·5	7·5	·5	20	...	1	3	8·5	1·5	14	...	·5	15·5	42	58	116	172	...
Per cent.			...	3	5	5	·3	13·3	...	·6	2	5·6	1	9·3	...	·3	10·3	28	38·6	77·3	...	114·6
4. Greeks—Constantinople	146	most m	1	6·5	12	5·5	4	29	...	1·5	7·5	7·5	3·5	20	...	2·5	15	28·5	51	97	147	...
5. Do. Brusa	99	most fem	...	2	10	7	...	19	...	...	6	4	2	12	...	1·5	5	27	34·5	68	107·5	...
6. Do. Renkioi	100	most fem	...	3	12·5	8·5	4	28	...	3	3	4	1	11	...	1	2·5	29	28·5	61	101·5	...
7. Do. Smyrna	148	most m	...	7	8·5	12	·5	28	1	·5	3	5·5	6	16	...	...	3	36	65	104	188	...
8. Do. Nymfi	37	most fem	...	·5	2·5	...	...	3	...	...	...	4	...	4	...	...	5	15·5	9·5	30	38	...
Total Greeks	530	...	1	19	45·5	33	8·5	107	1	5	19·5	25	12·5	63	...	5	30·5	136	188·5	360	582·8	...
Per cent.			·2	3·6	8·6	6·2	1·6	20·2	·2	·9	3·7	4·7	2·3	11·8	...	·9	5·7	25·6	35·5	68	...	109·9
9. Armenians — Constantinople, Brusa, Smyrna, Nymfi, and Konieh	196	m	...	3·5	8·5	14	3	29	...	...	6·5	6	1·5	14	1	...	3·5	38	110·5	153	283·5	...
Per cent.			...	2·8	4·3	7·1	1·5	14·8	...	...	3·3	3·3	·7	7·1	·5	...	2·8	19·3	56·3	78	...	144·6

	1	2	3	4	5	6	7	8	9	10	11	12	13	14	15	16	17	18	19	20	21	22
10. Bulgarians	20	m	...	3	5	1	...	9	...	...	1	1	...	2	...	...	2	4	3	9	9	...
Per cent.	...	...	...	15	25	5	...	45	...	...	5	5	...	10	...	...	10	20	15	45	...	45
11. Crim Tartars	45	most m	...	·5	6	3·5	1	11	...	...	1	3	3	7	...	...	1·5	13·5	12	27	51·5	...
Per cent.	...	...	...	1·1	13·3	7·7	2·2	24·4	...	...	2·2	6·6	6·6	15·5	...	...	3·3	30	26·6	60	...	114·4

Notes on Tables for the Levant.—These materials were almost entirely gotten during the Crimean war, in 1855-56. The Arnauts (Skipetar) were mostly from the neighbourhoods of Monastir and Ochrida. Two types seemed to prevail among them: one fair, with Slavonic features; the other, sharper-featured, with lank, russety-black hair. In both types the nose starts out from the forehead at a large angle. The Osmanli Turks, except the soldiers, almost all shave their heads. The proportions of the eyes in 400 shaven men were: light 14·7, neutral 10·5, dark 74·7. The Greeks at Smyrna seem darker than the others. Those at Renkioi, on the Dardanelles, may have a little Slavonic admixture. Those at Nymfi (east of Smyrna) have most of the old classic features. The Armenians are the darkest race in the Levant: they have large coarse aquiline features; but their women are often beautiful. Those at Smyrna, and the hamals (porters) from Konieh, seemed to be even more uniformly dark than the rest of them. Among the few Bulgarians I saw, the fairer men generally leaned to the Slavonic; the darker, to the Tartar type. The Crim-Tartars, by the way, are *not* very *Tartar* in physiognomy; their faces are often handsome, somewhat broad, round and full, the jaw having a round sweep, the cheek-bones not very largely developed; but the eyes are often small, and, in the action of winking, give one the idea of obliquity. The hair and beard, when allowed to grow, are not coarse or lank. I do not think the blood of the Tetraxitic Goths, whom the Tartars absorbed, has been entirely worked out.

I unfortunately lost my notes on the Bosnians, Circassians and Lazes. Of the first, I think I saw more chestnut-haired than dark-haired men; in the second, dark hair and eyes preponderated, but chestnut-brown hair and blue eyes were common, and blond and red hair occurred. Of my few Lazians some were decidedly blond, very blond.

COLOUR OF HAIR AND EYES, FROM PERSONAL OBSERVATION.—THE JEWS.

Colour of Hair	Number	Sex	EYES LIGHT.					Eyes Light.	EYES INTERMEDIATE OR NEUTER.					Eyes Neuter.	EYES DARK.					Eyes Dark.	Index of Nigrescence.	
			Red	Fair	Brown	Dark	Black		Red	Fair	Brown	Dark	Black		Red	Fair	Brown	Dark	Black		Gross.	Per cent.
1. Brusa	54	...	1	1·5	9·5	4·5	2·5	19	...	...	3	1	...	4	...	...	5·5	10·5	15	31	48·5	...
2. Constantinople	33	...	2	...	2·5	2·5	...	7	...	...	...	2	...	2	...	...	·5	7·5	16	24	42	...
3. Dardanelles	54	...	2	·5	·5	3	...	6	...	...	1·5	4	·5	6	1	1	1·5	20·5	18	42	60	...
4. Smyrna	92	...	1	1	5	6·5	·5	14	1	2	4	5	...	12	1	1	7	28·5	28·5	66	91	...
Oriental Jews, total	233	...	6	3	17·5	16·5	3	46	1	2	8·5	12	...	24	2	2	14·5	67	77·5	163	241·5	...
Per cent.	...	...	2·5	1·3	7·5	7	1·3	19·7	·4	·8	3·6	5·5	·2	10·3	·8	·8	6·2	28·7	33·2	70	...	103·6
5. Prague	100	...	1	1	10·5	8·5	4	25	...	...	4·5	5	2·5	12	...	...	1	38	24	63	110·5	...
6. Vienna	50	...	...	...	7	7·5	·5	15	...	...	1	7·5	1·5	10	...	...	...	13	12	25	56	...
7. Do. (many Polish)	65	...	1	4·5	11·5	9	2	28	1	...	2	6	1	9	...	...	3·5	11	13·5	28	53·5	...
8. Amsterdam	13	...	...	...	...	·5	·5	1	...	...	...	...	...	...	...	...	1·5	10·5	...	12	12	...
9. Rome	7	...	...	...	...	1	...	1	1	...	...	1	1	3	...	...	...	2	1	3	6	...
10. Bristol	50	...	...	1	4	4	1	10	1	...	3·5	1	1	7	...	...	1	16	16	33	56	...
11. London	100	...	...	2	6·5	12·5	2	23	1	1	2·5	1	1·5	14	...	...	2·5	22	38·5	63	122·5	...
12. Do., Portuguese	50	...	...	2	2	5	2	11	...	...	2	8	1·5	8	...	1	1	8·5	20·5	31	63	...
Total of Jews	668	...	8	13·5	59	64·5	15	160	4	3	24	45	11	87	2	3	25	188	203	421	721	...
Per cent.	...	...	1·2	2	8·8	9·6	2·2	23·9	·6	·4	3·6	6·7	1·6	13	·3	·4	3·7	28	30·4	63	...	107·9

If the Roman and London-Portuguese Jews are classified with the Orientals as Sephardim, we have indices of 107 and 108·6 for the Sephardim and the Ashkenazim respectively, or as nearly as possible the same. The head-forms of the Jews of different countries seem to me to be more variable in proportion than the hair-colours. See, for exact statistics of the Hungarian and Polish (Galician) Jews, the work of Körösy, and that of Professors Majer and Kopernicki; the latter, dealing with several hundreds of individuals, found 54·5 per cent. with dark eyes, and 65·2 with dark hair, proportions much larger than in the Ruthenians, and about double what prevail among the Poles. In Bavaria (Georg Mayr) 49 per cent. of the Jewish children have brown eyes, against 34 of the German, and 50 have brown and 20 black hair, against 41 and 5 respectively; the blond being 30 against 54 per cent. Thus, in all northern countries, the Jews are much darker than the Gentile inhabitants, while in the Levant they are, on the other hand, lighter than the Armenians, the Turks, or even, it would seem, the Greeks; their type remaining uniform to an extraordinary degree.

TABLE ILLUSTRATIVE OF THE GERMAN METHOD OF EXHIBITING RACIAL COLOUR-TYPES.

Colour of Hair	Number	Sex	BLUE EYES. BLUE-GRAY EYES separately.					Total Blue Eyes.	GRAY EYES, Including Light and Dark Gray, Ashen-Gray, Sea-Gray, Green.					Total Gray Eyes.	BROWN EYES, Including Black, Hazel, Light Hazel, Light Brown, Green-Brown, Dark Brown-Gray.					Total Brown Eyes.	Index of Nigrescence	
			Red	Fair	Brown	Dark	Black		Red	Fair	Brown	Dark	Black		Red	Fair	Brown	Dark	Black		Gross.	Per Cent.
1. Bristol, and surrounding counties	533	m	11	43·5	78·5	45·5	·5	182	10	26	71	61·5	4·5	173	5	8·5	42·5	95	27	178	168	28
2. Do., blue-gray eyes ...	67	m	1·5	18·5	24·5	22	·5	67	...	...	...	...	...	...	...	...	...	...	...	...	...	...
3. Ireland	84	m	1	2	11	10	2	26	4	1·5	10·5	15·5	4·5	36	1	...	4·5	8·5	8	22	...	65
4. Do., blue-gray eyes ...	16	m	...	1	3	11·5	·5	16	...	...	...	...	...	...	...	...	...	...	...	...	...	...
5. Wales (South)	69	m	...	2	5	4	...	11	3	1	6	9·5	2·5	22	1	1	7	19	8	36	45	60
6. Do., blue-gray eyes ...	6	m	·5	2	1·5	2	...	6	...	...	...	...	...	...	...	...	...	...	...	...	...	...

Table illustrative of the German Method of Exhibiting Racial Colour-Types—(continued).

Colour of Hair	Number	Sex	BLUE EYES. BLUE-GRAY EYES separately.						GRAY EYES, Including Light and Dark Gray, Ashen-Gray, Sea-Gray, Green.						BROWN EYES, Including Black, Hazel, Light Hazel, Light Brown, Green-Brown, Dark Brown-Gray.						Index of Nigrescence	
			Red	Fair	Brown	Dark	Black	Total Blue Eyes.	Red	Fair	Brown	Dark	Black	Total Gray Eyes.	Red	Fair	Brown	Dark	Black	Total Brown Eyes.	Gross.	Per Cent.
7. Scottish Highlands ...	44	♂	3	4·5	5	6	1·5	20	...	...	6·5	7·5	1	15	...	...	1	6	2	9	20·5	41
8. Do., blue-gray eyes ...	6	♂	1	1·5	1·5	2	...	6	...	...	...	...	...	...	...	...	...	...	...	...	...	...
9. Islay and Colonsay — Hebrides (McLean)	95	♂	3	9	8	7·5	1·5	28	6	7·5	7·5	20	11	52	...	3	5	3·5	2·5	14	38	33·6
10. Do., blue-gray eyes ...	18	♂	1	3	6	6·5	1·5	18	...	...	...	...	...	...	...	...	...	...	...	...	...	...

Notes on Table illustrative of the German Method of Exhibiting Racial Colour-Types:—

Virchow, in a paper lately read to the Royal Prussian Academy of Science, expresses regret that in the Belgian enquiry into the colour of hair and eyes in school-children, Vanderkindere adopted a different system of schedules from that employed in Germany and Switzerland, and more recently still in Cis-leithan Austria. I confess that to me Vanderkindere's plan seems preferable, by reason of its greater simplicity, in neglecting the difference between fair and dark skins, and between blue and gray eyes. In many parts of the British Isles, not to speak of the difficulties caused by one person calling that blue which another calls gray, a large proportion of irides are grayish-blue.

My own statistics are gotten from adults, not from children, besides being differently arranged. I believe, however, that the "grau" of the Germans and Swiss nearly corresponds with my own "neutral."

In order to get some data for comparison between Britain and Germany, &c., I have put together a few observations taken on school-children in Bristol, a city where the prevailing complexional colours are probably not far from the average of the United Kingdom.

250 children, about equally divided as to sex, and belonging partly to the upper, but chiefly to the lower and lowest classes, all attending school at Bristol, but not all natives of that city, yielded me the following percentages:—

REINBLOND.
Blue Eyes.

Red Hair.   Fair Hair.
·6   17·2

17·8

REINBRUNET.
Brown or Dark Eyes.

Brown Hair.   Dark Brown Hair.   Black Hair.
11·8   10·6   1·4

23·8

As children usually grow a shade darker in becoming adults, let us try the percentage of *blue* eyes with red, fair, or *brown* hair in a body of men: it should correspond nearly to that of red and fair in the same persons when children. Similarly, we should retrench from the brown type, in adults, those with brown (chestnut) hair, which was pretty certainly fair in childhood, leaving only the dark brown and the black.

In the great prison at Wakefield, where Dr. Milner observed the colours for me with great accuracy, the following were the results:—

Types as just now defined for adults:—*Reinblond*, 16·5; *Reinbrunet*, 18·6.

In this case most of the subjects were drawn from the North of England, which is a comparatively blond area; on the other hand, criminals,

Notes on Three Illustrations of the German Method of Exhibiting Racial Colour-Types (continued).

Careful observations on 464 convicts, in the Perth Prison—Scotch, Irish and English, but mainly Scotch—by Mr. James Bruce Thomson, gave the following results:—

Types as just now defined for adults—

	Reinblond.	Reinbrunet.
318 Scotch	27	11·3
51 English	29·4	15·7
96 Irish	15·8	10·5

Here the Englishmen were mostly from the North of England.

I have also constructed a table on this plan from a series of careful observations on adults, who were being subjected to other investigations: they were examined in Bristol, but the majority of them were natives of the surrounding English counties. To this are added analogous figures for my Scottish Highlanders, and for a certain number of Irishmen and Welshmen, examined with the same care (34 of the Irishmen were natives of the county Kerry), and for the natives of Islay and Colonsay, in the Hebrides, from the notes of Mr. Hector Maclean.

The resulting proportions for Virchow's two types are as follows, those for the blond element varying according as the men with bluish-gray eyes are or are not included:—

	REINBLOND TYPE.		BRUNET TYPE.
	Without bluish-gray.	With bluish-gray.	
S.W. England	22·1	29·6	20·3
South Wales	9·3	14·6	36
Ireland (Munster)	14	18	16·5
Scottish Highlands	25	33	16
Islay and Colonsay	17·7	26·5	5·3
Germany in general (Virchow)	31·8		14·0
Austria " "	19·8		23·1
Switzerland	11·1		25·7
Belgium	?		27·5

As applied to the British races, this method appears to me to have but small recommendations. It is true that the abundance of the dark and the scantiness of the fair element in South Wales is brought out clearly; but neither Ireland nor the Highlands takes its true position, owing to the fact that in these Gaelic countries so much of the dark and black, and especially the coal-black, hair, is combined, not with brown, but with gray or even blue eyes. This characteristic comes out very remarkably in Islay and Colonsay; and so it comes to pass that these islands show the ridiculously small percentage of 5·3 brunets less than is given in this plan to East Friesland, where I did not see a single black-haired individual.

The national differences in the British Isles in the proportion of blue and of gray eyes are not striking or characteristic. Blue is comparatively uncommon in South Wales, and common in the south and east of England; hazel, as distinguished from brown, is rather common in England and South Wales, and uncommon among the Gaels. But special varieties of eye-colour, too minutely discriminated to be brought to the test of numbers, do occur in special districts, and attract the attention of travellers. Thus, a kind of muddy brownish-gray is common in Wiltshire and the West Riding; clear china-blue in some of the Saxon counties; violet in Munster; both gray and blue, with a surrounding dark ring, in most parts of Ireland; a large blue iris, reticulated with gray or yellowish fibres, in North Devon. Greenish-gray is thought to prevail where Scandinavian blood is potent.

DATA CONCERNING CHANGES OF COLOUR-TYPE, AND RELATION OF COLOUR TO DISEASE.

Colour of Hair	Number	Sex	EYES LIGHT.						EYES INTERMEDIATE OR NEUTER.						EYES DARK.						Index of Nigrescence	
			Red	Fair	Brown	Dark	Black	Eyes alone	Red	Fair	Brown	Dark	Black	Eyes alone	Red	Fair	Brown	Dark	Black	Eyes alone	Gross	Per Cent.
1. National Portrait Gallery, and Worcester Exhibition, 16th and 17th centuries	80	most m	1	10	15·5	3·5	...	17	...	1	6	4·5	·5	2	...	1	8·5	20	8·5	19	33	...
Per cent. ...	...	...	1·2	12·5	19·3	4·3	...	...	...	1·2	7·5	5·6	·6	...	...	1·2	10·6	25	10·6	...	...	41·2
2. Chamberlain's Holbein — Court of Henry VIII.	36	m	1·5	6·5	10	1	...	3	·5	·5	1·5	3·5	...	2	1	1	3·5	5	1·5	...	1·5	4·1
	14	fem	4	4	1	1	...	4	1·5	·5	1	...	...	...	1	...	...	...	...	...	-8·5	-70
3. Mr. Rowlatt's lists, 16th and 17th centuries ...	40	m	2	18	4	1	...	5	2	2	2	5	...	...	1	...	1	...	2	...	-15	-37
4. Do., 18th century	31	...	3	6	2	6	...	16	3	...	2	1	...	...	...	...	...	6	2	...	+5	+16
5. Do., 19th-century	93	...	6	21	12	20	...	21	3	3	4	8	3	4	1	...	2	6	4	1	14	15
6. Do., mostly 18th and 19th. Pugilists, and other men remarkable for physical endowments	123	...	5	31	15	13	3	17	6	6	11	16	1	4	4	...	1	5	9	6	2	1·6

RELATION OF COLOUR TO DISEASE.—PHTHISIS AND CANCER.

	Number	Sex	EYES LIGHT.						EYES INTERMEDIATE OR NEUTER.						EYES DARK.						Index of Nigrescence	
			Red	Fair	Brown	Dark	Black	Eyes alone	Red	Fair	Brown	Dark	Black	Eyes alone	Red	Fair	Brown	Dark	Black	Eyes alone	Gross	Per Cent.
1. Phthisical adults of all British nationalities	500	both	16·5	49·5	106	69·5	8·5	...	4	7·5	21·5	37·5	3	...	5·5	3·5	29·5	103	35	...	214·5	...
Per cent.	...	...	3·3	9·9	21·2	13·9	1·7	50	·8	1·5	4·3	7·5	·6	14·7	1·1	·7	5·9	20·6	7	35·3	...	42·9
2. Scotch, included above...	250	both	10·5	27·5	53	32·5	7·5	...	2	6·5	7·5	11·5	·5	...	4	1	19	52	15	...	90·5	...
Per cent.	...	...	4·2	11	21·2	13	3	52·4	·8	2·6	3	4·6	·2	11·2	1·6	·4	7·6	20·8	6	36·4	...	36·2

3. Irish, partly included	65	...	...	1·5	11	12·5	12	...	37	...	...	3	12	2	17	...	...	...	5	6	11	30·5	47
4. Welsh and Cornish	42	...	...	...	4	7	4	...	15	...	...	·5	4·5	1	6	...	...	...	16·5	4·5	21	35	83·3
5. English, mostly at Bristol ...	200	m	6	22	59	34	·5	...	...	1	5	18	2	...	...	1	8	32	11·5	...	82	...	...
Per cent.	...		3	11	29·5	17	·2	60·7	·5	2·5	9	1	13	·5	·5	4	16	5·7	26·2	...	41	
6. Do.	300	fem	12	29·5	62	42	2·5	...	1·5	6·5	14·5	26·5	2	...	1	1	16	70	13	...	118·5	...
Per cent.	...		4	9·8	20·6	14	·8	49·3	·5	2·1	4·8	8·8	·6	16·8	·3	·3	5·3	23·3	4·3	33·6	...	39·5
7. Do., Brompton Hospital, London, by Dr. E. Liddon	72	both	2	3	18	5	...	28	...	...	11	4	2	17	1	...	18	7	2	28	18+	24·7+
8. Cancer (English and Scotch)	67	both	2·5	4·5	17	8	2	·34	...	...	1·5	7·5	1	10	1	·5	16·5	5	23	40	...
Per cent.	...		3·7	6·7	25·5	11·9	3	50·7	...	...	2·2	11·2	1·5	14·9	1·5	·7	24·5	7·5	34·3	...	59·7

Notes to Table on Changes of Colour-Type, and Relation of Colour to Disease.—There is a prevalent idea that the English are gradually changing from a fair to a dark race, while the sanguine is giving place to the nervous or nervo-bilious temperament. I confess to holding this opinion myself, but rather as a matter of speculation and conjecture than as a well-grounded belief. In my experience as a physician, it has appeared that, on the whole, dark-complexioned children have more tenacity of life than fair ones, under some of the unfavourable conditions connected with town-life; and it is conceivable that natural selection, working thus in conjunction with the rapid growth of towns at the expense of the country population, might in the course of a few generations considerably alter the proportions of the prevailing types. Here might be considered the various differences in physical and moral character which more or less associate themselves with the different complexions, some of which may have an effect upon their ratio of propagation. I once thought it possible to prove that conjugal selection had an influence in this direction; but more careful examination shook the value of the evidence, which at first seemed convincing.* That the influence is possible, however, cannot be gainsaid; and I think that the prevalence of red hair, for example, has been lessened in this way in those countries where it is an unpopular colour.

The differences between the blond and the brunet type may be considered with regard to their genesis and to their nature. On the former of these subjects, the paper of Professor Buchan, of Toronto, is the most valuable known to me. He believes the xanthous variety of man to have been developed by natural selection in the northern temperate zone, where dark pigment was least required as a protection against sunshine and dry air; but that, once established, climate has little further effect on it, at least in cognisable periods. I see no considerable objection to this opinion, unless it be the testimony of the Chinese annals to the xanthous complexion of the Woosun and Jingling tribes. On Mr. Buchan's hypothesis, xanthosity should not be an unfavourable or unhealthy characteristic in the region which gave it birth, whatever it may be elsewhere.

* See the table and note on Conjugal Selection. † "Complexion, Climate and Race," *Proc. Canad. Institute.*

Notes to Table on Changes of Colour-Type, and Relation of Colour to Disease (continued) :—

Dr. Sorby's investigations showed the existence of three pigments in hair—a black, a red, and a yellow colouring matter. The presence of the black pigment in large quantity obscures or conceals that of the red or yellow, which may nevertheless be in large proportion. The red often, perhaps usually, abounds in negro hair.

Pale shades in the hair, and indeed in the eyes also, are therefore in some sense the results of a defect—a defect of secretion ; but it does not necessarily follow that they are disadvantageous, or that they are a mark of weakness.

There are, however, several facts which may point in that direction, such as the alleged physical and constitutional inferiority of albinoes, to which there is, however, a signal exception in a distinguished modern statesman ; the comparative lightness of the hair of children—not only the black, but the red and yellow pigment, seem to be less in quantity in very young children ,* the changes which take place in disease, which are generally in the direction of dulness and paleness of hue ; the alleged inferior density of blood and of milk in blonds as compared with brunets ; the higher pitch of voice which has been said to characterise both fair-haired men and tribes in the dawn of civilization. Baxter (vol. i., p. 73) states that in the American Federal army more fair than dark men were rejected for every large class of disease, with the single exception of chronic rheumatism. This statement he qualifies, however, by the remark that there were other exceptions, in diseases of rarer occurrence, and mostly of an acute or inflammatory character.

On the other hand, it may be said that, with a few notable exceptions, conquering and ruling races have always been fair, while the vanquished and submissive races have been dark. The supposed superiority of blonds in stature is, as Dr. Baxter remarks, an affair of races, rather than of individuals. He found that among the Americans the dark-complexioned had even a slight superiority. Is it possible that this is due to ever so small an admixture with the tall Redskin race ? In British-Americans, among whom, of the leading race elements, the British is taller than the French, he found the proportions *reversed* (vol. i., p. 24). In most parts of Great Britain I have found that the higher stature goes with the fair complexion ; but there are important exceptions to the rule in particular districts, which shall be noted in their place, and which I suppose to have a racial origin.

There is a general consensus of opinion as to the superiority, as marksmen in shooting, of men with light blue and light gray eyes. As a rule, arctic navigators testify to the superior hardihood and power of enduring exposure possessed by light-complexioned, red-bearded men ; but they are not unanimous on this point. The northern races, we know, are less able to resist malaria than the southern ; but how far this is connected with the fair complexion is not clear ; strangely enough, blonds are said to stand the climate of West Africa better than brunets.

I publish a list, compiled by the Rev. J. H. Rowlatt, of the complexional colours of 123 natives of the British Isles who have been distinguished for physical superiority, which in many cases has been conjoined with conspicuous courage and intrepidity. His way of using terms is evidently not identical with mine, but there can hardly be a doubt that the list includes many more fair than dark men, and that red hair particularly abounds among these athletes and champions.† If anything can be confidently predicated as to the two principal complexions, it is that the fair goes more usually with active courage and a roving adventurous disposition, the dark with patient industry and attachment to local and family ties—the one with the sanguine, the other with the melancholic temperament. The temperament of genius and of intellectual development is a large subject, too large to be entered on here. One small contribution to it may perhaps be admitted :—Persons in Zoological and Physiological Sections of British Association, Manchester Meeting ; more than one-third women ; hair only observed—

No.	Red.	Fair.	Brown.	Dark.	Black.	Index.
120	3·5	23·5	47·5	43·5	2	20·5=17·1

* It is a mistake to suppose that women have lighter hair and eyes than men : they have even a slight excess of dark eyes.

† The great number of the persons in the lists I have abstracted from those of Mr. Rowlatt, who are credited with neutral eyes, arises from my having placed under this

I have said already that the greater liability of light-complexioned persons to disease, which Dr. Baxter found to exist in the United States, does not probably extend to this country. For an example, see the accompanying statistics of the liability of the different colours to phthisis, or to the diseases which are commonly included under that name. It will be seen that the index of nigrescence in phthisical persons in both England and Scotland is considerably greater than that of healthy persons in the regions about Edinburgh and Bristol, which supplied the greater part of the cases noted, or than that of the general run of hospital patients in those cities. The excess of persons with black hair is especially large. The figures for Wales and Cornwall are at least equally strong, but the number of cases is insufficient for generalisation; in Ireland there is more room for doubt, there being an apparent excess of both blonds and black-haired persons. I have added some statistics from the Brompton Hospital, London, by Dr. Edward Liddon, of Taunton, which point in the same direction, though Dr. Liddon evidently calls some shades "brown" which for me would be "dark."

Cancer is another disease to which in this country brunets are more liable than blonds. The table shows a great preponderance of persons with dark hair, often black, and frequently combined with dark eyes and complexion. But as cancer for the most part selects its victims from those who have passed the age of procreation, it can hardly affect the processes of natural selection, whereas phthisis may do so.

In order to test directly the question whether, through natural selection or any other process, the colour-type has altered among our upper classes during the last three or four centuries, I have tabulated a number of facts derived from the inspection of portraits, mostly of distinguished men. I have already remarked, however, that this is not so satisfactory a test as might be supposed. Age and smoke and varnish obscure the colours; and painters used to be, nay, sometimes even now are, careless, or flatter by following the fashion. My list, put together without selection, indicates, contrary to expectation, a greater prevalence of dark hues in the 16th and 17th centuries than in the 19th. The 18th is scarcely available, owing to the practice then in vogue of wearing wigs or powder. Holbein, as rendered by Chamberlain, gives only doubtful adumbrations of the colours, and in the case of women gives hardly any but reddish and golden tints. I do not think these can be trusted, any more than the flaxen and yellow of the Venetian ladies of old, which were certainly artificial or imaginary, seeing the men of that place and period were almost all painted with dark hair. I have thought it fair, in this connexion, to print Mr. Rowlatt's lists of distinguished men for the 16th, 17th, 18th and 19th centuries. One may be permitted a little to doubt whether he They differ from mine in indicating a preponderance of light colours in the first two centuries. One may be permitted a little to doubt whether he carried out his selection with the perfect fairness which he doubtless intended; the criterion of distinction is itself indistinct.

On the whole, the results of this part of the investigation are unsatisfactory; nor should I have thought them worth publishing, were it not that they may help others to succeed where I have failed.

The most promising line in this direction is the comparison of country-born with town-born adults. The reader will find some material for this purpose in the West of England table, compiled at Bristol. There are some indications therein that the people of town-birth are more often dark-eyed, but certainly not darker, perhaps rather lighter, in hair, than those born in surrounding country districts. Still, supposing this to be proven, it may be due to no influence of media, but to the ascertained fact that the towns of the West of England contain far more persons of East-English or of Welsh descent than their rural neighbourhoods; and that dark eyes are disproportionately common in Wales and in some eastern counties.

TABLE ILLUSTRATING POSSIBLE EFFECTS OF CONJUGAL SELECTION.

The material for this table was derived from the female patients of the Bristol Royal Infirmary, during a period of about nine years. In these statistics all women over 20 years of age were originally included, and the apparent result was that the fair-haired women remained single in larger proportion than the dark-haired ones, or than the red-haired. Some correspondence with Mr. Darwin, who was interested in the matter, led me to reconsider the facts, and to discover that my inference was not warranted by them. I had been misled in consequence of not having made allowance for the darkening process which goes on in the hair of most persons for many years beyond the age of 20, wherefore light-haired persons are more numerous, proportionally, at young ages, when many women who ultimately become married are still single. The present table includes only women over 35 years, and tends to show that the darkening process had not quite ceased even at 35 :—

COLOUR OF HAIR.

35 to 45—	Red.	Fair.	Brown.	Dark.	Black.		Total.	Index of Nig.
Single ...	4·5	5	11·5	20·5	7·5	=	49	26 = 53 per cent.
Married ...	23·5	41	134·5	128·5	32·5	=	360	129 = 36 "
45 to 50—								
Single ...	1·5	·5	6	3	1	=	12	3 = 25 "
Married ...	5·5	12·5	49	85·5	11·5	=	164	90·5 = 55 "
Totals—								
Single ...	6	5·5	17·5	23·5	8·5	=	61	29 = 47 "
Married ...	29	53·5	183·5	214	44	=	524	219·5 = 42 "
Percentages—								
Single ...	9·8	9	28·7	38·5	13·9			
Married ...	5·5	10·2	35	40·8	8·4			

These figures, if they show anything, show that among the working classes of Bristol, women with red and women with black hair do not marry in quite so large proportion as those with hair of other colours. If this be the fact, it does not *necessarily* imply preference for other colours on the part of the men. Comeliness and intelligence, especially when combined, are certainly not particularly conducive to matrimony in the classes under consideration : it is even doubtful whether they are so in other ranks of society. The diminution in size of the female head, as compared with the male, in certain civilized countries, may have some import in this connexion.

To return—the question is probably one more of temperament than of preference. But it is obvious that if in several successive generations the same relations of complexion to matrimony were to continue, red and black hair would probably become somewhat less prevalent. This would imply, according to Dr. Sorby, a diminution in the production of the two most abundant kinds of hair-pigment; and we should have a general prevalence of dull shades of brown.

MEASUREMENTS OF BRITISH SKULLS, ANCIENT, MEDIÆVAL AND MODERN.

	Number	LENGTHS				BREADTHS						CIRC.			HEIGHT		ARCS.			INDICES.		Capacity, Cub. Cent.
		Glab. Max.	Front. Inial.	Glab. Inial.	B. D.	Front. Min.	Steph.	Zygo.	Aur.	Max.	Mast.				Basio-Bregm.	Basio-max.	Naso-occip.	Biaur-Bregm.	Biaur-sup.-cil.	Latit.	Altit.	
1. Rothwell, males ...	15	7·31	...	...	...	...	...	...	...	5·75	...	...	...	...	...	...	...	...	...	78·7	...	1374
2. Micheldean, males ...	5	7·47	7·24	7·22	7·38	4·02	4·72	5·12	4·46	5·59	5·06	...	...	...	5·34	5·36	13·24	13·14	11·36	74·8	71·5	...
3. Do., females ...	2	7·35	7·15	7·05	7·35	3·85	4·55	4·90	4·35	5·50	5 ?	...	...	...	4·85	4·95	13	13·10	11·30	74·8	66	...
4. Hythe, males... ...	11	7·06	...	...	...	...	...	...	...	5·74	...	...	...	...	5·23	...	...	...	...	81·3	74·4	...
5. Do., including irregular and defective measures ...	11	7·06	6·98	6·94	...	3·93	4·84	5·32	4·67	5·74	5·12	...	...	...	5·23	...	12·6	12·65	...	81·3	74·4	...
6. Do., females ...	10	6·86	...	...	...	...	...	...	...	5·48	...	...	...	...	5·10	...	...	...	...	79·9	74·3	...
7. Do., children... ...	8	6·48	...	...	...	...	...	...	...	5·50	...	...	...	...	4·95	...	...	...	...	84·7	76·3	...
8. Do., other, selected, males...	3	7·35	7·41	7·2	7·2	4·2	5·03	5·56	4·96	6·10?	?5·25	21·23	...	...	5·61	...	13·1	13·4	...	83·3	76·8	...
9. Do., elliptic form ...	1	7·1	7	7·2	7	4·1	5	5·4	4·8	5·7	5	...	...	...	5·4	...	13	13·1	...	80·3	76	...
10. Do., quadrate form ...	1	7	...	...	...	3·9	4·6	5·2	4·7	5·8	4·8	...	...	...	5·3	...	12·5	13	...	82·8	75·7	...
11. Aran, Galway Bay, males ...	4	7·53	...	...	...	...	...	...	...	5·59	...	...	...	...	?5·27	...	...	...	...	74·25	70 ?	...
12. Silurian or Dobunian (?) skulls, from Gloucester, males ...	7	7·32	7	7·05	...	3·82	...	?5·29	4·26	5·51	...	20·86	...	...	5·14	5·34	13·20	...	10·75	75·27	70·22	...
13. Mediaeval, Bristol, males ...	3	7·35	7·16	7·21	7·30	3·81	...	...	4·73	5·63	5·16	21·30	20·56	20·76	5·20	5·45	12·80	12·43	11·03	76·60	70·75	...
14. Older skulls from St. Werburgh's, Bristol, males	28	7·34	...	...	...	...	...	...	...	5·88	...	...	...	...	...	5·56	...	...	...	80·1	72·9	...
15. Do., females	8	6·95	...	...	...	...	...	...	...	5·56	...	...	...	...	...	5·10	...	...	...	79·9	73·2	...
16. Do., both sexes ...	36	7·26	...	...	...	...	...	...	...	5·81	...	...	...	...	...	5·30	...	...	...	80	73	...

MEASUREMENTS OF BRITISH SKULLS, ANCIENT, MEDIÆVAL AND MODERN (continued).

Number	LENGTHS					BREADTHS					CIRC.	HEIGHT		ARCS.			INDICES.		Capacity, Cub. Cent.
	Glab. Max.	Front. Inial.	Glab. Inial.	B. D.	Front. Min.	Steph.	Zygo.	Aur.	Max.	Mast.		Basio-Bregm.	Basio-max.	Naso-occip.	Biaur-Bregm.	Biaur-sup.-cil.	Latit.	Altit.	
17. Recent, St. Werburgh's, males	10	7·58	...	...	7·27	...	...	...	...	5·94	...	...	...	5·40	...	...	...	78·1	71·2	...
18. Do., females	7	7·18	...	...	...	...	...	...	...	5·33	...	...	...	5·15	...	...	...	74·2	71·7	...
19. Do., both sexes	17	7·43	...	...	...	...	...	...	...	5·69	...	...	...	5·30	...	...	...	76·6	71·3	...
20. Anglian, males (*see note*) ...	10	7·34	7·12	6·98	7·27	3·86	4·59	5·11	4·52	5·57	4·9	?21·11	5·25	5·35	12·95	12·75	11·10	75·8	70·9	...

Notes on the Table of British Skulls.—Rothwell is a large village, or small town, in Northamptonshire; once larger still. In a crypt under the church, whose existence had been forgotten and rediscovered, was found in the last century a large collection of human bones. It can hardly be doubted that this was a mediæval ossuary. The skulls are on the whole rather short and broad; their capacity appears small. The method I employed for ascertaining the capacity was that of Professor Busk, the material was rape seed, and the instrument one of Mr. Busk's own construction, which he kindly lent me. See a paper on some of the Rothwell skulls, by Sir William Grove and Mr. Busk, in the *Journal of the Anthropological Institute*, vol. i. Mr. Busk, operating on eight skulls, some of which were female, found a breadth index of 78·2, an altitudinal of 75·4; I do not know what method he adopted in measuring the height. Skulls of older date, lying singly or in small groups, are not unfrequently disinterred in Southern Northamptonshire, about Towcester; they are supposed to date from the time of Edward the Elder's campaigns, and are generally of the Anglian or Graverow type; a specimen in my possession measures 7·7 × 5·9, indexing 75·3.

Micheldean is a small town in the Forest of Dean, the most north-western part of Gloucestershire, west of the Severn. This district was probably conquered by the English soon after the battle of Deorham (A.D. 577), but the population continued mainly Welsh, and the features and hair-colour indicate that it remains so still. These skulls are from a small charnel-house attached to the church, and are doubtless of considerable age. They are almost all phanerozygous, and have prominent nasal bones; the norma occipitalis tends to be rounded, the norma verticalis varies, but on the whole may be said to be ovoid. So far as I can judge, these characteristics remain in the bulk of the present population of the Forest. I have excluded from computation one aberrant skull, which had a breadth-index of 91; it was without doubt that of a rickety youth. For details, see a paper in the *Trans. Bristol and Glost. Archæol. Soc.*, 1881-2.

Hythe is a port on the south-eastern coast of Kent, said to have been more important during the middle ages than of late. The collection in the charnel-house of the church is of some celebrity, and has been visited by several anthropologists. See two papers by Dr. Robert Knox (*Trans. Ethn. Soc. Lond.*, i., 238, and ii., 136), and an interesting note by Barnard Davis, in the *Thesaurus Craniorum*, pp. 45, 46. There were six skulls from Hythe church in the B. Davis collection, of which four masculine ones yielded average indices of breadth and height of 82·8 and 76·7; while two female skulls yielded indices of 85·2 and 75·5. Five of the six were brachycephalic; they were all rather large, and had probably been selected as fine specimens.

My visit to the charnel-house was short, and the opinion I have formed is given with some reservation. It is, that the bones are mostly those of the mediæval population of Hythe, but that mixed with these may be those of a considerable number of Frenchmen, said to have been slain in an unsuccessful descent on Hythe. A great part of the skulls have a cuboid or quadrate form, such as is common in France and Switzerland; others, especially among the women, are elliptic or cylindroid; the latter form may be a variety of the Saxon or Frisian, or Jutish type; others, ... The males are a large majority. As many of the female and most of the juvenile skulls I had time to look at ... the former can hardly be so.

Notes on the Table of British Skulls (continued) :—

as those we have of the old Kentish Jutes are long, I am disposed to think that Hythe may have received a good many French emigrants during the centuries subsequent to the Norman Conquest.

From the manner in which the Hythe ossuary is arranged, it is impossible to be sure of having gotten a fair sample of the whole. It is much to be desired that some anthropologists having sufficient leisure would devote several days to its examination.

The four skulls which I measured in Aran were found in the dry sand which has gathered within the small and ancient ruined church of St. Enery, Aranmore. I have already spoken of the Aran people, who are reputed Firbolg, but whose remarkably long-featured long-headed type, with light eyes and generally dark hair, though like enough to that of some continental Belgæ, hardly agrees with McFirbis's description of the Firbolg.

The skulls here called Silurian were found at Gloucester, in 1881; and a full account of the locality and circumstances, by Mr. John Bellows, appeared in the *Transactions of the Bristol and Gloucester Arch. Society* for 1881-2, accompanied by details of my measurements. He was of opinion that the bodies were those of insurgent Britons, from the Silurian side, who had attacked the wall of the Roman city at its weakest point; that a number of them had been slain, and buried where they fell. It is certain in any case that they belonged to the Roman period. Curiously enough, there was among them one skull, that of a young person, probably a boy, which was brachycephalic (index 85), seemingly from hydrocephaly or rickets; just as there is in the charnel-house of Micheldean, among the crania of, probably, the posterity of the same tribe that furnished these skeletons, one, almost globular, also belonging to a boy. These have been excluded from computation.

The other Gloucester skulls are pretty uniform in type. They are rather small, moderate in height and breadth, the forehead is rather low and narrow, the point of maximum breadth is set rather far back, the temporal region is flattish, the dolichocephaly is occipital, and there is more or less of parieto-occipital flattening.

Three series of Bristolian skulls follow. The first, a small one of three, was discovered in digging for foundations in the centre of the city, where St. Leonard's church once stood. These three were more or less ill-developed, especially in the anterior region.

The second series was gotten from below the vaults which underlay the church of St. Werburgh's, when it was demolished. This church dated from Edward II.'s reign, but had been *partially* rebuilt in 1761. These thirty-six skulls must all, therefore, have been prior to 1761, and many of them appeared to be, and I have no doubt were, of much greater antiquity, if not truly mediæval, as is still more likely.

The next series, of seventeen, consisted of skulls from the churchyard of St. Werburgh's; they were of various dates, but comparatively recent. For details respecting both series, see *Bristol and Glos. Arch. Trans.*, 1878-9. There was a remarkable difference between them, the older heads being, for the most part, quite unlike the more recent, and unlike the Bristolian heads of to-day, so far as I can judge. They were short, broad, rounded, rather flat, with rather small frontal region; but otherwise well filled. Of the thirty-six, thirteen were decidedly brachycephalic, one reaching 90, and three more yielded the neutral index of 80, while only two were truly dolichocephalic, or below 75 in index. A curious aberrant skull, very long, measuring 82 × 5·3 x 5·3, with indexes of 64·6, was excluded; it was probably Spanish. Similarly, a negro skull was excluded from the seventeen, of which only two were brachycephalic, and which exhibited some of the types common in the neighbourhood at the present day, but not one distinct example of the small round type described above.

The numbers here dealt with are probably sufficient to bear some weight of inference, especially as they included the whole of the skulls from St. Werburgh's that were capable of measurement. The great diminution of the short broad type in modern times does not seem to corroborate Schaafhausen's theory of its increase with the advance of civilization. It might be alleged, indeed, that the bodies beneath the vaults belonged to a period when immigration from the rural districts was smaller, and those in the churchyard to the modern period of rapid urban growth by immigration from the long-headed population of the surrounding counties; and that the older type was the result of centuries of city breeding. I should be more inclined to think, however, that it depended on a great influx of artizans and others from the Continent, during the centuries which succeeded the Norman Conquest, when Bristol was a very important place politically and commercially; and that the alien stock was very gradually dispersed, extinguished, or incorporated with the native majority.

The Anglian type, as represented here, is introduced for the sake of comparison, and as a standard. Unfortunately the number is too small, and the sample perhaps unduly depressed by the presence of one or two very poor specimens. Five of the ten are from the Museum at York; the other five are from Northumberland and Oxfordshire, and are in the Museum of the University of Oxford. The principal characteristic which comes out from my measurements is the considerable projection of the upper occipital region beyond the vertical plane of the inion. Still, even this is not universal in Anglian skulls, any more than the elliptic form, or the rounded orbits.

SKULLS FROM DAVOS, IN GRAUBUNDEN, SWITZERLAND.

	LENGTHS					BREADTHS					HEIGHT		CIRCUMFERENCE				ARCS								INDICES	
	Glab. Max.	Fron. Inial.	Glab. Inial.	Bar. Dav.	Fron. Min.	Step.	Zyg.	Aur.	Max.	Mast.	Bas. Bregm.	Bas. Max.	Glab. Max.	Fron. Inial.	Glab. Inial.	B. Dav.	Fro.	Par.	Sup. Occ.	Sub. Inial.	Tra.	Ant.	Bas. Cranii.	Nose.		
1. Disentis type	157	158	152	156	92	120	120	109	N.N.E. p. 151	113	124	124	499	494	474	489	120	110	80	30	347	250	89	St. ?	96·1	78·9
2. Do.	178	177	174	175	104	131	133	126	t. N. by E. 152	128	126	130	532	534	530	530	128	122	60	46	335	283	99	O.	85·4	70·9
3. Hohberg type	195	188	187	190	95	112	?	119	p. N. by E. 138	126	123	124	548	534	540	542	125	137	73	45	337	290	105	O.	70·7	63·1
4. Disentis-Hohberg	180	179	175	178	105	132	134?	127	nearly N. 156	134	138	139	540	546	536	540	128	135	67	50	360	300	102	Aq.	86·6	76·6
5. Sion type	182	172	174	175	102	120	146	126 (130)	t. N. by E. 150	139	141	142	540	532	540	523 (301)	128	130	62	50	343	303	106	Aq.	82·4	77·6
6. Belair type	191	192	187	190	105	124	136	117 (20)	t. p. N. by E. 151	122	136	138	555	556	548	555	146	134	63	52	345	312	108	St. ?	79	71·2
7. Neutral	182	180	178	180	91	114?	132?	116?	144	124	142	142	526	532	526	526	138	140	56	52	354	286	98	sl. Aq.?	79·2	78
Averages	185	178	175·3	179	99·1	122	133?	118·5	149	126·5	133	134	534	532·5	527·7	529	130·4	130	66	46·4	346	289	101	…	82·8	73·7

These skulls were chosen by myself out of a number in the bone-house at Davos, as specimens of types. 2, 3, and 7 were most numerously represented. I believe them all to be masculine except No. 1. No. 3 is a true Hohberg, though not lofty. No. 4, a very fine skull; the nose and occiput rather Hohberg than Disentis. No. 5 is extremely thick and heavy, weighing (without mandible) 34 ounces. The supraciliar ridges are extremely large and prominent, and in other respects, except in breadth, it conforms to the Sion type, and in all respects to the Bronze type of Great Britain. No. 6, though masculine and somewhat broad, has the points of the Belair type; but I suppose Von Hölder would call it Sarmatic, the norma verticalis being somewhat quadrangular, and the ear and the maximum breadth far back. No. 7 is a common form in England. I am indebted for the collection to the municipality of Davos, through the kind offices of Dr. Ruedi.

PRINCIPAL MEASURES OF BRITISH HEADS.

DISTRICTS, &c.	Number	Max. Length	Max. Breadth	Zygo.	Mast.	Circumference	Index. Lat.
		Inches.	Inches.	Inches.	Inches.	Inches.	
1. Kerry	20	7·81	6·07	...	...	22·63	77·8 ⎫
2. Munster	46	7·71	5·96	5·45	5·18	...	77·30 ⎬77·27
3. Rest of Ireland	9	7·78	5·91	5·41	...	...	76 ⎭
4. South Wales	66	7·67	5·98	5·42	5·21	22·50	77·96
5. Cornwall	17	7·72	6·01	5·49	...	22·67	77·90
6. South Devon	42	7 66	6	5·40	...	...	78·30 ⎫78·20
7. North Devon	56	7·75	6·05	5·52	5·26	...	78·13 ⎭
8. West Somerset	71	7·66	5·88	5·37	5·12	...	76·8
9. South Somerset	32	7·56	5·94	5·34	...	...	78·57
10. East Somerset	94	7·67	5·96	5·41	5·16	...	77·7 ⎫
11. Bristol	80	7·70	5·98	5·39	...	...	77·65 ⎬77·65
12. Gloucestershire	77	7·70	5·98	5·44	...	...	77·59 ⎭
13. Wiltshire	55	7·76	5·96	5·44	5·15	...	76·82
14. E. Glos. and E. Wilts	17	...	...	...	...	...	78·3
15. East of England ...	30	7·65	6·01	...	...	...	78·6
16. Yorkshire	11	7·70	6·02	5·48	5·33	22·84	78·18
17. Cumberland and ⎱ Lancashire ... ⎰	10	7·74	6	...	...	...	77·5
18. Educated Englishmen	40	7·78	6·09	...	...	...	78·25

DETAILED MEASURES OF BRITISH HEADS.

	Number	LENGTHS					BREADTHS					CIRCUMFERENCE				ARCS			Index.
		Glab. Max.	Fron. Inial.	Glab. Inial.	Bar. Dav.	Vert. Men.	Fron. Min.	Zyg.	Aur.	Max.	Mast.	Glab. Max.	Fron. Inial.	Glab. Inial.	Bar. Dav.	Nas. Occ.	Tra.	Aur. sup.	
1. Highlanders	55	7·88	7·69	7·66	7·76	10·03	4·15	5·50	5·24	6·01	5·23	22·76	22·39	22·34	...	14·21	14·30	11·89	76·27
2. Eyemouth and Burnmouth, Berwickshire	18	7·86	7·74	7·68	7·76	10·05	4·17	5·58	5·36	6·04	5·35	22·76	22·55	22·53	22·65	14·19	14·43	12·15	76·77
3. Berwickshire, inland	12	7·80	7·58	7·58	...	...	4·19	5·54	5·27	6	5·23	...	...	...	...	...	...	...	76·92
4. Educated Scotchmen	20	7·93	7·76	7·71	7·84	10·15	4·29	5·54	5·35	6·15	5·36	22·98	22·67	22·67	22·75	14·50	14·56	12·1	77·5
5. Irish, mostly Munster	27	7·77	7·63	7·52	7·68	9·97	4·19	5·50	5·32	5·99	5·22	22·67	22·44	22·37	22·51	14·07	14·21	...	77·09
6. Cornish	10	7·74	7·50	7·53	7·58	9·88	4·18	5·53	5·34	6·02	5·29	22·65	22·37	22·45	22·46	13·97	14·5	11·6	77·7
7. Devon	15	7·79	7·54	7·50	...	9·83	4·11	5·52	5·39	6·05	5·22	22·75	22·34	22·37	...	...	14·14	...	77·76
8. Somerset and Gloucestershire	40	7·77	7·65	7·52	7·72	10·05	4·18	5·44	5·24	5·96	5·17	22·67	22·46	22·50	...	14·16	...	...	76·7
9. South Wales (including Monmouthshire)	16	7·64	7·52	7·44	7·60	9·63	4·27	5·47	5·24	6·04	5·22	22·52	22·33	22·23	22·36	13·71	14·14	...	79·05
10. Wilts	20	7·76	7·56	7·52	7·70	9·89	4·18	5·48	5·25	6	5·16	22·65	22·42	22·36	22·50	13·87	...	...	77·3
11. East of England	30	7·65	7·53	7·45	7·60	9·90	4·15	5·43	5·28	6·01	5·18	22·41	22·18	22·14	22·23	14	...	...	78·56
12. Yorkshire, and North of England ...	15	7·71	7·53	7·48	7·62	10·01	4·19	5·44	5·27	6·01	5·26	22·73	22·42	22·48	22·49	14·08	14·31	...	77·75
13. Educated Englishmen	40	7·78	7·66	...	...	...	...	5·53	...	6·09	...	22·88	...	...	...	...	...	...	78·25

DETAILED MEASURES OF HEADS OF CONTINENTAL PEOPLES.

	Number	LENGTHS.					BREADTHS.					CIRCUMFERENCE.				ARCS.			Index.
		Glab. Max.	Fron. Inial.	Glab. Inial.	Bar. Dav.	Vert. Men.	Fron. Min.	Zyg.	Aur.	Max.	Mast.	Glab. Max.	Fron. Inial.	Glab. Inial.	Bar. Dav.	Nas. Occ.	Tra.	Aur. sup.	
1. Walloons	10	7·76	7·52	7·60	...	10	...	5·61	5·39	6·02	5·38	22·4	22	22·05	...	14·06	...	...	77·57
2. Norwegians	11	7·77	7·52	7·54	...	10	4·25	5·56	5·39	6·12	5·48	22·60	22·34	22·45	22·47	13·72	14·44	...	78·76
3. Swedes	33	7·65	7·51	7·50	...	...	...	5·51	...	6·06	5·23	22·46	22·17	22·27	...	13·90	...	...	79·2
4. Danes	28	7·66	7·45	7·42	7·59	9·68	4·21	5·52	5·36	6·17	5·27	22·66	22·42	22·34	22·50	14·02	14·38	...	80·5
5. Hanover and East Friesland ...	13	7·89	7·62	7·66	7·83	9·87	4·21	5·59	5·43	6·25	5·39	23·18	22·91	22·74	22·94	14·27	14·58	12·1	84·11
6. Nassau	13	7·49	7·36	7·34	7·41	9·82	4·3	5·67	5·43	6·3	5·41	22·72	22·55	22·48	22·56	13·58	14·49	11·9	79·2
7. Pfalz	10	7·46	7·34	7·28	7·44	9·77	4·19	5·47	5·30	6·21	5·19	22·20	21·99	21·72	22·15	13·61	14·28	11·65	83·11
8. Finns	12	7·52	7·43	...	...	...	...	5·67	...	6·23	5·49	22·52	22·41	...	...	14·06	...	...	82·80
9. Do. (included)	4	7·56	7·40	7·41	7·48	9·97	4·29	5·72	5·49	6·16	5·50	22·35	22·25	22·25	22·07	13·60	...	...	81·48
10. Italians, various	10	7·36	7·28	7·26	7·29	9·69	4·14	5·49	5·20	6·01	5·18	22·03	21·92	22	...	13·37	14·28?	...	81·62

HEAD MEASUREMENTS OF SCOTTISH HIGHLANDERS.

(See Chapter on "METHODS.")

MEASUREMENTS OF THE HEAD.

		Stature barefoot	Eyes	Hair	Complexion	LENGTHS. Glab. Max	Fron. Inial	Glab. Inial	Bar. Dav.	Vert. Men.	Fron. Min.	Step	BREADTHS. Zyg	Auric.	Max.	Mast.	CIRCUMFERENCE. Glab. Max	Fron. Inial	Glab. Inial	Bar. Dav.	ARCS. Nas. Occ.	Tra.	Aur. sup.	Jaw.	Face.	Forehead.	Brows.	Nose.	Cheek bones.	Mouth.	Chin.	Head.	Back-head.	Inion.	ORIGIN OF FAMILY.
1	McF.	…	Gray	Dk.Br.	Dk.	7·9	7·8	7·7	7·8	10·2	4·2	…	5·6	5·3	6·15	5·2	23	22·5	22·5	22·3	14·1	15·2	12·2	…	Ob.O.	R.	…	C.	…	…	R.	R.O.	…	…	St. Fillan's
2	McK.	…	Gray	Gray	F.	8·1	7·9	7·9	8	9·8	4·1	…	5·3	5·2	6·1	5	22·8	22·6	22·5	22·6	14·5	14·2	12·3	…	Ob.	R.	…	…	…	…	R.	…	…	…	St. Fillan's
3	D.	…	Gray	Brown	Int.	8·1	8	8	8	10·1	4·2	…	5·4	5·1	6	5·4	23	22·9	22·9	22·9	13·9	14	12	…	L.	Sq.	…	L. Si.	Pr.	Prog.	Ang.	…	Pr.	…	High	Glenlednock
4	F.	…	Lt.Br.	c. Dk.Br. Dkish.	Dk.	8	7·9	7·8	7·9	10	4	…	5·4	5·1	5·9	5·25	23	23	22·8	22·2	14·5	14·5	11·5	…	L.Sp.	Sq.	M.	L. Si.	Pr.	Prog.	…	O.	Pr.	…	…	St. Fillan's
5	F.	…	Blue	Dkish. Brown	F.	8	7·9	7·8	7·9	9·6	4	…	5·3	5·1	6	5·2	22·4	22·1	22·8	22·2	13·8	14·2	12·2	…	O.	R.	…	L. Si.Aq.	M.	Prog.	N.	O.	O.	M.	…	St. Fillan's
6		…	Blue	Brown	F.	8	8·1	8·1	8	9·9	4·1	…	5·7	5·5	6·1	5·4	23	22·9	22·9	22·9	14·1	14	12·2	…	R.	R.	Fl.	Str.	M.	…	…	O.	M.	…	…	St. Fillan's
7	C.	…	Blue	Lsh.Br.	F.	7·8	7·6	7·4	7·7	9·8	4·1	…	5·2	5·2	6	5·1	22·5	22·2	21·9	22·3	14	15	12·2	…	R.	R.Re.	Pr.	L. Si.	Pr.	…	Pr.	Hig.	…	Pr.	High	Nr. St. Fillan's
8	C.	…	Blue	Dark	I.	7·7	7·7	7·6	7·6	9·7	4·15	…	5·4	5	5·6	5·1	22	22	21·7	21·7	14	13·6	11·3	…	L.O.	I.	Arc.	L.Aq.Si.	Fl.	…	…	Hig.	…	…	…	St. Fillan's
9	McE.	6·1	D.Bl.	Yellow	F.	8·	7·8	7·7	7·9	10	4·3	…	5·7	5·4	6·15	5·5	23·2	22·8	23	22·9	13·7	14	11·7	…	Sp.	Sq.	Arc.	Str.	Pr.	…	Pr.	…	Py.	Pr.	…	St. Fillan's, ¼ Dumfriesshire
10	G.	5·8	alm. Hazl.	Brown	F.	7·75	7·5	7·5	7·7	9·8	4·1	…	5·5	5·2	5·9	5·25	22·3	…	23	21·7	14	13·5	11·4	…	Pent.	I.	Obl.Arc.	L.Aq.Si.	B.	…	Ang.	O.	…	Rd.	High	Durinish, Isle of Skye
11	McD.	5·6	D.Gr.	Dk.Br.Bk.	I.	7·7	7·6	7·6	7·6	10·1	4·1	…	5·5	5·2	6	5·3	22·5	22·1	22·3	22·9	14·1	14·2	11·9	…	Ob.	Br.	r. Pr.	Sh. St. Pt.	B.	…	Sq.	O.	Pr.	Rd.	…	Glencoe and Glenelg
12	C.	5·5	Brwn.	c. Dk.Br.	L.	7·75	7·6	7·6	7·8	9·7	4·1	…	5·5	5·2	6·05	5·2	23·2	22·8	22·4	22·1	14·2	14·2	11·7	…	O.	M.	r. Pr.	Si. Pt.	r. Pr.	…	N.	L.O.	Pr.	…	Gr.	Glenorchy and Lorne
13	McD.	5·5¼	Blue	I.Gray	F.R.	8·1	8·1	8	8	10	4·25	…	5·9	5·6	6·2	5·2	23·7	23·4	23·3	22·2	15·1	14·5	12·5	…	R.	B.	M.	St. Pt.	M.	…	B.	Ov.El	R. m.P.	…	Sm.	Glencoe and Lochcreran
14	C.	5·9¼	Blue	Brown	F.	8·6	8·2	8·1	8·4	10·8	4·2	…	5·7	5·3	6	5·5	24·1	23·4	23·1	22·9	16	14·7	12·2	…	L.O.	U.Sq.	Str.	Str.	Pr.	…	r.N.	L.O.	R. v.P.	Gr.	…	Lismore & Appin
15	McI.	5·8¼	Gray	I.Gray	I.	8·2	8·1	8·1	8	10·4	4·1	…	5·8	5·5	6·25	5·6	23·5	23·1	23	23·1	14·6	14·2	12·2	…	Loz.	Re.S.	v.P.	Aq.Po.	B.P.	…	N.	L.O.	v.P.	Sm.	…	Lismore & Appin
16	R.	5·6	Blue	Fair	F.	8	7·8	7·6	7·9	10	4·25	…	5·4	5·2	6	5·2	23	22·4	23	22·1	14·6	14·6	11·1	…	Sp.	B. U.S.	M.	Str.	M.	…	N.	O.	Pr.	…	…	Pure Glencoe
17	McI.	5·4½	Brwn.	Black	D.	7·5	7·2	7·2	7·4	9·7	4	…	5·1	4·9	5·9	4·9	21·9	21·7	21·3	21·7	13·9	14·3	11·8	…	L.O.	Re.S.	Pr.	L.Aq.Po.	M.	…	N.	O.	Pr.	…	…	Glencoe
18	C.	5·5	Blue	Gray	F.	7·6	7·3	7·2	7·5	9·6	4·1	…	5·4	5·2	6	5	22·3	21·6	21·3	22·1	14	13·9	11·9	…	O.	Sq.	M.	Str.	Pr.	…	r.N.	O.	r. P.	Sm.	…	Pure Glencoe
19	McK.	…	Gray	Brown	F.	7·7	7·6	7·5	7·65	10	4·1	…	5·1	4·9	6	5	22·6	22·6	22	22·1	14·2	14·6	11·8	…	O.	Sq.	Str.	Aq.	M.P.	…	N.Pr.	O.	M.	Gr.	…	NetherLochaber
20	McL.	5·6	Gray	Dk.Br.	I.	8·2	8	8·2	8·1	11·2	4·2	…	5·9	5·7	6·25	5·7	24·4	23·9	24·5	24·3	15	14·9	13·1	…	L.Sp.	S.Re.	Ar. P.	Aq. Si.	Pr.	…	N.Pr.	H.Py.	M.	M.	…	Ardgour
21	McK.	…	Neut.	Dk.Br.	F.R.	7·3	7·1	7·1	7·2	9·7	4·2	…	5·2	4·9	5·6	5	21·3	21·2	21·2	…	13·9	13·7	11·1	…	L.Sc.	B.	Str.	Aq.	M.	…	Ang.	H.Py.	r. P.	Gr.	Gr.	Lochaber (500 yrs.)
22	C.	5·7	Blue	Red	F.R.	7·7	7·7	7·8	7·9	10·4	4·3	…	5·8	5·6	6·25	5·5	23·3	22·9	22·9	22·9	14·1	14·7	12·5	…	Sp.	B.	Str.	C. Si.	M.	…	R.	O.El	Sm.	R.	Sm.	Glencoe and Glen Nevis
23	McI.	5·4½	Bl.Gr.	Dk.Br.	D.	7·7	7·5	7·7	7·65	9·9	4·2	…	4·8	4·8	5·7	5·1	21·3	21	21·9	21·9	13·7	14	14·7	…	Ob.O.	B.Do.	Arc.	Si.Po.	B.	…	N.	O.El	R.	…	…	Lochaber
24	C.	6	Bl.Gr.	Red	F.R.	8·1	7·8	7·8	7·8	10·8	4·2	…	5·3	5·3	5·9	5·1	23·1	22·3	22·8	22·8	14·7	14·1	11·5	…	L.O.	S.Re.	Str. P.	Aq.Si.Po.	Pr.	…	L.Py.	O.	r. P.	Gr.	Gr.	Pure Appin
25	A.	5·4½	Brwn.	I.Gray	D.	7·2	7·1	7·1	7·1	9·2	4	…	5·2	5·1	5·9	4·9	21·4	21·1	21	21·1	13·3	14·7	11·4	…	Pent.	S.Re.	Str. P.	Pr. Si.	v.Pr.	…	A.	Py.O	Pr.	…	…	(Lochaber and …)

25	McL.	5-8	Bwn.	Dk.Br.	D.	...	7·95	7·8	7·9	7·8	10·1	4·5	...	5·8	5·6	6·2	5·2	·234	·22·9	22·6	...	12	Aq.	Pr.	...	M.	Ang.	?	M.	...	Cruachan-ben
29	C.	5-9	D.Gr.	Gray	D.	...	7·4	7·2	7·9	7·8	10·1	4·5	...	5·8	5·6	6·2	5·2	·234	·22·9	22·6	14·6	14·5	12	Sp.	Sq	Pr.	Si.	N.	O.	Pr.	...	Lochaber
30	McF.	5-7¼	Gray	Brown	I.	...	7·4	7·2	7·1	7·2	9·3	4	...	5	4·85	5·6	5	21·4	21	20·7	14	13·9	11·3	Sp.	...	M.	Si.	N.	O.	Pr.	...	Glen Etive, pure
31	McC.	6-1	Blue	Red	F.R.	...	7·8	7·6	7·7	7·7	10	4·5	...	5·6	5·25	6	5·4	22·7	22·3	22·6	14·4	14·1	12·4	Sp.	Sq.	B.	Aq.	A.	O.	M.	...	Lochaber
32	C.	5-4	Gray	Gray	?	...	7·7	7·4	7·6	7·6	9·7	4·1	...	5·4	5·1	5·9	4·9	·225	21·7	21·7	14·1	14·2	11·6	Ob.	M.	M.	St.	R.	Ell.	Pr.	...	Lochaber (?)
33	McK.	5-7	Blue	Fair	F.	...	8·1	8	7·8	8	10·2	4	...	5·5	5·2	6·1	5·1	·239	22·6	22·9	14·7	15·1	11·9	Ell.	...	r.Pr.	Si.Po.	r.N.	O.Fl.	r.P.	...	Onich, Lochaber
34	McK.	5-9¼	Bl.Gr.	Lsh.Br.	F.	...	7·9	7·8	7·8	7·8	9·9	4·5	...	5·35	5·2	6·3	5·1	·239	24	23·4	14·5	13·5	12·8	Sp.	B.Re.	Arc.	Si.Po.	B.	Si.	Pr.	...	Lochaber and Arisaig
35	C.	6	Blue	Red	C.	...	7·8	7·5	7·7	7·6	10	4·5	...	5·2	5·2	4·9	5·1	23	·22·5	22·3	14·5	15	12	Ob.O	B.H.R.	M.	Si.	M.	Si.	Pr.	...	Lochaber and Arisaig
36	C.	...	Bl.Gr.	Brown	I.	...	8·05	7·9	7·9	7·9	10·1	4·5	...	5·6	5·3	6·05	5·6	23·3	23	23·3	14·3	14·9	12·5	O.	...	Pr.	P.A.Si.	N.	O.	Py.	...	Glendochart and Appin
37	McN.	...	Gray	Dkish. Brown	I.	...	7·8	7·7	7·6	7·6	10·1	4	...	5·2	4·8	5·8	4·9	22·5	21·9	21·4	14·8	15	12	L.O.	Sq.	r.Pr.	Si.	M.	A.	r.P.	21·9	Upp. Nairnshire
38	McG.	5-7	D.Bl.	Dk.Br.	I.	...	8	7·6	7·6	7·6	10·3	4·55	...	5·75	5·5	6·15	5·1	23·3	22·6	22·8	14·4	14·7	12·4	Sh. Pent.	B.R.	B.	Str.	A.	Ell.	M.	...	Ardnamurchan and Lochaber
39	McN.	5-7¾	Gray	Brown	F.	...	7·9	7·7	7·5	7·9	10·3	4·5	...	5·6	5·4	6	5·3	23	22·5	22·3	14·1	14·4	12·1	Ob.O	Bor.	Fl.	Sh.St.Po.	M.	Ell.	r.P.	...	Lorne and Lochaber
40	McD.	5-6¾	Bl.Gr.	Dk.Br.	D.	...	7·85	7·8	7·85	7·8	10	4·5	...	5·6	5·3	6	5·3	22·5	22·5	22·5	14·2	14·4	11·7	O.	Sq.	r.B.	Si.Po.	M.	Ell.	Pr.	Gr.	Lochaber
41	McI.	5-11	D.Bl.	Black	Sw.	...	8·2	8·1	8	10·4	4·5	...	5·5	5·25	6	5·4	23·1	22·6	22·8	14·2	14	12	O.	Sq.	M.	L.Aq.	M.Pr.	O.	Pr.	...	Pure Appin
42	McI.	5-10½	Bl.Gr.	Fair	F.	...	8·15	7·9	7·8	7·9	10·3	4	...	5·5	5·5	5·9	5·15	23·6	·22	22·4	14	14·2	11·3	L.O.	N. R.R·x.	Pr.	Po.L.Aq.	N.	O.	Pr.	4·6	High
43	McN.	5-6	D.Br.	Br.Bk.	Sw.	...	7·6	7·6	7·6	7·6	10·2	4·5	...	5·5	5·2	6	5·3·5	22·6	22·8	22·6	14·3	14·3	11·9	L.Pn.	U.S.	M.	Aq.Si.	A.	...	M.	...	Glendochart and Appin
44	McD.	5-5	L.Br.	Br.Bk.	I.	...	7·5	7·2	7·5	7·5	9·4	4·5	...	5·3	5·5	6	5·15	22·1	22	21·8	14·4	14·2	11·3	Sq.	Sq.B.	Pr.	Sh.C.	Sq.	...	Pr.	...	Moidart and Ardnamurchan
45	McL.	5-7	Blue	Dk.Br.	F.	...	7·8	7·3	7·25	7·7	9·9	4	...	5·5	5·2	5·8	5·1	21·9	21·3	21·4	14	13·7	11·3	L.O.	N.F.	Fl.m.Ar.	L.Si.	N.	L.O.	P.	...	Moidart, pure
46	McI.	6-3	Blue	Brown	F.	...	8·6	8·55	8·5	8·5	10·6	4·6	...	6·4	6·1	6·9	6·25	...	22	22	14	15·3	13·1	Ell.	Dorn.	Ar.P.	Str.	R.	Ell.	R.	H.Sm	Argyle. Perthshire, and Inv.
47	C.	5-10	Brwn.	Dk.Br.	D.	...	8·3	7·9	8·25	8	10	4·5	...	6	5·15	6·15	5·3	23·1	22·6	23	15·5	14·3	13·2	O.	R.Re.	Arc.	L.Aq.	O.	O.	r.P.	Gr.	Inveraray
48	McB.	5-7	Gray	Gray	I.R.	...	7·55	7·9	8	7·5	10	4·1	...	5·5	5·5	6	5·35	23·1	21·8	21·9	15·6	14·3	12·2	R.Re.	Ir.	C.	...	N.A.	R.	r.F.	v.H.	Upp. Nairnshire
49	McPh.	5-8	Gray	Brown	R.	...	8	7·8	7·5	7·6	10·2	4·1	...	5·6	5·3	6·1	5·1	22·6	21·8	21·8	12·9	14	11·8	Sc.	Re.	Arc.	L.Aq.	N.A.	O.	O.	Low	Laggan, pure
50	R.	5-8	D.Gr.	Dk.Br.	I.R.	...	7·55	7·8	7·6	7·4	10	4·2	...	5·2	5·2	6·05	5·5	·22·7	21·8	22·3	14	14·1	12	O.	R.Re.	Pr.	Sh.C.	M.	Ell.	Pr.	Pr.	Ross and Blair-Athol
51	R.	5-6	Blue	Red	F.	...	7·6	7·4	7·4	7·4	10·1	4·1	...	5·2	5·2	6·05	5·5	22·8	22·4	22·6	13·8	14·2	11·8	Ell.	B.	Str.	B.P.	M.	B.A.	Pr.	...	Edderton, Ross, pure
52	C.	5-7	D.Gr.	Gray	I.	...	7·5	7·6	7·7	7·55	9·5	4·2	...	5·2	5·2	6·2	5·1	22·2	22	21·7	14·1	14·3	11·8	Sq.	B.	M.Fl.	C.Si.	N.	Pr.	Sm.	...	Strathspey, pure
53	G.	6-·•	Gray	Brown	F.	...	7·8	7·9	7·45	7·45	9·5	4·6	...	5·9	5·5	6·2	5	22·1	22·1	21·6	13·2	14·2	11·6	Br.	Fl.	C.Si.	N.R.	N.R.	B.	...	Strathspey, pure
54	McD.	5-11	Gray	Br.Bk.	I.R.	...	7·8	7·8	7·75	7·6	10·5	4·3	...	5·5	5·3	6·15	5·4	22·6	22·4	22·2	14	14·9	11·9	L. Ob.O.	B.Re.	Pr.	St.Si.	M.	Ell.	r.P.	4·6	Strathspey and West H.
55	McV.	5-7¾	Blue	Dk.Br.	I.	...	8	7·85	7·8	8	10·4	4·5	...	5·5	5·3	6·15	5·2	22·7	22·5	22·3	13·8	14	12	L.O.	U.Sq.	Iri.	St.P.P.	N.	Ell.	M.	...	Glenfyne
56	C.	5-6	D.Bl. Gray	Black	I.R.	...	7·8	7·5	7·5	7·7	9·6	4	...	5·2	5	5·8	5·1	22·4	22	22	13·1	13·6	14·1	O.	R.	Pr.	Aq.Si.	N.Re.	O.	Pr.	High	Lochaber and Lochgoil
57	Bl.	5-10	Blue	Lsh.Br.	F.	...	8·15	7·65	7·6	7·6	10·1	4·5	...	5·55	5·3	6·05	5·45	23	22·3	22·5	14·5	14·5	11·3	O.	N.Re.	B.r.P.	Str.	M.	O.	Pr.	...	Mull & Lochgoil

9. Profile Greek, aspect Scandinavian, not Highland. 10. Turanian type. 11. Beard dark red. 12. Good type of the small, active Highlander. 13. North Devon family. 14 Straight profile; remarkable occipital projection. 16. Old Glencoe family, but race of Dumfriesshire blood; resembles 14. 20. Very powerful man; large-boned, rickety. 22. See 46. 24. Very fine specimen of the red Gaelic type; ? Caledonian of Tacitus. 25. Belonged to an old Helot race. 27. Powerful man; of the pure old Keppoch race. 28. Dark handsome Iberian (?) type.

29. Very fine man; bold Roman profile. 31. From one of the later xanthous races, probably. 35. Scandinavian type. 36. Gaelic type of feature. 38. Brachycephalic Celt of Hector McLean, referred by him to the Eastern Highlands especially; whence this gentleman came. 41. Very fine specimen of the handsome dark race; but 42, a good-looking fair man, with nothing Iberian about him, was his brother. 44 and 45, from the West coast, with more of the aboriginal aspect; especially 44. 46. Colossal every way; very pure Highland ancestry.

but might be a Yorkshire Anglian. 48. Something of the Bronze or Borreby type. 49. Variety of Gaelic type, apparently, but less angular. 52. Perhaps hydrocephalous in childhood. 56. Very typical.

I am indebted, for assistance in obtaining these measurements, verifying pedigrees, &c., very specially to the well-known Highland naturalist, the Rev. Alexander Stewart, of Nether Lochaber; also to the Earl of Cawdor, to Dr. Campbell, of Craigrannoch, and to Messrs. Davie and Currie, at St. Fillan's and Ballachulish.

HEAD MEASUREMENTS ON THE LIVING.—SWITZERLAND.

	LENGTHS					BREADTHS							CIRCUMFERENCE				ARCS			Eyes	Hair	Complexion	Face	Forehead	Brows	Nose	Cheek bones	Chin	Head	Back head	Index
	Glab. Max	Fron. Inial	Glab. Inial		Vert. Men	Fron. Min	Steph.	Zyg.	Aur.	Max	Mast.	Jaw	Glab. Max	Fron. Inial	Glab. Inial	Bar. Dav.	Nas. Occ.	Tra.	Aur. sup.												
1. Davos, Grisons	192	190	188	190	252	99	141	141	136	150	130	…	579	579	574	…	358	373	307	Hazel	Thick v.d.Br	D. Ry.	Sp.	…	Pr. m.Ar.	B. Aq.	…	A.	…	R. Pr.	78·1
2. Davos, "	193	192	190	192	248	110	142	145	139	156	135	106	576	576	569	574	353	370	309	Dark Gray	Str. Black	Sw.	Ov.	M.	M.	St.	M.	R. Pr.	Ell.	…	80·8
3. Prättigau, "	188	192	183	188	242	101	146	140	134	156	118	…	579	593	576	581	363	365	305	Blue	Brwn.	Fr.	Ov.	Up.	m.Ar. not P.	LN Si.	…	Pr. M R	…	…	82·8
4. Disentis, "	183	188	182	185	234	108	148	144	137	162	125	92	564	574	574	571	355	375	305	Blue Gray	Str. Iron Gray	Ry.	Sp.?	B. Up.	m.Ar. Fl.	St.	Sm.	RN.	…	…	88·5
5. Disentis, Argau	187	183	179	183	241	106	140	136	132	152	140	101	570	…	…	…	365	370	315	Light Gray	Str. Light Brwn.	Fr.	Ov.	Up.	r. F.	C.	Sm.	M.	M.	M.	81·3
6. Finstermunz, Tyrol }	188	188	182	183	260	116	154	150	135	167	138	114	584	592	584	581	376	398	327	Blue	Dksh. Brwn.	Il.	Sq.	Br.	Fl.	St. Sh.	r.B.	B.	Sq.	…	90·7

1.—Sion type; profile convex, inion high placed, large. 2.—Opisthognathous; brother of 1. 3.—Nose nearly straight, slight bulb; glabella flat; mouth fine; parieto-occip. flattening. 4.—Small old man; ears long; forehead bombé. 5.—Tall man, of northern type. 6.—Very powerful, thickset man.

NOTES ON TABLES OF HEADFORM.

For the mode of examining the living head adopted by the author, see the chapter on Methods. As time went on, and new lights were obtained, I dropped some measurements, as uncertain or unfruitful, and adopted others; those whose results are here published are, I think, about the best and most important, but are insufficient at the best. They have the advantage of being practicable with instruments that can be carried in the pocket.

Quetelet's favourite number of examples, 10, would be very insufficient for this purpose. The principal ethnical elements in Britain are too much alike in headform to yield their differences to an average constructed on but a few living heads. 50 is not a superfluously large number.

With respect to breadth-index, it is evident that the Scottish Highlanders have a remarkably small one; due, however, to the great length of the head rather than to its narrowness. Nearly the same may be said of the Berwickshire people, whether fishers or peasants, who, though different in race and complexion, have indices little larger than the Highlanders. The Irish also have long and narrow heads, except perhaps the people of Kerry, where, contrary to what occurs in Islay and in the West of England, the black-haired people have a little broader heads. The natives of West Somerset and of North-west Wiltshire have narrow heads; the former have them both small and narrow; in them a Gaelic type is common, but this can hardly be said of the Wiltshire men. South Wales, Devon, and Cornwall (though here the numbers are far too small) seem to form a group in which the breadth-index is about 78. Bristol, with the two counties whence its population is fed, yields an index of 77·65—almost identical in the three cases. In the East of England we may probably be pretty confident that the index is larger than 78. The educated Englishmen, chiefly professional men and merchants, but partly men of a lower class with a better education than usual, have heads both longer and broader than any other series of Englishmen measured; their index of 78·25 is scarcely larger than the average of the counties to which they belonged; a good proportion of them were from the east.

The results of some of the more exact measurements will be noted in the general commentary on the tables, which will form the last chapter but one. Certain differences come out between the Anglian or Anglo-Danish Eyemouthers and the Gaelic Highlanders. In the former the head is slightly broader, especially about the base; the forehead is a little more and the occiput a little less developed.

In the Irish the forehead is upright, the occiput protuberant, the head rather low. The South Welsh seem to differ from the Cornish by the greater breadth of the forehead and less prominence of the brows; the head is smaller and probably lower; the face short; but larger numbers are needed. The North Devon heads are decidedly large. The Wiltshire heads are long, narrow, and apparently rather low. The extreme narrowness appears to belong to the western side of the county only; this is shown, not only by my own figures, but by the fact that the late Thurnam, having measured for me the heads of all the Wiltshire lunatics in the public asylum who were in good bodily health and not imbecile—a set of subjects who, of course, came in pretty equal proportion from all parts of the county—obtained an average breadth-index of 77·5. The East of England heads are short, but not narrow; they seem to be higher than the Welsh ones, and more rounded in the norma verticalis, whereas the Yorkshire heads are more inclined to be oblong: this I infer from the proportion borne by the circumference to the other dimensions.

The educated Scotchmen—or should I say, the better-educated Scotchmen?—like the corresponding class in England, surpass their less educated countrymen in every point of measurement; they also surpass the Englishmen. Their breadth-index is 77·5, larger than that of either the Highlanders or Berwickshire men; but I doubt whether it be larger than that of the Lowland Scotch in general.

The measurements do not enable me to prove, what nevertheless I hold for certain, that elliptic and ovo-elliptic forms, such as some of those I have figured after Gildemeister, prevail in the east, pyriform and ovo-pyriform ones in the west. The nearly oblong form, which includes both the Belair type of His and the Sarmatic of Van Hölder, seems to belong to both races, and is especially frequent in the North of England. As Rolleston expressed it: "Though skulls very closely similar to the typical representatives of either of the prehistoric races (the neolithic and the bronze) might be found upon living shoulders among the present population of this country, the elongated and fairly well-filled oval Anglo-Saxon cranium is the prevalent form among us in England at the present time."*

The inference is obvious; it is stated by Rolleston in another place: "The Saxon or English conquerors of this country have been shown, from the examination of their burial-grounds as well as of other evidence, to have displaced the population they found in occupation of it as entirely and completely as it has ever. been found possible for invaders to do. · · · · But marshes and forests · · · must have made the entire extirpation of the Romano-British population an impossibility," &c.

These statements respecting the craniological evidence are certainly

* Greenwell and Rolleston, *British Barrows*, p. 646.

strong, perhaps a little too strong; but they were made by a master of the subject.

The measurements of continental races do not call for much remark. Those of the Walloons indicate a long face, a receding forehead, broad zygomata and base of skull. The subjects were taken from the vicinity of Furfooz, during a visit to M. Dupont; and it is evident from M. Honzy's extensive enquiry into the subject that the Walloons in general have much broader heads than these.

My Norwegians exhibit a broad skull-base, a rather low skull and a projecting occiput.

The Swedes have broader heads, I suspect, than the average Swedish population. They were all sailors. Several of them had the inion placed high, so as to diminish the apparent occipital projection.

The Danes have been spoken of in a separate paper.

The Hanoverian heads are long and broad, with prominent occiput and somewhat receding forehead; the head is not low.

The Nassau heads are short and broad, glabella and frontal prominence moderate, forehead and zygomata broad, occiput flattish, skull-base broad.

Pfalz: short and broad; forehead prominent, glabella flat, head rounded, probably rather low than high.

Finns: short and broad; base, cheek-bones and forehead broad, head rounded and pyramidal; *no remarkable prominence of brows.*

Italians: short; small in all measurements except the height and the maximum breadth (this probably indicates a pyriform or heart-shaped head); occiput very flat.

It will have been observed that the last four series bear very little resemblance to the several British series, while there is more or less of resemblance between all the latter. The Scandinavian and Hanoverian series are all slightly broader than any of the British ones, but otherwise are not dissimilar to them. Nevertheless, some of the Southern Germans (Nassau and Pfalz men) were very English in facial features; we might, perhaps, apply to them what Ranke says of the Bavarians: that a Northern face is wedded to a short (Southern) brain-case.

The examination of the living head affords opportunity for the study of the features. Of these the form of the nose may easily be stated in a tabular form. I have taken 50 subjects, and raised the numbers to percentages :—

	Aquil.	Aq. Sin.	Sinuous.	Straight.	Sin. Co.	Concave.
			FORM OF NOSE.			
Irish	20	...	42	20	...	18
Highlanders	24	10	26	26	6	8
Welsh	26	6	30	20	2	12
English, Glo'stershire	28	2	14	36	...	20
Do., East and North	40	2	20	20	...	18

The most notable difference brought out here is the abundance of "sinuous" noses among the two Gaelic series, and in a slightly less degree among the Welsh, while they are comparatively uncommon among the English, in whom they are replaced by aquiline or straight ones. Concave noses are far from being so common among the Irish as is generally supposed; the really predominant form is long, sinuous, and prominent, especially at the point, with long nostrils.

Now let us compare the English forms with those of North-western Germany, and of the Scandinavian countries :—

	Aquil.	Aq. Sin.	Sinuous.	Straight.	Sin. Co.	Concave.
N.W. Germany	48	...	16	23	3	10
Denmark	40	...	10	30	...	20
Sweden	23	...	13	36	3	23

FORM OF NOSE.

There is certainly a good deal of resemblance, especially with the North-German forms. Everywhere the aquiline and straight forms predominate. But what I here call aquiline might more correctly be styled " slightly convex ;" as a rule neither the bridge nor the point can be called prominent, nor would the nasal bones probably appear so in the skull. In one of the Danish types a considerable prominence of the glabella and brows accompanies that of the nose ; but in the Swedes, North Germans, and English this is not so common.

On the whole, both the form of the head and that of the nose indicate a close relationship between the people of North-western Germany and of a great part of England.

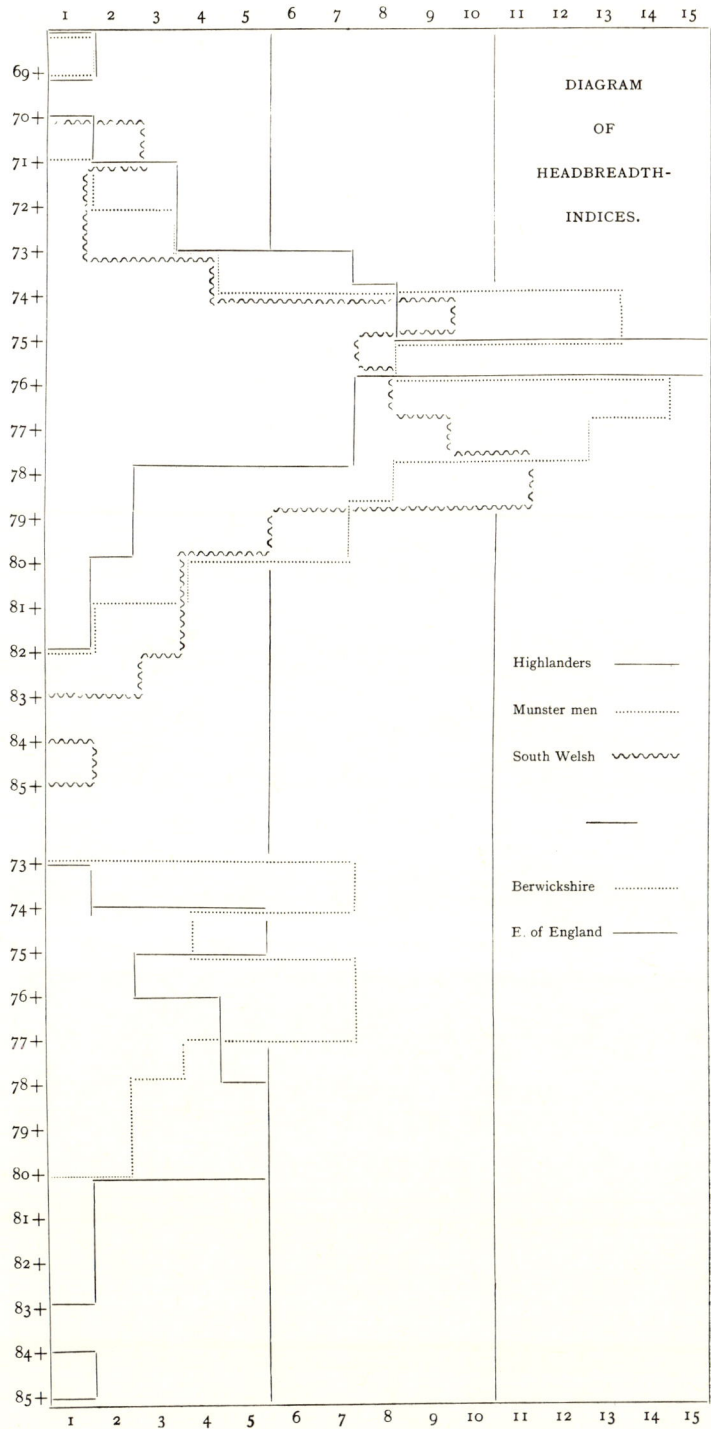

DIAGRAM

OF

HEADBREADTH-

INDICES.

Highlanders ————

Munster men ....

South Welsh wwwww

————

Berwickshire ....

E. of England ————

CHAPTER XIV.

General Commentary on the Tables.

THE Shetlanders are unquestionably, in the main, of Norwegian descent, but include other race-elements also; and though something has been done, much remains to be done for their anthropology. My only visit to Shetland was made thirty years ago: the observations here published were the first I made systematically; and I did not divide the black from the dark-brown-haired. See the account of the Shetlanders in the *Crania Britannica*, and the colour-statistics of Dr. Arthur Mitchell, quoted there; also the statistics of the Committee, which, probably with truth, make the Shetlanders the fairest population in the British Isles; also *Stature and Bulk of Man in the British Isles*, p. 13. The eyes—usually, I think, light gray rather than blue—are often of an indeterminate greenish or brownish-gray *(cæsii)*, a colour which seems to be a Scandinavian mark. Black hair does occur, and not *very* unfrequently. It is usually found in persons of decidedly Ugrian aspect and melancholic temperament. The same type may be found at Wick, and I have seen it in several persons from north-eastern Sutherland and from the Gaelic parish of Latheron, in Southern Caithness. These people may be relics of the Ugrian thralls of the Norse invaders, or possibly descendants of some primitive Ugrian tribe, whose enigmatic name remains to us in Ptolemy as dwelling in the far north (No. 1). The excessive use of tea, the one luxury of Shetland, probably only aggravates a constitutional tendency to nervous disorders, which is more prevalent among the few dark than the many fair Shetlanders. The people of Coningsburgh, near Lerwick, are said to be darker than the Lerwick and Scalloway men, and less mild and peaceable; some say that descendants remain there of the crew of one of the Spanish Armada; but *quien sabe?* Any peculiar customs of the Coningsburghers are said to be old Norse. The heads of the Shetlanders are larger than the average of Scotland, and slightly broader in proportion.*

The history of Kirkwall, and the family names there, testify to much immigration from Scotland into that city; but the Orcadians in general so much resemble the Shetlanders, that if the latter be pretty purely Scandinavian, I think the bulk of the former must be so too. The angular bony Scotch chin and cheekbones, and the prominent glabella,

---

* Dr. Cowie, *Shetland and its Inhabitants,* p. 300; authority, an Edinburgh hat manufacturer.

are perhaps as rare out of Kirkwall as they are in Shetland. Sometimes the malar bones are broad and rounded, and the face flattish; and my late friend, Mr. G. Petrie, of Kirkwall, told me this was particularly noticeable in the pure-blooded Orcadians of North Ronaldsha. On the whole these islanders are quite as much English as Scottish in aspect, dialect, voice and character; fair, smooth-featured, and comely, they resemble the fairer individuals among the eastern English. Probably the number of light-haired persons in Orkney would have been put a little higher, had I visited the islands after more experience in observation (Nos. 2, 3, 4).

The Outer Hebrides (the Long Island, as they are collectively called) have a population doubtless differing much in its several divisions, which has been much studied by Captain Thomas and Dr. Mitchell.* My personal knowledge of it is confined to Stornoway and the immediate neighbourhood, and to a few photographs from other parts. Two or three strongly contrasted types are met with in the Lewis. There is the large, fair, comely Norse race, said to exist almost pure in the district of Ness,† at the north end of the island; the short, thickset, snub-nosed, dark-haired, often even dark-eyed race, probably aboriginal, and possibly Finnish, whose centre seems to be in Barvas; and the West Highland type, which has gradually filtered in, and is usually characterised by an athletic figure, of medium size, a bony face, long sinuous pointed nose, gray eyes and dark hair. On the whole, I think the Norse type still predominates at Stornoway, though its language was swamped by the Gaelic centuries ago. The incongruity of these types comes out in my Stornoway observations, the Ness type appearing in the abundance of fair hair, the Barvas in that of black, and perhaps also in that of red hair, the union of both in the great number with hazel or brown eyes and brown hair.‡

The Harris men are described as differing from all the types just mentioned. They are a rather dark people, with handsome elongated features; probably an old race with a Norse cross, moulded into a distinct type by ages of seclusion, for Harris is a very mountainous country.

* Summaries of their observations may be found in the *Crania Britannica*. I regret much that neither of these gentlemen has published a monograph on the anthropology of the Hebrides. See also *Stature and Bulk*, pp. 12, 13.   † Worsage, *Danes in England*.

‡ The red is a yellowish sandy-red, not the flaming Highland colour; the fair is generally pale yellowish brown; the black occurs chiefly with sharpish features and prominent straight brows, and is usually curly, but does not seem to be an importation from the mainland, for most of my specimens were country folk; lighter colours are also pretty often curly. The eyes are blue, sea-gray, hazel, not seldom dark hazel, or even what is called black. One black-haired countrywoman had large eyes, curly hair, a broad face with a tapering chin, not at all English or Scotch, but much like some Basques I have seen in photographs, Campbell, of Islay, and I think other observers, have made the same remark on some of the Long Islanders. In five heads, mostly of boys, the indices of breadth were 74, 75, 75, 76, and 81; all five were of the Norse type.

SHETLANDER.   LEWIS
                  (SCANDIN.)

LEWIS   (SCANDINAVIAN TYPES).

LEWIS   LEWIS   HARRIS.
(GAELIC).   (BARVAS).

The two returns from Skye differ rather widely. The one from Strath, gotten many years ago, probably represents the native breed of the more accessible parts pretty fairly. My notes speak of the commonly lightish hue of their lank abundant hair, the shortness of their noses, and less prominence of their brows, compared with those of West Highlanders. Portree is proved by the surnames to have a very mixed population, with a large contingent from the mainland (Nos. 6, 7, 8).

The isles of Seal and Luing, and the neighbouring islet which is called Easdale, apparently for the confusion of etymologists,* have a considerable population of slateworkers, whose ancestry is believed to be in the main local, or from the neighbouring mainland and islands, with a small English cross apparent in the surnames. The people are handsome, more generally fair than most Highlanders, and with straight, high features (No. 9).

West of Argyle are a number of islands, for the anthropology of which we must look principally to Mr. Hector McLean. These are Islay, Jura, Mull, Coll, Tiree, &c. They vary among themselves in the proportion of the Norse and so-called Celtic elements; but, generally speaking, that of the former is much less than in the Lewis. Captain Thomas's papers on place-names in the Hebrides show that while a large majority of the names of farmhouses in the Lewis are Norse, in Islay the majority are Gaelic. Mull and Jura are probably more Gaelic than the fertile Islay, Colonsay more Norwegian. McLean's account of the Colonsay people is very distinct, and may be quoted here as an excellent description of a Scandinavian type. " They are generally fair and florid," he says, " and the skin is remarkably white. The hair is flaxen and light red, passing into shades of brown, seldom black. The face is oval, and generally long for its breadth. The cheekbones are rarely broad or prominent, or the eyebrows prominent. The chin is seldom very broad, narrow, or prominent. The profile is usually straight, or nearly so; the forehead high for its breadth; the reflective faculties (frontal eminences) nearly as prominent as the perceptive. Hair, soft and glossy, and often curly. Blue eyes not so common as in Islay, where the people are darker and more Celtic." So far as I can judge from Mr. McLean's statements respecting colour, the index of nigrescence may be about 10 in Colonsay, and 30 or more in Islay. Brown eyes are uncommon in both islands. The measurements bring out the important facts that the blackhaired men are considerably shorter than the rest, their heads narrower, and the circumference of their pelvis smaller, both absolutely and in relation to that of their shoulders.

The eastern, more level and less inhospitable portion of Caithness is

* Easdale is the Celto-Norse name of a glen near Dunmailraise, in Westmoreland (*eass*, a waterfall or torrent); but there is absolutely no water on the island. The name is said to be modern, and, so to speak, accidental.

occupied by a very fine English-speaking race of Norse descent. They are represented, not very purely, by the observations taken at Wick (No. 10). But the three western parishes of Caithness, Reay, Halkirk, and Latheron, are Gaelic; perhaps they always were so, in spite of the name of the second. On both coasts of Sutherland, Cromarty and Ross, the Scandinavians have left plenty of local names; and the native race shows unmistakable symptoms of a northern cross, as far down as the southern part of Ross. Dr. Christison, who is well acquainted with my method of working and standards of colour, observed for me 111 persons, including 31 women, in the western parts of Sutherland. The results, reduced to percentages, were as follows :—

WEST SUTHERLAND.

Colour of Hair	Red.	Fair.	Brown.	Dark Brown.	Black.		Index.
	3·6	30·6	29·7	29·7	6·3	...	8·1

This part of Sutherland lies opposite the Lewis, and Assynt was formerly the patrimony of a branch of the MacLeods, the same Norse-descended clan who ruled the Lewis. Further south, at Ullapool, in Cromarty, I saw a generally blond population, many of whom, by their clear blue eyes, without any dark ring, their soft features, elliptical facial outlines, flaxen or pale red hair, were unmistakably discriminated from any common West Highland type. But I believe, from what I have seen of men from north-eastern Sutherland, that the race thereabout, consisting chiefly of Mackays, is different, and resembles the dark-haired people of Western Caithness. The Sutherlanders, of whatever complexion, are a very fine, stalwart people, as the 93rd Highland Regiment and the Edinburgh police used to exemplify (Nos. 11, 12).

The eastern part of Ross is fertile and genial, and its people have absorbed the blood of the old Scandinavian lords of Tain and Dingwall, as well as that of more recent Lowland colonists (Nos. 14, 15). The MacRaes, in the south-west of the country, are a fine breed of Highlanders, tolerably pure, and very frequently gray-eyed and dark-haired (No. 13).

Inverness, as the centre and capital of the Highlands, has of course a mixed population, but the non-highland element is comparatively small (Nos. 16, 18, 18B).

From Nairn (No. 17), a little east of Inverness, round Buchan Ness to the Tay and the Forth, extends a broad band of English-speaking country (or, perhaps one should rather say, Lowland-Scotch-speaking), which, though in parts decidedly mountainous, is considered to belong to the Lowlands. In the centre of this curved band, the great mountain masses, and the upper valleys, radiating thence, of the Spey, Doveran, Don, Dee, and the tributaries of the Tay, have hitherto remained Gaelic. The composition and descent of the Lowland population have been much debated, and extreme views have been put forth by both

Philogaels and Philangles. Those who used to claim them for almost unmixed Picts, attributed to that nation a Teutonic tongue, and so got over any difficulty as to the introduction of the present form of speech. That speech differs from other Scottish dialects by some peculiarities, seemingly borrowed from Gaelic vocal organs, such as the use of *f* for *wh*. All the way round from Nairn (where Highland features seem to wear Lowland complexions) to the Forth, it seems to me that the physical characteristics indicate an admixture of two or more elements, whereof two are both very strong. The Teutonic may have included Angles, Flemings, and Norsemen or Danes: of the Pictish element I will speak presently. The colouring throughout the whole region,* except about Keith and Huntley, seems to be light. In approaching Aberdeen from the side of Inverness I was struck by the breadth of the foreheads and chins, and the roundness of the faces; but no such idea had occurred to me when I had visited Aberdeen on my return from Orkney and Caithness. Such of the peasantry as I saw were mostly stoutly-built men, not tall, but long-backed, broad and burly. Fair complexions and light eyes were extremely prevalent, but hair of a darkish brown was not seldom conjoined. Flaxen was more common than yellow hair, and dull red was frequent (Nos. 21, 22).

The people of Moray are not very dissimilar to the Aberdonians. The large number of dark eyes in the gathering at Brodie may be partly accidental; but dark eyes are certainly more prevalent among the middle than among the lower classes of Scotchmen; probably in part from their being more mixed in blood (Nos. 20, 20B).

Keith and Huntley are in an elevated country near to the hills; the district remained Gaelic later than Moray or the Lower Don; and though Celtic patronymics are not very common there, no doubt the blood is mainly Pictish. It is interesting to note that the colours are nearly those of the West Highlanders; and I thought the forms inclined towards the same type (No. 19).

The townspeople of Angus incline to the Teutonic characters. Observe the difference between the people of Arbroath and the neighbouring rural parish of Arbirlot (Nos. 23 to 29).

On the coast of Fife there are similar local differences. Wherever the increase of hazel eyes raises the percentage of dark ones, it seems to me that smoother features, less sunken eyes, and broader, rounder jaws are the rule. This was noted particularly at Pittenween, Anstruther and Arbroath: all these old towns used to have much commerce with the Easterlings (Nos. 30 to 33).

Stirling I have visited three or four times, in order to correct or confirm my first observations; the result has been their confirmation. I think that either the Angles of Lothian pushed *en masse* in this direction

---

* I have never been able to visit Buchan; but am told that the people there resemble the other Aberdonians.

to the ford of the Forth and the Campsie Fells,* or the royal residence at Stirling attracted citizens from the same quarter (No. 34).

Perth, no doubt, and its fertile neighbourhood, early received English settlers. Swan, the ancestor of the Ruthvens, did not come alone; Dunning was occupied about the same time, and its "Saxon" tower, with masonry not unlike Colswegen's, at Lincoln, built early in the 12th century; but the Ochills were, roughly speaking, the boundary of the languages after Fife had been Saxonized. Accordingly the people of Strathallan and Auchterarder (No. 37) are rather Gaelic in appearance and colour. The Forteviot schedules are curious (No. 38). I cannot explain them, but they were very carefully and leisurely taken. The number of hazel eyes among the women is remarkable. At Perth the type has somewhat altered since I first knew the city. I am confident that both dark eyes and dark hair are more common than formerly; there has been an immigration of Highlanders, and to a smaller extent of Irishmen (Nos. 35, 36).

We come now to the true Highland country of Scotland, the abode of the Gaelic tongue and people. In attempting a description of their physical type, one feels a difficulty, less indeed than has to be encountered where the subject is a more mingled and heterogeneous race, but perhaps, for that very reason, more clearly defined.

Most travellers, on entering the habitat of a race strange to them, quickly form for themselves from the first persons observed some notion of the prevailing physical type. This idea serves as a peg whereon to hang subsequent observations, but is seldom materially altered. Doubtless this is one reason why such descriptions vary so much *inter se*. On the other hand, those who belong to the race, or have lived long surrounded by it, see more of the differences than of the points of agreement. I confess that the longer I have known the Scottish Highlanders the more diversity I have seen among them.

Nevertheless, there certainly is a central type round which the subordinate ones cluster. The diagram of the indices of latitude, which accompanies this chapter, indicates a very homogeneous race, *quoad* head-breadth, the ratios varying only between 69 and 82 as extremes, and culminating very distinctly at 76. The average is 76·27 (so that in the skull it will hardly exceed 74; in 40 West Highland men it is only 75·87, in 16 from the eastern districts it rises to 76·9. The head and face are long and rather narrow, the skull-base rather narrow, the brows and occiput prominent; further than this the figures do not guide us. The eyes are generally light;† of the 55 whose heads were measured, they were blue or bluish-gray in 30, gray in 19, light brown or dark brown in 8, of which only 1 was true hazel. The hair in 48 was thus divided: 5 red, 4 fair, 3 lightish brown, 11 brown, 17 dark brown,

* Note the word *Fell*. Was it brought hither by the Yorkshire refugees?
† See the tables for Scotland.

5 brown-black, 3 coal-black. The resulting index is 41·6. These proportions are very nearly those which prevail throughout the Highlands.*

When we talk of a race mixed from two or three stocks, we are apt to forget that even these parent stocks were not absolutely homogeneous. Their own sagas and poems show that neither the Norsemen nor the ancient Gaels were so in respect of colour; nor do I believe that there was ever a period when, for example, all the Caledonians were red-haired. Similarly of the skulls; assuredly there was never a time since the dawn of history when most, if not all, of Kollmann's five types could not have been found within the limits of any one race. The variations, therefore, which are allowed in the description I am going to quote, with slight abridgment, from Hector Maclean,† are not greater than necessary to correctness:—

"The dolichocephalous Celt," he says, "is of various sizes, but often tall; he is of various complexion, the colour of the skin ranging from a ruddy white to a swarthy hue; the shape of the body is often graceful; the head is high and long, often narrow, seldom broad in proportion; the face is frequently long, and the profile more or less convex; the lips are usually full, often thick and more or less projecting; the chin and lower jaw are obliquely placed, and *the contour of the lower jaw, taken from its junction with the neck, is but slightly curved, and often looks to the eye as if it were a straight line;* the chin is seldom round, and generally somewhat trapezoidal; the forehead, viewed in profile, gradually increases in prominence from the coronal region towards the eyebrows; face, from the external orbital angles to the point of the chin, long—a characteristic of which the old Gael, Feinn, or Scots seem to have felt rather proud (see 'Lay of Diarmaid,' *West Highland Tales,* translated by J. F. Campbell). The nose is frequently large and prominent; eyebrows prominent, long, slightly arched, *sometimes closely approaching a straight line;* cheekbones large and prominent; eyes most frequently gray or bluish gray, sometimes dark gray or dark brown; hair reddish yellow, yellowish red, but more frequently of various shades of brown, of which yellow‡ is the ground colour; sometimes, when it appears altogether black, a yellow tinge is discovered when it is closely examined; when mixed with other types the hair is coal-black, but hardly ever so when pure. Leg and foot usually well-developed, thigh long in proportion, instep high, ankle well-shaped and of moderate size; step very elastic and rather springing, the heel being well raised and the knee well bent. Quick in temper and very emotional, seldom speaking without being influenced by one feeling or another; more quick than accurate in observation; clear thinkers,

---

* In explanation of the extreme darkness of the hair of the Argyle men in my military schedules, it may be right to say that I rejected a large number of men with distinctly Lowland names, natives of Dunoon and other places on the Clyde, which are really outlying suburbs of Glasgow, rather than Highland villages.

† *Anthropological Review,* vol. iv., p. 129.   ‡ I should read here *red* or *reddish-yellow.*

but wanting in deliberation; they have a fertile and vivid imagination; love the absolute in thought and principle; dislike expediency and doubt; sympathetic with the weak, patriotic, chivalrous. Disposed to a sentimental melancholy, yet hopeful and sanguine. Often witty and eloquent; lovers of the animal kingdom, sometimes excel in zoological science."

Maclean describes with equal minuteness and accuracy another type, which he calls the brachycephalous Celt, and which is, he says, frequent in the eastern and northern parts of the Highlands. In this the head is broad (comparatively), the profile straight, cheekbones broad and large, nose generally sinuous, face tapering rapidly to the chin, which is often prominent and angular; the skin is dark; the eyes deepset, often small, dark-gray or dark-brown; the hair reddish-brown, red, or raven-black; the lips seldom prominent; the hand square, large-jointed; the chest square and broad; the calf large, and foot well-formed. The gait is easy and shuffling. These people have strong attachments and feelings, but much forethought and self-control; are gloomy, fervent, humorous.

I have met with good examples of this type, but do not think it is anywhere very numerous. My No. 38 belongs to it. It may be assigned to a Finnish rather than to an Aryan stock.

Maclean's third "Celtic" type is that of Sancho Panza, already described, and said to be especially prevalent in the outer Hebrides, as well as in the west of Ireland.

A fourth type, which has entered more largely into the constitution of the Highland people than is generally supposed, is the Scandinavian. I have given some specimens of this, from Shetland and the Lewis; but cannot refrain from again quoting Maclean as to some of its points:—
"Generally tall," he says, "and long-armed, profile straight, forehead arched horizontally, brows more arched and less prominent than in the 'Celts'; face square, oblong, or tapering *in a curve* towards the chin (my spade or scutiform face), cheekbones broad and flat; nose sometimes large, usually of average size, varying from being slightly sinuous to being considerably aquiline. Mouth well-formed, seldom large; lips seldom thick; chin often prominent, and semi-circular; lower jaw strongly arched. Eyes blue and bluish-gray; occasionally hazel or brown; larger and more prominent than in the 'Celtic' type, but flatter and less lustrous. Hair flaxen and sand-colour (pale red, I suppose), passing into various shades of brown. Gait firm, often awkward; little bending of knee, calf and foot not so well formed. Strong digestive organs. 'Doubts numerous, convictions few.' Accurate and impartial observers. Powerful local memory, which gives a talent for geometry, astronomy, navigation. Firm, self-reliant, truthful; less irritable than the Celt, and less ready to forgive."

These types and their descriptions very nearly correspond with those of Captain Thomas and Dr. Mitchell; but the Spanish Celt of Captain

Thomas, dark and well-featured, has not so extensive a range in characteristics as Maclean's "dolichocephalous Celt." The problem of the origin of this last is not, I think, as yet ripe for solution; but I believe it to comprehend both Galatic and Iberian elements, if not others. Some of its leading points, such as the formation of the brows and of the lower jaw, are extremely prevalent throughout Ireland, and wherever else the Gaelic tongue is known to have existed.*

Every here and there a decidedly Iberian physiognomy appears, which makes one think Professor Rhys right in supposing that the Picts were in part at least of that stock, or that the longbarrow race has left relics of itself here in the far north-west, as well as in South Britain. No. 28 of my series is a very pure specimen of this type, with a long, high, narrow head (index 73·7), handsome features and dark complexion.

At a considerable distance in type from this is the large-boned, harsh-featured, red-haired Gael, whereof No. 24 is an excellent specimen, and who might represent the Caledonian of Tacitus. So indeed might two or three more of my men; but though 31 may perhaps come within the limits of the first Gaelic type, 35 has certainly a Scandinavian cross, as many of the Arisaig and Ardnamurchan people have. 29 represents, even better than 31, the very fine martial type, resembling the Swiss type of Sion, which is more common in Perthshire than in the west, and which may also have been Caledonian or Brythonic. 8, 12, 17, 23, 54, 56, all belong to McLean's first type. So does 41, who verges on the Iberian, and is exactly Captain Thomas's Spanish Celt, while his brother, 42, is almost Scandinavian. 14 and 16 are two very fair men, nowise related, but noteworthy for their straight profiles and great supra-occipital projection. 44 is the "Irish Celt or Fin" of Captain Thomas, said to abound in the Hebrides. 22, 35, 39, 46, perhaps 45 and 50, are among those who partake of the Norse type. 46 is a gentleman of thoroughly known ancestry, entirely Highland; yet there is nothing about him, except his colossal size, that would strike an observer who encountered him in (say) Tamworth or Chichester market.

The average stature of 43 of my men was 5 feet 8 inches exactly, without shoes (1·727 metre). There was no selection for size; but I think this average is quite high enough. The Anthropometric Committee's report, however, which includes those published in my *Stature and Bulk*, gives 5 ft. 8·45 in. for Inverness, and 5 ft. 8·63 in. for Argyle and Bute (Nos. 39 to 71 of the Tables of Colour). In explanation of the fairness of the people of the Great Glen (54—57), it is said that English excavators in great numbers sojourned here during the making of the canal, and that some settled down here. About Abernethy, in Strath-

* Observe the near resemblance of the Highlanders and Munstermen in respect of headbreadth, as developed in the diagram of breadth-indices.

spey, I collected a number of observations, which were lost; the index of nigrescence was about 27.

Proceeding to the south-east, at Stirling Bridge we cross an ethnological frontier, that of the flaxen-haired Angles and Anglo-Danes, who extend without interruption as far as the Mercian Fens. Repeated visits have convinced me that they continue in great force as far west as Stirling, if not further, though, of course, in the towns, and especially in Edinburgh, a blending process has long been going on (Nos. 82—88).

The Lothian peasantry are generally tall, large and muscular; their figures and features are rounder, and their cheekbones less prominent, than those of their western and northern countrymen. Their complexion is usually very fair, eyes blue or light gray, or sometimes hazel, and hair varying from light red and flaxen-yellow through divers shades of brown, often dull, but seldom very dark. The overhanging penthouse brows, so common among the Scottish Gael, are less so here, the eyes being less sunken; the nose is straightish, rather short than long, with nostrils and tip more rounded; the forehead is often dome-shaped, the chin and lower jaw broad and rounded, the profile nearly straight (No. 89).

Wherever this race predominates, it seems to run into the two principal types distinguished by Gildemeister at Bremen.[*] Of these the longheaded one is by far the more numerous. In the Merse (the low country of Berwickshire) it is so potent that, both in the rural and the fishing population, I found the breadth-index under 77. The fisherfolk, both here and to the north of the Forth, form, as is well known, separate communities, commonly supposed to have been recruited, if not founded, by immigrants from the Dutch and Norwegian coasts. Be that as it may, they are a very fine people, and the women are particularly comely, after the Frisian style of beauty, with blue or hazel eyes and hair varying from yellow to deep chestnut. Their surnames are those of the neighbouring country, whatever their race may be (Nos. 90, 94 and 97).

Roughly speaking, this Anglian or Anglo-Scandinavian race, however diluted by the immigration during centuries past of the other elements of the Scottish nation, may be said still to occupy the three counties of Lothian and the four of Tweeddale (Nos. 95, 96, 98—115). The eastern part of Dumfriesshire is possessed by nearly the same breed of men, with the same preponderance of the Norse element that exists in Cumberland (Nos. 117—120). Further west the race changes, though traces of the conquest of Kyle and the coast of Galloway by the Northumbrians, and of the settlement of Upper Clydesdale after the Norman Conquest,[†] may perhaps be still observed. The blood is

---

[*] Ante, pp. 43, 44, 45.

[†] Note such local names as Dolphinton, Symington, Thankerton.

mainly Brythonic, Strathclydewallian. As Broca found the stature
higher in some of the Cymric or Belgic departments of France than in
the more Germanic ones, so here the Welshman of Upper Galloway
excels in stature, though not in bulk, the stalwart Anglians of the
Merse. It is doubtful whether anywhere else in Europe could be found
a population like that of Balmaclellan,* who average 5 feet 10·46 inches
(about 179 centimetres) without shoes; and those of Dundonald and
Lesmahagow are not much smaller. The prevailing combination of
colour hereabout is that of blue or gray eyes, with dark-brown or even
coal-black hair: the last is very common about Lesmahagow, which is
a sequestered hilly district; and on the whole the tallest men seem to
be the dark-haired ones. Probably the primitive Brythons of these
parts—Ottadini, Attacotti, &c.—were tall, gray-eyed and dark-haired.
One is reminded of the Britons whom Strabo saw at Rome, who were
half a foot taller than other people; Strabo also says that the Britons
were not so light-haired as the Gauls (Nos. 72—80).

In Lower Galloway (Wigtonshire especially) the ethnology is complicated by the presence of a population formerly called Pictish, and
who appear to have crossed over from Ulster. Their clan nomenclature
resembles that of the Highlands, but they are oftener dark-eyed than
the true Highlanders. This is what we might expect to find, if the
Cruithne or Picts were really Iberians (No. 77).

In Ayrshire, when the hair is light, it is often of a beautiful bright
yellow. I have no measurements of the heads of south-western Scotland, but, judging by the eye alone, I should say the hexagonal form
prevailed here; whereas the Berwickshire form inclines to be elliptical.

The mental and moral attributes of the two divisions of the Southern
Scots might be the subject of a very interesting enquiry. I will simply
point to the fact that the strong religious feeling which developed itself
in the Covenanters and Cameronians belonged to the west rather than
the east. Both divisions have the glory of having produced much of
our finest poetry. Burns was not, however, I believe, of Ayrshire
descent, whereas Scott was a pure Borderer. The west has produced
many minor poets; but the finest of our ballads had their birth in the
fair land of the Tweed. Their characteristic merits, their force and
simple pathos, are Anglo-Danish rather than Gaelic or Kymric, and
would have been marred, perhaps, by the exuberant fancy of the livelier
races. The nearest likeness to them is found in the old ballads of
Denmark.

Northumberland is strongly Anglian, and much like Berwickshire
anthropologically; the Danish element, which is apparently rather
more potent in the blood than in the history of the county, may have

* Or, perhaps, even in America, among whites. See Peckham, *Growth of Children*,
p. 31.

given to the Northumbrians their characteristic *burr*,* which results from an inability to pronounce the letter *r* properly. Local authorities— *e.g.*, Mr. Ralph Carr, of Hedgley—think there is a notable proportion of old British blood in Tynedale, along the Roman wall, and on the western Border. The rural population round Hexham is, however, fair, and apparently Teutonic; and Hexham was very early Anglicized (Nos. 121, 129). Of the Cumbrian region much has been said in the historical chapters. Fine specimens of the old bronze type, with prominent brows and nose, occur there pretty frequently; but the prevailing type has a straight profile and a long, fine, straight nose, with fair hair and gray eyes, and is in the main Scandinavian, though crossed with the Kymric (Nos. 130, 145).

Durham county is nowadays a centre of immigration, but the old race was Anglian in the main, with the Danish element increasing in force towards the frontier of Yorkshire. It is curious, that whereas Durham was among the first, and was actually the last, among the counties of England, to offer resistance to the Conqueror, it was perhaps also the one in which the native English retained most of their lands and their political importance, and in which the foreign settlers were fewest (Nos. 146—148).

The North and East Ridings of Yorkshire have an Anglo-Danish population, in which there are probably but scanty remains of the primitive races. It is likely enough, however, that the descendants of the citizens of York and Catterick survived to amalgamate with the earlier swarm of conquerors; and that a considerable number of Norman invaders—rather Norman in this case than French—settled here after the ravages of the great Bastard. The prevailing types are certainly Anglian and Danish; the chief one is thus described by the late Professor Phillips, than whom no man knew the county better: "Tall, large-boned, muscular persons; visage long, angular; complexion fair or florid; eyes blue or gray; hair light, brown or reddish." The local variations are considerable, and some of them may date from the Conquest. The features of the famous Captain Cook, who was a Whitby man, are frequently reproduced; they resemble those of a Scandinavian type, found in the Lewis, which has been figured. The average stature

---

* The relation to race, in the British Isles, of differences of intonation, accent and pronunciation, apart from those of dialect, has been comparatively little studied. The late Angus Smith was at work upon it a little before his lamented death.

The sing-song intonation found in parts of the Border country, and perhaps in Suffolk, has been said to resemble that of the Swedes. Want of a musical ear has prevented me from following up this part of my subject. The "burr" (thick indistinct pronunciation of the *r*), which is peculiar to the natives of Northumberland and Berwick-upon-Tweed, ought to be found in Sleswick or Jutland. The mismanagement of the aspirate, common in Southern England, extends to Yorkshire (thus 'Ul for Hull); but not, I think, beyond the river Wear. All this might probably be explained by a minute Scandinavian scholar.

and weight are apparently the largest in England; the Anthropometric Committee give the height and weight as 5 feet 9 inches (1·754 metre) and 164 lbs. (74·5 kilos).*

Upper Teesdale was a desert at the date of *Domesday;* it had probably been swept clean by Malcolm Canmore; and the modern inhabitants may be a colony from Westmoreland or Durham; they are a very blond race (No. 140). The small, round-faced, brown, dark-haired men, with dark almond-shaped eyes, whom Phillips met with especially in the vale of the Derwent and the level lands south of York, are by him ascribed to a Romano-British or Iberian origin. I am more disposed to believe that the old Brigantians were a tall race, like the other northern Brythons, and that this dark type may be at least partly French in origin.

The remaining type of Professor Phillips belongs chiefly, he said, to the elevated districts of the West Riding. " Person robust, visage oval, full and rounded; nose often slightly aquiline; complexion somewhat embrowned, florid; eyes brown or gray; hair brown or reddish." This brown, burly breed he thought Norwegian. I believe it to be a variety of the Anglian; it abounds in Staffordshire, a very Anglian county. A notable point about it is the frequency of eyes of a neutral undecided tint, between light and dark, green, brown and gray; the hair being comparatively light; this is the " Wiltshire eye." In Craven, the Brigantian, or Romano-Briton, certainly survives in some force; the hair is oftener dark, and the features high. In the ancient kingdom of Loidis and Elmet, from Tadcaster and Leeds westwards up Airedale and the Worth Valley to the Lancashire frontier, the fair race predominates to a remarkable degree. I can see nothing British or Iberian about them; they are the bold, rude, obstinate race so well depicted by Charlotte Brontë, who lived among them. I conjecture that Edwin of Deira expelled the British inhabitants of Elmet, driving them across the mountains, and that the Angles of the plain of York took refuge here from the subsequent invasion of the Danes.

Another type (plate 2) does probably descend from an ancient race; it seems to occur especially in the south-western part of the West Riding.

In few parts of Britain does there exist a more clearly marked moral type than in Yorkshire. To that of the Irish it has no affinity; but the Scotchman and the Southern Englishman alike recognise the differences which distinguish the Yorkshire character from their own, but are not so apt to apprehend the numerous respective points of resemblance.

---

* The population of the fishing village of Flamborough, which has been examined by General Pitt-Rivers, differs remarkably from the general population of the East Riding. They have long been a separate race, but the constitution of the village was apparently subsequent to the Conquest. They are mostly very dark. (*Journal of Anth. Inst.*, vol. xi., p. 469, &c.).

The character is essentially Teutonic, including the shrewdness, the truthfulness without candour, the perseverance, energy and industry of the Lowland Scotch, but little of their frugality, or of the theological instinct common to the Welsh and Scotch, or of the imaginative genius, or the more brilliant qualities which sometimes light up the Scottish character. The sound judgment, the spirit of fairplay, the love of comfort, order and cleanliness, and the fondness for heavy feeding, are shared with the Saxon Englishman; but some of them are still more strongly marked in the Yorkshireman, as is also the bluff independence —a very fine quality when it does not degenerate into selfish rudeness. The aptitude for music was remarked by Giraldus Cambrensis seven centuries ago, and the taste for horseflesh seems to have descended from the old Northmen, though it may have been fostered by local circumstances. The mind, like the body, is generally very vigorous and energetic, and extremely well adapted to commercial and industrial pursuits, as well as to the cultivation of the exact sciences; but a certain defect in imaginative power must be admitted, and is probably one reason, though obviously not the only one, why Yorkshire, until quite modern times, was generally behindhand in politics and religion (Nos. 151—169).

North Lancashire resembles Cumberland and Westmoreland, ethnologically. Here, as there, the Norwegians have been strong enough to change the names of even considerable rivers—*e.g.*, the Greta, *great water*. In the prevailing type the profile is straight; the nose of good length, straight or slightly aquiline, rather narrow, not sharply pointed, nostrils roundish; brows not prominent; mouth and chin medium; eyes *à fleur-de-tête*, often of a muddy gray; ears oval, well-formed; hair generally straight and blond, but not bright-coloured. The face is either oblong or scutiform; the head apparently oblong or elliptic (No. 149).

In the southern part of Lancashire there is now a congeries of people from all parts of the three kingdoms. The prominent type in the old native breed is the heavy Anglian one, much like the West Riding type of Professor Phillips. An ancient, so-called "Celtic" one, with dark hair, is said to prevail in the high moorland valleys; but I cannot say whether this is really so (No. 150).

Nottinghamshire and Lincolnshire are Anglo-Danish counties; in the latter, as far as to the borders of the Fens, the Danish element is particularly strong. Lëndum may have survived the Anglian conquest; but the modern population of Lincoln yields no traces of the fact. They are a fair and handsome people, with regular features; blue-eyed, says Professor Phillips; blue or light hazel, I should say; the latter hue is very conspicuous at Boston, where the countryfolk remind me strongly of the peasantry about Antwerp.

From Lincoln to Nottingham, along the vale of the Trent, the same breed of men prevails. Mr. D. Mackintosh, who has studied the features

BOSTON.   LINCOLN.   LINCOLNSHIRE.

WEST-RIDING TYPES.   NOTTINGHAMSHIRE.

JUTE ? KENT.   SUSSEX.

more than I have, makes the leading points of his Danish type a long face, high cheekbones, with a sudden sinking in above on each side of the forehead, high and long nose, head elevated behind, reddish hair. There is a traditional attribution of red hair to the old Danish invaders, in some parts of the country; but I do not think the colour is common in Lincolnshire nowadays. The high finely-formed nose and prominence of the superciliary ridges, yet with fairly arched brows, not the straight penthouse of the Scotch and Irish, are frequently seen in Denmark;* and where they are very prevalent among the Anglians, a Danish cross may be suspected (Nos. 170—181).

Derbyshire has, at least in its north-western mountainous district, a good many Celtic local names; but the physical type of the population is certainly Anglian. My own observations, the military statistics, and those of the Anthropometric Committee, all agree in representing the Derbyshire people as having lighter hair than all but a very few English counties;† but between this county and Cheshire there seems to be a kind of racial frontier.‡ Here, as well as in the West Riding, the Danish invasion probably drove the Anglian population of the plains into the thitherto thinly-peopled hill country. Longdendale was entirely waste when *Domesday* was compiled; the origin of its famous archers might be an interesting subject of enquiry (Nos. 182, 183).

East Staffordshire is also very Anglian, but nowise Danish; its people resemble those of the West Riding. The Mercians probably settled thickly along the Trent, whose course they may have followed upward from the Humber. Repton and Tamworth were the royal residences. Till lately the crypt of Tamworth church was full of fine ovo-elliptic skulls, which were all buried, I regret to say, just when I had been making arrangements to measure them (Nos. 187—197).

Leicestershire was largely colonized by the Danes; Rutland was not so. The former differs from the other North-Midland counties, apparently, by having retained a good proportion of the dark pre-Anglian stock. See pages 23, 24, on this point. I doubt whether Professor Phillips was right as to the smaller proportions of the dark stock in this part of England (Nos. 184—186).

The northern part of Cambridgeshire (the Isle of Ely) is also supposed to retain a large proportion of British blood. See the reports of Dr. Clapham, of Thorney, and Dr. Stuckey, of Parson Drove, in my

* Mr. Park Harrison lays great stress upon this feature as Danish. It is common to the Borreby race, and to the British bronze men, to the Sion type of Switzerland, and to many modern Savoyards (Hovelacque), perhaps to the Arvernians, but not to the Disentis, nor, I think, to the Ligurian type. In one of the Anglian types, very abundant about Leeds, the glabella is quite flat.

† Barnard Davis found the index a minus number at the village of Youlgrave (see Appendix).

‡ Observe the high index of nigrescence at Leek, on the frontier of Cheshire, Staffordshire, and Derbyshire (No. 187).

Stature and Bulk, pp. 76, 77. They found more hazel and brown than blue or gray eyes. The southern part of the county is more like Norfolk and Suffolk, anthropologically (Nos. 222, 223).

These two counties are more Anglian than either Danish or British. Mr. Grant Allen, whose summary of the Brito-Saxon controversy, in his excellent little book on Anglo-Saxon Britain, is about the fairest we have, dwells perhaps a little too much on the British element in East Anglia. It is perhaps stronger in Suffolk than in Norfolk. The following are my notes on the people of Norwich and its vicinity :— "Approach the northern (Northumbrian) types; frames bulky; faces of short-oval or oblong form; jaws rather massive; noses short, and usually straight; brows arched; foreheads and chins broad. Complexions generally light; eyes much more often light gray than blue; various shades of grayish-hazel and light brown are common, but brown more common than clear hazel; the eyes are often full and prominent. Hair of a light sandy-red is common; so are flaxen-yellow and dull brown; black is rare." A remarkably tall blond race occupies the hundreds of Flegg, in the north-east of Norfolk, where the local names are Danish.* On the other hand, the people of Yarmouth seem to be comparatively dark†; and so, it is said, are those of Brandon, a small town where flint-working is thought to have been carried on since prehistoric times‡ (Nos. 224—228).

In Essex I think that there was a considerable survival of the Romano-Britons; and that though the invading Saxons preponderate near the coast, it is not so in the interior forest country. At Braintree, a Huguenot colony have left their surnames and complexions (Nos. 229—233).

I do not believe that the Saxons ever destroyed London; but they seem to have settled numerously round about, in Middlesex, and perhaps in Surrey.

In the midland and south-midland counties, from the river Lea to the Warwickshire Avon, and from Banbury to Peterborough, it is reasonable to suppose that the British or pre-Saxon element would remain in larger proportion than in most parts of England. This region lay remote from the great foci of invasion, from the Southampton Water and the Humber: it was cut off from East Anglia by the almost impassable fens, and many parts of it were densely wooded. It probably long protected both its own natives and British fugitives from other less fortunate districts. Accordingly we find here, at and about Stratford, Rugby, Heyford, Northampton, and Dunstable, a larger proportion of dark hair and a higher index of nigrescence than elsewhere. In the

---

* See Mr. Waller's Report in *Stature and Bulk*.

† My observations there, however, cannot be relied on, as they were taken when the town was full of strangers from London and elsewhere.

‡ Mr. Park Harrison.

south-eastern portion of the region both the darkness of the hair and eyes and the breadth of the head may have been further increased by the French immigration after the Norman conquest, which has been shown to have been large in Bedfordshire and some adjoining counties. If Aylesbury is an apparent exception, we must remember that its rich vale very early tempted the West Saxons to occupy it, as the Chronicle specially informs us they did (Nos. 212—216, 220, 221).

East Worcestershire, again (No. 209), was one of Ceawlin's acquisitions; and that he not merely conquered, but also colonised it, would appear from the fact that its dialect is still Saxon rather than Anglian, still of the southern type, though it was early transferred from the sovereignty of Wessex to that of Mercia. Accordingly, its index of nigrescence is somewhat lower than that of the region to the east of it. The physical type here seems to be a cross between the Saxon and the Iberian,* forms not too dissimilar, except in colour, to blend easily; and the resulting features are more regular and comely, on the whole, than those of the mingled breed in Central Mercia.

Cheshire and Salop were colonised, apparently, by the Mercian Angles from Staffordshire.† Patronymics in SON are pretty common here, which is one of the reasons that incline me to think that termination was Anglian, and not only Scandinavian.‡ On the Dee, and along the western border of Salop, the British population must have remained on the land; and I have no doubt that in the hilly country west of the Severn, in Worcestershire as well as Shropshire, they were always the majority. This applies also to the whole of Herefordshire, of which indeed Archeafield (the Trans-Wye country) and some portions of the west border, beyond Offa's Dyke, were never Saxonised. I have spoken already (cap. xii.) of the long-continued reflux of the Welsh over the whole of the Marches, which has rendered the preponderance of native physical types, especially in the lower and middle classes, very conspicuous (Nos. 198—204, 208, 210).

In Oxfordshire, at least in the central part (No. 217), the West-Saxon element is very strong; and hence, extending up the valley of the Thames, it affects a great part of the Cotswolds, the hill country of Gloucestershire, and even the Severn valley, as far as to the Severn. The city of Gloucester is supposed to have survived its conquest by Ceawlin: its market and streets stand pretty much on the original sites. To the Forest of Dean, the part of the county beyond the river, applies

* Hyde Clarke conjectures that the natives of the Severn valley were Iberians, not so thoroughly Celticised, even in the 6th century, as to prevent their joining the Saxons against their Cymric rulers; they were, he thinks, the Lloegrians of the early Welsh poems. One may go so far with him as to recollect, and lay some stress upon, the recency of the Cymric conquest.

† See, however, p. 70 for a possible qualification of this statement.

‡ It is true there was a small Scandinavian settlement in Wirrall, the peninsula between the estuaries of the Mersey and the Dee.

what has been said of Herefordshire. The peculiar institutions of the miners there date back to a Roman or pre-Roman period,* and the physical type of the inhabitants does not seem to have altered materially in the meanwhile. The hair is generally dark, the head long, the cheek-bones prominent in the face: on the whole, the aspect is perhaps rather Gaelic than what we call Iberian (Nos. 293—298). The Severn is a distinct ethnological frontier: the contrast between the country people in the Eastgate Street of Gloucester, on a market-day, and those who come across the Bridge from the Forest side, is extremely striking.

Returning eastwards, to London, neither my own figures, nor the military statistics, nor those of the Anthropometric Committee, indicate any great difference between the Londoners and the inhabitants of the British Isles taken generally, as regards colour of hair and eyes. Perhaps the eyes are a little darker than they should be by calculation. If, however, we restrict the examination to the twelve or fifteen counties immediately surrounding London, from which more than half of its immigrants are drawn,† we shall find that the difference is quite small, as most of the sixteen south-eastern counties of England have an excessive proportion of dark eyes. And perhaps the foreign immigration is, or has been, sufficient to account for any excess of dark hair.

In some of the central, yet, if one may use the word, secluded, districts of London, such as Clerkenwell—where, if anywhere, the genuine hereditary London artisan is abundant—I am satisfied that the colours are a little darker than elsewhere. On the other hand, in the upper classes met with in the West End, at garden *fêtes* and in fashionable streets, who are generally, of course, not natives of London, the colours of both hair and eyes are considerably lighter (Nos. 234, 237).

There is still room for much investigation in Kent. In the north and east Teutonic types preponderate, with light or brown hair: one in particular, with very prominent profile, is claimed by Mackintosh and Harrison as Jutic (plate 2), and is said to be frequent also in the Isle of Wight and the land of Meon in Hampshire. With regard to the question of Norman-French immigration, see the table of surnames and the notes on the skulls of the Hythe ossuary. Romney Marsh and the neighbouring portion of the Weald seem to be much more British, if we may judge by the darker hues‡ (Nos. 238—241).

So are parts, at least, of the Weald of Sussex, the Andred's Wald, into which Ella drove the natives; but the greater part of Sussex is pretty strongly Saxon. About Chichester, the starting-point of the Conquest, the Saxon type is very conspicuous. Regular features; elliptic

---

* See the papers of Mr. John Bellows on the local archæology and the table of measurements of skulls in this work.

† Ravenstein, p. 21.

‡ Dr. F. Cock, in *Stature and Bulk*, pp. 90, 91. Mr. Grant Allen colours this district as probably British.

head and face; brows moderately arched; nose straight, often rounded or bulbous at point; mouth well moulded; complexion fair, and transparent; eyes well opened, iris seldom large, of a beautiful clear blue, but sometimes brown or hazel; hair flaxen or brown of various shades, seldom bright, curly, or abundant (Nos. 242—246).

Hampshire also, another starting-point of Saxon colonisation, bears witness to the fact by the blond character of the population. The "Jutic" type is said to abound in the Isle of Wight. About Southampton the one just described is prominent, with a frame not very tall or broad, but plump and rounded. The Hampshire peasantry are accused of being stolid and selfish; they require cultivation to develop their better qualities* (Nos. 250—252).

The New Forest is said to have retained a primitive population; I have never visited it. But the Saxon and Frisian types undoubtedly spread from this centre far to the north and west, predominating in a great part of Berkshire and central Oxfordshire, and occupying in force the valleys which radiate from Salisbury among the Wiltshire downs. The differences between the several districts of Wiltshire are curious, yet almost always easily explicable. Thus the Heytesbury and Wilton valley has a blond population; in and around the royal manor of Chippenham a Saxon type predominates. On the other hand, the secluded vale of Calne, the frontier town of Devizes ("the Divises"), and Malmesbury, with its old abbey of Celtic foundation, all yield higher indices of nigrescence. Were the Malmesbury men still Wealas in any sense, when "Athelstan, the bracelet-giver," bestowed on them the lands they still enjoy, as a meed for their loyal prowess at the Brunanburgh fight? (Nos. 247—249, 253—259).

Immediately to the south-west of the Saxon vale of the Wiley lies a hilly tract, respecting which Rowland Williams, then vicar of Broad Chalk, told me he thought his parishioners were of pre-Celtic race. Beyond this again, beyond Mere (the Mark), about Wincanton in Somerset and Gillingham in Dorset, the dark hair and high cheekbones (perhaps a legacy of the Belgæ) have nothing in common with the blond, smooth-featured Saxons of Wilton. Selwood and the hills protected these parts for a while, I doubt not, both from those invaders who pushed up the Wiley, and from those who swarmed up the Dorsetshire river-valleys from Poole Harbour, and who have made the blond types common from Wareham to Yeovil. Between these last and the sea, again, according to Mr. Kerslake,† the dedications of the churches to

---

* Very light brown or flaxen hair, with little mixture of red or yellow, such as is common in the Saxon part of England, is not seldom conjoined with beard and whiskers of a *darker* shade of brown. Flaxen hair is uncommon in the so-called Celtic countries, where a very pale yellow seems to take its place, accompanied usually by a *red* beard. See some remarks of Mme. Clemence Royer, in the discussions of the Paris Society, reported in their *Bulletins.*   † *The Welsh in Dorset,* by T. Kerslake.

British saints indicate a later period and a more merciful character of conquest (Nos. 260—262).

Proceeding westward, and passing by Bristol for the present, we find the index of nigrescence slowly increasing. Almost everywhere in Somerset it is greater than in Wiltshire, or than in Gloucestershire east of the Severn; nevertheless, everywhere perhaps, except in the S.E., about Wincanton, and in the western mountainous district about Exmoor, the Saxon type is more or less represented (Nos. 281—286).

Devon comes next, a county whose ethnology has been much fought over. Here the military schedules desert me, and agree better with those of the Anthropometric Committee, which give this county a medium position as respects colour. As my hospital statistics bear out my local observations, I have no doubt of the correctness of the latter, which embraced over 2,000 individuals. The people of Devon are for the most part dark-haired, and the Gaelic combination of blue or gray eyes with dark brown or blackish hair is very frequent among them. When the eyes are hazel, on the other hand, the hair is not seldom lightish. In the district about Dartmouth, where the Celtic language lingered for centuries, the index of nigrescence is at its maximum, exceeding 50. But around the estuaries of the Taw, the Torridge, the Tamar, and perhaps the Exe, Frisian or Danish settlements seem to have been effected. In these localities there is a large proportion of blonds, which in the case of Plymouth affects the neighbouring part of Cornwall to some extent. The anomaly in the military statistics is partly explicable by the large number of men enlisted for both army and navy at Plymouth. The Devonians are usually rather short and strongly made, with heads of good size and considerable occipital projection. The singular beauty of the women depends in great part, apparently, on the very soft and mild climate, whence a peculiar delicacy and softness of both outline and complexion (Nos. 263—273).

Cornwall nourishes a stalwart race, superior to the Devonians in stature and length of limb; the miners, again, seem to surpass the agricultural population, though of this I have not statistical proof. In each case there may have been a process of selection, for Cornwall probably gave the last refuge to the free British warriors, who were gradually forced back by the West Saxons into the peninsula, while their serfs, accustomed to the yoke, may have bowed their necks for the most part to that of the strangers. The stature, as deduced by Roberts and Rawson from 305 observations, is 5 ft. 7·9 in., or 1·726 metre; and I do not think this is over the mark. The Cornish are generally dark in hair and often in eye: they are decidedly the darkest people in England proper; they resemble the Scottish Highlanders in their warmth of colouring, and probably Dr. Sorby would find a large substratum of red or yellow under their dark brown and black. The point which comes out most distinctly from my head-measurements is

DEVONSHIRE.   CORNWALL.   CORNWALL.

BRONZE TYPE, FROM CUMBRIA.   SC. HIGHLANDS.

WEST OF KERRY.   ARANMORE I.   SC. HIGHLANDS.

the prominence of the glabella and (probably also) of the brow-ridges. To these may be added, more doubtfully, a receding forehead, a head much arched longitudinally, and broad about the parietal eminences. All these points, it will be observed, are common to the bronze race. A fine specimen was portrayed by Holbein, in the person of John Roscorla. All the British types, however, occur in Cornwall, and the most characteristic is, I think, Iberian with a dash of the Semitic; of this a fine example has been figured in the person of one John Penhaligan. Barnard Davis was struck with the heaviness of the mouth and lower part of the nose; this is a common feature among the earlier races of Britain, but is certainly not universal in Cornwall (Nos. 274—280).

The observations made at Bristol are very numerous (Nos. 287—291). The colours come out very much like those of the surrounding districts; so do the head forms. The differences between the sexes are the usual ones, but are very small; the males have, if anything, the darker hair, the females the darker eyes. The middle are slightly, the upper decidedly, fairer than the lower classes.

This may be the best place for referring to the West of England table, whereof the materials were collected at Bristol, the birthplace of every individual having been ascertained. It very strongly favours the influence of race on colour, as opposed to that of media. What is otherwise a bewildering confusion of figures, falls into something like order when viewed in connexion with ethnographical history and probabilities. These explain at once how it is that the natives of towns, descendants of a shifting and migratory population, almost always tend more towards the general standard of the country, than do those of the neighbouring rural districts. The hypothesis—the truth of which few, if any, doubt—that the invading Teutons were fairer than the prior inhabitants of this part of Britain, explains at once why we find a regular gradation from light to dark as we proceed from the Saxons and Frisians* of Wiltshire through Gloucestershire and East Somerset to North Devon, and then to West Somerset (Exmoor, &c.) and South Devon, a gradation which appears to me to be attended with a gradual change in the prevailing form of the cranium, if not of the trunk and limbs. Beyond the Severn, in like manner, the type becomes more purely Welsh as we proceed from the coast towards the interior. In the warm low lands of Monmouthshire and Glamorgan, the ancient seats of Saxon, Norman, and Flemish colonisation, I find the index of hair-colour so low as 33·5, and the proportion of dark eyes to light, 63; while in the cold, rainy, and mountainous interior, if we exclude the children of English and Irish immigrants, the figures rise to 57·3 and 109·5, the last ratio indicating a prevalence of dark eyes

---

* I do not, of course, mean that the Wiltshire men are anything like *pure* Saxons or Frisians. I should be quite satisfied if it were granted that they were at least half Saxon.

beyond what I have met with in any other part of Britain. There is no possible explanation of these phenomena except that of heredity.

The statistics for Wales give several very distinct indications; they represent the Welsh as a generally dark-haired and often dark-eyed people, among whom the Gaelic combination is common; but the opposite one, of dark eyes with chestnut or lightish hair, is by no means rare. This latter is not derived from a Flemish cross, for it is equally noticeable in North Wales, where no Flemings settled. It is generally accompanied by broad cheekbones and a short compact build, and by the dark complexion prevalent among the Welsh; and the whole aspect is suggestive of a Turanian origin.*

The inferences that can be drawn from my head-measurements respecting the Welsh are but scanty. From the larger series, of 66, almost all South Welshmen, we may with some confidence put the index of breadth at about 78, somewhat greater than that of the Irish or of the Wiltshire or West Somerset men, but below that of the Eastern Englishman. From the smaller series, of 16, which is included in the greater one, we may infer with less certainty a broad forehead, a small glabella, a somewhat low head, a somewhat short face, and a considerable lateral development of the zygoma. Dark complexions, square foreheads, and sinuous noses prevail; noses more or less aquiline are more common than the concave.

But, in truth, the Welsh are anything but a homogeneous race. The diagram of head-breadth indices confirms other lines of probability, and points towards the presence in force of at least two races in South Wales, not yet thoroughly amalgamated. The characteristics of several types are doubtless smoothed over, and to a great extent neutralised in these averages. Those which come out are not those of the dominant race, the true Kymry, whose purest representatives should be sought in the tall, long-faced, light-eyed, darkish-haired population of Nithsdale Upper Galloway, and the neighbouring region.

For descriptions of the types, the careful observations of Mr. D. Mackintosh,† and the works of Mr. Wirt Sikes, may be consulted with advantage. The meso-cephalic type of the Denbighshire caves (figured by Boyd Dawkins) certainly survives among them; so does the Gaelic, and here and there the long-headed one of the chambered barrows. A very Welsh feature, noted by Mackintosh, and belonging to more than one of his types, is the hollowness of the cheeks, the sudden sinking-in below the malar bones.

The account which Giraldus de Barry gives of his countrymen is extremely interesting, and may still, after 700 years, be read with instruction. Incidentally he lets us know that they were then, as now, of swarthy complexion. "Nature," he says, "has given to the Welsh,

---

* See cap. ii., pp. 9—12.

† "Comparative Anthropology of England and Wales," *Anthrop. Review*, 1866, p. 8.

of all ranks, boldness of speech and confidence in answering before princes and nobles: we see that the Romans and French have the same gift of nature, but not the English nor the Germans." He ascribes this, not to servitude, but to a liquid and cold complexion of nature, derived from their neighbourhood to the pole, whereas the Britons "ex calidâ et adustâ Dardaniæ plagâ,* quanquam in fines hos temperatos advecti, quia cælum non animum, &c., tam exterius fuscum illum cognotumque terræ colorem, quam etiam naturalem interius et adusto humore colorem, unde securitas, originaliter trahunt."

The rest of his description of their character is so vivid and striking that it may be quoted with advantage. It presses very hardly on the worst points of the Welsh character; but some of the vices which he alleges are those with which their enemies still charge them.

" They are inconstant," he says, "mobile: they have no respect for their oaths, for their promises, for the truth: they will give their right hands in attestation of truth, even in joke: they are always ready for perjury."

" They attack fiercely, with much noise; if repulsed, they flee as in terror, but as readily return to the charge. They are given to digging up boundary fences, and removing landmarks: they are continually having lawsuits about land. They are abstinent in need, and temperate by habit; but will gorge themselves at another's expense: no one wastes his own substance out of gluttony as the English do; but they are ostentatious in vieing with others." He mentions their love and talent for music, and says that they could sing in three parts, whereas the English, *except the Northumbrians,*† could only sing in one: the Northumbrians sang in two parts.

Vengefulness is also noted as a characteristic by Giraldus, and withal love of race and family, regard for high birth and carefulness about genealogies. This last quality does undoubtedly belong to the Welsh, and makes it strange that they have not contrived for themselves a better system of surnames.

Miss F. P. Cobb,‡ comparing them with the Irish, denies to both of these races the possession of any love of order and regularity, or of æsthetic capacity except in music, while allowing to both an imaginative temperament, a quick understanding, a strong religious instinct, and warm domestic affections. "In both," she adds, "the love of justice and of truth, the backbone of every worthy Englishman's nature, is replaced by the imperfect substitute of personal loyalty or general kindliness." Prudence, frugality, caution, and secretiveness distinguish the Welshman, however, from the Irishman. They have a common element, in both physical and moral nature; but their

* Whence he conceived them to have immigrated.
† The Yorkshiremen are still the most naturally musical people in England.
‡ " The Celt of Wales and the Celt of Ireland," *Cornhill Magazine,* 1877.

differences are as well marked as their likenesses, and there is said to be more antipathy than sympathy between them, whereas the Irishman and the Scottish Highlander easily coalesce.

I have said little of differences between the North and the South Welshman. They are not greater, I think, than obtain between several districts of the two main divisions. The Flemings of the south have been spoken of. The Kymric type is stronger in the north-eastern counties than elsewhere. The Snowdonians, in spite of the Rev. T. Price, the earliest regular observer of eye-colour, are a very dark race (Nos. 300—325).

Though the ethnological history of Wales, so far as it goes back, is simple enough, while that of Ireland is very complicated, the descriptive anthropology of the latter is a much easier subject.

Throughout the greater part of Ireland one distinct type of man decidedly predominates; and to describe it is easy, though to explain its origin and constitution may be difficult.

As regards colour, the frequency of light eyes and of dark hair, the two often combined, is the leading characteristic. Sir W. Wilde found in 1,130 Irishmen, from all parts of the country, but in large proportion from Dublin and its neighbourhood, the following averages:—Blue Eyes, 34·1 per cent.; Gray Eyes, 54·6; Hazel Eyes, 2·4; and Brown Eyes, 8·8. Doubtless many of these grays must have been of a deep shade, but it would be difficult to find so small a proportion of really brown eyes anywhere, except in the Western Highlands and in Scandinavia. The Anthropometric Committee found in 346 persons, 25·6 per cent. of brown or hazel eyes. The Military Statistics, dealing with upwards of 2000, yield less than 30 per cent. of "dark" eyes; and my own, including 700 of the upper class and 9,266 of the general population, give for the former 10·6 neutral and 24·3 dark, and for the latter 14·3 neutral (mostly dark gray) and 18·3 dark, some of which may have been dark blues, grays, or violets, indistinctly seen, rather than brown or hazel.

It is worth noting that the upper class of the Irish are darker in eye, though considerably lighter in hair, than the lower classes. Thus the indices of nigrescence of the upper, in Dublin and in Cork, were 14 and 21·4 (see Irish table), and those of the lower class in the same cities respectively 33 and 34·2. The cause of the discrepancy is the large infusion of English blood in the landed and professional classes of Ireland. In 1,181 persons, who attended a ball given by the Lord Mayor of Dublin, an archery meeting at Kilkenny, and an agricultural show meeting in South Mayo, the proportions of the surnames were as follows:

English and Scotch.	Doubtful.	Irish.
78·9	3·7	17·3

and those of the three lists taken separately were nearly the same.

I have already shown that the proportion of native surnames among Irish recruits, on an average of the whole country, is about 58 per cent.; and even this ratio I believe inadequately to represent that obtaining among the peasantry.

In the personal observation table for Ireland, the localities are arranged in an ascending scale of depth of colour of hair; and it will be seen from the figures, and from the illustrative maps, that blonds are most numerous on and near the eastern coast, and brunets towards the west, whither they have been driven by successive invasions. There are a few exceptions to the rule, mostly explicable.

Under 30 per cent. of nigrescence come, as has been already stated, the upper classes in Dublin and Cork, with the people of Enniskillen, Youghal, Cloyne, and the neighbourhood, of Cashel and Cahir in Tipperary, of Charleville in Limerick, of Waterford town and Wexford county, of Kilkenny, and of some other parts of Leinster. The index in these cases is comparable with that found in most parts of England; but in no case is it nearly so low as in many parts of the north and east of that country or of Scotland.

Between 30 and 50 per cent. ranks the general population of Cork and Dublin, of Drogheda and Kildare, of Killarney in Kerry, of Collooney in Sligo, of Joyce's Country in Galway, of some districts about Cork, and of the county of Fermanagh with Western Cavan; also the people of the fishermen's quarter in Galway, called the Claddagh. Most parts of the Scottish Highlands would come in here.

Between 50 and 70 ranks the largest number of districts; viz., the counties of Longford and Leitrim, most part of those of Sligo, Roscommon, and Galway, with the town of Galway and the Aran Isles, Athlone, Pettigo in South Donegal, Dingle in Kerry, and Cappoguin in Waterford. The indices here equal those met with in Wales and Cornwall. Lastly, over 70 come several districts in the west of Kerry, with Clifden in Connemara, Jar-Connaught, Moytura in the hills between Sligo and Roscommon, and Mallow in county Cork. Such a preponderance of dark hair does not, I believe, occur anywhere in Great Britain; it ranges with that found in Auvergne, Savoy, and Northern Italy.

The colour of the iris tends on the whole to be darker where the hair is darker; but there is no approach to uniformity in this respect. The largest proportion of dark eyes was found at Moytura and at Pettigo. But there is no exception to the rule that light eyes greatly preponderate, and that the hair, except in the upper class, is pro-portionally much darker than the eyes.

The Irish skull inclines to be long, low, and narrow, but little more so than the English or Welsh skull: the average latitudinal index is about 75; the size and capacity are good; the point of maximum breadth is usually placed far back; in profile the prominence of the upper occipital region, and the flattening about the after part of the sagittal suture, are the most notable points; in a vertical view, the flattening of the temporo-sphenoidal region, and the somewhat angular salience of the part abaft the ear, noticed by Daniel Wilson and Massy as belonging to their Celtic type. The cheekbones are prominent in the face, but the zygomata not much expanded.

This form prevails extensively in most other parts of Ireland, as well as in the west, and is identical with that exhibited by most of the few primeval Irish skulls I have had the opportunity of examining, and which may be seen in the museums of Dublin and Kilkenny.*

Of forty-one skulls in the Barnard Davis collection, only two were brachycephalic; and of thirty-eight heads measured by us in Kerry, only one would have been brachycephalic (exceeding the index of 80) in the skull. Yet, as has been stated already, the average Irish skull is not very much narrower than the average skull of Great Britain.† The Irish are more homogeneous, and extremes in the form of the head are rare, as are also extremes in stature.

The physiognomy of the Irish, as distinguished from the English, Welsh, and Scotch, is best studied in the west and south-west, where there has been least immigration. Apart from that, one type probably predominates in almost all parts of the country. Davis well says‡ that it is easily seen to be derived from the cranial conformation. The leading feature is the level eyebrow, surmounting low deep orbits.

The average stature of the 346 Irishmen included in the final report of the Anthropometric Committee amounts to 5 ft. 7·9 in. (1·725 metre). I found that of 1,500 adult Irish recruits to be 5 ft. 7·25 in. (1·709 metre). This is raised by the existence of a minimum standard. Baxter, dealing with upwards of 30,000 recruits of Irish birth, got an average of 5 ft. 6·74 in. (1·696 metre), that of his Englishmen being only 5 ft. 6·58 in. Taking these data, and comparing those gotten from Irish criminals and lunatics, and their ratios to the same classes in England and Scotland, I do not believe the entire male adult population would average over 5 ft. 7 in. (1·703 metre), though Mr. Roberts would put it higher.

We may now sketch rapidly a few of the local varieties:

The people of Forth and Bargy baronies, which form the southern peninsula of the county of Wexford, are said to be descendants of a

---

* See Carter Blake's description of the Louth Abbey skull, in vol. ii. of the *Anthropological Memoirs*.

† Of thirty-nine English skulls in the Barnard Davis collection, about seven appear to be brachycephalic.

‡ *Thesaurus Craniorum*, p. 70.

colony from Pembrokeshire. Their character is said to be more English than Irish, and I should say the same of their appearance. It will be remembered that southern Pembrokeshire is more Anglo-Flemish than Welsh.

North and west of these baronies, in the county of Wexford, and in the city and neighbourhood of Waterford, appears, as I have said elsewhere, a tall fair race, which extends, with some modification, up the northern bank of the Suir, across the Golden Vale of Tipperary, into the county of Limerick. The Wexford men, among whom countenances quite Norwegian in aspect are pretty numerous, have the reputation of being peaceable and industrious, but bold and fierce when roused: they were the backbone of the rebellion of '98. There is said to be much Cromwellian blood in southern Tipperary, and undoubtedly the English surnames in the Golden Vale are numerous; but the prevailing type, though very often brilliantly fair, is not English. The turbulence and pugnacity of the Tipperary men is proverbial.

In Kilkenny the English element is very strong, and of old date.

I know very little of Ulster. Though there are in it large districts where the majority of the population is of English or Scottish descent, this is far from being the case in other parts of the province. Donegal, for example, is pretty purely Irish. In the west of Cavan may be found, I think, the breed to which Sir William Wilde referred, as the descendants of the Tuatha de Danaan. They are fair, large-limbed, comely, smooth-featured, and *appear* to have broader heads than other Irishmen·

The Hiberno-Norse type appears in other neighbourhoods besides Wexford and Waterford. It is not extinct about Cork,* nor yet about Limerick, where, after the sack of the city by the Munster Irish, the annalists say, with their usual hyperbole, that there was not a dwelling without a woman of the Gentiles grinding at the hand-mill.

Though there are other primitive types of feature in the west of Ireland, the one already referred to as correlated with the skull-type is by far the most conspicuous. The following description was drawn from the people about Ventry and Cahirciveen, in the far west of Kerry: The men are of good stature, and many of them approach 6 feet; they have square, but not very broad, shoulders. Their heads are long; they project about the occiput, but are not large in the cerebellar region. The nasal notch is deep, the brows are prominent and square; but the frontal sinuses apparently not large, the glabella being inconspicuous. The forehead is flat, of good breadth apparently; it recedes somewhat, and the hair, which is profuse and wavy, but seldom strongly curled, grows low upon it. The upper part of the head presents a regular gentle curve. The nose is generally long and sinuous, except in those

* The type is well represented in many of the pictures of Maclise, especially in his last work, "The Earl of Desmond and the Butlers." Maclise was a native of Cork, and drew Cork features.

(a decided minority) who are notably prognathous, in whom it is generally of moderate length and somewhat concave: in either case it is
pointed, and has the true Gaelic nostril, which is long and narrow, and
often conspicuously visible. Quite a due proportion, perhaps more, of
the fairer people belong to the prognathous class. This is a little
strange, as in the west of England prognathousness goes with dark hair.
The eyes are light gray, bluish-gray, ash-gray, dark sea-gray (*bleu de mer
foncé* of De Belloguet), often with a dark rim round the iris, or brown;
hazel is rare, and so is clear china-blue; they are narrow in men, and
wrinkles appear about them early. The common colour of hair is a
dark brown, approaching black; but coal-black is very frequent. Red,
and a sort of sandy-flaxen hue, also occur pretty often; medium brown
is (comparatively) rather uncommon. The cheek bones and zygomata
are rather broad; the mouth coarse, often open; the lips thick; the
teeth good; the chin rather narrow, with little depression between it
and the lip. The lower jaw is narrow, and ascends steeply from near
the chin to the ear, and there is often but a slight fold between this and
the stemomastoid muscle.

Intermixed with this type, which is evidently closely related to the
one which dominates in the West Highlands of Scotland, occurs, in
smaller proportion, the Sancho Panza type of H. Maclean,* with short
stature, large head, shorter and squarer face, coarse features, and cocked
nose; also, more rarely, one which reminds one of the true Celtic type
of France, with a large and broad head, and a face rather broad than
long: in this the lower jaw, though broad, is angular, not rounded with
a regular curve as in the Batavian. There are several local variations
in county Galway. In its eastern part, and in the east of Clare, there
is more fair and light red hair. In the Claddagh (fishermen's quarter)
of Galway, there is more of yellow and less of dark hair than in the
town, and the observation applies to other fishing villages in Ireland.
In the limestone country about Cong, and in Joyce's Country, the
colours are lighter and the features less angular: the Joyce clan are
English on the paternal side. Here and among the O'Flaherties the
people are tall; but the Connemara people are generally short, and
depart in some respects from the common type, having less angularity
of cheek bones and chin, and less prominence of mouth; the forehead
looks broad and low; the greatest breadth of face is at the level of the
eyes. Light eyes predominate, as usual; the combination of dark-gray
with black hair is very common, and dark hair and complexion attain
their maximum. There are in Connemara clans considered as of servile
origin.†

* See Ante, table on the Highland types.

† *E.g.*, the Kinealys. One of these, who was pointed out to me as a specimen, was
short, with a broad round face, shortish head, and oblique eyebrows: altogether a
Turanian aspect. I had no opportunity of measuring his head.

The people of the Aran Isles, in Galway Bay, have their own very strongly marked type,* in some respects an exaggeration of the ordinary Gaelic one, the face being remarkably long, the chin very long and narrow, but not angular ; the nose long, straight, and pointed ; the brows straight, or rising obliquely outwards ; the eyes light, with very few exceptions ; the hair of various colours, but usually dark brown. We might be disposed, trusting to Irish traditions respecting the islands, to accept these people as representatives of the Firbolg, had not Cromwell, that upsetter of all things Hibernian, left in Aranmore a small English garrison, who subsequently apostatised to Catholicism, intermarried with the natives, and so vitiated the Firbolgian pedigree.

The military returns show that the people of Mayo have the Irish colour-type in a high degree. Further east, in the mountains about the battle-field of the northern Moytura,† between Sligo and Roscommon, I met with the swarthiest people I have ever seen. Seven out of thirty-three had quite black hair, and many had dark eyes. A few had handsome features of the so-called Kimbrian type, rather short heads, spade faces, and aquiline noses, and might have been Walloons ; but most of them approached the commoner types ; still, I was more reminded of the South Welsh than anywhere else in Ireland.

There are several islands off the west coast, besides Aranmore, which it might repay an anthropologist to visit. I have had the privilege of seeing but one of them, Inismurray, county Sligo. There "the barbarous people received us with no little kindness." Barbarous they were, however, inasmuch as they grew up, as the "Queen" of the Island told me, "all the same as cattles." They were a decidedly fair race, and not uncomely : a few had remarkably long faces, narrow, but with the usual projection of the malar bones, very pointed chins, and aquiline noses. They might have been descendants of the savage men whom Giraldus's informants met with in a skin canoe, off the coast of Connaught, who rarely wore clothing, but "had long yellow hair, like the Irish, falling below their shoulders and covering most of their bodies."‡

I cannot recollect that Giraldus, who is so distinct as to the complexion of his own countrymen, ever alludes to that of the Irish, unless in the above passage. Neither does Froissart, nor, perpaps, any other mediæval writer ; though several of them speak of their stature, strength and agility. The following is a numerical expression of the complexions

* See table of skull measurements for mediæval or ancient skulls from Aran.

† Part of No. 43 in the Irish table. See Sir W. Wilde's address in the Military and Militia Statistics. Sligo and Roscommon show a larger proportion of dark eyes than most parts of Ireland.

‡ Giraldus, quoted by Elton, *Origins of English History*, pp. 178—9.

or colour of skin prevalent in several parts of Britain.   They are given
in percentages ; but in each case the number observed was 50 :

COMPLEXION.

	Fair.	Intermediate.	Dark.
E. and N. of England...	74	14	12
Wiltshire	54	30	16
Bristol	54	24	22
Highlands	48	30	22
Munster	38	26	36
Devon	36	22	42
South Wales	24	28	48

Here both the men of Munster and of Devon come out darker than
might have been expected, considering the soft moisture of the climate.
The colour of the skin seems to be correlated with that of the hair
more nearly than with that of the eyes ; but where both these are
comparatively dark, as is the case in South Wales, the maximum of
swarthiness is reached.

Ancient Irish poetry indicates that there was always great variety of
complexion and hair-colour among the people, but that blue eyes and
yellow hair were most characteristic of the higher ranks, or ruling caste.
Some heroes however are described as having blue eyes and *black* hair,
with a clear skin and ruddy cheeks, a combination very rare out of
Ireland.

I think it probable that the military caste or stratum of the Irish, at
the time of the Anglo-Norman invasion, was fairer than the bulk of the
population, and that it has been more reduced, in comparison, by
slaughter and emigration, while at the same time the fairer races of
Great Britain have largely supplied its place.

FINAL CHAPTER.

Conclusions and Inconclusions.

THAT the colour of the hair is so nearly permanent in races of men as to be fairly trustworthy evidence in the matter of ethnical descent.

That nearly as much may be said for the colour of the iris.

That the Index of Nigrescence, even when uncombined with any system of appraising the colour of the iris, but still more decidedly when so combined, is preferable, for the exhibition of race-differences, to the Rein-blond and Rein-brun method.

That in Britain, and especially in Ireland, the colour of the hair and of the iris are very far from varying in direct ratio with each other.

That though blonds may have been numerous among some earlier races of invaders, and particularly among the bronze race, the greater part of the blond population of modern Britain—or, at all events, of the eastern parts—derive their ancestry from the Anglo-Saxons and Scandinavians. That a comparison of the Indices of Nigrescence in the continental regions whence these last-named invaders came with those found in the parts of the British Isles where they settled, and those of the purest Gaelic and so-called Celtic stocks, leads towards the conclusion that in some parts of the east and north Anglo-Saxon or Scandinavian blood predominates, and that in the greater part of England it amounts to something like a half.

For example, if we put the index of Friesland and Lower Saxony at about − 20, and that of West Cornwall and of Carmarthenshire (neither of which districts is free from Anglo-Saxon intermixture), at + 60, the mean, + 20, may be expected to represent a mixed population, in which these two stocks are of nearly equal potency. On examination of the coloured map, constructed from personal observation, it will be found that a very large part of England, and almost the entire east of Scotland, yield indices lower than + 20, and, by hypothesis, should have a larger proportion of the Saxon than of the Welsh element in the blood of the people.*

* It is not very long since educated opinion considered the English and Lowland Scots an almost purely Teutonic people. Now the current runs so much the other way that I have had to take up the attitude of an apologist of the " Saxon " view.

That the prevailing head-forms and facial features in England are such as to fortify the conclusion arrived at by the study of hair-colour.

That though the heads of educated men in Great Britain are somewhat larger than those of the uneducated, there is no evidence to support Schaafhausen's notion that civilisation turns dolichocephals into brachycephals.

That the French immigration, subsequent to the Norman Conquest, was large enough to produce a definite ethnological effect in some of the eastern and southern parts of England. That this effect was greater in North and East Yorkshire, and less in most parts of Kent, than the respective positions of these counties would have led one to expect.

That the proportion of English and Scotch blood in the present inhabitants of Ireland is, probably, not much less than a third.

That a large proportion—in some parts as large as a third—of the present inhabitants of the counties adjacent to Wales is descended from Welsh immigrants.

That in the absence of trustworthy evidence as to a change of colour-type in Britain, in the direction from light to dark, it is best to rest upon the undoubted fact that the Gaelic and Iberian races of the west, mostly dark-haired, are tending to swamp the blond Teutons of England by a reflux migration. At the same time, the possible effects of conjugal selection, of selection through disease, and of the relative increase of the darker types through the more rapid multiplication of the artizan class, who are in England generally darker than the upper classes, should be kept in view. The effect of phthisis in this direction is *nil*, as it is more prevalent among the dark-haired.

That sundry important problems respecting the Picts; the origin of the modern Gaelic type, and particularly of the prognathous element therein; the complexion of some of the " Celts " of history; the presence of Ugrian or Turanian tribes in Britain, &c., &c., remain yet unsolved. The Iberian origin of the Picts is somewhat favoured by the colour phenomena in Wigtonshire, and Keith and Huntley. The physical type of the modern Gael in Ireland and Scotland, and of their apparent kinsmen in parts of Wales and the West of England, is, on the whole, best accounted for, perhaps, by a cross of the Iberian with a long-faced, harsh-featured, red-haired race, who contributed the language and much of the character. If only the Belgæ had spoken Gaelic, as Dr. Guest believed, the difficulty might not have been so great: the attendants of Jovinus are not unlike modern Gaels, and the Milesians may have been a tribe of the same cross, who passed through Spain. The great geographical extension of this type in the British Isles makes it more likely that it was generated by a crossing effected on the Continent than that it was produced *in situ*. So does the similarity in colour, though the effect of climate through selection during many ages may, possibly, have lightened the eyes. All our Gaels dwell in moist climates and under cloudy skies, and all have light eyes and dark hair—or, at least, eyes lighter than their hair.

But a truce with speculation! It has been the writer's aim rather to lay a sure foundation; rather to test, and reject unsound material; rather to prepare some small part of a solid platform, whereon insight and genius may ultimately build, than himself to erect an edifice of wood and stubble, which may make a fair show for a day, and then be consumed by the testing fire. If these remaining questions are worthy and capable of solution, they will be solved only by much patient labour, and by the co-operation of anthropologists with antiquarians and philologists; so that so much of the blurred and defaced prehistoric inscription as is left in shadow by one light may be brought into prominence and illumination by another.

FINIS.

APPENDIX A.

Part 1.

MALMESBURY—TENANTS OF THE ABBEY, 12TH EDWARD (II.?)

NORMAN : *doubtless*—De Ba.

        believed—Malone, Katelyne.

        probable—Blaunchard, Spigurnel, Patyne, de la Loupe, de Schowell.

        nicknames—le Jevene, la longe, Bonenfaunt.

LATIN :   "

SAXON :   "   —Aylwyne, Edrich, Sebern, Wolrich, Aldwyne[2], Harding, Alneth, Edwy, Aylmere, Selewyne, Serich, Colewyne.

        probable—Wixi, Cunn, Wygewold.

ENGLISH : *nicknames*—la Rede[2], la Red[21], Snel[2], Tredegold ? la Stronge, le Mey[2], Springald, Niweman, Broun, Red[3], le Oter, le Wyte, le Fader, le Wyse, le Flynt, le Fox, Broun[2]?, Mydewinter, le Byrd, le Gouk, le Overniweman.

LOCAL : *specific*—de Wyntone, de Cerneye, de Auste[21], de Bathon, de Hanendon, de Cleye, de Wodewike, de Hundle, de Bradefeld, de Bradenstoke, de Chelewrth[2], de Morcote, de Bradenbroke, Dunpory, de Hurdley, Leveslane, de Mordone, de Pyriton, Calston, de Thekedon, de Hanekinton, de Morle, de Hund-lavinton, de Charleton.

        general—de la Wyke[3], North, de Doggedich[3], de Angulo[2], in la Hele[2], de Albomolend, de Ponte[2], de la Pyrie, de Aqua, West, de Fonte, de la Pleystede, de la Lake, de la Chereche, de Fraxino, de Porta, South[2], de la Lane, in la More, Est, de Cimiterio, de Bosco[2], Oppehule[3], de Dounhulle[2], de Mora, de la Forde[2], Halfmark, de Puteo, de Pyro, de la Hethe[2].

        of county—

        of nation (Fr.)—Daungier.

        of other—le Scot.

PATRONYMICS : *general*—Gerard, Herewy, Cunnild, Vincent, Elys[2], Josep, Matheu[2], Payn, Arnald, Bernard[2], Hamund, Clement, Helewys, Ewestas.

    Do. *in* FITZ—F. Henr, F. Helene, F. Alic, F. Helene.

TRADES : *French*—le Vithelare, la Mounere, le Carpenter.

        English—le Irmongar[2], le Chepman, la Coliare, le Wyn.

        Latin—Faber[2].

RURAL : *French*—
    English—le Akerman, Hogeman, le Bor[2].
    Latin—Molendinar[2], Messor, Molend.

OFFICES, &C.: *French*—Marescal, le Bedel, le Paumer[2], le Palmare.
    English—la Frye, Wodeprest, Archer, Alderman[2], le Synegare.
    Latin—Scolas, Propositus[2], le Porter, Capellanus.

DOUBTFUL : le Egede, Sturewowe, Bovetoun, Boye, le Cuf, Doun[2], Pouke, la Bartur[2], Waye, le Suriman, le Cuf.

NAMELESS : Edward.

NORMAN : *doubtless*—
    believed—le Gag, Treypas, Walerond.
    probable—Garleck, Sodel, de Scalera, de la Loupe, Paynel.

FRENCH : *nicknames*—le Noble.

LATIN :   "

SAXON :   " —Cole[2], Ordrich, Dunnig, Donning, Alfred, Alwy.
    probable—Weceke, Blakeman[2], Balle.

ENGLISH : *nicknames*—Niweman, le King, la Wyte Gode, Wreanne, le Hog[2], le Lutle.

LOCAL : *specific*—de Ovorde, de Radeweye[2], de Toghull[3], de Benhull[2], de Wodeford[2], de Gosemere, de Wytechurche, de Radestrop, de Pevenhulle[2], Baseli, Schyrwold, Wateforde, de Wydyhull, de Chippenham.
    general—le Treys, de la Lane, Atthedichende, de la More, de la Hulle, de Pole, de Hoggeslane, de Husted, de la Forde[2], de Puteo.
    of county—
    of nation (Fr.)—Angewyne.
    other—Waleys.

PATRONYMICS : *general*—Stevene, Topas, Ingram, Umbald, Perys, Beneyt, Hereberd, Godefray.
    Do. *in* FITZ—Fil Nichi.

TRADES : *French*—le Barbur, le Carpenter.
    English—le Hattare, le Coliare, le Bothwebbe.
    Latin—Faber.

RURAL : *French*—le Cartare.
    English—Rodeman, le Bor, la Daye.
    Latin—Molend.

OFFICES, &C.: *French*—le Panmer, Frankelayn.
    English—le Ridare, le Buriman, le Bonde, le Frye.
    Latin—

DOUBTFUL : le Pyk, Gorebagge, Blakemore, Wygun, Lynyot, le Mop[2], le Cur[2], Cobbe, le iard, Sodemer, Wrenche.

part 2.

PARISHES OF WILDEN AND RAVENSDEN, IN BEDFORDSHIRE (NORTH), RATEPAYERS.

NORMAN : *doubtless*—Gammons, Lovel[6].

    believed—Horrell[3], Gillett[2], Breary, Boyse.

    probable—Cambers[2], Geer, Hillyard, Cope[3], Joyce.

FRENCH : *nicknames*—Favell[2].

LATIN :   "

SAXON : *doubtless*—Billing, Goodwin.

    probable—Whittamore, Holding.

ENGLISH : *nicknames*—Pope[3], Brown, Lightfoot, Armstrong, White, Wildman[2], Bull, King[2], Inskip.

LOCAL : *specific*—Loxley, Fensom[7], Hartop[3], Kirby, Stanton[2], Sunderland, Harlow[2],Whyley,Westley[3], Fensome[6], Gadsden[2], Laughton, Quenby, Stafford.

    general—Green, Woods, Mead, Wythes, Street.

    of county—

    of country—

    France—

PATRONYMICS : Allen, Peacock[6], Hawkins, Gilbert[2], George[2], Ives[3], Nichols, Austin, Franks[6], Bartram, Pete[4], Bennett, Goddard, Swales, Osborn, Syer, Allen.

Do. *in* SON : Williamson[2], Richardson[2], Harrison[2], Dawson[3], Johnson[3], Simpson.

DOUBTFUL : *Welsh*—Daniels, Jeffries[2], Rogers, Simons[2].

TRADES : *French*—Farrer[4], Cox[3], Draper[5].

    English—Harper, Smith[4].

    Latin—Fuller[3].

Do. RURAL : *French*—

    English—

    Latin—Foster, Carter[4].

OFFICES : *French*—Marshall, Page, Franklin.

    English—Mayes[6], Churchman[2].

    Latin—

DOUBTFUL : Wiles[3], Lumbis, Rust[2], Pell[7], Byles, Chalk.

WELSH : Jones, Lloyd.

SCOTCH : Ballingall, McLachlan.

IRISH : Higgins.

FRENCH :

GERMAN : Creamer.

JEW :

APPENDIX B.

CONTRAST OF ANGLIANS AND WELSHMEN.

DR. BARNARD DAVIS'S OBSERVATIONS.

		EYES LIGHT.						EYES NEUTRAL.						EYES DARK.						Index of Nigrescence.	
		Red.	Fair.	Brown.	Dark.	Black.	Total.	Red.	Fair.	Brown.	Dark.	Black.	Total.	Red.	Fair.	Brown.	Dark.	Black.	Total.	Gross.	Per cent.
Village of Youlgrave, Derbyshire	61	5	9	26	3	...	43	...	...	7	1	1	9	...	...	4	5	...	9	−3	...
Per cent.	...	8·2	14·7	42·6	5	...	70·5	...	...	11·5	1·6	1·6	14·7	...	...	6·5	8·2	...	14·7	...	−4·9
Carnarvonshire	440	11	25	63	44	6	149	3	5	48	65	9	130	1	...	7	96	57	161	+304	...
Per cent.	...	2·5	5·7	14·3	10	1·3	33·8	7	1·1	10·9	14·8	2	29·5	·2	...	1·6	21·8	12·9	36·6	...	+·69